Welcome back to Orange **Line**!

In Band 5 findet ihr viel Neues. Hier ein kurzer Überblick:

Die vier **Topics** (Kapitel) können in beliebiger Reihenfolge bearbeitet werden. Innerhalb jedes Topics gibt es obligatorische Teile und 2 **Options** (Themen zur Auswahl). Zu jeder Option gibt es **Tasks** (Aufgaben). Diese werden in einer Gruppe bearbeitet und schließen immer mit einer **Presentation** in der Klasse ab.
Ein Topic besteht aus:

Check-in	Einstimmung auf das Hauptthema anhand von Fotos
Aspects	Kurze Texte und Verständnisübungen
Options (x2)	Texte, Übungen und Aufgaben
Words in action	Wortschatzarbeit
Check-out	Selbstüberprüfung
Test yourself!	Vorbereitung auf Abschlusstests

In den zwei Teilen **A literature project** findest du jeweils nach den Topics 1 und 3 einen Lesetext. Diese Texte sind nicht obligatorisch und sind thematisch von den Topics unabhängig. Sie bieten dir die Möglichkeit, dich mit literarischen Texten zu beschäftigen.

Nach den Topics findest du folgende Teile:
Skills (Arbeitstechniken und Fertigkeiten) und **Grammar** (Grammatik). Bei manchen Übungen und Aufgaben innerhalb der Topics findest du Verweise auf diese Teile.
Der **Skills**-Teil beinhaltet Tipps zu Lern- und Arbeitstechniken und nützliche Ausdrücke.
Im **Grammar**-Teil kannst du nachschlagen, wenn du dir unsicher bist, z. B. beim Verfassen von eigenen Texten. Dort findest du auch neue Grammatik-Themen. In dem Teil **Overview** (Überblick) kannst du z. B. Aktiv und Passiv in einer Tabelle zusammengefasst anschauen.
Der Teil **Grammar practice** bietet darüber hinaus Übungen zu jedem neuen Thema an.

Weitere Übungen findest du in dem Teil **Mediation and communication**.
Am Ende des Buches befindet sich der Teil **Vocabulary** (Vokabelliste). Hier findest du nicht nur alle neuen Vokabeln, sondern auch Wortfeld- und Wortbildungsübungen sowie Kästen zu *Everyday English*. Das **Dictionary** (Wörterbuch) listet die Vokabeln alphabetisch auf. Es ist zum Nachschlagen gedacht.

Erläuterungen:

Let's talk	Lasst uns reden	CD-Nummer → 1, 1 (Track-Nummer)	Übung auf CD
Let's listen	Lasst uns zuhören		Einzelarbeit
Work with a picture	Vorbereitung auf mündliche Prüfung		Partnerarbeit
Task	Hauptaufgabe bei einer Option		Gruppenarbeit
Presentation/ Choose a presentation	Arbeitsergebnisse in der Klasse auswählen bzw. präsentieren		
Online link	⇨ 547550-0001		
Skills	2, 18		
Grammar	G 5, 7		
Overview	Ov 3		
Workbook-*Verweis*	(→ p. 9/ex. 14)		

4 Topics

Maybe these photos and comments can help you to choose.

Topic 1 – Oz 4 us!

Have you ever been to Australia? Do you know anything about the animals there? What do young people do there?

▶ If you choose Topic 1, we'll take you Down Under.

Topic 2 – Chilling-out time

Kids today can chill out in lots of different ways: They can have a good time with friends, do sports or help other people.

▶ In Topic 2 you can find out more about kids today and maybe get some ideas.

AUSTRALIA & NEW ZEALAND
TIMOR
NEW GUINEA
PACIFIC OCEAN
CORAL SEA
INDIAN OCEAN
GOLF OF CARPENTARIA
GREAT BARRIER REEF
Great Dividing Range
Darwin
Kakadu National Park
NORTHERN TERRITORY
Cooktown
Cairns
A U S T R A L I A
QUEENSLAND
WESTERN AUSTRALIA
Alice Springs
Uluru National Park
Uluru (Ayers Rock)
SOUTH AUSTRALIA
Brisbane
NEW SOUTH WALES
Sydney
CANBERRA
Australian Capital Territory
Perth
GREAT AUSTRALIAN BIGHT
Adelaide
VICTORIA
Melbourne
TASMAN SEA
TASMANIA
Hobart
NEW ZEALAND
Auckland
WELLINGTON
Christchurch
SYDNEY
Manly
Bondi Beach
Rockdale
BOTANY BAY
0
200
400
600
800
1000 km

Orange **Line**

Grundkurs 5

Herausgeber: Dr. Frank Haß

Ernst Klett Verlag
Stuttgart • Leipzig

Orange Line 5 für Klasse 9 an allen differenzierenden Schulen

Herausgeber: Dr. Frank Haß, Kirchberg
unter besonderer Mitwirkung von Harald Weisshaar, Bisingen

Autorinnen und Autoren: Holly De Marco, Cambridge; Elizabeth Rutledge, München
unter besonderer Mitwirkung von Hamida Aziz, Tübingen; Sheila McBride, Stuttgart

Beratung: Anette Christiani, Dortmund; Ulf Degen, Braunschweig; Ingrid Hartmann-Scheer, Kaarst; Margitta Kuty, Greifswald; Monika Teichmann, Wuppertal; Annegret Preker-Franke, Bielefeld

Zusatzmaterial für Schülerinnen und Schüler zu diesem Band:

Workbook mit Audio-CD und Lernsoftware	978-3-12-547655-4
Workbook mit Audio-CD	978-3-12-547555-7
Fit für Tests und Klassenarbeiten	978-3-12-547584-7

1. Auflage ISBN 978-547550-2 (fester Einband) 1 7 6 5 4 | 2016 2015 2014 2013

1. Auflage ISBN 978-547650-9 (flexibler Einband) 1 8 7 6 | 2016 2015

Alle Drucke dieser Auflage sind unverändert und können im Unterricht nebeneinander verwendet werden. Die letzte Zahl bezeichnet das Jahr des Druckes.

Redaktion: Susanne Steiert; Cornelia Schaller, Lektorat editoria, Fellbach

Gestaltung: Ulrike Wursthorn
Illustrationen: Sylvia Wolf, Wiesbaden; Christian Dekelver, Weinstadt (Karte vorne); Scivos/Klett Perthes (Karte hinten)

Umschlaggestaltung: Koma Amok, Stuttgart
Umschlagfoto: Avenue Images GmbH (Photodisc), Hamburg
Reproduktion: Meyle + Müller, Medien-Management, Pforzheim
Druck: Stürtz, Würzburg

Printed in Germany
ISBN 978-3-12-547550-2 (fester Einband)
ISBN 978-3-12-547650-9 (flexibler Einband)

9 783125 475502

9 783125 476509

Topic 3 – Freedom's just another word for ...

There are lots of different ideas of freedom: But how did people in the past fight for freedom?

▶ Read more about these and other views of freedom in Topic 3.

Topic 4 – Global matters

We all live in a modern world and many of us can enjoy the good things that life gives us.
But not everything that we do is good for the Earth.

▶ Topic 4 tells you more about our world and its problems.

Topic 1 Oz 4 us!

1 *Bondi Beach, Sydney*

1. Look at the title. Where or what is Oz? What do you think?
2. Work with a picture:
   a) What can you see in photo 1? Collect words. Now describe the picture.
   b) Why is there a tree in the middle of the picture?

1, 1 ◎ 3. Look at all the pictures and listen. Which announcement matches which scene? (→ p. 2/ex. 1)

2 *Ayers Rock (Uluru)*

3 *A kangaroo in the Outback*

4 *Sydney: The Opera House*

5 *A diver at the Great Barrier Reef*

⇨ 547550-0001/0002

40,000 years ago	1770	1788	1842
The first people – Aborigines – lived on the Australian continent.	Captain James Cook discovered Australia and claimed it for England.	First convicts arrived at Sydney Cove on the First Fleet. Many had escaped jail or the death sentence.	The colony at Sydney Cove became the city of Sydney.

A

Fact Card No. 23 Australia — **Creatures Down Under**

Why do tourists always want photos of koalas? Well, they look really cute. Often this animal is called a koala 'bear' by people, but it isn't one. And these cute, little animals are threatened, not by crocodiles or snakes, but by farmers. Every year they cut down thousands of eucalyptus trees. The koala only eats the leaves from these trees. Today, the koala is protected by laws.

When a koala baby is born, it's as tiny as a jelly bean!

➔ Option 1

B

JOBS on the Great Barrier Reef

Two new reef rangers are urgently needed at the Great Barrier Reef Marine Park.
'Reef programmes' and activities for tourists, pupils etc. are organized by us.
So applicants should
– know about activities that can destroy the Reef (e.g. it's damaged by fishing).
– work with a team to protect the Reef.
For more information please contact the Job Centre in Townsville.

➔ Option 2

1 Texts about Oz 1, 5, 6 G1, 2

a) *Read texts A and B. What are they about? Match each one with a heading.*

Cute 'bears' • School in the Outback • A job in Oz • A message home

b) *Read all the texts again carefully. Choose the best word to complete each sentence.*

1. Koalas are threatened by	a. farmers	b. crocodiles	c. snakes.
2. So koalas are protected by	a. tourists	b. laws	c. farmers.
3. At the Marine Park they need	a. pupils	b. fish	c. rangers.
4. The Reef is damaged by	a. fishing	b. applicants	c. teams.

2 Timeline info G1 (→ p. 3/ex. 2)

Look at the photos (D) and match each of them with a date on the timeline.

The 'School of the Air' started – a school for Outback kids who learn from home.
1951

The Great Barrier Reef Marine Park opened.
1975

The Summer Olympics took place.
2000

C

Sydney, 5th Jan.

Hi Mum!
I've been 'Down Under' for two weeks and we've had sun every day. The beaches are fantastic! People are often invited to 'barbies' (barbecues) by their friends – I've been to 3! Last week we visited a museum in Sydney. Imagine: There was a woman on the First Fleet called Margaret Dawson! We're going to Taronga Zoo tomorrow, so I'll try and send you a postcard of a cute baby koala!
Love to all at home,
Paula

Mrs M. Dawson
163 Wordsworth Way
Bristol
BS 67 4JK
UK

D

1

2

3

4

5

6

1, 2 ◎ **3 Let's listen: Death or the First Fleet** G1

a) *Read the postcard (C). What are people often invited to do 'Down Under'? What did Paula visit a week ago? What will Paula send next?*

b) *Listen. A guide is talking about Margaret Dawson, a convict on the First Fleet. Listen and match his report with a date on the timeline.*

c) *Listen again. Which sentences are correct?*
1. Margaret Dawson worked in Liverpool.
2. She stole a clock, jewellery and money.
3. The police caught her on her way to Liverpool.
4. She did her sentence in London.
5. She met a doctor called William.
6. Margaret died in January 1816.

4 Let's talk: Typically Australian 2, 4 (→ p. 3/ex. 3)

a) *Look at the texts again. What things there don't you find in your country? Make a list.*

b) *Would you like to live 'Down Under'?*
A: I think it would be great – … .
B: But it's better here because … .

Deadly Down Under

Sydney Funnel Web Spider

If you are bitten by this spider, you can die in just 15 minutes unless anti venom is used.

Advice: Leave them alone and don't play with them.

Blue Ring Octopus

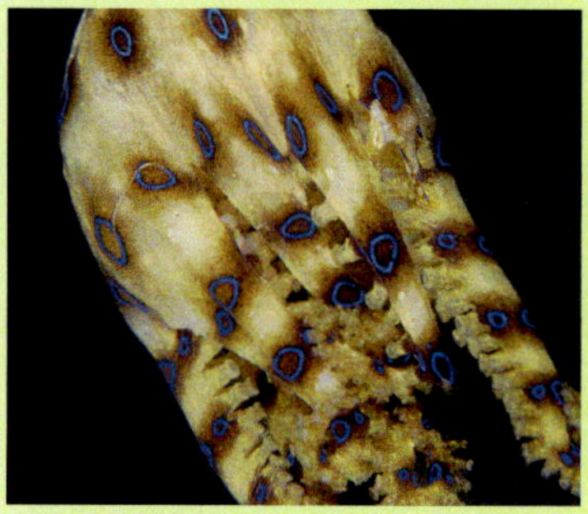

There is no anti venom, but only two deaths are known in Oz. Aussies know what to do if someone is stung.

Advice: Never swim alone. Remember: It only stings if it is disturbed.

Saltie

Every year people are attacked and killed by saltwater crocodiles. They are called 'salties'.

Advice: Don't swim in the evening or at night or near warning signs.

Sea Wasp Jellyfish

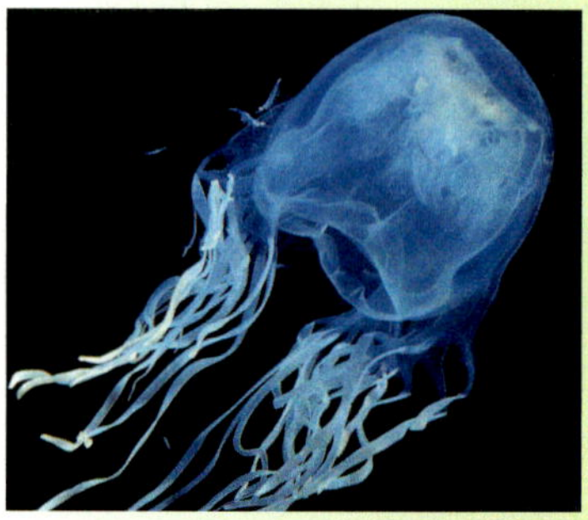

There **is** anti venom, but many swimmers die every year. Surfers once wore tights.

Advice: Always carry vinegar and use it if you are stung. Wear a 'stinger' suit if you want to survive!

Brown Snake

You can get anti venom but there are still 1–2 deaths from bites every year in very remote areas.

Advice: Keep away from snakes and they will keep away from you!

Great White Shark

Every year 1–2 people are attacked by this shark. It is found in warm water near the coast.

Advice: Don't swim near seals or sharks.

 Für diese Topic brauchst du: Voll- / Hilfsverben → G1 • Passiv → G2 • mod. Hilfsverben → G3 • Adjektive → Ov5

Task: To find out about dangerous creatures

1 The photos 1 Ov5 (→ p. 4/ex. 4)

I'm frightened of … . • I hate … . • Its teeth look … . • Its body looks … . • It looks so big / deadly / unfriendly / … .

a) *Look at the photos and read the names.*
Which creature do you find most frightening? Why?

b) *Which do you think is the biggest/smallest creature? Put the creatures in order starting with the biggest. Check your answer at the bottom of this page. Were you right?*

c) *Which deadly creatures are there in your country?*

2 Deadly facts 2, 5 G2, 3 (→ p. 4/ex. 5)

a) *Read the info about the different creatures and match the sentence parts.*

1. The Sea Wasp Jellyfish	can kill you in 15 minutes.
2. Aussies know what to do if someone	isn't found in cold waters.
3. The Sydney Funnel Web Spider	are called 'salties'.
4. Saltwater crocodiles	kills 1–2 people each year in very remote areas.
5. The Great White Shark	is called a 'stinger' by Australians.
6. The Brown Snake	is stung by a Blue Ring Octopus.

b) *Read the advice for each creature carefully. Your partner closes his/her book. You 'give advice'. Your partner has to say which creature you mean.*

Example: You mustn't swim after dark. – This advice is for **salties**.

3 Presentation: A quiz 3, 10, 18 G1, 2, 3 (→ p. 5/ex. 6–7)

a) *Form groups of six. In your group each of you chooses one of the six creatures and collects all the facts about it in a grid like this one:*

The creature is called …	If you are bitten / stung / attacked / …,	You are advised …
… the Sydney Funnel … .	… you can die within 15 minutes. … you should use … .	… to leave them alone. … not to … .
…	…	…

b) *Look for one or two more facts about your creature. You can use books, brochures or the Internet. Make a fact card with a picture and info about the animal.*

c) *Look at all your info and write two questions on your creature. Compare your questions with the questions of others who chose the same creature.*

d) *Collect all the questions in your option group and make a quiz for the rest of the class.*

e) *Display your fact cards. The class has ten minutes to study them. Then they can do the quiz.*

GREAT WHITE SHARK

This shark has thousands of teeth – in rows, but many are hidden. When it loses a tooth, a new one comes in its place.

saltie 7m, shark 6.5m, snake 1.5m, jellyfish 30cm across, octopus 20cm, spider 4.5cm

Jobs Down Under

Goldcoast Water Sports Centre

Reference: Vacancy No. V09/304

A new water sports centre has opened this month near Brisbane. They need an assistant to sell surfboards in their shop. Applicants must be interested in water sports. But you needn't have shop experience – training is given. The job is permanent, part-time and at least 20 hours per week.

Hours: 3 hours on weekdays, 3½ hours at weekends.
Pay: A$ 23 per hour.
Closing date: 27 July

Please contact the Job Centre if you want to apply.

Davy Jones' Dive Centre

German and English-speaking diving instructors are wanted to teach in our centre in Cairns and on the Great Barrier Reef. If we've interviewed you before, you needn't apply again. Applicants must have:

- a full instructor certificate
- insurance
- a valid working visa
- a driving licence.

Hours: F/T (30 hours), temporary (permanent contract possible)
Pay: around A$ 40 per hour
For further info please contact our training manager Connie MacDonald.
e-mail address: jobs@davyjones.com.au

Australian JobSearch

job seeker info | find a job | job details | provider search

Green Corps helper
Tasmania – Franklin
Pay: A$291 per week / Hours: full-time (35 hours per week)

Jobs at Green Corps are supported by the Australian Government. The job is open to young Australians (17 – 20) who are interested in the environment. With Green Corps you can get 6 months paid work experience on exciting projects. Successful applicants must go on a professional training course before they start. Your job will be to look after trees, to check lakes and rivers and help to save old historical buildings.
We also welcome young people with disabilities.
Interested? Then please call us (0394799595) or apply online to greencorps@cvgt.com.au.
For further information please call 1300658272 or check our website www.cvgt.com.au and click on the Green Corps link.

similar careers | e-mail contact | >> back to search results

Task: To learn about job applications

1 Job ads 4, 2, 6 G2, Ov5 (→ p. 6/ex. 8)

a) *Think: What information is important for job seekers? Make a list.*

b) *Look at the ads on page 14. Which jobs are offered?*

c) *Read the ads. Find a word or phrase which means:*
1. to need 2. not full-time 3. through the Internet 4. teachers 5. not permanent

d) *Read the ads again carefully and choose the best word/phrase to complete each sentence.*
1. Professional training is given at a *dive centre/water sports centre.*
2. At Goldcoast Water Sports Centre they require an assistant for their *pool/shop/café.*
3. Davy Jones needs *driving/diving/language* instructors to teach in Cairns.
4. The Green Corps job is open to people who are interested in the *government/environment.*
5. Successful Green Corps applicants must go on *a historical tour/training course/long trip.*

e) *Pair: Copy and complete the grid to sort all the information from the ads.*

Info	ad 1	ad 2	ad 3
job title	shop …	…	…
…	A$23/hour	…	…

f) *Look at the grid together. Which of the jobs would you like to do and why? Which one(s) would you find terrible? Why? Talk about the work, the pay and how the ad is written.*

g) *Share: Discuss in your group. Take a vote on the most and least popular jobs.*

2 A CV 13 (→ p. 6/ex. 9; p. 7/ex. 10)

a) *Read Manuel's CV. What's missing?*

b) *Look at page 14 again. Which job should Manuel apply for? What do you think? Why?*

c) *Write your own CV.*

d) *Hang up all the CVs. What's good about each one? What could be better?*

3 Presentation: A job application 3, 10, 13,14, 18 (→ p. 7/ex. 11)

a) *Choose the best CV in your group and explain to the class how a good CV is written.*

b) *Write an e-mail to apply for one of the jobs.*
Say you're interested in the job. Say why.
Where did you see the ad (newspaper, job centre, Internet …)?
Write about your skills.
Do they take people from abroad?
Discuss the e-mails in class.

CURRICULUM VITAE (CV)

Name:	Manuel Hassel
Address:	
Tel.:	
E-mail:	
Date of birth:	
Place of birth:	Düsseldorf
Primary school:	
Secondary school:	Brücken Gesamtschule
Exams:	
Skills:	PC
Certificates:	Advanced Life-Saving Certificate Beginner's Diving Certificate
Work experience:	Shop assistant in sports shop
Hobbies/interests:	Swimming, sailing, reading
Referees:	1. Dr. Schmidt, Brücken Gesamtschule 2. Thorsten Weidmann, Fitfun Sports

1 Creatures

a) *Sort the letters and find the names of the creatures.*

1. aalko
2. leyjl fhsi
3. kesna
4. doilccoer
5. khasr
6. aislte
7. idrspe
8. psoucto
9. asle
10. ragookna

b) *Which ones can be deadly?*

2 Don't be a silly tourist!

Read the newspaper summary. Replace the highlighted words / phrases with ones from the box.

no food and water • destroyed • bitten • isn't hurt • typical • were lost • swimmers • be sensible • are told • survives • saltwater crocodile

Every day we **get information** about tourists in Australia who do silly things. This is a **normal** week:
It's 10:30 a. m. on Monday: A woman is attacked by a **saltie** near Darwin. She is lucky. She **doesn't die**.
It's 4 o'clock on Tuesday: A man is **hurt** by a shark near Melbourne. His surfboard is **useless** but he **is OK**.
It's 12 o'clock on Wednesday: Some **people in the sea** near Cairns are stung by jelly fish.
It's 6 p.m. on Thursday: A boy is killed by an octopus.
It's 8 o'clock on Friday: Six tourists who **couldn't find their way** in the Outback are found again after two days. They had **nothing to eat and nothing to drink** and no map.

Please don't be in our report for the weekend.
Use your head and you'll be safe!

3 The odd one out

Which word doesn't belong in the group?

1. CV, interview, die, application
2. part-time, permanent, form, temporary
3. manager, pay, hours, closing date
4. licence, visa, insurance, reef
5. river, remote, lake, ocean
6. bite, sting, kill, hurt, swim
7. require, need, contact, want
8. saltie, octopus, shark, bird

4 The same or different?

a) *Find the nouns for these verbs. (Some may sound the same but the noun is spelt differently!)*
Examples: to train – training, to exercise – exercise, to practise – practice

1. to advise
2. to apply
3. to help
4. to interview
5. to describe
6. to sound
7. to begin
8. to survive
9. to choose
10. to report
11. to search
12. to meet
13. to sting
14. to die
15. to bite

b) *Choose three words from above. Write one sentence for each (verb and noun).*
Example: I **exercise** every day. – Which **exercise** do we have to do for homework?

5 How?

Complete the sentences with the best word from the box.

1. Venom can kill you … .
2. The Corps needs a helper … .
3. Be sensible and you'll get home … .
4. Remember: Write your CV … .

carefully • quickly • urgently • safely

OPTION 1

✔ … describe a picture.

Describe the picture. Who and what can you see? Where are they? What are they doing?

✔ … talk about the history of Australia. G1, 2

Match the words with the dates and write a sentence for each.

1770 • 1788 • 1842 • 1951 • 1975 • 2000

school • city • Olympics • convicts • reef • discover

✔ … talk about activities in Australia.

Name two things which you would/wouldn't like to do there. Say why/why not.

✔ … talk about creatures in Australia. G2, Ov5

1

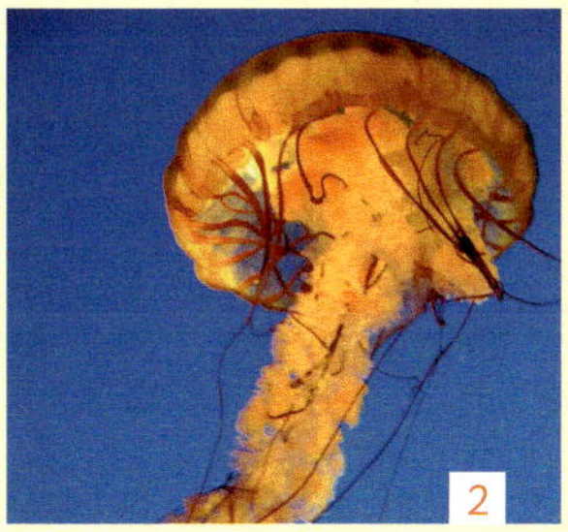

2

3

What are these three creatures? What advice/info would you give about them?

OPTION 2

✔ … understand a job ad.

Look at the ad. Which of these applicants would probably get the job? Why?

1. Mat is 17, has a swimming certificate and is looking for a part-time job in Townsville.
2. Sharon is 15, has a valid life-saving certificate and is looking for a permanent job in Townsville.
3. Cora is 18, is looking for a temporary job and has a life-saving certificate.
4. Mark is 17, has a valid life-saving certificate, is looking for a job between March and July.

Swimming instructors needed for sports centre in Townsville. Age 16+.
P/T – (24 hours/wk)
The job is temporary (Nov. to Jan.)
Pay – A$35 per hour
You must have a valid life-saving certificate. For more information please contact the Job Centre.

✔ … apply for a job.

You want to apply for the job above. What would you write in your CV about your skills and your work experience? Write three questions which you could ask.

(→ p. 8/ex. 12; p. 9/ex. 13)

A competition[1] with BYTE! (→ pp. 10–12)

Truckies[2] Times' reporter Judie Lennox interviewed Tom Dawson from Hervey Bay. He was one of the best drivers at this year's BYTE (Best Young Truckies Event), which is a national competition to find the best road train[3] driver in Australia.

Tom's dream to become a truck driver started when he was five. At the age of 16 he began to drive for his parents' company on the east coast. Three years later he got his special driving licence and soon after that he bought his own truck. That's when he started to do the long trips up north.

We asked Tom about the competition:

"Well, there were 16 finalists[4] from about a thousand young drivers from all seven states in Australia," he explained, "so I'm really pleased to be second. Jake, the winner, is a great road train driver who has much more experience in the job!"

As[5] Tom has only just become 21, he should be pleased: The winner, Jake Lee, is seven years older than Tom!

"It's hard to drive a monster road train! It can be 50 metres long with up to five or six trailers[6], Tom told us. "You can't just overtake[7] when you want to and sometimes you can't see because there's so much dust[8]. But luckily at BYTE we each drove a 19-metre trailer!"

During the event each driver is asked questions about road trains and rules of the road. In the driving part they have to pass five tests. This year one test was to drive all eleven wheels[9] of the left side of their truck along a 20-centimetre line. If a wheel came off the line, they lost points. Tom got full points on that one. But there was one test which he found very difficult: With their front wheel they had to knock down[10] only *one* of three little metal sticks on the ground.

Tom remembered: "I watched Jake and thought, wow, not one mistake! So when it was my turn, my God, I was scared!" But Tom didn't have too many problems with this test.

The organizers of BYTE want to show that a truck driver's job needs lots of skill and that most truckies are experts and safe drivers who love their job. So what did Tom think about that?

"Well, that's right. One bad driver doesn't mean we're all bad! I'd never swap my job for anything else: I enjoy driving and being alone out in our huge, fantastic Outback! And in a few years I'll be back at BYTE, this time to win the 'King of the Road' crown!"

Blue skies, white heat and red dust of the Outback: Some reasons[11] why Tom Dawson would never swap his job!

[1]competition [ˌkɒmpəˈtɪʃn] – *Wettbewerb,* [2]truckie [ˈtrʌki] – *LKW-Fahrer/in,* [3]road train [ˈrəʊd ˌtreɪn] – *Fernlastzug,* [4]finalist [ˈfaɪnəlɪst] – *Finalist/in,* [5]as [æz] – *hier: da,* [6]trailer [ˈtreɪlə] – *Anhänger,* [7]to overtake [ˌəʊvəˈteɪk] – *überholen,* [8]dust [dʌst] – *Staub,* [9]wheel [wiːl] – *Rad,* [10]to knock down [nɒk ˈdaʊn] – *umwerfen,* [11]reason [ˈriːzn] – *Grund*

A Reading

1 Read the text and find the best answer.

a. The article is about …
1 the Outback. 2 a truckie competition. 3 computers.

b. Tom Dawson is …
1 a company owner. 2 the king of Australia. 3 a truck driver.

c. He was only 19 when he …
1 got a special driving licence. 2 started work in a company. 3 bought a company.

d. For Tom, Jake is …
1 just a good driver. 2 a good friend. 3 a real winner.

e. Tom was a good driver who came …
1 second. 2 first. 3 last.

f. A difficult part for Tom was to …
1 answer questions. 2 drive along a line. 3 knock down a metal stick.

2 Answer the questions. Don't write complete sentences.

a. Where is Tom Dawson from?
b. When did Tom's dream start?
c. How many drivers were there in BYTE in the end?
d. Where did they all come from?
e. How old is Jake?
f. What part of Australia does Tom love?
g. What does Tom want to do in a few years?

B Language

1 Find the words in the text with the same or a similar meaning.

a. truck drivers *(lines 1–5)*
b. happy *(lines 10–15)*
c. marks *(lines 30–35)*
d. hard *(lines 30–35)*
e. frightened *(lines 35–40)*
f. change *(lines 40–45)*

2 Find a word or phrase in the text which means …

a. … something you take part in and try to win.
b. … a long truck.
c. … different parts of a country with their own names.
d. … a short exam.
e. … someone who knows all about a job and is very good at it.
f. … without other people.
g. … dry, open lands in Australia, where very few people live.
h. … something a king wears on his head.

1, 3

C Listening

Urgent job search: A young truckie

1 Listen to a guest on the radio programme "JobSearch". Right or wrong?

a. Ella is a radio reporter.
b. She's looking for a new job.
c. She's 16.
d. The people are friendly in her job.
e. She doesn't want to work in the city.
f. Her dream is to drive a big tourist bus.
g. Ella's father is a truckie.
h. Her plan is to share a job with her boyfriend.

2 Listen again and answer the questions.

a. Where did Ella do training after school?
1 in a transport company
2 in a department store
3 in a radio studio
4 in a shoe shop
5 in an info centre
6 in a school

b. Ella passed a test. What licence did she get?
1 a licence for cars
2 a train driver's licence
3 a trucker's licence

c. What does she want to save money for?
1 to get another special licence
2 to buy a car
3 to travel

d. What does Ella's boyfriend do?
1 He works on a cattle station[1].
2 He drives a road train.
3 He's a radio DJ.

D Speaking

A

B

1 Describing

a. Look at the two pictures. Make a grid and collect at least five words to describe each situation.

b. How do the people see their jobs? What do you think? Write three sentences for each scene.

2 Role play

Rod from 'Sydney Transport' calls into JobSearch and has some questions. Give Ella's answers.

Rod: I hear you now have a normal trucker's licence. But have you got truckie experience?
You: (*Sage nein. Erkläre, dass du die Straßen kennst, weil du oft mit deinem Bruder und deinem Freund unterwegs bist, die LKW-Fahrer sind.*)
Rod: We're looking for a driver to start next month. Can you start then?
You: (*Sage, dass das kein Problem ist, und, dass du schon an deinen Chef geschrieben hast.*)
Rod: So you're planning to take the test for the road train licence?
You: (*Sage, dass du planst, das erst in ein paar Jahren zu tun, weil der Unterricht sehr teuer ist.*)
Rod: Yes, well, have you got any questions?
You: (*Frage, welche Städte du besuchen wirst. Frage auch, was du transportieren wirst. Frage nach der Bezahlung und der Arbeitszeit. Frage, ob du immer denselben LKW fahren würdest.*)

[1]cattle station ['kætl ˌsteɪʃn] – *Rinderfarm*

E Mediation and communication

Your family wants to drive through Australia. You have found some rules of the road on the Internet. Answer your parents' questions about these helpful tips:

Rules of the road in the Australian Outback

If you follow these easy rules, you can help the truck driver – and protect your life at the same time!

- On a highway: Stay on the left* of your lane. When a road train overtakes, it needs at least the whole of its lane. So always give road trains LOTS of space!
- On one-lane highways: Slow down if a road train is coming towards you and move onto the emergency lane until the truck has passed.
- If you want to overtake a road train, check that you have enough space on the road in front of you. That means leave LOTS of space! Remember: It takes some time to pass a 50-metre train if you are only a bit faster than the trucker.
- When you overtake a train, also leave LOTS of space between you and the truck as you go back into your lane. (Check that you can see the truck lights in your mirror before you start to go back.)
- Road trains sometimes switch on a warning sign if they are turning left. Never overtake a train at this time because it needs LOTS of space (sometimes two full lanes) to turn left!
- From behind a road train on bad roads, you can't see because there's so much dust. Keep a safe distance and put your lights on. Then the truckie knows you're there, too! Or just stop (off the road) and have a break: It's really no fun to drive behind a road train for hours in a cloud of dust!

* For our visitors from abroad / Europe: Remember, we drive on the left in Australia (like in the UK).

a. Auf welcher Seite fährt man in Australien?
b. „Lane“ ist doch ein Gässchen: Gibt es dort auf der Autobahn Gässchen?
c. Was heißt „overtake“?
d. Was dauert einige Zeit?
e. Was für ein Schild schalten die Laster manchmal ein und warum?
f. Was darf man dann auf keinen Fall machen?
g. Wann muss man die Scheinwerfer unbedingt einschalten?

F Writing

1 Skills

What important information do you need to give when you apply for a truck driver's job? Collect words and phrases and make a profile.

2 A job ad

You are looking for a job as a truck driver. Use your profile and write a job ad for the notice board in your local job centre.

1, 4–11 ◎ # The kiss 5

1 The title

Before you read the story, look at the title. What could the story be about?

2 The text

It happened yesterday, but it started weeks before. I've never had any friends at school. My face isn't the same on both sides, it has a strange colour and you can just see my top lip[1] – that's because my big sister played with matches[2] when she was three and my buggy[3] caught fire with me in it. I can't do sport because the skin[4] on my feet is all funny and even when I'm laughing, my face doesn't look happy. I can't show my feelings. It doesn't mean I don't feel things.
It was the middle of last term when they started. Spike and his gang, I mean. At first they just called me names – Ugly[5] Face, No Lip – and grabbed my books and threw them over the wall. But then it got worse …

a) *What could happen? What do you think?*
1. They could hit the boy.
2. They could ask him to join the gang.
3. They could become the boy's friends.

It was Science with Mr Conway. What he does is, he grabs one of you and uses you as an assistant in experiments. It was my turn that day:
He lit[6] a match, some stuff caught fire and I screamed[7]. Well, to be honest, I did more than that – I shouted and ran out of the room.

b) *Why does the boy do this? Choose the right answer.*
1. He does not like Mr Conway.
2. He is scared of fire.
3. He does not want to be an assistant.

I can't remember the fire in the buggy, but Dad thinks my body does. I see a flame and alarm bells ring. I never even go near a barbecue.
From that minute, Spike and his gang had me just where they wanted me.
On the way home that afternoon they stopped me and Karl pulled out a box of matches. Luke and Adam pushed me against a fence[8] and Spike grabbed the matches from Karl, lit one and held it up to my face.
"See this?" he asked and waved the flame near my right eye. "Now watch me as I burn off your eyelashes[9] with this."
I felt hot all over.
"Well?" Spike went on. "Yes or no?"
"Wh…wh…what do you mean?" My heart[10] was so loud that I couldn't hear my own voice.
"Burn – or do what we say!" said Karl.
I didn't answer. I felt sick.
"More!" Spike told Karl.

I fought. I promise you I did. I turned my head, I kicked with my feet, I even tried to pull my arm round and knock the matches from Karl's hand. But when the flame of the fourth match touched the eyelashes of my

[1]lip [lɪp] – *Lippe,* [2]match [mætʃ] – *Streichholz,* [3]buggy ['bʌgi] – *Kinderwagen,* [4]skin [skɪn] – *Haut,* [5]ugly ['ʌgli] – *hässlich,* [6]to light, lit, lit [lait, lɪt, lit] – *anzünden,* [7]scream [skri:m] – *schreien,* [8]fence [fens] – *Zaun,* [9]eyelashes ['aɪlæʃɪz] – *Wimpern,* [10]heart [hɑ:t] – *Herz*

left eye, I screamed a few times, "OK, OK, I'll do anything – stop it – please!"

"I think," Spike said, "we've got a result."

c) *What is the result?*

And that's how it started. At first it was cigarettes, then they wanted booze[1], too. The first few times I didn't steal from shops – I took cigarettes from Mum's bag and a bottle of whisky from the drinks cupboard.

But in the end I had to use shops because Spike wanted stuff we never had at home. I went to Mr Patel's at the corner of our street. And all the time I felt sick and the words 'thief[2], thief' went around in my head.

Then, last week, I left the shop with some cigarettes and Mr Patel shouted, "Hey you!" and I ran down the street, round the corner and was sick[3] over my trouser leg.

I didn't sleep that night and the next morning I was sick again and Mum kept me at home. The doctor asked all those silly questions – "Anything wrong?" (Like, you want a list?) and "You can always talk about your problems, you know." (Oh sure, and then wait for Spike's revenge[4].)

I was away from school for three weeks and when I went back, there was this new girl in my class. The moment I saw her, I knew what all those love songs were about. Her name was Shelby. She was from Montana, which is in America – because her father now works on some project at the college.

"Hi," she said to me that first morning at break.

She just said, "Hi." It may be nothing special to you, but you probably look normal.

d) *Why is it something special to the boy that the girl says 'Hi!'?*
1. The girl does not speak English.
2. Usually nobody says 'Hi!' to the boy because they don't like his face.

Most people look away when they first meet me, or they offer me seats and smile sweetly to show how good they are with the disabled[5]. Shelby didn't do anything like that.

She just spoke to me normally.

"Hi," I answered.

Then we joked a bit.

And she laughed. Not the awful embarrassed[6] laugh[7] at my lips, but a real kind of laugh.

And that's how *we* started. We were just friends, of course – nothing more, but it was nice. At lunchtime we hung out and talked and it was cool.

Until Spike and his gang noticed us.

"We've got a job for you, Ugly Face," Spike said at lunchtime last Wednesday. "Adam is having a party and we need booze. So get it."

He was looking not at me, but at Shelby, who looked shocked. "Or else!"

Then the gang left.

"Chris," Shelby asked, "what does all this mean?"

[1]booze [bu:z] – *Alkohol,* [2]thief [θi:f] – *Dieb/in,* [3]to be sick [sɪk] – *sich übergeben,* [4]revenge [rɪ'vendʒ] – *Rache,* [5]disabled [dɪs'eɪblt] – *Behinderte/r,* [6]embarrassed [ɪm'bærəst] – *verlegen,* [7]laugh [lɑ:f] – *lachen*

e) *Why is Shelby shocked? What do you think?*

"Him?" I said. "Oh, my dad sells booze and he lets my friends have …"

"Chris Matthews, I'm not an idiot," she said. "They want you to steal it, right?"

"What do you think I am?" I said. "A thief? Well, thanks very much!"

And then I walked away.

She didn't look at me for the rest of the day. Or the next day.

"Got the booze?" Spike asked at lunch break.

"No," I said. "I'm not getting any more."

They couldn't do much at school, but they got me after school. They held me on the ground and they kicked me and then lit a match and burned the ends of my hair. That's when I went crazy. I screamed and shouted "Help!" a few times until Adam put his hand over my mouth.

"Wait!" The way Spike spoke made the other two stop. "Got an idea."

f) *What do you think Spike wants him to do? Why?*

"You like Shelby, right?" Spike said.

"She's OK," I answered. There was blood on my lip and I was in pain.

"This is what you have to do," Spike said. "Kiss her."

"What?" The idea had been in my mind for days, but the reality was hopeless[1]. I can't even do the kiss shape in the mirror[2].

"Tomorrow. After school, at the sports hall," Spike said. "Be there or die!"

"Shelby," I said the next morning. "I need to talk to you."

"To say what?" she asked. "How good you can steal stuff?"

"No," I answered quickly. "I'll never do that again as long as I live."

"Is that really true?"

"Sure," I said. "It was stupid. It's just that when you look like a freak …"

"You don't look like a freak[3] and if you want to feel sorry for yourself[4], I'm not hanging around," she said. "Now what did you want?"

So I told her.

"And you, Chris Matthews, want me to kiss you just because they want you to? Well, thank you for nothing!"

She turned and walked off. I ran after her.

"It's not like I don't want to. I want to a lot but …"

"You do?"

I nodded[5] sadly. "But I can't do it. I don't know how."

"Right," she said. "Be there."

g) *What happens next? What do you think?*

1. Shelby kisses Chris.
2. Shelby kisses Spike.
3. Shelby tells a teacher about Spike.
4. …

At four o'clock, we got to the sports hall. Spike and the gang were there – and also about fifty other kids.

[1]hopeless ['həʊplɪs] – *hoffnungslos,* [2]mirror ['mɪrə] – *Spiegel,* [3]freak [friːk] – *Monster,* [4]to feel sorry for yourself [fiːl 'sɒri fə jɔːˌself] – *sich selbst bemitleiden,* [5]to nod [nɒd] – *nicken*

"So what are you all looking at?" Shelby shouted. "We're not doing anything."

"Do it or die," Spike said.

"By fire," added Adam.

"Slowly," said Karl.

That's when I saw the fireworks in Spike's pocket – the ones called Flame Thrower[1] that have blue and yellow flames.

"I'll do it," I said quickly.

"No," shouted Shelby. "What are you? A wimp[2]?"

I stopped. A wimp? Yes – but I loved Shelby and I wanted her to have respect for me. But then Spike put a firework in the ground next to my foot.

Karl lit a match. "Kiss!" shouted Spike. "Or we light it."

"Kiss, kiss, kiss," the kids shouted. I was scared. I turned towards Shelby and tried to make my lips the right shape. I didn't do it very well, so the kids laughed.

Then I saw Shelby's eyes wide with horror[3]. Out of the corner of my eye I saw Karl as he lit the firework.

"Move!" Shelby shouted.

She pushed me to one side and put out her hand towards the firework.

"Noooo!" I screamed.

But it was too late.

[adapted[4] from *The Kiss* by Rosie Rushton]

3 Right or wrong?

1. Chris' buggy caught fire when he was three.
2. Chris is scared of fire.
3. Chris does not like Science.
4. Shelby's dad is a teacher.
5. Chris steals things for Spike and his friends.
6. Shelby helps Chris to get the booze for Spike.
7. The kids shout, "Kiss, kiss, kiss."
8. Shelby doesn't kiss Chris because of[5] his lip.

4 Chris' problems

a) *What problems does Chris have? Choose the right numbers.*

1. He's scared of fire.
2. He can't do sports.
3. He's a bully.
4. He looks strange.
5. He can't show feelings.
6. He's boring.

b) *Add more ideas if you can. Write in your exercise book.*

5 The ending 10

Write an ending for the story (4–5 sentences). The phrases in the box can help you. But your story can also end differently.

… lay on the ground • … called an ambulance • … was hurt / burnt • police arrived • pupils laughed • fire went out – nothing happened • … kissed … • … fell in love with[6] … • police / teacher talked to … • Spike and his gang did not bully … from that day on

6 A discussion[7] 3, 19

What can you do if somebody bullies you? Collect ideas in class and write them on a poster.

[1]thrower ['θrəʊə] – *Werfer,* [2]wimp [wɪmp] – *Weichei, Feigling,* [3]wide with horror [ˌwaɪd wɪθ 'hɒrə] – *weit aufgerissen vor Furcht / Horror,* [4]adapted [ə'dæptɪd] – *angepasst,* [5]because of [bɪ'kɔːz‿əv] – *wegen,* [6]to fall in love [ˌfɔːl‿ɪn 'lʌv] – *sich verlieben,* [7]discussion [dɪ'skʌʃn] – *Diskussion*

Topic 2 Chilling-out time

1. Work with a picture:
What's happening in photo 1?
What do you think?
I think two kids are … . A girl is … . Maybe they are … .

2. Guessing game: Say one sentence about one of the photos. The class guesses which photo you're talking about. 3

3. Prepare interviews for a school magazine. Each of you chooses a different photo. Pretend you are one of the people in your photo. Find sensible answers to your partner's questions. 2 (→ p. 13/ex. 1–2)
Where are you? Are you having fun? Why? Why not? Who are you with? What …?

1 *Messing around in the playground*
2 *Watching videos at home*

3 *Shopping in town*
4 *Having fun at the pool*
5 *Hanging out at a party*

⇨ 547550-0003/0004

A Chilling out in a gang?

UK GANG FACTS

For 80% of kids in some UK cities chilling out means hanging around in a gang. 3 in 5 gang members carry a gun. Few girls are members of gangs. They often hang out in peer groups. There are 3 groups which kids can belong to:

- Peer groups – small groups with the same background; seldom use crime.
- Street gangs – crime is important. Usually they have a name and carry knives.
- Organized groups – only want money through crime. They carry guns.

B What's attractive?

Home | Dating | Chat | Groups | Greet

Re: What do you find attractive? 27.11.

I hate dating guys who smoke or wear cowboy boots. And going on a date with a guy who gets jealous is no fun! He needn't have a six-pack but he should be fit. And he should smell good – body odour is a real turn-off! There's no need for flowers but if a guy opens the door for his girl, that's really nice.

Re: What do you find attractive? 27.11

I like dating girls who are fun! Laughing together is important. A funny text message is cool! I find some girls boring – for example if they like shopping with other girls all the time! And, sorry, but I'm not crazy about girls with short hair.

1 Different texts 5, 8

a) *Look at each text. Where could you find texts like these?*

b) *Which one tells you about:* 1. volunteer jobs 2. finding a girl/boyfriend 3. how kids hang out?

2 Chilling out in gangs? 1 (→ p. 14/ex. 3)

a) *Read text A. Which word or phrase is wrong in each sentence? Correct them.*

1. In some UK cities 80 % of girls hang around in a gang.
2. Small groups with the same background are called street gangs.
3. In peer groups there is a lot of crime.
4. Street gangs usually have a name and carry guns.
5. Organized groups only want guns through crime.

b) *Look at the photo. Which of the three groups do you think the kids belong to and why?*

3 Who thinks what? G6 (→ p. 14/ex. 4)

Read text B. Who wrote these things? Start like this: Tammy/Judd wrote that she/he …

1. didn't like cowboy boots.
2. wasn't crazy about short hair.
3. thought laughing was important.
4. hated dating somebody who smoked.
5. said body odour was a real turn-off.
6. found funny text messages were cool.

C The American City of Murals

Help

Tammy
Age: 15

Judd
Age: 16

→ Option 1

We need volunteers!

Do you want to do volunteer work? Can you find a few hours each week? Could you help with an event once or twice a year? Are you good at office work, organizing or painting?

The Mural Arts Program in Philadelphia is looking for artists, office assistants, and event assistants. Interested? You can e-mail or phone us or send a completed Volunteer Application.

http://www.muralarts...

→ Option 2

1, 12 ◎ **4 Let's listen: A volunteer?** 15, 6 (→ p. 14/ex. 5)

a) *Read text C and find the two possible answers.*
Volunteers can …

1. film a programme.	2. write to artists.	3. help at an event.
4. get in the way.	5. get experience in mural art.	6. have an office.

b) *Look at the questions below.*
1. Who told Aidan about the Mural Arts Program?
2. How old are the kids in the program?
3. When does Aidan want to leave school?
4. What does the Mural Arts Program do in the summer?
5. When can new students start on the program?
6. Where can you get an application form from?

c) *Listen to a telephone call and write notes. Answer the questions.*

5 Activities 4 G6, Ov3, Ov4

a) *Think: What do you do/would you like to do as a free-time activity?*
b) *Pair: Talk to your partner about his/her activities and what he/she would like to do.*
c) *Share: Tell the class about these activities.*
d) *Write two lists: 'Activities you do' and 'What you would like to do'. Which are the most popular ones?*

Torn between …

Miguel, Zach, Sandy and Jaden loved painting so they formed the 'Brushstroke Gang'. And they were really excited when they heard about a local mural painting competition. The council gave them a wall and soon after that they started painting. Suddenly Jaden said he had to leave …

Task: To put a text into a different form

1 Important qualities 2

a) *What is a 'friend' for you? Choose five important qualities from the boxes below.*

A good friend:

lends you his/her mobile phone if your batteries are dead is someone you can do crazy things together with helps you to fix your computer/when you move/… doesn't let you pay in the café/cinema/… every time is interested in your ideas and listens to you gives you advice, even when you don't want it doesn't laugh about you behind your back supports you in a fight, doesn't walk away	has the same hobbies is a member of your gang wears the same clothes likes the same music understands your problems spends every free minute with you notices your feelings does what he/she promises

b) *Compare your lists of qualities. Which is the most important one for each of you? Why?*

2 The story remixed G8 (→ p. 15/ex. 6–7; p. 16/ex. 8)

a) *Read the comic and then these sentences. Use them to tell the story.*
Example: Jaden tells the gang that he has to leave. – Jaden **told** the gang that he **had** to leave.

1. He remembers that he has to meet Chloé.
2. He explains to her why he is late.
3. She says she doesn't like wasting time.
4. Sandy tells Jaden that they need him.
5. But Jaden says that he hasn't got time.
6. Later Jaden decides that he has to go back.
7. He doesn't know that Sandy is there.
8. She tells the gang where Jaden is.
9. The judges think that their mural is good.
10. Jaden doesn't know which girl is better.

b) *Jaden wrote to a friend about the mural, but he lied about some things.*
Read the e-mail and correct his 19 mistakes.

Hi, Jules. Last week our gang heard about an international mural painting competition. We were really bored, so we decided to take part in it. Just imagine, a TV company gave us three walls and we could paint anything we wanted. We were in the middle of it, when I suddenly remembered that I had to leave. I explained to the others that I had to meet Chloé, a famous actress, in a hotel. She told me that she wanted to be in the movies. I knew that the others were happy for me. But later they needed me to sign the mural, so they all called and asked me to come back. I said 'of course' and Miguel was so pleased that he finished the mural. I decided to go back to the wall at once! It looked really awesome. I looked at it for hours. And next day we got first prize! Chloé was so excited that she threw her arms round me and kissed me …

c) *Why do you think Jaden lied – to make an impression, so that his friend is jealous, to show him that the gang is good, …?*

3 Choose a presentation 3, 10, 18 (→ p. 16/ex. 9)

1. *A performance: Practise the comic and act it for the class.*
   OR
2. *A reading: Write the comic as a story. Record it and play it or read it out to the class.*

The perfect job? A few examples from the UK

You're not sure what job you would like to do? Our tip is: Don't just look at school subjects, think about your free-time activities, too. They can often help you to see what your talents are. Ask adults who are close to you, too. Maybe they can tell you what a job is really like.

I did voluntary part-time work in our local zoo because I wanted to see what a zookeeper does. I knew that they look after animals and feed them but I didn't know that they have to clean their cages. The worst job was cleaning out the tiger cages. They stink!! But it wasn't all bad. The keepers let me help when they did a health check on the baby animals. I liked being with the sea lions best. After two weeks I could answer most visitors' questions.

Karim, 15

➜ You don't need: A-levels
➜ You need: at least 3 GCSEs (Maths, English and Science).

➜ You don't need: good exam results
➜ You need: technical and photography skills

TV Studies is my favourite subject at school. I'd like to work as a cameraman for music videos because I think that's more exciting than films or TV. I've already made three videos for friends. So I've had some practice. Qualifications aren't important – but you can't just go in and start filming. I've applied to twenty TV studios to do an apprenticeship but all I get are 'no's'! I think I'll put the videos on YouTube and see if that helps.

Mike, 16

I wanted to be a chef, so I did three weeks work experience in a local hotel. I worked full-time in the team for vegetables or salads. Other teams did things like bread and cakes. It was really boring. Have you ever cleaned and prepared carrots for a week?
The chef planned the menus, ordered the food, checked the meals and organized all of us. He also told us if we did something wrong, like cooking without our hat!
I still want to become a chef but I never want to eat carrots again!

Olivia, 14

➜ You don't need: A-levels
➜ You need: NVQs in Cooking or Nutrition. There are courses you can do while you're training.

 Für diese Topic brauchst du: Gerundium → G6 • indirekte Rede → G7 + G8 • Verlaufsform → Ov 3 + Ov 4

Task: To find a suitable job or career

1 The photos and the texts 5 Ov3, Ov4

a) *Look at the pictures. What are the people doing? What do you think?*

b) *Choose a caption that describes their activities best for you. The ones in the box can help you.*

c) *Now read the texts. Were you right about the pictures? Do you still agree with the caption which you chose?*

At the zoo • A zookeeper's job • Fun with animals • Lights! Camera! Action! • Give me a camera – I'll make you a star • Behind the camera • A hotel chef at work • King of cooks • Food star • …

2 Job talk 2 G8 (→ p. 17/ex. 10)

a) *What did they say about their 'perfect' jobs? Complete these statements.*

1. Karim thought that the worst job at the zoo
2. He also said that he
3. Mike explained that he
4. He said that qualifications
5. Olivia realised that preparing food
6. She also said that she

a. weren't important for a cameraman's job.
b. was sometimes boring.
c. still wanted to become a chef.
d. was cleaning out the tiger cages.
e. liked being with the sea lions.
f. wanted to make videos.

b) *Read the texts again.*
What do people do in each job? What qualification(s) do they need? Make a grid like this:

Job	What the people do	Qualification(s)
zookeeper	look after …	…

3 A job for me G6 (→ p. 17/ex. 11; p. 18/ex. 12)

Before you can find a job, you need to think about skills, likes/dislikes, health, … .
Answer these questions.

1. What are your special skills / talents?
2. What do you like doing in your free time?
3. What are your best / worst subjects at school?
4. How fit are you?
5. Do you like working in a team?
6. Are you better working alone?
7. Do you like working outside?
8. Are you happier working in a building?

4 Choose a presentation 3, 18 (→ p. 18/ex. 13)

Use the questions from Ex. 3 and make a questionnaire for the other groups.
Then do one of these activities:

1. *A PowerPoint presentation: Inform the others about the three jobs on page 32.*
   Say what people have to do, what qualifications they need, … .
   The others then use their answers to the questionnaire and choose a job that suits them.
   OR
2. *A talk: Explain what you have to do in the three jobs. Use the grid from Ex. 2. Say which one(s) each of you would/would not like to do and why. The others in the class then use their questionnaires to choose a suitable job. Which job is most popular in your class?*

1 Word pairs

a) *Use a word from each of the boxes and put them together to make a new word or word pair. Some have a hyphen:* six-pack

six ✔ • body • peer • turn • chilling • mural • sea

painter • off • group • lion • odour • pack ✔ • out

b) *Match each of the answers in part a) with one of these meanings.*

1. hanging around
2. an animal
3. a hard stomach
4. pictures on a wall
5. it smells bad
6. something that isn't cool
7. kids of the same age

2 Notices in a youth club

Read what they said and put the words in the correct places.

I'm looking for a holiday (1) from July 10th to September 2nd. I'm 16 and I would like to work outside, if possible. I did (2) work on a project for the town (3) last year and I also helped at our school fair. I'm interested in a (4) job.

council
job
full-time
volunteer

ARE YOU INTERESTED IN STYLE? Do you like meeting people? What about an (1) in a hairdresser's? We're looking for two young people for our shop in town. You needn't have any (2). We'll (3) you. Please (4) to the manager at the shop.

train
apprenticeship
apply
experience

Fed up with (1) or just hanging around and (2) time with the (3)? **Why don't you** come to the club at the weekend? We do sports events and (4) trips to interesting places during the school holidays.

gang
chilling out
wasting
organize

Are you worried about (1) in your (2)? Are you frightened of gang (3) in your school? Then our (4) on Friday is for you. Come to the café at 6 p.m.

meeting
crime
members
area

3 Let's talk: Different activities G6

a) *How do Chloé and Jaden feel about these activities? Example:* Chloé **doesn't like wasting … .**

☹ ☹ = hates ☹ = doesn't like ☺ = isn't crazy about ☺ = is good at ☺ ☺ = loves

Chloé

Chloé	Things they can do	Jaden
☹	waste time	☺
☺	date guys / girls who smoke	☹
☺ ☺	shop with other guys / girls	☹ ☹
☹ ☹	paint murals	☺ ☺
☹ ☹	chill out with the gang	☺ ☺
☺	do volunteer work	☺

Jaden

b) *What about you? How do you feel about the activities in part a)?*

OPTION 1

✔ … use a picture to interview someone. G 6, Ov 3, Ov 4

Pretend your partner is a member of the gang in the picture. Ask him/her these questions.

Which one is you?
Who are you with?
Where are you all?
What are you doing?
Why are you doing that?
What else do you like doing in the gang?

✔ … choose a good friend.

Which of these people would/wouldn't you like to have as a friend? Why?

✔ … tell a story in your own words. Ov 3, Ov 4

Tell the story behind one of the pictures in three sentences. What happened? What did the people say and do?

OPTION 2

✔ … talk about job qualifications.

a) *What exams are there in your country which are like these?*

A-levels | GCSEs | NVQs

b) *Give one example of a job you can do with each qualification.*

✔ … choose a job which you would be good at. G 6

What are the jobs in the pictures? Which would you be good at? Think about your special skills, your hobbies and where you would like to work.

(→ p. 19/ex. 14–15; p. 20/ex. 16)

Breaking down barriers[1] (→ pp. 21–23)

A Peterborough newspaper did a series in which they asked young people to talk about their lives. Here are two of them.

OUR 'YOUNG BRITS TODAY' SERIES PART 5

WORK WITH AN ENEMY

Hi! I'm Riz Mirza. I'm 16 and a member of the Unity Youth Crew (UYC). We work with the City Council to help teenagers like me. I didn't know a lot about the crew until I took part in one of their projects. I felt they did a great job. Getting together young people from different communities isn't easy. So when the project finished I did a training course.

My own project, a rap workshop, starts next week. I'm running it with Greg Reidy, 16, who was once my greatest 'enemy'. We hated each other. Our gangs were often in fights. We were shocked when we found we were on the same project. I thought: "No way![2] I'm out of here!" Well, now we're both in the crew!

I'm good at organizing, so I help in the office where we plan projects for kids like cycling[3], acting and team games.

OUR 'YOUNG BRITS TODAY' SERIES PART 6

WORK IS CHILD'S PLAY

My name's Miriam Norton and I'm 16. I was bored after GCSEs, so I got a job in a shop. It's part-time[4] but I now have money for my hobbies – photography and painting. At the moment I'm trying to use both skills in my pictures. I spend all my money on art materials. I'm preparing an art folder. I have to present it when I apply for an Art course at college next year.

On Saturday mornings I do voluntary work in a women's refuge[5]. The women are usually there because they have problems at home. I love being with the kids in the play group. Even the five-year-olds can take great photos! Some spend hours with finger paints or making models. I'm sure it helps them to forget their difficult family situation.

The council is planning to show the kids' work in the town hall.

[1]breaking down barriers ['bæriə] – *Barrieren/Grenzen einreißen,* [2]No way! [nəʊ 'weɪ] – *Auf keinen Fall!,* [3]to cycle ['saɪkl] – *Rad fahren,* [4]part-time ['pɑ:ttaɪm] – *Teilzeit-,* [5]women's refuge ['refju:dʒ] – *Frauenhaus*

A Reading

Read the profiles and find the best answers.

a. Riz Mirza is a teenager who …
1 loves acting. 2 runs projects for kids. 3 hates projects.

b. The members of UYC are …
1 big enemies. 2 from different communities. 3 all rap artists.

c. Greg Reidy is …
1 in the Crew. 2 his biggest enemy. 3 on the City Council.

d. Miriam Norton is 16 and she …
1 has to take her GCSEs. 2 goes to college. 3 works in a shop.

e. Her hobbies are …
1 taking photos and painting. 2 art and technology. 3 working in a shop.

B Language

1 Who or what could these be? Find a word or phrase in the texts.

a. Members of the UYC work with them to help teenagers.
b. Riz didn't know a lot about them until he did a project.
c. They are both working on the same project.
d. Miriam was bored after she had finished them.
e. She has to present it next year.
f. Some kids spend hours with them.

2 Find the words in the texts which are the opposite of these words.

a. terrible	b. the same	c. started	d. friend	e. loved
f. interested	g. full-time	h. save (money)	i. to remember	j. easy

1, 13–14

C Listening

1 Part a: Miriam's plans

Listen to Miriam and Mr Smith. Find the best answer.

a. What kind of dialogue is it? It's …
1 a discussion[1]. 2 an argument. 3 a phone call. 4 a radio chat show.

b. What is it about? It's about …
1 her old school. 2 an interview. 3 an office job. 4 a secretary.

c. What does the other person want to change? He wants to change …
1 his secretary. 2 his number. 3 Miriam's course. 4 an interview date.

d. What will also be different? The thing that will be different is …
1 the room. 2 the letter. 3 the course. 4 Miriam's phone.

2 Part b: Two weeks later …

a. Listen to part b. Who is Mrs Monte? She's …
1 a college secretary. 2 an Art teacher. 3 a play group leader.

b. Where is Miriam? She's ...
1 in a play group. 2 in a shop. 3 in an interview.

c. Listen again. Right or wrong?
1 Mrs Monte is one of the secretaries.
2 Mrs Monte thinks Miriam's ideas are interesting.
3 The two girls in one of her photos are from a playground.
4 Miriam took the photo in a role play session.
5 The shadows in the picture came from the sun.
6 Miriam wanted to underline the colours.
7 The kids in her play group really hate singing.

[1]discussion [dɪ'skʌʃn] – *Diskussion*

D Speaking

1 Describing

a. Describe the scene above as the teenager on the left/right could see it.
Write two sentences.

b. Now choose two other people in the picture. They are watching the scene.
What are they saying? What do you think?
Write a text for speech bubbles for them (one sentence for each person).

2 Role play

You are in the group above. Two of the other girls, Zara and Ruby, start to argue. You try to mediate[1].

Ruby: You're an hour late, Zara. And you promised to be on time.
Zara: I wanted to come earlier, but I couldn't. I had to – er – help – er – a friend.
Ruby: A friend? Is my brother, Neville, a friend? Someone saw you in a café with him.
You: Hey, you two. *(Sage, dass Ruby aufhören soll, zu schreien. Frage, was los ist?)*
Ruby: She's an hour late. And she lied. She said –
You: *(Sage, dass Zara dir erzählen soll, was passiert ist.)*
Zara: Well, I'm sorry I'm so late. But I didn't lie! Maybe you lied, but I –
You: *(Sage Zara, dass sie sagen soll, wo sie war.)*
Zara: OK, if you must know: It's Ruby's birthday soon, right? So Neville wanted some help with a present for her!
You: *(Sage Ruby, dass du glaubst, dass sie sich entschuldigen soll.)*
Ruby: Oh! I didn't know! I'm sorry, Zara.
Zara: That was the idea: He wanted to surprise[2] you!
You: *(Sage, dass du froh bist, dass die Sache jetzt geklärt ist.)*

[1]to mediate ['mi:dieit] – *vermitteln,* [2]to surprise [sə'praiz] – *überraschen*

E Mediation and communication

Your younger brother has heard of Eminem but he doesn't know the film 8 Mile. He sees this photo and asks questions about the film. Read the text and answer his questions.

8 Mile (Curtis Hanson, USA 2002)

The story takes place in Detroit in 1995. 8 Mile Road is a road in the city between the areas where most Blacks and most white Americans live. It is a line which it is difficult to cross.

The film starts at a rap battle[1] where Jimmy B. Rabbit Smith Jr (*played by Eminem*) is so nervous that he has to leave the competition. Jimmy works in a factory and he has a lot of problems. He lives with his mother (*Kim Basinger*), who drinks, his sister and his mom's boyfriend.

At first he thinks others make his problems but slowly he begins to see that he can control his own life. He is fed up with his gang, who do nothing. His dream is to be a musician but he decides to become more serious[2] about his job and his future.

He and his gang often have fights with the members of another gang called the 'Leaders of the Free World'. His greatest enemy is a member called Papa Doc (*Anthony Mackie*).

At an important battle he and Rabbit have to fight against each other. Everbody is frightened of Papa Doc. They think he's a dangerous gangster but Rabbit knows this isn't true. He tells them this in the battle and Rabbit wins it.

His friends in the gang want him to have a big party but Rabbit decides to leave them. He goes back to the factory to work.

[1]battle ['bætl] – *Wettbewerb, Kampf,* [2]serious ['sɪərɪəs] – *ernst*

a. Ich erkenne Eminem, aber wer ist der andere auf dem Foto?
b. Was machen die beiden?
c. Was bedeutet der Titel des Films?
d. Welche Frauen spielen in dem Film?
e. Was passiert am Ende des Films?
f. Warum macht er das?

F Writing

1 Skills

Collect information about you. Think about:

NAME → AGE → HOBBIES → FAVOURITE SUBJECT → INTERESTING JOB FOR ME?

2 Your own profile
Write four to five sentences about you. Use the information from part 1.

Topic 3 Freedom's just another word for …

1

1. Think about your idea of freedom.
   a) What is freedom for you?
   b) Where and when do you feel most free?

   For me freedom is having enough money / no school / staying out late / … .
   I feel most free on holiday / at weekends / on my own / with my friends, … .

2. Which of the photos is nearest to your idea of freedom? Why?

3. Read the captions in the box on the right. (→ p. 24/ex. 1–2)
   a) Try to guess the new words. Check at the back of your book.
   b) Match each photo with a caption.

Free with music • Free of borders • Free fall • Free to protest • Free and equal?

4. Sort the photos under 'political' and 'personal' freedom.

5. Work with a picture: Photo 1 is from an advert.
   a) What do you think it was for? Look for ideas in the box on the right.
   b) Collect more advertising photos which use the idea of freedom for a product and make a collage.

airport • parachuting club • adventure holiday • sports clothes • bank • paragliding club • …

2

3

4

5

1 *Snowboarding in the Rockies*
2 *Racial discrimination in the US*
3 *Young man playing the guitar*
4 *An anti war protest*
5 *The fence along the border between Mexico and the US*

➪ 547550-0005/0006

WE OFTEN THINK OF FREEDOM AS A RIGHT: THE RIGHT TO BE HAPPY, TO DO THE JOB WE LIKE, TO PRACTISE OUR RELIGION, TO MARRY THE PERSON WE CHOOSE, ...

A The song for freedom

→ Option 1

Martin Luther King

MARTIN LUTHER KING (1929 – 1968) fought against the discrimination of Blacks. In his opinion we must always fight for our rights and the rights of others. But we should do this without violence. The fight may take many forms: demos, media reports – even a song can help.
There are, in fact, a number of songs about M. L. King. One example was by Bono from the group U2. In 1984 he wrote a song called 'Pride (in the Name of Love)[1]'. The last verse is about King's murder.

Bono

Early morning, April 4
Shot rings out in the Memphis sky
Free at last, they took your life
They could not take your pride

Another example are the words at the start of a song called 'Death Of Martin Luther King[2]'. Champion Jack Dupree recorded it just after King's murder:

Well the world lost a good man
When we lost Doctor Martin Luther King
A man who tried to do everything
He tried to keep the world in peace
And now the poor man is gone to rest
But go on, Doctor Martin Luther King, take your rest
There will always be another Luther King

1 M. L. King and a song 5 G3

Read text A. Choose the ending for each sentence.

1. Martin Luther King said that we …
   a. must fight for our rights. b. should hate others. c. may use violence.
2. King felt that the fight …
   a. mustn't take different forms. b. may take many forms. c. must end in violence.
3. The song 'Pride' is about the day King …
   a. had a fight. b. wrote a song. c. died.

1, 15 2 Let's listen: Two reactions to murder 15

a) *Before you listen, read the song texts (A) again. What could these words mean?*
   1. rings out (You know 'a bell rings'.) 2. at last (You know 'at first'.)
   3. to rest (You know 'rest area'; here it is about the end of life.)
   Check in a dictionary.

b) *Now listen to Bono's verse.*
   1. When, where and how did King die? 2. What couldn't the killer take from King?

c) *Listen to Dupree. Right or wrong? In Dupree's opinion:*
   1. King lost a good man. 2. King tried to keep peace in the world.
   3. It's OK for King to take his rest. 4. There will never be another Luther King.

d) *Correct the sentences which are wrong in c).*

 Für diese Topic brauchst du: modale Hilfsverben → G3 • Adjektive → Ov5

... BUT IT WASN'T ALWAYS LIKE THAT. MARTIN LUTHER KING FOUGHT FOR OUR RIGHTS (FOR EXAMPLE THE RIGHT TO VOTE). WE OWE OUR FREEDOM TO PEOPLE LIKE HIM.

B Careers: Going it alone

++ CAREERAID ++ CAREERAID ++ CAREERAID ++ CAREERAID ++ CAREERAID ++

Your website for careers info – including advice, profiles, your experiences, tips and tricks ...

our team | training & jobs | careers advice | **profiles** | e-mail us

Steve Fosset (1944–2007)

THIS WEEK'S PROFILE: A man who never gave up easily: Steve Fossett

A FIGHTING SPIRIT FOR QUICK SUCCESS

Like the old American pioneers Steve Fossett tried everything. He was adaptable and didn't give up easily. At school he wasn't good at sports but he climbed some mountains and after four attempts he swam the English Channel. His solo, non-stop balloon flight round the world made him famous but he had to try six times before he was successful.

He had a good job at IBM but he soon decided to 'go it alone' because he wanted to be his own boss. That way he was free to try out his own ideas.

He set up several businesses and in the early 80's made a lot of money. He was enterprising and his fighting spirit brought him quick success. The money he made helped him to follow his dreams.

→ Option 2

3 Profile of a man 5

a) *Read the article (B) and list 2–3 facts about Steve Fossett.*

b) *Match the sentence parts.*

1. Fossett was like a pioneer, which meant that	was successful after he had tried six times.
2. Fossett was terrible at sports but	before he swam the English Channel.
3. He needed four attempts	to follow his own dreams.
4. His solo balloon flight around the world	because he wanted to be his own boss.
5. He left his job at IBM	which helped him follow his dreams.
6. 'Going it alone' meant that Fossett was free	he climbed some mountains.
7. He made a lot of money,	he tried everything and didn't give up easily.

4 Describing a pioneer 10 (→ p. 25/ex. 3–5)

a) *Read text B again. Choose five words or phrases which describe Steve Fossett best for you and write sentences. You can choose from the ones below or you can find your own words.*

independent • unfriendly • loved adventure • scary • enterprising • angry • sporty • lucky • successful • famous • terrible • bored • brave • proud • dangerous • good with money

b) *Compare with your partner. Did you choose the same words? What was different?*

c) *Think of people in your neighbourhood/family/... who have decided to 'go it alone'. What are their jobs (e.g. shop owner, cook, hairdresser, ...)? Write 3–5 sentences.*

Milestones: From slavery to citizen's rights

1929 In 1865 US slaves get their freedom but Blacks don't have the same rights as white Americans. Blacks may vote but there is **discrimination** in jobs (e.g. less pay for the same work).
When **Martin Luther King** is born in 1929, there is a policy of **segregation**: Blacks must go to different schools. They mustn't mix with white people in public places.

1954 Segregation in schools and universities officially ends. They must now let black students in. Many Americans – black and white – feel that Blacks should have the same rights as white people. The **Civil Rights Movement begins**.

1955

1955 **Rosa Parks** doesn't give up her seat to a white person in the 'colored' part of a bus. The police arrest her. As a protest the black people of Montgomery, Alabama, decide that nobody should use the buses. The bus service ends segregation on its buses a year later.

1957

1957 **Martin Luther King** and others found a non-violent protest group. Some US states don't accept the new laws against segregation. So many black students can't enter their schools. One such group is the **'Little Rock Nine'**. The National Guard has to help them to get in!

1963 Shocked by scenes of police violence on TV, people start to support the protesters. About 200,000 march for jobs and freedom in Washington DC. There King gives his famous **'I have a dream'** speech.

1963

1964 King gets the 1964 **Nobel Peace Prize** because he fights with words – not with weapons.

1965 Los Angeles, California, August 1965: **Race riots** break out in a Black part of the city.

1965

1968 Memphis, Tennessee, **4th April**: Martin Luther King is shot dead. There are riots in many cities all over the world.

Today The US government **bans** racial discrimination. And by law there should be equal pay. Black Americans work in all areas of society and some have top positions in firms and in the government. There are still reports of discrimination especially by **the police**.

 Für diese Topic brauchst du: modale Hilfsverben → G3 • Adjektive → Ov5

Task: To find out about civil rights

1 Your civil rights 2 (→ p. 26/ex. 6)

a) *Which of these rights do you have?*

The right to:
use public transport • vote • carry a gun • go to school • protest peacefully

b) *What other rights do you have in your country?*

2 Key words 5 (→ p. 26/ex. 7)

a) *The words in the box are from the text. Match them with the right meaning.*
1. working without pay or rights
2. unfair treatment of one group of people
3. a policy which, for example, makes one group sit on different seats
4. the rights which you have as a citizen
5. violent protests by a crowd of people

segregation • riots • slavery • civil rights • discrimination

b) *Use each of the key words from a) in a sentence.*

3 Things have changed G3 (→ p. 26/ex. 8; p. 27/ex. 9–10)

Read the milestones again and choose the best words to complete the sentences.
1. Until 1865 there was slavery in the US, but now no one *(may/must)* keep slaves.
2. Today all US citizens *(mustn't/may)* vote but before 1870 only white people had this right.
3. Now, by law, Blacks *(should/can't)* get the same pay as Whites.
4. Blacks *(mustn't/can)* go to all schools and colleges today, but before 1954 there was segregation.
5. Today bus companies *(must/mustn't)* let people sit where they want.

4 Choose a presentation 2, 3, 18 (→ p. 27/ex. 11)

1. *A quiz:*

a) *Your group writes a date or a key word (name or event) on cards. (Use one card for each piece of info).*

b) *In your group write notes for each card.*

c) *The others in the class each choose a card and ask a question about it in turn.*

d) *Your group uses its notes from b) and answers the questions.*

OR

2. *A gallery walk (poster profile of Martin Luther King):*

a) *Work with a partner. Use part A on page 42 and the milestones opposite and start a mind map about M. L. King.*

b) *Use your mind map for a poster about King. Find one or two photos and a good title.*

c) *You and your partner use your poster to tell the class about King.*

d) *Put your poster up in your class. The class looks at all the posters and votes for the best one.*

Careers advice

A Cartoon

"I see... and any ideas *other than* Supreme Ruler of the Universe?"

C An employee's view

Emilio Conte, one of Jo's employees

B Should you 'go it alone'?

"OK, I'm not rich but I'm my own boss!"

A US survey showed that almost 8% of the working population wanted to start their own business. The reason for a third of them was 'to make more money'. Other reasons were 'to be my own boss' and 'to fulfill a dream'. One of our readers, Jo Delaney, owns a bistro bar. This is what she told our reporter:

As a child I was very independent. My mom had a small hotel and was always busy, so I organized my own life a lot.

My dream was to open my own snack bar. I did a catering course at high school. Later I worked in a restaurant in Hollywood. When their chef quit one night, I took over the kitchen. I liked the work but the hours were crazy and I didn't earn much! Also, my employer was always in a bad mood. So I decided to go it alone.

There were lots of different bars in my town but none of them were good. Many Americans like French food, so I thought a French bistro would be a good idea. I worked out a business plan and looked around for a place to rent.

Luckily my bank manager gave me a loan and two months later we opened.

That was three years ago. It was really hard at first. You can't take a vacation or have a day off if you're ill. But it's going well now. We have a lot of regular customers: We're near the college, so students come for breakfast or get takeaways for lunch.

OK, I'm not rich but I'm my own boss. And I'm never in a bad mood! Ask Emilio! He sees me every day.

Task: To find out about self-employment

1 A cartoon: The right job? 2, 7 (→ p. 28/ex. 12)

a) *Who and where are the people? What's happening? Compare your answers.*

b) *What jobs could the young man do? Tell your group. Do they have different ideas?*

2 An employer 3, 5 (→ p. 28/ex. 13)

a) *Read the title of the article (B). What do you think it could be about?*

b) *Read the text. What does Jo say about the pros and cons of her job? Collect them in a grid.*

c) *Discuss in the group. Have you missed anything? Add your own ideas to your grid from part b).*

1, 16 3 Let's listen: An employee 15 (→ p. 28/ex. 14)

a) *In part C Emilio talks about his job at Jo's bistro. Before you listen, match the words and meanings.*

to give orders • baguette • a slug • temporary

a small creature that loves lettuce • not for always • to tell others what to do • it's long, it's bread and it's French

b) *Listen and find the best answer.*

1. Emilio likes his job because *(he's happy to do what Jo tells him / he loves paper work).*
2. He wouldn't be a good employer because *(he doesn't like customers / he hates giving orders).*

c) *Which job would you rather have – Jo's or Emilio's? Why?*

4 If you start a business, ... 4 G3, Ov5 (→ p. 28/ex. 15; p. 29/ex. 16)

a) *Think: Read the tips and put them in order of importance for you.*

Good with money	→ Good business sense is important: You mustn't spend all your money!
Organized	→ For example: Keep careful records of everything.
Independent	→ Remember: You are the boss now. You must decide.
Trained	→ You should train to do the job. But find out about exams etc. first!
Adaptable	→ You must know how to act in an emergency.
Legal	→ You should know about the age limits: For some jobs you must be over 18. Or you may not borrow money either till then.
Outgoing	→ You must know your customers and find out what they want or need.
Enterprising	→ You shouldn't be afraid of new ideas.

b) *Pair: Compare your list with your partner's list. Do you want to change your list?*

c) *Share: Decide in your group which three tips you think are most important.*

5 Presentation: Self-employment 3, 18 (→ p. 29/ex. 17)

a) *Use your grid from Ex. 2 and tell the class the pros and cons of self-employment.*

b) *Give the class the above list of tips. Which three do they think are most important? Why? Tell them what your group thought was most important and why.*

c) *Do a class survey: How many would like to 'go it alone'? Why? What would they like to do?*

1 Odd one out

Find the one word or phrase which doesn't fit in the group.

1. angry – equal – free – happy
2. radio – TV – reporter – newspaper
3. reports – laws – rules – limits
4. solo – alone – double – one
5. to tell – to say – to text – to protest
6. catering – slug – bistro – restaurant
7. discrimination – university – violence – segregation
8. independent – angry – enterprising – adaptable
9. government – career – advice – job
10. employer – boss – director – technology

2 Different people

Look at the definitions. Who are the people?

1. They are people who belong to a country.
2. They have a job and an employer.
3. They are the first to try out or do something new.
4. They show they are against a policy or an idea.
5. They are people at the head of a country.
6. They decide what a group of people should do.
7. They are a special kind of police.
8. Reporters write articles for these people.

employees
leaders
pioneers
citizens
readers
protesters
National Guard
rulers

3 Remembering M. L. King

Choose the right words for this report about Martin Luther King.

Martin Luther King was an American civil rights *(winner/leader)*. He *(fought/sang)* against the discrimination of Blacks. He was for *(violent/non-violent)* protest. In 1963 there was a huge march for jobs and *(discrimination/freedom)* in Washington. King gave his famous 'I have a *(friend/dream)*' speech there.

A year later he got the Nobel *(People's/Peace)* Prize because he fought for people's rights without using *(weapons/demos)*. Martin Luther King died in Memphis, Tennessee on April 4th. After his murder there were *(milestones/riots)* all over the world.

Now, every year, Americans *(remember/believe)* this great man on the third Monday in January – on Martin Luther King Day.

4 Steve, Jo or Emilio?

Make a grid with the headings Steve Fossett, Jo Delaney and Emilio Conte. Choose words/phrases from the box which describe these people and put them under the right heading. (Some can go under more than one heading.)

independent person • no formal training • worked for IBM • wanted to earn more • wasn't good at sports • couldn't be boss • did catering course • adaptable person • hates paper work • outgoing person • wanted to be his/her own boss • left school at 16 • didn't give up easily • made a lot of money in different businesses • did temporary jobs • found the work hard at first • opened bistro bar • had quick success • isn't good at giving orders

OPTION 1

✓ … write about important events in the American Civil Rights Movement.

Name four important dates in the history of the CRM in the US. What happened then? Write one sentence about each.

✓ … recognise important figures in the CRM.

a) *Who is the man in the photo? What is he doing and why?*

b) *Name one more important figure in the CRM. Say why he/she was important. (2 sentences)*

✓ … write about civil rights and freedom. G3

Write four sentences about civil rights and freedom in your country. The phrases in the box can help you. Start like this:

In my country you can/can't/may/may not/must/mustn't/should/shouldn't … .

show discrimination because of colour, age, religion • vote when you are 18 • choose a job you like • marry who you want • …

OPTION 2

✓ … compare employers and employees. G3

a) *Name one thing you can do and two things you can't do if you are an employer.*

b) *Name one thing you may do and one thing you shouldn't do if you are an employee.*

c) *Look at the photos. What must the 'secretary' do for her boss?*

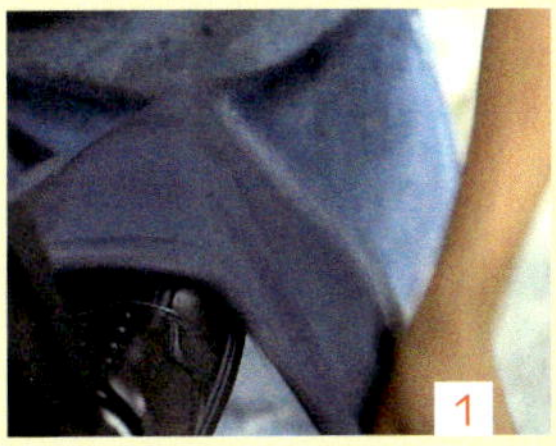
1

2

3

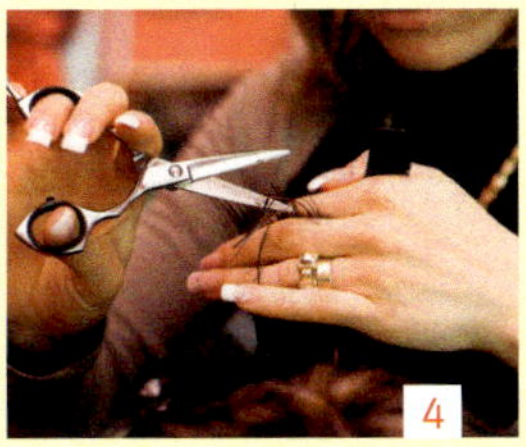
4

d) *Would you like to be the 'secretary' or her boss? Why/Why not?*

✓ … give advice on starting a business. G4, Ov5

What sort of person should you be if you want to start a business? Choose five words from below.

beautiful · legal · organized · independent · trained · intelligent · enterprising · careful · adaptable · rich

(→ p. 30/ex. 18; p. 31/ex. 19)

A child of the 'Stolen Generation' – A short biography[1]

(→ pp. 32–34)

Archie Roach wasn't a real orphan[2]. He was a child of the Stolen Generation. Roach was born in 1956 in Mooroopna, Australia. As a small boy he lived in a mission house. Later he stayed with foster[3] parents, the Coxes, in Melbourne.

There Roach learned to play the guitar and the keyboard from Mary, the Coxes' oldest daughter. He loved music.

When Roach was older, he got a letter from one of his sisters. She told him about their real family. He was upset with his foster family and their lies: He left them and tried to find other family members[4]. But his parents were dead and the only person he found was one of his sisters.

With only his guitar in his hand, he travelled to Sydney and Adelaide. Of course, he had no money so he lived out in the streets. It was a difficult time in his life and he drank a lot. But he began to make his own music and he met his future[5] partner, Ruby Hunter. At the end of 1980 Roach and Hunter started a band, the 'Altogethers'.

One of Roach's first songs was called *Took the Children Away.* It was about his own past. But it was more than that: It told the story of the Native Australian people's fight for their rights. It moved many Australians across the country, both native and white, when he played it on a TV show.

Roach won an international human rights award for *Took the Children Away.* For the first time the award went to someone for a song!

In the year of the Olympics in Sydney (2000) Roach became famous around the world. This was because 'Time Magazine' did an article about him and put his photo on the front cover.

Today Roach and Hunter live with their children near Berri, South Australia. They keep their home open to Native Australian kids and offer them a break from life out on the streets.

INFO BOX: The Stolen Generation

'Aboriginal'[6] people (or 'Native Australians') were the first people who lived in Australia. Between 1869 and 1969 white officials took tens of thousands of 'Aboriginal' children from their parents. The parents couldn't stop them. They took the kids to missions or gave them to white foster parents. The children often had to do all the housework there. They were very unhappy and missed their families. These children were called the 'Stolen Generation'.
In 2008 the Australian Prime Minister[7] Kevin Rudd said sorry to families of the Stolen Generation. He wanted Australians to 'turn[8] a new page' for a better future.

[1]biography [baɪ'ɒgrəfi] – *Biografie,* [2]orphan ['ɔ:fn] – *Waisenkind,* [3]foster ['fɒstə] – *Pflege-,* [4]member ['membə] – *Mitglied,* [5]future ['fju:tʃə] – *zukünftig,* [6]Aboriginal [ˌæbə'rɪdʒnl] – *Ureinwohner/in,* [7]prime minister [praɪm 'mɪnɪstə] – *Premierminister/in,* [8]to turn [tɜ:n] – *umblättern*

A Reading

1 Find the English words in the text for these German words.

Lüge • Generation • Mission • Keyboard

2 Read the text and find out …

a. the name of Roach's foster family.
b. the places he went to with his guitar.
c. the song for which he won an award.
d. the place where he now lives.
e. the band he formed with Ruby.
f. the magazine that did an article on him.

3 Read the text again and choose the right word to complete each sentence.

a. When he was a small child, Archie Roach lived in …
1 a mission house. 2 Scotland. 3 Sydney.

b. Children who had to leave their families were called …
1 Blues Artists. 2 Street Kids. 3 the Stolen Generation.

c. Archie left the Coxes because …
1 he was afraid. 2 he was upset. 3 he had to do all the housework.

d. He became famous because …
1 a magazine printed his photo. 2 he sang a song. 3 he made a film.

e. He opens his home to Native Australian kids who …
1 can play the guitar. 2 are orphans. 3 live on the streets.

B Language

1 Find phrases from the text which mean the same as …

a. a children's home.
b. became known in many countries.
c. wrote about him.
d. a lot of listeners[1] cried.
e. to give them a short holiday.

2 Which word(s) in the text mean the opposite of the word(s) in bold[2]?

a. **real** parents b. an **easy** time c. drinking **very little** d. the **back page of a book**

1, 17 ◎
C Listening

Listen to three teenagers – Angie, Trevor and Mike. They are talking about Prime Minister Kevin Rudd's speech on the Stolen Generation.

Listen again and complete the sentences with the correct endings.

	+	
a. Angie listened to Rudd's speech		just before she died.
b. Rudd said he was sorry		from outside the building where he spoke.
c. They took away Trevor's aunt		when she was a baby and they changed her name.
d. Angie's grandad found his mother		about the terrible life which the Stolen Generation had.

[1]listener ['lɪsnə] – *Zuhörer/in,* [2]in bold [bəʊld] – *fett*

D Speaking

1 Fighting for your rights

a. Look at the photos. What's happening? What are the people fighting for/against?

1

2

b. Choose one of the photos for a flyer about the protest. Say why you chose it. Give two reasons.

2 Role play

You and your German cousin see a protest when you are on holiday: Some skaters want a place where they can skate in their town.
Your cousin wants to find out more but he/she can't speak English. Help him/her.

Cousin: *Hey, was ist denn hier los? Kannst du bitte mal nachfragen?*
You: Hi, there. …?
Protester: There's a great place behind the concert hall. We always skate there. Now the town wants to stop us.
You: *Es gibt einen tollen Platz … .*
Cousin: *Oh, das ist Pech. Warum ist die Stadt dagegen?*
You: Oh, that's …?
Protester: We're pretty loud – but we never skate when there's a concert. I guess some people think we're dangerous!
You: *Sie sind …!*
Cousin: *Warum schreiben sie nicht einen Brief an die Zeitung – oder erzählen einem Reporter von dem Problem?*
You: Why don't you …?
Protester: Well, the local radio is doing an interview with us tomorrow at 5:15 pm. Maybe you can listen to it!
You: *Sie geben morgen …!*
Cousin: *Sag danke und sag, dass wir das Interview anhören werden.*
You: …!

E Mediation and communication

You are talking to another German tourist who doesn't speak English. Someone gives you a flyer. Try to answer the tourist's questions about it.

Help us to save our disco now!

- **DON'T** let the town close our only disco!
- **SIGN** our supporters' list. Find more supporters to sign!
- **SUPPORT** our action group! Tell your friends and family!
- **COME** to our 'Disco in the Park':
  Info, music, food and drinks and more!
  WHEN? 12 o'clock, 10th November
  WHERE? King's Park, Littleton

Who are we?
We're young people who live in this area.
We love music, dancing and meeting friends.

Why do we need you?
If the disco closes, we'll have to travel miles to get to the next disco.
That means we'll need night buses. We can't afford[1] taxis!
We're also afraid of a rise in 'drinking and driving'!

How can you support us?
- Discuss the problem at school and in your family:
  How will YOU get to the disco in the next town if they close our disco?
- Write to your local newspaper about the problem.
  Find as many reasons as you can for the disco to stay open.
- Take part in our action in the park.

a. Wer hat diesen Flyer geschrieben?
b. Was fordern die Verfasser?
c. Was für eine Aktion planen sie?
d. Welche Probleme gibt es? (2 Dinge)
e. Wie kann man sie unterstützen? (3 Sachen)

F Writing

1 Skills
Your town wants to close your youth club/build offices on fields where you play football … .
You want to plan a protest with a summer fair at your youth club/a sports event on the fields.
You decide to write a leaflet[2] (like the one in part E) about your protest action. Make a list of the information you will need to put in the leaflet. (Who is protesting? Why? What? When? …)

2 A leaflet
Use your ideas and write a short text (50 – 60 words) for your leaflet.

[1]to afford [ə'fɔ:d] – *sich leisten,* [2]leaflet ['li:flet] – *Flugblatt*

1, 18–24 ◎
Joy riding[1] 5

The main characters:

Max – gets bored easily, is soft on someone[2]

Jake – Max's friend, loves big burgers

Kayla – cool, a bit of a show-off[3]

Lucy – Kayla's friend, Kayla is her big star!

1 The story

A It was Saturday night in downtown[4] Chicago. Max and Jake decided to hang out at the Big Bite Burgers. Jake wanted to go there for one of their 3B 'specials'. Max wasn't hungry, but he decided to hang out with his friend. He had his own reason[5]: The burger bar was across the street from the movie theater. And that's where Kayla and her friend, Lucy, will be. Then they'll certainly come in here after the movie, he thought. Or, at least, he *hoped* they would …

Max ordered a coke and watched as Jake began to eat his huge burger. The burger bar began to fill up with kids, so the film was over, thought Max. He looked over his friend's shoulder and kept an eye on the door for Kayla. Could it be that the girls had other plans for the evening?

"You are soft on that Kayla, eh?" said Jake, like he could read Max's mind.

"No, where did you get that stupid idea?" said Max, not laughing. "Come on, Jake, let's get out of here before I yawn[6] myself to death!"

[1]joy riding ['dʒɔɪ ˌraɪdɪŋ] – *eine Spritztour machen,* [2]to be soft on sb [sɒft] – *für jmdn. schwärmen,* [3]show-off ['ʃəʊɒf] – *Angeber/in,* [4]downtown [daʊn'taʊn] – *Stadtzentrum,* [5]reason ['ri:zn] – *Grund,* [6]to yawn [jɔ:n] – *gähnen*

B A few blocks south of downtown, a car stopped outside Lucy's home. Lucy opened the car door and climbed in.

"Wow, Kayla!" she said. "How did you get your daddy's car? Where are we going?"

"Now, that's for me to know and for you to find out," answered Kayla in a voice full of mystery. "But let's check who's at the 3Bs first!" …

C Max and Jake walked along the street silently. Suddenly a car stopped in front of them.

"Hey, look, Jake! It's Kayla and Lucy," said Max, in a cool voice. He didn't want Jake to see how excited he was.

"Hi, Kayla! That's your daddy's car, right? So you two are going somewhere fast in the middle of the night, eh?" Jake laughed.

"Yeah, he was asleep so I just 'borrowed' it from him, you know. I'm showing Lucy how to drive. Then she's gonna[1] take me for a ride[2]," answered Kayla, and smiled.

Max thought, 'I'd like to take Kayla for a ride, too.'

Instead[3], he said, "Now that's strange. Jake and I are also going for a ride. Isn't that right, Jake?"

"What? Oh … er … yeah, Max. We're just getting the car …" answered Jake. But he didn't really understand what his friend meant.

"Yeah, you got it, Jake," said Max with a smile[4]. "Lucy, just stay around here and practice your driving, and we'll be back in a few seconds!"

a) *Stop! What do you think the boys will do?*

D As the boys walked away, Jake turned to Max and said, "Now, how are we gonna get a car? And who's gonna drive? You know that you don't have a driver's license any more …"

"So you want to hang out here doing nothing, eh? Don't spoil[5] the fun! Don't tell me that *you* can't drive, Jake! Who needs a license?!" said Max.

"Well …, yeah, of course, I can drive. My brother showed me, but …"

"No 'buts' Jake! We told the girls that we're going for a ride. And that's what we're doing, OK?"

They chose an old Chevy that stood in a dark side road. Jake stood at the end of the road to check that no one came around the corner.

Max worked quickly. He got the door open and started the engine for Jake.

Then he got into the passenger seat and said, "Hey, Jake, what are you waiting for? Let's get away from this place!"

At the end of the road they turned into Main Street. Suddenly Max saw Kayla's car. It stood on the side. Lucy was now in the driver's seat.

"Hey, cool!" said Lucy when she saw Jake at the wheel[6]. "Let's go, you guys!"

[1]gonna ['gɒnə] – *umgangssprachlich für* going to, [2]to take sb for a ride [ˌteɪk fər‿ə 'raɪd] – *mit jmdm. eine Spritztour machen,* [3]instead [ɪn'sted] – *stattdessen,* [4]smile [smaɪl] – *Lächeln,* [5]to spoil [spɔɪl] – *verderben,* [6]wheel [wi:l] – *Lenkrad*

E The boys were close behind the girls' car.

"They're too slow," shouted Max. "Flash them!"

He put his head out of the window and shouted, "Hey, Lucy, the gas pedal[1] is on the right!"

"What do they want?" Lucy asked Kayla. "Max is shouting something but I don't know what …"

"Hell! They're too close to us. Faster, Lucy," said Kayla as she turned up the music even louder and started to sing at the top of her voice.

Lucy put her foot down on the gas. Now they were much faster than the speed limit[2]. Still the boys stayed close behind them.

"Come on, girl, go fast. We're first and they're last. I know them, come on, let's show them!" rapped Kayla to the rhythm[3] of the music.

Then suddenly she shouted at her friend,

"Hey, don't let them overtake[4]!"

There were just the two cars on the road. The guys were now in the fast lane[5]. Suddenly there was a bend[6]. Jake noticed too late. He put his foot down on the brakes[7]. The car swerved and hit the side of the other car. Lucy had no time to think. Their car crashed[8] into the barrier[9] and came to a stop. Everything went silent …

b) *Read part E again. Which picture describes the accident correctly?*

F Somehow Jake stopped the car. Max got out. He had blood on his clothes and on his hands. That scared him because he couldn't work out where the blood came from. He looked around wildly and started to walk away.

Jake got out of the car.

"Hey, Max!" he shouted. "We must get help!"

But Max didn't hear him. His head was hurting and his body was cold. He couldn't walk right. Something was wrong with his right leg.

My cell phone. That's right – I have to get help, thought Jake. He called an ambulance. Then he went over to the wreck[10].

"Lucy? Kayla?" he shouted.

But there was no answer. He tried to get them out but he just couldn't open any of the doors. He started to run.

[1]gas pedal ['gæs ˌpedl] – *Gaspedal,* [2]speed limit ['spi:d ˌlɪmɪt] – *Geschwindigkeitsbegrenzung,* [3]rhythm ['rɪðm] – *Rhythmus,* [4]to overtake [əʊvə'teɪk] – *überholen,* [5]fast lane ['fɑ:st ˌleɪn] – *Überholspur,* [6]bend [bend] – *Kurve,* [7]brake [breɪk] – *Bremse,* [8]to crash [kræʃ] – *krachen,* [9]barrier ['bæriə] – *Leitplanke,* [10]wreck [rek] – *Wrack*

G Lucy woke up in a clear, sunny room.

The light hurt her eyes so she closed them again. She tried to think: Where am I? This time she opened her eyes more carefully. She saw someone next to her bed. It was a nurse.

"A police officer will be here soon," said the nurse quietly. "She wants to ask some questions. But, my dear, if it gets too much for you, tell me – or just look at me. And I'll send the police officer away."

I don't know what she's talking about, thought Lucy. Her head hurt really badly. She couldn't remember anything! Then it came back to her suddenly, scene for scene. She began to cry.

"Kayla? What about Kayla?" she whispered.

"Now, don't worry about your friend. She's going to make it, I'm sure. Just try and rest."

[adapted[4] from *Joy Riding* by Hamida Aziz]

2 Right or wrong?

1. Max and Jake go to the movie theater.
2. Max isn't very hungry.
3. Max is soft on Kayla.
4. Lucy got her daddy's car.
5. Max takes Kayla for a ride.
6. Jake has a driver's license.
7. The cars are too fast.
8. Jake notices the bend too late.

3 A chat room message

Does this chat room message describe Kayla and her friends' accident correctly? Write a short text. Say why/why not.

>>> Hi! Did you hear about Lucy, Jake and Max? They had a terrible accident with Lucy's mother's car. They crashed into another car. But they were lucky. Nothing happened to them. <<<

4 Who made a mistake?

a) *Make a grid in your exercise book and write down which mistake each of the four characters made. Use your grid and write a short text.*

Max	Jake	Kayla	Lucy

b) *Discuss in your group who made the worst mistake. Start like this:* I think … made the worst mistake because he/she … /didn't … .

5 An ending 10

How does the story end? What do you think?

a) *Write an ending for the story. Write at least four or five sentences.*

b) *Get together in groups of four or five and read all your endings in your group. Choose the best ending and present it in class.*

6 A class discussion[2] 3, 19

Kids in the US can drive alone at the age of 16. Do you think this is a good/bad idea? Why?

[1]adapted [əˈdæptɪd] – *angepasst,* [2]discussion [dɪˈskʌʃn] – *Diskussion*

Topic 4 Global matters

dirt / chemicals in the water / air • trade • opportunities • pollution • energy from the sun or wind • climate changes • poverty • inter-cultural exchange • talking to / contacting people • international business

1. Work with a picture: Look at photo 1 and its caption. Read the words in the box. Which words go with the photo?
2. Look at the other photos. Match each one with a word or words from the box. (→ p. 35/ex. 1–2)
3. Which photo goes best with each of these four headlines? What do you think?

Satellite links …

DEATH BY OIL?

Cocoa on the move!

Wind or sun: Which one?

3

4

1 + 2 *Modern communication in Mongolia*
3 + 4 *Oil pollution*
5 *Alternative energy: Solar panels and a windmill*
6 *World market: Worker on a cocoa farm in Ghana*

5

6

⇨ 547550-0007/0008

'Products' of globalisation

INFO CARD

PROS
- News travels fast (Internet and satellite).
- You can watch TV from different countries.
- You can send e-mails in seconds.
- Many companies are multinational.
- Cheap flights to everywhere!
- We can buy the same products everywhere and they're often cheaper.
- Millions in poor countries get jobs.
- Shipping gets products to us quickly.

INFO CARD

CONS
- Millions of workers in poor countries are paid very badly.
- Multinational goods make local ones expensive.
- TV: More is not always better!
- Criminals can use the Internet, too!
- Multinational companies 'control' the world.
- Shipping causes pollution: Some ships dump dangerous rubbish or their oil in the sea.
- More travel means more greenhouse gases.
- News travels fast but 'rubbish' travels faster!

A We are the world

Young people from different countries met in London last month. They all agreed: If governments worldwide cared more, young people would have a better and healthier future. Two speakers there were:

Kofi, 16, is from Ghana, West Africa. He worked on a cocoa farm. His talk was about the situation of slaves there.

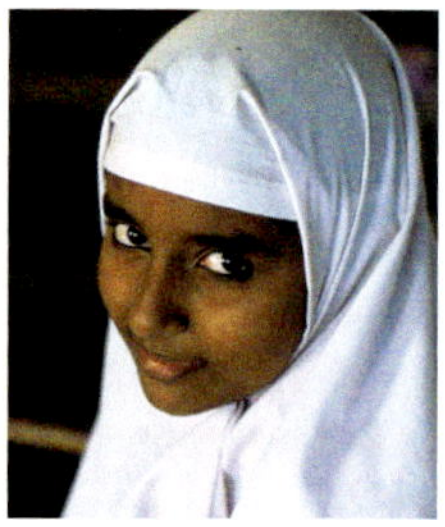

Zameera, 17, is from the Maldives. Her talk was about some of the environmental problems in her country.

→ Option 1

1 The price of globalisation 2, 5

a) *Look at the info cards at the top of this page. Match each photo with a fact from the cards.*

b) *Read the facts again and match each pro with a con.*

c) *Which two pros and which two cons are most important for you? Write a short text. Compare it with your partner's.*

1, 25–26

2 Let's listen: We are the world 15 (→ p. 36/ex. 3–4)

Read about Kofi and Zameera (A). Then listen and find the right sentence endings.

1. In the city some men offered Kofi	a. money.	b. cocoa.	c. a job.
2. Workers in the cocoa fields were	a. slaves.	b. farm owners.	c. company workers.
3. Kofi escaped after	a. 4 years.	b. in a van.	c. with a friend.
4. Zameera is worried about	a. holidays.	b. the future.	c. boats and ships.
5. The sea level is rising because	a. it rains.	b. there's no sun.	c. there are climate changes.

B A global disaster

Some Australian kids see this advert and decide to go there. It'll be a holiday that they'll never forget – but more like a nightmare than a dream for some of them!

*Imagine beaches with white, coral sand and clear, blue water with colourful fish near beautiful reefs – all free of pollution: A dream holiday that you'll never forget! But hurry – or you'll miss the chance to see this paradise!**

* Most islands there aren't more than 1 metre above sea level. And the sea is rising at almost 1 cm/year. Scientists have warned: If global warming continues, the Maldives will disappear by the end of this century! And that's just one of many environmental problems these islands have today.

➜ Option 2

C A new 'eco' car

New eco sports car: But is it really eco?

A US company plans to launch an eco sports car this year. They call it 'eco' because it runs on electricity – not on fossil fuel. Other US companies are now testing a new model which looks more like a plane than a car. The 'flying' car will be much lighter than cars we know. The question is: If they built such a car, would it *in fact* be better for the environment? Companies like using the word 'eco'. But do they really understand – or care – what that means?

3 Paradise lost? G4, 5, Ov3, Ov4

a) *Look at the advert (B). If you visited the Maldives, what would you do there?*

If I went there, I would ...

go swimming/diving/... • take photos of the fish/scenery/coral reef/... • like lying ... • enjoy watching/looking at ...

b) *Read the advert again. What could stop people from living on the Maldives one day?*

1. too many cars
2. global warming
3. not enough jobs
4. dream holidays
5. colourful fish
6. too many beaches

c) *What could happen to the Australian kids? What do you think?*
Example: They could have an accident. / Someone could steal ... . / They could lose ... . / ... .

4 A new 'eco' car 5

a) *Read the short article (C) and list 3–4 key words.*

b) *Correct the sentences.*

1. A US company wants to launch an eco sports car next year.
2. They say it's 'eco' because it runs on fossil fuel.
3. Other US companies are testing a new plane.
4. The new model looks more like a spaceship.
5. The reporter thinks that people like using the word 'eco'.
6. The reporter is not sure if the car would in fact be better for companies.

Sweet and fair trade

HOME | About Us | News | Products | Contact us

A

TRANSFAIR
FAIRTRADE

Guarantees
a **better deal**
for Third World
producers

FAIRTRADE conditions

Labels with this logo started in the late 1980s. The logo tells you that the farmers work under good conditions and get a fair price for their work.

FAIRTRADE chocolate is made from cocoa beans which are bought under fair trade conditions like:

- a guaranteed price for beans
- extra pay for farmers
- good working conditions
- support for farmers' communities.

B

From farm to co-operative to fair trade

Chocolate is now Ghana's second most important export. But in the past the farmers there got very little money for their cocoa beans – until they realised: If they had bigger farms, they would make more money! So they made one big farm out of their small farms and sold their beans together. They called this co-operative Kuapo Kokoo. Then, four years later, they decided it would be better if they produced their own chocolate bars.
Together with three British organisations, which supported projects in Africa, they founded the 'Day Chocolate Company'. It launched its first FAIRTRADE® chocolate bars in the UK.
On 1st January 2007 the company changed its name to 'Divine Chocolate Ltd.'. They now have offices in the US, too.

The company has a turnover of more than 20 million pounds. Their mission is to make good, fair trade chocolate, to make farm workers' lives better and to tell people about FAIRTRADE®. Here are two of the company's successful products:

Divine:
Classic milk chocolate bar, launched in 1998

Dubble:
A chocolate bar for kids

Source: www.bized.co.uk

Task: To find out about a fair trade company

1 Fair trade 2, 5

a) *Do you think it is good to buy fair trade products? Why? Why not?*

b) *Read text A. What is special for farmers who produce the cocoa beans for fair trade chocolate?*
They get … .

2 A fair trade product 4, 5 (→ p. 37/ex. 5–7)

a) *Think: What do you know about chocolate? (What's in it? Where does it come from? …) Start your own chocolate fact card.*

b) *Read text B and the chocolate facts on the right. Add any new info to your fact card.*

c) *Pair: Compare your facts.*

d) *Share: In your group make a list of popular chocolate bars. Which is your group's favourite chocolate bar? Vote on it.*

Chocolate facts! INFO card

Did you know that …
… cocoa beans grow on trees?
… farmers first grew these trees in South America?
… chocolate came to Europe in 1528?
… in Spain they once used cocoa beans as money?
… an English company made the first chocolate bar in 1830?

3 Let's listen: At a trade fair 15 (→ p. 38/ex. 8)

1, 27

a) *A reporter interviews Mr Buah from Kuapo Kokoo. Listen and list some of the things they talk about.*

b) *Choose the correct phrase.*
1. The reporter says that the company's stand looks *very nice/busy.*
2. He also says that Divine Chocolate *is doing very well/makes you happy.*
3. The company will spend the money which they made on new *chocolate/schools* for kids.
4. They also plan to support water *sports/projects.*
5. Mr Buah says that the company wants to *get more of the US market/open a market stand.*

4 A 'chocolate' job G5

Abeeku is a young man who lives in Ghana. He would like to work for the Divine Chocolate Company. What is he thinking?
If I worked for this chocolate company, I could eat … . / I would support … . / I could help with … . / I would have good … .

fair trade | lots of chocolate | projects which the company supports | working conditions | …

5 Presentation: A sales talk 2, 18 (→ p. 38/ex. 9–10)

a) *Form pairs. Each pair designs a fair trade chocolate advert. Think of a name and a caption. The ideas in the box can help you. Use your chocolate fact cards and the company profile (text B).*

crunchy • yummy • tasty • nutty • smooth • a dream • a piece of paradise • healthy • milky • dark • …

b) *Write notes about what is special/good about your product. Some ideas to help you: Where is it from? How much is it? What are the pros of fair trade? How does it taste? …*

c) *Each pair presents its advert and tries to sell the product to the class. The class votes on it.*

1, 28–32

Danger in paradise *(adapted from 'Deep, blue and deadly' by Hamida Aziz)*

1 Before you read

a) *Where are the Maldives? What can you do there? (Use the Internet, books or travel brochures.)*

b) *Look at the photos. Would you like to go there? Why? Why not?*

Zach, Amber and her boyfriend Joel are teenage tourists from Australia. They are on a holiday on one of the islands in the Maldives. It's a real paradise, at least that's what they think at the beginning of their holiday. But then why are large numbers of the fish in the area dying? The islanders – fishermen and local people – are worried. And, of course, the hotel manager and staff (like Zahra, who works in the spa) don't want the tourists to find out: That could be very bad for business!
When the Australian group go diving with their instructor Abu, they have a great underwater experience which turns dangerous …

It was the diving group's fourth day in the Maldives. They were on the boat at a different reef that day. It was a warm, sunny morning. But the sea wasn't as calm as on the days before. Amber was glad that she didn't get seasick. She put her wetsuit on […]
"OK, guys," said Abu, their dive instructor. "We're visiting a 'cleaning station' today. And I hope we'll see some manta rays. So get your camera ready, Amber. We're not diving deep – about ten metres. But the current here is very strong."

"I'd say we're up current now," guessed Zach, "so won't we hit the reef with a crash?"
"No, there's a sand channel behind some coral heads. That's where we want to land," explained Abu. "The idea is to let out all the air in your jacket, so you drop quicker than the current carries you along. Then stop at about ten metres. That should get you to the sand channel. As I said, we're not deep but we could be down there for some

time. So your decompression stops on the way up are important. OK? Let's go!"

They went down almost together. Amber felt the strong current right away. It pushed her along. She was really excited but also a little scared. The others were in front of her. No! Hang on! Where was her buddy, Joel?
At that moment he went past and dropped far below her. The current moved her along. Now she could see the sand channel. Just then Joel took her hand and she pulled him with her. The two of them went with a crash into the channel. Joel hit his left hand on some coral and it was a bit bloody.
They joined the group and waited behind a couple of coral heads. Twenty minutes passed, and there wasn't a manta in sight.

Joel swam into the channel to explore the coral life there. He pointed to something, maybe to some colourful fish. Amber got a shot of him as they moved around him.
But then Abu gave a sign and pointed out of the channel and into the deep blue sea – just as a large, cloudy creature came out of the shadows! It was about five metres long and blue-grey. Its fins were like the wings of a fantastic, huge bird out of some myth. The manta swam towards them easily, as if there was no current at all. Amber got as many shots as she could.
Now the manta was directly above the coral head. Amber watched, surprised, as lots of smaller fish began to 'clean' the huge creature.
The divers weren't very deep down, but they had spent a very long time in the channel. Abu decided that it was time to go back up again.

2 The story up to now 5 (→ p. 39/ex. 11)

a) *Read the introduction on page 64 again. Then correct the one wrong word in each sentence.*

1. Amber is a teacher from Australia.
2. Zach is her boyfriend.
3. The fish are swimming on the island.
4. The local people are happy about that.
5. It could be very bad for energy.
6. Abu is the group's driving instructor.

b) *Make a grid with these headings: 'Before the dive', 'Dive to sand channel' and 'The cleaning station'. Look at the notes about what has happened and sort them under the right heading.*

all got to sand channel • worried local people • saw manta at cleaning station • went to different reef • warned about strong current • took photos • dead fish bad for local business • hoped to see manta • put wetsuit on • Amber excited but also scared • manta ray came near them • Abu gave diving instructions • lots of dead fish

c) *What could happen in the next part of the story? What do you think? Discuss with your partner and write five sentences.*

They find some dead fish. • Something happens on their way up again. • They can't find the boat because of the current. • Joel's hand gets worse. • A diver doesn't do the correct decompression stops. • A sea creature attacks them. • …

The boat picked them up some distance away from where they had gone down. As they took off their wetsuits, the divers talked about their adventures.
"I've never seen a manta before!" said Amber.
"Hope you got lots of shots!" said Zach.
As they talked, Joel sat down with the logbook and wrote the day's entry – or tried to write it: He wasn't feeling too good. He couldn't think right. His body itched, his left hand felt dead, his knees hurt terribly – and it felt like his heart was running a race! Abu came over to him.
"Are you OK, mate?" asked Abu.
"No, er … I feel sick … My body hurts," said Joel weakly.
"OK, just lie down," said Abu. "You need decompression: We'll get you to the dive base and they'll fly you out!"
At the base things happened very quickly. Amber wanted to go with Joel, but they assured her that he'd be OK.
She watched the plane as it got smaller and smaller. When it was just a tiny dot in the sky, she turned to the others.
"He'll be OK, Amber," said Zach. "It's not dangerous and it's only for a day!"
"Yes, don't worry," added Abu. "Joel sometimes dives down too fast, I've noticed. Then he comes up too fast. But your buddy will be back soon, you'll see."
"Joel loves that 'diving' feeling – me, too. Only, I'm just that bit more careful, I guess," laughed Amber. But, in fact, there were tears in her eyes.
"Well, OK," said Abu, "I'll take you back to Suvaruge Fushi now: I think you all need to rest a bit."

* * *

Back on the island, Amber went and looked for Zahra. She found her in the juice bar.
"Hi, Amber! Oh, what's wrong?" Zahra asked.
"Joel …" said Amber quietly.
"Oh, Amber – OK, listen," said Zahra quietly. "The spa closes in a few minutes. I'll just clean the bar and close it. Then I'm free to talk."
They sat in the shade behind the spa. Amber told Zahra what had happened …

3 After the dive (→ p. 39/ex. 12; p. 40/ex. 13)

Read from line 74 on this page to the end again.

1. How does Joel feel? Collect all the words and phrases which describe the problems which he has.
2. What do Abu, Zach and Amber think about Joel's problem?

worried / hopes he'll be OK • Joel needs decompression • it's not dangerous

4 Dead fish – sick tourist

Is there a link between the dead fish and Joel's problem? What do you think? If you want to know what really happens: Read the Klett reader 'Deep, blue and deadly'!

Task: To retell a story in your own words

5 Islanders or tourists? 2, 5

a) *Who are islanders and who are tourists in the story? Why do they 'need' each other?*

b) *Look back at the story. Who was it?* This person …
1. had never seen a manta before.
2. thought they were up current.
3. tried to write in a logbook.
4. took lots of photos.
5. had to leave in a plane.
6. pointed to the manta.

c) *Make a grid with 'Islanders' and 'Tourists' and sort the phrases from the box under the right heading. Think of more phrases about each group.*

d) *Why don't the islanders want the tourists to see the dead fish? What do you think?*

are on holiday • worry about the dead fish • enjoy underwater life • are fishermen • work on the islands • go diving • stay in hotels • don't want tourists to know about dead fish

6 Sum up the story 2

Read about the divers' trip again. Put the sentences in the right order to get a summary of the divers' underwater adventure.

1. Smaller fish begin to clean the manta.
2. Joel comes up again too fast.
3. Joel feels very sick after the dive.
4. Amber gets a shot of Joel with some fish.
5. Joel drops lower than Amber.
6. Then a huge creature comes out of the shadows!
7. The divers wait behind some coral heads.
8. But he and Amber get to the sand channel safely.
9. Joel has to leave the island by plane.
10. Abu tells the divers what to do before the dive.

7 Paradise in danger? 4 G5, G6

a) *Think about these two questions:*
1. What is 'paradise' for you?
   Example: For me **paradise is chilling out** in my messy room / living in a clean environment / … .
2. What dangers would destroy your paradise?
   Example: **If I had to** clean my room, **that would destroy** my paradise. / If there was more pollution … .

b) *Pair: Tell your partner about your idea of paradise. Your partner listens and writes notes.*

c) *Share: Tell your group about your partner's paradise. Which was the most popular idea?*

For me paradise is 'hanging out' in the garden!

8 Presentation: An e-mail 2, 10, 18 Ov3, Ov4 (→ p. 40/ex. 14)

Abu wants to tell a friend about the dive. Use the summary from Ex. 6, add what happened to Joel and write Abu's e-mail. Compare with your partner and read it out in the class.

1 Rhyming words

Find the words which rhyme. Example: reef – grief

reef ✓ • thank • blue • fuel • nightmare • slave • shot • criminal • dump • fin • bean • price • trade • organize • worldwide • mission • export • swam	grave • scene • grief ✓ • fair • bump • lamb • shoe • bank • inside • realise • afraid • twice • condition • bought • mule • mineral • tin • got

2 Good news!

Terry, from England, wants to go to Ghana for a year's work experience in a fair trade co-operative there. He gets a positive answer from the company and writes to his friend about it. Put in the correct words.

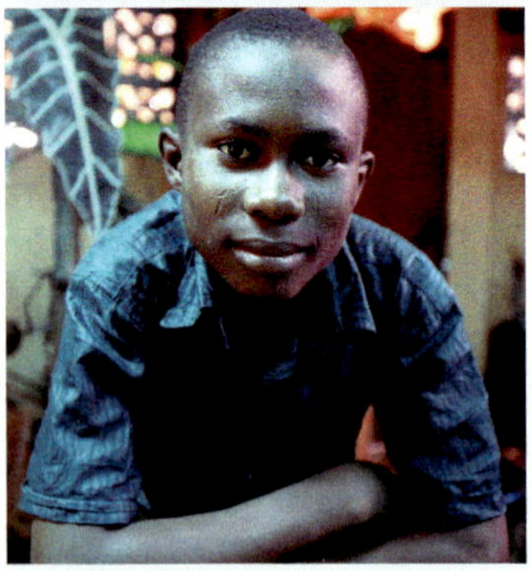

Hi Dave,

Can you imagine: I got the job *(in/at/from)* Ghana! I have to be there *(at/on/in)* 1st December.
So I must go *(in/for/to)* the travel agency soon and ask *(about/on/over)* flights. I'm really excited *(for/about/on)* this trip because I'm interested *(about/for/in)* fair trade. And I love chocolate!

Just think: I can stay *(with/by/between)* a farm worker's family in the village! They've a kid my age who also loves football. But I'm sure there's a big difference *(from/between/in)* living in a city like London or living in a small village. And maybe the food there will be very different *(from/as/through)* what we eat here. So it'll be an exciting experiment.

Of course, the co-operative offices all have computers so I can always contact you *(in/on/from)* the Internet. Maybe I can even send you lots of photos *(from/of/through)* the farm, the people and the scenery.

I'll call you as soon as I've booked the trip *(after/to/for)* Ghana.

Bye,
Terry

PS What do you think of the photos?

3 Word pairs

a) *Find the word pairs. Example:* extra – pay → 'extra pay'

environmental • coral • working • local • global • farm • sea • dream • 'eco' • fossil • extra ✓ • manta • cocoa • greenhouse • decompression • underwater • juice • fair	conditions • products • problems • ray • level • reef • bar • trade • workers • pay ✓ • fuel • beans • camera • gases • stops • holiday • sports car • warming

b) *Make a grid with the headings 'Holidays', 'Work' and 'Environment'. Put the pairs from a) under the right heading.*

c) *Choose five pairs from your grid and write a sentence for each.*

OPTION 1

✔ … understand some aspects of globalisation.

a) *Start a mind map on globalisation.*

b) *Write two sentences each for the pros and cons of globalisation.*

✔ … talk about the 'Fairtrade' label and chocolate. Ov5

a) *Say when using labels first started.*

b) *Explain who it helps and how it does this.*

c) *Describe your favourite chocolate: Is it sweet, dark, not so dark or white? Has it got lots of milk/pieces of fruit in it? Is it soft/hard inside? Is it in pieces/a long bar/…? Is it expensive? Do you often buy it or do you only buy it on special days? …*

✔ … give a profile of a company.

a) *Name three important things about Divine Chocolate Ltd. (e.g. Where? Who? Turnover? …).*

b) *Name two things that you like about the company.*

✔ … say what would happen if … . G5

Look at the pictures. What would happen if some other farmers in Ghana did these things?

1

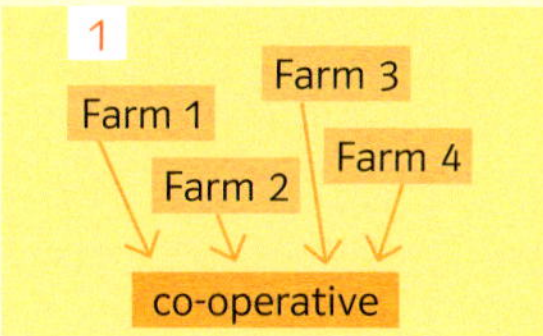

to put … together / to make

2

to grow / to produce

3

to change / to be

4

to open / be in Sydney

OPTION 2

✔ … describe an island in paradise and dangers to it. G5

a) *Name – three things that you could/would see or do if you were on an island in paradise.*
– two environmental problems which islands like the Maldives have.

b) *Would it be the place for a dream holiday? Why/why not?*

✔ … understand new words in a story.

Sort the words into three groups: sea, hotel and people.

islanders • manta ray • coral • juice bar • fisherman • diving group • tourists • wetsuit • current • spa • manager • fin • decompression • underwater shots

✔ … talk about the characters in a story. G1

Talk about the islanders', Amber's and Joel's feelings.
For example: The islanders feel … because large numbers … . Zahra feels … because … . Amber feels … . Joel … .

angry | worried | scared | sad | sick | frustrated | excited | unhappy | …

✔ … retell a story in your own words. G1

Retell the story of an exciting film which you've seen: Where did the story happen? Who were the main characters? What happened? Why did you like it?

(→ p. 41/ex. 15; p. 42/ex. 16)

Greenford Ecovillage, Australia (→ pp. 43–45)

Our Motto: The Earth is Our Future!

HOME | NEWS & EVENTS | GALLERY | ECO-DATA | MAP | JOIN US | CONTACT

Beginnings
Today
Our future

It all started on 1st January 2000. In the morning we – five good friends from Melbourne – talked about what the future would bring us. We decided that we had to form our future and not let it form us! Our deep worry about globalisation and its effects[1] on the environment made us[2] become active[3]. That's how the project 'Greenford Ecovillage' began. Since then we have never looked back!
It took a lot of time to decide how to organize our village. We read about the land where we planned to live. The scientists in our project group presented ideas and models of other eco-communities in the world.
Today, Greenford is 'our dream come true': We are a community of 15 families and we all have respect for nature[4]. We want to bring back the balance[5] in our environment. The idea behind our village is that "pollution is energy in the wrong place". So we use bio fuels and solar energy, and our farming is organic[6] (see our eco-data page). Also, we don't have TVs or mobile phones, which lots of people find crazy!
Anyone who lives here must believe in our motto: 'Our Earth is Our Future'! The Earth can go on without us but we can't live without it! So we have to help to correct the harm humans have already done – and are still doing!

HIGHLIGHTS[7]

Live Music in our Info Café from 3 p.m. every Saturday …

Summer Fair with a farmers' market plus stalls selling organic food, local art and jewellery – and sports & games for all …

Experience[8] Week: A chance for young people to live and work in the village for a week. Learn about the eco-community first hand. If that doesn't get you hooked[9] …

[1]effect [ɪ'fekt] – *Auswirkung,* [2]made us ['meɪd‿ʌs] – *veranlasste uns,* [3]active ['æktɪv] – *aktiv,* [4]nature ['neɪtʃə] – *Natur,* [5]balance ['bæləns] – *Gleichgewicht,* [6]organic [ɔː'gænɪk] – *organic,* [7]highlight ['haɪlaɪt] – *Höhepunkt,* [8]experience [ɪk'spɪərɪəns] – *Erfahrung,* [9]to get hooked [hʊkt] – *süchtig werden*

A Reading

Read the website and find the best answer.

a. The Ecovillage is a …
1 big city in Australia. 2 community which respects nature. 3 disco.

b. The people care about …
1 the future of the Earth. 2 models. 3 televisions.

c. They use …
1 mobile phones. 2 microwaves. 3 solar energy.

d. To live there you have to …
1 bring your own mobile. 2 believe in the motto of the village. 3 be over 18.

B Language

1 Find the words in the text with the same or a similar meaning.

a. began
b. mates
c. chatted
d. group of people living together
e. energy from the sun
f. people

2 Find the sentences in the article with a similar meaning.

a. We thought about our life and that we have to change it for a better future.
b. We spent a long time before we got all the ideas together for our Ecovillage.
c. The village which we made is what we had always wanted.
d. Anyone who moves here has to respect nature and what we believe.
e. We need the Earth to live but it doesn't need us.

3 What would the five friends say? Find the two right sentences.

a. "Biofuels and solar energy are great!"
b. "We need roads for our cars!"
c. "We don't care about pollution!"
d. "Everyone should think about the future and care about the environment."

1, 33–34

C Listening

Part I: Planning Greenford Fair

1 The people at Greenford Ecovillage are planning their next summer fair.
Listen to three of them – Karen, Mike and Angela – and choose the right ending.

a. For this year's fair Angela wants to decide about
1 posters and people. 2 visitors and events. 3 stalls and events.

b. At last year's fair the kids – and the adults[1] – really enjoyed
1 the photos. 2 the games. 3 the food.

2. Listen again. Which word in each sentence is wrong?

a. The people are meeting to talk about the football match this year.
b. Karen and Mike are officials in the village.
c. The best thing last year was the farmers' tractor.
d. In the three-legs football match two animals play with three legs.
e. They had a disaster before the end of the match.
f. Suddenly two people destroyed the tea tent.

Part II: At the summer fair

Listen and choose the right person / people.

a. *Karen/Mike* hasn't sold many things at the stall.
b. *A couple/Angela* bought a picture hours ago.
c. *Karen/Angela* fell and hurt her arm.
d. *Mike/Angela* wants Karen to move her fingers.
e. *Mike/Mike's dad* wants to get some organic oils for Karen.
f. *Mike's dad/Angela* will look after the stall until they come back.

[1]adult ['ædʌlt] – *Erwachsene/r*

D Speaking

1

2

1 Describing

a. Look at the two photos. Who and what can you see in each one? Where are the people? What do you think they are doing and why? Make three sentences.

b. Now choose one of the people from one of the photos. What do you think he / she is saying right now? Make three sentences.

c. Give two pros and two cons each for shopping in a supermarket or at a market stall.

2 Role play

You are near the woman in photo 1. You are arguing with a friend about what to buy.

Friend: Let's buy some pizzas for supper. Look they're really cheap.
You: *(Sage, dass du zuerst lesen möchtest, was in den Pizzen enthalten ist.)*
Yes, OK. But first I'd like to … .
Friend: Why are you so interested in what is in them?
You: *(Oft sind viel Zucker[1] und ungesunde Sachen in diesen Pizzen.)*
Well, because there's often … .
Friend: But it says here on the front of the packet that they have no sugar[1] in them.
You: *(Sage, dass könnte heißen, dass sie vielleicht andere Sachen enthalten, die nicht gesund sind.)*
Yes, but that could mean that maybe they …
Friend: How can I know that my supper is healthy?
You: *(Sage, dass er / sie immer nur Bio-Produkte kaufen soll. Dann weiß man, dass es gesund ist.)*
Only buy … . So then you … .
Friend: But how do you know it's organic? Just because it says 'organic' on the packet?
You: *(Sage ja, du denkst, dass es stimmt, was auf der Packung steht. Es gibt dafür strenge Regeln.)*
Yes, I think what they write on the … .

[1]sugar ['ʃʊgə] – *Zucker*

E Mediation and communication

You've found a short summary of a student's project week at an eco-village in New Zealand. Your uncle is interested in eco-communities but his English isn't very good. Answer his questions.

My 'eco-experience'

The eco-village is on an island in New Zealand. The community needs no electricity from power stations[1] because all the buildings have solar panels. Some even have windmills.
Luckily the island has enough rainfall[2], so the village isn't connected to[3] the public water system. Instead[4], rain is collected from roofs in huge tanks. Most showers are outside behind people's houses, open to spectacular views of mountains: But don't worry, you can enjoy the scenery privately: You have your own special shower time!
There's no fast food here, of course. It's all organic, the meat is local – and it's all home cooking, too. I've learned to prepare a lot of simple but really tasty meals.
Digging in the garden was my early morning task. Then we had eco-classes. There we learned how to make mud bricks[5] or how solar panels work. I got quite good at making the bricks! I even helped to set up a windmill water pump[6] at my guest family's house. I was so proud when it went into action.
In the first few days I missed my family and friends back home. But people here made me feel welcome. And if you grew up[7] here, family and friends would be in the village, too, right?

A windmill for a water pump

It was fantastic that there was no traffic in the eco-village. Now, back in Sydney, I miss the peace and quiet. Also, you feel special because you helped to build your community. And you eat the food you grow. Now I feel strange each time I buy food in a big supermarket!

[1]power station ['paʊə ˌsteɪʃn] – *Kraftwerk,* [2]rainfall ['reɪnfɔːl] – *Niederschlag,* [3]to be connected to [kə'nektɪd] – *verbunden sein mit,* [4]instead [ɪn'sted] – *stattdessen,* [5]mud brick [mʌd 'brɪk] – *Lehmziegel,* [6]pump [pʌmp] – *Pumpe,* [7]to grow up [grəʊ‿'ʌp] – *aufwachsen,* [8]reason ['riːzn] – *Grund*

a. Liegt das Ökodorf in Deutschland?
b. Woher bekommen sie ihren Strom?
c. Wie werden sie mit Wasser versorgt?
d. Ist der Anbau dort biologisch?
e. Was hat der Student im Projekt gelernt?
f. Was findet er im Ökodorf besser als in der Stadt?

F Writing

1 Skills
You would like to do a project week in an eco-village. Write a list of reasons[8] why. Think about what you could learn during the week there.

2 An e-mail
Write an e-mail to an eco-village. Write 4 – 5 sentences: Say who you are. Say you would like to do a project week there. Say why you would like to do it at their eco-village. Write when you would like to do the project week. Remember to be polite.

Sozialformen

1 Einzelarbeit (1 Person)

2 Partnerarbeit (2 Personen)

3 Gruppenarbeit (3+ Personen)

4 Think-Pair-Share (1; 2; 3+ Personen)

Arbeitstechniken und Fertigkeiten

Folgende Techniken und Fertigkeiten trainierst du in den Topics besonders:

Lesen	5	Einen längeren Text verstehen
	6	Eine Stellenanzeige verstehen
	7	Einen Cartoon verstehen
	8	Lesetexte unterscheiden
Schreiben	9	Einen englischen Text zusammenfassen
	10	Texte verfassen
	11	Eine Postkarte schreiben
	12	Einen Rap schreiben
	13	Einen Lebenslauf (*CV*) auf Englisch schreiben
	14	Eine formelle E-Mail schreiben
Hören und Verstehen	15	Hörtexte verstehen
	16	Öffentliche Ansagen verstehen
Sprechen	17	Ein Interview mit jemandem führen
Arbeitsergebnisse vorstellen	18	Eine Präsentation vorbereiten
	19	Eine Diskussion durchführen

1 Einzelarbeit

Manchmal, z.B. bei Hausaufgaben, musst du eine Aufgabe allein erledigen. Folgende Tipps können dir helfen, effektiver und sicherer zu arbeiten.

	Fragen	Tipps
1.	Welche Aufgaben machst du gern allein? Z.B. ein Bild malen, einen Rap schreiben.	Überlege, wo du eventuell Probleme haben könntest.
2.	Verstehst du die Aufgabe?	Lies zunächst alle (Teil-)Aufgaben. Wenn du etwas nicht verstehst, kannst du deinen Lehrer / deine Lehrerin oder deine Eltern fragen.
3.	Was musst du machen und in welcher Reihenfolge?	Schreibe einen kurzen Arbeitsplan.
4.	Welche Hilfsmittel benötigst du: Laptop? Internet? Wörterbuch? …?	Achte darauf, dass du das notwendige Material in Reichweite hast.
5.	Wie viel Zeit brauchst du?	Mach dir einen Zeitplan und schätze ab, wie viel Zeit du für die Teilaufgaben brauchst.
6.	Kannst du etwas verbessern? Hast du etwas vergessen?	Lies deine Arbeit am Schluss noch einmal durch und sei dabei kritisch. Spiele deinen eigenen Lehrer! Vergleiche noch einmal mit der Aufgabenstellung.

2 Partnerarbeit

Viele Aufgaben kannst du in Partnerarbeit lösen. Auch hier kannst du die Tipps zum selbstständigen Arbeiten anwenden. Gleichzeitig musst du darauf achten, was dein Partner / deine Partnerin sagt oder sagen möchte und dies berücksichtigen. In dem Infokasten sind einige nützliche Ausdrücke:

Los geht's!	*Let's read the exercise / task … again.* *I think we have to … .*
Ideen sammeln	*What do you think? / Have you got any ideas?* *I think we should … . / Let's … .* *OK. That sounds good. /We could also … .*
Besprechung	*What do you think of my answer / picture / …?* *I'm not sure about … .* *Oh, dear! I think this word / spelling / … is wrong.* *Hey, that's great. That looks / sounds really interesting / … .* *I think we should change the word … the text / … .*
Zeitplan	*We've only got … minutes left.* *Let's hurry!*

3 Gruppenarbeit

Diese Tipps sollen dir helfen, effektiver und mit mehr Spaß in einer Gruppe zu arbeiten.

Tipps	Ausdrücke
Begrüßt euch, bevor ihr anfangt, z. B. *Hi, G'day* oder mit Handschlag bzw. einem *high five*.	*Hello, I'm … .* *And I'm … . Hi!*
Die Arbeitssprache kann Deutsch oder Englisch sein. Die Ausdrücke hier und am Ende des Buches können euch helfen.	*What's the English word for …?* *How do you say … in English?*
Wer soll die Gruppe leiten *(group leader)*? Wer soll den Zeitplan überwachen *(time keeper)*? Wer soll Sprecher / in *(messenger)* sein, falls es z. B. Fragen oder Probleme gibt?	*Who wants to be group leader / …?* *Not me. I did it last time. … can do it.* *OK. I'll do it.*
Was ist das Ziel / die Aufgabe der Gruppe? Schreibt dies am besten für alle auf.	*We have to … .* *I'll write that on the board / … .* *Are there any questions?*
Alle müssen verstehen, wozu sie diese Aufgabe erledigen sollen.	*Does everyone understand?* *We have to find out about … / so that we can … .*
Wer soll welche Aufgabe übernehmen? Woher könnt ihr Infos bekommen? Wie viel Zeit habt ihr?	*Who wants to …?* *Where can we find out about …?* *How long have we got?*
Wie wollt ihr die Aufgabe erledigen, d.h. welche Teilaufgaben wollt ihr in welcher Reihenfolge bearbeiten?	*We've got to … and … .* *I think we should do / read / … first and then … .*
Hast du etwas vergessen? Kannst du etwas verbessern?	*Is this OK?* *Maybe you should add / say something about / … .*
Ein Austausch innerhalb der Gruppe ist notwendig, bevor ihr der Klasse über eure Arbeit berichtet.	*Can you check my work, please?* *What do you think?*
Berichten könnt ihr der Klasse auf unterschiedliche Art und Weise. Wichtig ist, eine Form zu wählen, die euch liegt (siehe *Skill* 18).	*Our task was to … .* *We would like to tell you about it in a talk / dialogue / … .*
Die Klasse soll Lob aussprechen bzw. Verbesserungsvorschläge machen. Merkt euch diese für die nächste Aufgabe.	*That was great! / Interesting! / … .* *I think you should leave out … .* *Why didn't you talk about …?* *I didn't understand … .*

4 Think – Pair – Share

Manche Übungen sind so unterteilt, dass du einen Teil der Übung
→ allein (*Think*),
→ einen Teil mit einem Partner / einer Partnerin (*Pair*),
→ und einen Teil in der Gruppe (*Share*) erledigen musst.

1 Think

Manche Aufgaben in diesem Buch machst du am besten allein, z. B.:

- über etwas **nachdenken**,
- dich an etwas **erinnern**,
- dein **Wissen zusammentragen.**

Wenn du allein arbeitest, kannst du dir deine Arbeit selbst einteilen.

2 Pair

Für andere Aufgaben brauchst du einen Informationsaustausch mit einem Partner / einer Partnerin, z. B.:

- beim Rollenspiel,
- wenn du deine **Ergebnisse** mit jemandem **vergleichen** musst,
- um sie zu **vervollständigen** oder zu **korrigieren**.

Wenn du mit einem Partner / einer Partnerin zusammen arbeitest, musst du nicht nur zuhören, sondern auch verstehen können, was er/sie sagt und darauf reagieren.

3 Share

Umfangreichere Aufgaben musst du mit anderen in einer Gruppe erledigen, z. B.:

- eine **Umfrage**,
- eine **Diskussion.**

Die Arbeit in einer Gruppe kann schwierig, aber auch spannend sein. Jeder muss wissen, was er zu tun hat.

5 Einen längeren Text verstehen

Vor dem Lesen:

1. Woher kommt der Text: Zeitschrift? Geschichte? ...?
2. Handelt es sich um einen Sachtext oder um einen fiktionalen Text?
3. Schau dir die Bilder und den Titel an? Wird der Text sachlich, spannend, informativ, ... sein?
4. Weißt du etwas über den Autor und die Zeit, in der der Text spielt bzw. geschrieben wurde?

Beim ersten Lesen:

Lies den Text. Ist er so, wie du erwartet hast? Was ist anders?

Beim zweiten Lesen:

Wie kannst du die Bedeutung der neuen Wörter erschließen?

A crazy idea!
For centuries stories about UFOs and aliens have attracted people: Spaceships land on the Earth, people go out to take photos and never come back, aliens enter the brains of people and control their bodies, hideous creatures try to take control of our world. Many people all over the world believe that there are aliens on the Earth. There are thousands of stories from people who claim that they have seen UFOs, met aliens or been on an alien planet. But astronomers and other scientists are more sceptical. They want facts not fiction. They say that we will never meet an alien and that most of these stories come from people who have visions. Others have a lot of imagination and believe that what they imagined really happened.

Schau dir die markierten Wörter an und lies dazu folgende Tipps:

Logische Ableitung: Das Wort *body* ist dir bekannt. Was könnte dann *brain* sein, wenn es deinen Körper kontrolliert?
Kontext: Ein Wort wie *hideous* kannst du nur mithilfe der Wörter erraten, die es umgeben. Ist es wohl eher ein positives Wort wie *beautiful* oder ein negatives wie *horrible*?
Wortbildung: Du kennst bereits die Verben *to control* und *to take*. Was könnte der Ausdruck *take control* of bedeuten? Das Verb *to imagine* ist dir auch bekannt, so dass *imagination* leicht zu verstehen ist.
Deutsch: Drei weitere Wörter (*astronomers, sceptical* und *visions*) kannst du erraten, weil sie deutschen Wörtern ähneln, z. B.: *sceptical* = skeptisch.

Das heißt, du müsstest nur das Wort *claim* im Wörterbuch nachschlagen, falls du es doch nicht aus dem Kontext heraus verstehen kannst.

Nach dem zweiten Lesen:

1. Was ist das Hauptthema – *astronomers, the Earth, aliens?*
2. Was glauben manche Leute?
3. Was sagen andere dazu?
4. Was ist die Schlussfolgerung? / Wie endet der Text?

6 Eine Stellenanzeige verstehen

Eine Stellenanzeige ist ein Sachtext. Bevor du dich auf eine Stelle bewirbst, solltest du überprüfen, ob du alles in der Anzeige verstanden hast.

The word for the job	Weißt du, um was für eine Art Job es sich handelt? Englische Berufsbezeichnungen sind oft ungewöhnlich, z. B.: *builder* = Bauarbeiter / in (nicht Bauer) *shop assistant* = Verkäufer / in (nicht Assistent / in)
Qualifications / experience	Verfügst du über die gewünschten Qualifikationen? Brauchst du Vorkenntnisse?
Training	Wird ein Einarbeitungsseminar angeboten?
Age	Bist du alt genug, um dich zu bewerben?
Employer / advertiser	Mit wem sollst du Kontakt aufnehmen? Achte darauf, dass du die Adresse richtig schreibst.
Reference number	Achte auf die Referenznummer. Sie steht meistens in der Anzeige.
Important information	Wie sind die Arbeitszeiten? Handelt es sich um eine Voll- oder Teilzeitstelle? Was würdest du verdienen? Wann würdest du anfangen müssen?

7 Einen Cartoon verstehen

Cartoons findest du oft in einer Zeitung oder Zeitschrift. Sie haben normalerweise einen sehr kurzen Text *(caption)*. Dieser ist nur in Zusammenhang mit dem Bild zu verstehen.

Cartoons stellen etwas Aktuelles dar. Dabei vermischen sie oft Dinge aus dem wirklichen Leben mit unrealistischen oder übertriebenen Dingen. Deshalb müssen wir lachen.

"How may I hurt you?"

Um einen Cartoon zu verstehen, solltest du folgende Fragen beantworten:

1. Was siehst du?
   In the foreground / background I can see … .

2. Was wird gesagt bzw. ist zu lesen?
   The caption / text / character says: … .

3. Was will der Cartoonist damit sagen?
   He / she is criticising / laughing at / … .

4. Was ist deine Meinung dazu?
   I agree / don't agree with … . / I think it's funny / silly / … .

8 Lesetexte unterscheiden

1. Man kann Texte in zwei Hauptgruppen aufteilen: Sachtexte und fiktionale Texte.

Sachtexte / Nicht fiktionale Texte (*fact*)	Fiktionale Texte (*fiction*)
Anzeige, Zeitungsartikel, Bewerbungsbrief, Biocard, Lebenslauf usw.	Kurzgeschichte, Auszug aus einem Roman, Erzählung, Gedicht, Lied, Drama usw.

2. Die Texte in diesen Gruppen haben viele Gemeinsamkeiten, aber manches ist doch anders. Hier ein kurzer Überblick: Unten findest du zwei Beispiele.

Eigenschaften	Sachtext	Fiktionaler Text
❶ Titel	direkt und informativ	oft indirekt bzw. Wortspiel
❷ Bild(er)	Diagramme, Fotos mit klaren Aussagen	Zeichnungen, Stimmungsbilder
❸ Anfang	leitet das Thema ein	führt in den Handlungsrahmen ein
❹ Absätze	Es wird jeweils ein neuer Sachaspekt eingeleitet bzw. vertieft.	Es wird ein Wechsel von Ort, Zeit, Personen und Handlung angezeigt.
❺ Schluss	Schlussfolgerung	sehr unterschiedlich, z. B. Lösung, offenes Ende
❻ Ziel des Lesens	Argumente / Infos zur Weiterbearbeitung vermitteln	Unterhaltung, Kritik äußern, Lebenserfahrungen vermitteln
❼ Stil	berichtende, zumeist sachliche Sprache	erzählend, oft mit wörtlicher Rede, Fragen, Ausrufen

Tavistock Times

❶ UFO reported: 15-year-old missing

❷

A 15-year-old boy is missing after he went to look for a UFO on Friday. ❸ His parents contacted the police the next morning. Their son, Darly, went out in the evening with his camera. He wanted to take photos of a UFO. He did not come home later.❹ A neighbour last saw the pupil from a school in Tavistock on Friday night with two friends after supper. One of the friends phoned Darly at around six o'clock. He said that there was a UFO over the moors.
The three boys set off on their bikes but only two of them came home at ten o'clock.
❺ The parents are certain that aliens have taken their son. ❻ + ❼

❶ A Sci-Fi adventure story:

How we lost Darly

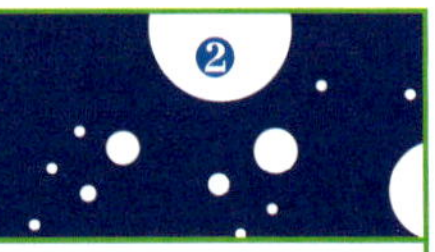
❷

When I phoned Darly that night, I knew that he would go with us to the moor. ❸
❹ "Of course I'll come with you. I'll get my camera and meet you in ten minutes at the end of the road."
Around 7 o'clock we reached the place where we thought we would find the UFO. It was dark and windy. Then the rain started. It got so bad that we decided to wait under a big tree.
We all ran towards it but Darly fell. He got up again and followed us to the tree.
But then he shouted, "I've dropped my camera!"
He went back to look for it but he didn't come back.
❺ We looked everywhere for an hour but we couldn't find him.
That was the last time we ever saw him. ❻ + ❼

9 Einen englischen Text zusammenfassen

Wenn du eine Geschichte nacherzählst oder Informationen aus einem Text weitergibst, musst du den Inhalt immer kürzen. Dabei darfst du weder etwas Wichtiges vergessen noch etwas Unwichtiges beibehalten. Diese Tipps können dir helfen, Informationen zu sammeln bzw. eine gute Zusammenfassung zu schreiben.

	Fiktional	**Nicht fiktional**
1	Du kannst Textmarker verwenden oder Bemerkungen an den Rand schreiben. Setze verschiedene Farben für verschiedene Punkte ein.	
2	Hast du genügend Platz am Rand, um Bemerkungen zu schreiben? Ist der Zeilenabstand groß genug, um zwischen die Zeilen zu schreiben?	
3	Markiere wichtige Dinge / Stellen, z. B. Wörter, Sinnabschnitte und Textteile, Charakterzüge, Atmosphäre, spannende Sätze, …	Markiere wichtige Dinge / Stellen, z. B. Zahlen, Haupt- und Nebenthemen, Argumente oder Namen, die dir wichtig erscheinen, …
4	Wer sind die Charaktere? Wo befinden sie sich? Was machen sie? Was passiert? Wann passiert es? Warum passiert es? Wie endet die Geschichte?	Welche Infos gibt es zu dem Thema? Welche Argumente werden aufgeführt? Was ist die Schlussfolgerung?
5	Benutze deine eigenen Worte. Wähle einfache Vokabeln und Sätze. Sei sachlich. Füge **nicht** deine eigene Meinung oder die anderer ein.	
6	Zusammenfassungen sind immer kürzer als der Text. Lass Unwichtiges weg. Nenne z. B. keine Beispiele, Ausschmückungen, Zitate oder direkte Rede. Verwende auch sprachliche Kürzungen, z. B. das Zusammenziehen von Begriffen zu einer Sachgruppe *(milk, butter, bread = food)*.	
7	Verwende das *simple present*.	Verwende die Zeit, in der der Text geschrieben wurde.

10 Texte verfassen

Anbei findest du acht Schritte *(steps)*, die dir helfen können einen guten Text zu schreiben.

	Schritte	
1	**Aufgabe**	Was genau ist deine Aufgabe? Was für einen Text sollst du schreiben? Wozu? Worüber?
2	**Inhalt**	Welche Punkte musst du erwähnen?
3	**Textsorte**	Welche Merkmale hat ein solcher Text?
4	**Plan**	Mach einen Entwurf. Vergewissere dich, dass du keine Punkte vergessen hast.
5	**Wörter / Begriffe**	Welche *key words* gibt es zu dem Thema? Benutze ein Wörterbuch, falls du Hilfe brauchst. Fallen dir sogar schon ganze Sätze ein? Sammle alle Wörter, Halbsätze und Sätze in einer *mind map*.
6	**Erster Entwurf**	Schreibe einen ersten Entwurf. Lass zwischen den Zeilen Platz frei, damit du Korrekturen einfügen kannst.
7	**Partner-Check**	Bitte einen Partner / eine Partnerin, deinen Text zu lesen. Versteht er / sie ihn? Baue seine / ihre Korrekturen in deinen Text mit ein.
8	**Fertiger Text**	Schreibe den Text neu.

Vorsicht! Es gibt viele *false friends* und viele Fallen im Englischen. Das heißt, dass es manche gleich aussehende Wörter im Englischen und Deutschen gibt, die in den beiden Sprachen aber etwas anderes bedeuten. Hier sind ein paar Beispiele:

German	English	German	English
Handy	*mobile (phone)*	praktisch	*handy*
Gymnasium	*grammar school*	Turnhalle	*gym(nasium)*
Technik	*technology*	Methode	*technique*
Chips	*crisps*	Pommes frites	*chips*
Mappe	*folder*	Karte	*map*

The end of a beautiful friendship?

11 Eine Postkarte schreiben

Zwischen einer Postkarte aus dem englischsprachigen Ausland und einer Postkarte, wie du sie schreiben würdest, gibt es einige Unterschiede – und nicht nur sprachliche.

❶ *Hi*, oder *Hello*, mit Namen sind üblich. Du kannst auch *Dear …*, schreiben. Vergiss das Komma nach dem Namen nicht.
❷ Im *BE* schreibt man Ortsnamen und Datum oft oben rechts vom Text.
❸ Das erste Wort wird groß geschrieben.
❹ Sage, wie es dir geht und was du gerade tust. *(present progressive)*
❺ Ein oder zwei kurze Sätze genügen.
❻ Sage, was du an welchem Tag gemacht hast. *(simple past)*
❼ Sage, was du vorhast *(want to, will, would like to, …)* und wann.
❽ Es wird oft abgekürzt z. B.: *C U* (= See you) …, *Luv …*
❾ Vergiss deinen Namen nicht. (*X* = ein Kuss, *O* = eine Umarmung)
❿ Anreden wie *Mr, Ms* oder *Mrs* brauchst du in der Adresse nicht.
⓫ Schreib die Adresse genau so auf, wie du sie von deinem Freund / deiner Freundin bekommen hast.
⓬ Vergiss die Postleitzahl nicht. Sie steht **nach** dem Ort.
⓭ Wenn du aus dem Ausland schreibst, gib das Zielland an.

Hier ein Beispiel:

6th August, Dublin ❷

Hi, Henry, ❶
❸ *Just to say we are all well and we're having* ❹ *a cool time in Ireland. The weather is great! It has been sunny since we arrived.* ❺ *Yesterday we spent* ❻ *the day in the zoo. Tomorrow* ❼ *we want to go to the coast. We hope we can swim there. Hope* ❽ *all is well with you and the family. CU* ❽ *when we get back to Glasgow.*

❽ *Luv Fiona. XOX* ❾

❿
Henry Mc Farlane
209 Westwind Street ⓫
Glasgow
GL7 6YT ⓬
⓭ *Scotland*

12 Einen Rap schreiben

Raps werden nicht wie Lieder gesungen, sondern gesprochen. Sie haben immer einen ausgeprägten Hintergrundrhythmus, der aus Musik, *scratching* oder Auszügen aus anderen Songs bestehen kann.

1	Raps haben viele Reime. Mach dir eine Liste, bevor du anfängst, deinen Rap zu schreiben.	*limousine – hip-hop queen – just eighteen – …* *time – dime – I'm – …, bad – had – …* *bling-bling – sing, look back – short track*
2	Schreibe über etwas, was du erlebst oder erleben möchtest, z. B. über Freunde, Familie, Schule.	*She was just eighteen, a hip-hop queen* *with jewellery and a limousine.*
3	Normalerweise reimen sich bei Raps die ersten beiden Zeilen, dann die nächsten beiden. Die fünfte Zeile reimt sich häufig mit den ersten beiden.	*She told the world, "I'm,* *here to have a good time",* *but the drugs were bad,* *she lost all she had* *and very soon she didn't have a dime.*
4	Der Rhythmus der ersten und zweiten Zeile soll gleich sein. Der Rhythmus in den folgenden Reimpaaren kann unterschiedlich sein.	*Met a guy – he was her king.* *He was cool and he could sing.* *Then he gave her a ring.* *But he left her alone, she was all on her own* *Tried to finish her life in the bath with a knife.* *Then she started to cry,* *"No! I'm too young to die!"*
5	Der Takt kann überall unterschiedlich sein. Die Zeilen können kurz oder lang sein.	*And now she's clean, no longer a queen* *but happy and free in a little town in the* *South of Germany.*
6	Ein Refrain ist eine Gruppe von Zeilen, die regelmäßig im Rap wiederholt werden. Sie verändern sich innerhalb des Raps kaum.	*She was just eighteen, had a limousine,* *She took some drugs, but now she's clean.*

13 Einen Lebenslauf (*CV*) auf Englisch schreiben

Auf S. 15 siehst du einen teilweise ausgefüllten englischen Lebenslauf (*CV*).
Vorsicht! Es ist im englischsprachigen Raum nicht üblich, ein Foto mitzuschicken.

1	**Name**	Vorname, dann Nachname
2	**Address**	mit Postleitzahl und Land
3	**Tel.**	mit internationaler Vorwahl
4	**E-mail**	Prüfe, ob du sie richtig geschrieben hast.
5	**Date of birth**	*BE* = Tag / Monat / Jahr, *AE* = Monat / Tag / Jahr
6	**Place of birth**	Stadt + Land
7	**Primary school**	Voller Name und Adresse + Angabe der Jahreszahlen von … bis …
8	**Secondary school**	Voller Name und Adresse + Angabe der Jahreszahlen von … bis …
9	**Examinations**	Name und Datum der Prüfungen
10	**Skills**	Fähigkeiten und Fertigkeiten, die du beherrschst und die für den Job wichtig sind, z. B.: *Computer, photography*
11	**Work experience**	Praktika und Jobs, die du gemacht hast: Wo? Was? Wann?
12	**Hobbies/interests**	Hobbys, Sport, ehrenamtliche Tätigkeiten usw.
13	**Referees**	Lehrer, Trainer, Arbeitgeber, … (Name, Adresse, Telefonnummer)

Referees:
Falls der Arbeitgeber sich für dich interessiert, wird er sich mit deinen *referees* in Verbindung setzen. Du benötigst für deinen Arbeitgeber möglicherweise 2–3 Empfehlungsschreiben von *referees*. Sie sollten den Arbeitgeber über deine Persönlichkeit und deine Leistungen im Job informieren. Bei Bewerbungen im englischsprachigen Raum bekommst du deine Empfehlungsbriefe nicht zu sehen.

14 Eine formelle E-Mail schreiben

Wie bei einem formellen Brief, schreibst du in einer formellen E-Mail eine Anrede, eine Einleitung und ein paar abschließende Worte.

Die E-Mail-Adresse des Empfängers steht unter deiner E-Mail-Adresse. Der Betreff *(Re)* sagt, worum es geht.	*From:* *To:* *Re:*
Wenn du den Namen der angesprochenen Person nicht kennst, verwende die Form in Klammern. Vergiss das Komma nach dem Namen nicht. Das erste Wort wird groß geschrieben. Sei immer höflich, auch wenn du dich beschweren willst.	*Dear (Sir or Madam) Mr/Ms …,* *With reference to your … .* *Would it be possible to …?* *I'd be very grateful if you could … .* *I look forward to hearing from you.*
Verwende die richtige Schlussformel.	*Yours faithfully/sincerely,* *…*

15 Hörtexte verstehen

Diese Tipps sind besonders für die Arbeit in der Schule nützlich.

Vor dem Hören:
Es hilft dir, folgende Punkte zu klären, bevor du versuchst, einen Hörtext zu verstehen:

1. Kontext: Wo kommt der Text her? Was weißt du schon über solche Texte?

Medien			Öffentliche Ansagen			Persönliche Gespräche im Alltag		
Radio	TV	…	Bahnhof	Flughafen	…	live	Telefon	…
Hörspiel, Interview, Film			Z. B. Ansage			Anruf, Gespräch, …		
Oft handelt es sich um einen Bericht oder ein Interview.			Die gesuchte Info kann mit einem Schlüsselwort herausgehört werden. Der Rest ist unwichtig.			Du kannst immer nachfragen, wenn du etwas nicht verstanden hast.		

2. Vorwissen: Was kann dir sonst noch beim Erschließen helfen?

Der Titel	Ein Bild	Die Einführung	Sonstige Kenntnisse
… kann bei einem Film oder einer Sendung hilfreich sein.	… hilft oft dabei, sich ein Bild vom Sprecher / von der Sprecherin bzw. von einer anderen Person / Personen zu machen.	… gibt Hintergrund-informationen bzw. erklärt die Situation.	Wie ist die Person, mit der du redest? Wie könnte sie reagieren?

3. Was möchtest du von dem Text erfahren? (Wer? Wann? Was? Wie? Wo? Warum?)

Allgemeines	Bestimmte Details	Eine Information
Was ist das Hauptthema? Um welches Problem / welchen Inhalt geht es?	Wer redet? Welche Angaben werden zu einem Problem / Thema gemacht?	Detaillierte Angaben zu einer bestimmten Frage, z. B. „Wann fährt der nächste Zug?“

Während des Hörens:
Mach dir Notizen.
1. Falls du dir mehrere Punkte notieren willst, kannst du eine Liste, eine *mind map* oder eine Tabelle anfertigen.
2. Hör dir den Text bei einer Prüfung zwei- oder dreimal an. Im Alltag ist das nicht möglich, aber dann kannst du immer jemanden fragen.
3. Prüfe, ob du alle Infos hast, die du brauchst.

Nach dem Hören:
Erledige sämtliche Aufgaben mithilfe deiner Notizen. Falls du mit einem Partner / einer Partnerin zusammenarbeitest, vergleicht eure Ergebnisse.

16 Öffentliche Ansagen verstehen

a) Englische Ansagen auf Flughäfen oder Bahnhöfen sind auch für Muttersprachler schwierig. Diese Tipps können dir helfen, mit ihnen klar zu kommen.

	Tipps
1	Achte auf Schlüsselwörter (Personennamen, Ortsnamen, Zeiten, Flugnummern usw.)
2	Wenn du einen Teil der Nachricht verpasst hast, höre beim zweiten Mal besser zu.
3	Falls du die Info nicht verstehen konntest, bitte jemanden um Hilfe.
4	Falls du dir Sorgen machst, finde einen Beamten oder suche den nächsten Schalter auf.

b) Wenn du Wörter zum ersten Mal in einem englischsprachigen Land hörst, kann es sehr schwer sein, sie zu erraten. Die folgenden Tipps können dir helfen.

1. Es kommt darauf an, wo du gerade bist.

Du bist ...	**Du hörst ...**	**Bedeutung**
am Flughafen.	1. das Wort ‚*transfer*'	→ umsteigen
auf dem Sportplatz.		→ transferieren
auf der Bank.		→ überweisen
im Londoner Tower.	2. den Ausdruck ‚*A great fire*'	→ ein großer Brand
im Wohnzimmer.		→ ein tolles Kaminfeuer

2. Schreibe schwierige Wörter auf. Manchmal kannst du einen Laut falsch gehört haben. Hör genau hin.

3. Bei Anweisungen hörst du oft dieselben oder ähnliche Wörter. Wo könntest du diese Meldungen hören? Bahnhof? Schwimmbad? Museum? Busbahnhof? Flughafen?

> Do not **leave** your luggage anywhere at any time.
> Please **leave** your clothes and shoes in a locker.
> We are closing now. You are asked **to leave** the building quickly and quietly.
> Will Mr Jones please go to the **Left** Luggage Office next to the Ticket Office?
> This coach is for Glasgow only. We **are leaving** in five minutes.

17 Ein Interview mit jemandem führen

Bevor du ein Interview führst, ist es wichtig, dass du versuchst, im Voraus etwas über die Person bzw. das Thema zu erfahren. So kannst du leichter Fragen stellen. Das Interview wird dadurch interessanter.

Tipps	Im Studio	Auf der Straße
1. Be polite.		

2. Prepare your questions.		
Beginne mit einem Fragewort.	***Who*** *do you …?* / ***What*** *have you …?* / ***Why*** *did you …?*	***What*** *is your opinion on …?*
Beginne mit einem Verb.	***Can*** *you tell me …?* / ***Have*** *you ever …?* / ***Is*** *it true that …?*	***Do*** *you think people should …?* ***Can*** *you remember …?*
Beginne mit einer höflichen Einladung / Aufforderung.	***Please, tell*** *us about …* / ***explain*** *… .*	***Could you*** *say something about …?* ***Would you*** *be prepared to give us your opinion on …?*
3. Say goodbye.		
Bedanke dich und sage noch etwas Nettes.	***Thank you*** *very much … . That was very interesting / … .* ***We hope*** *you enjoy your stay in … .* 	***Thank you*** *Sir / Madam / … .* *You have been very helpful.* ***Have a nice day.*** 

18 Eine Präsentation vorbereiten

Wenn ihr eine *Option* bearbeitet habt, müsst ihr die anderen, die diese *Option* nicht gewählt haben, darüber informieren, was ihr gelernt habt. Hier findet ihr einige hilfreiche Tipps.

1. Schreibt zunächst ein Handout und macht Kopien für die Klasse. Hier ein Beispiel:

	Handout	
The title →	*Deadly creatures*	← Schreibt den Titel der *Option* als Überschrift auf die Seite.
Part A →	***Important words:*** *shark = Hai* *snake = a long creature without legs*	← Wählt 10–12 wichtige Wörter bzw. Wendungen aus der *Option* aus und erstellt eine Wortliste.
Part B →	***Facts:*** *The Great White Shark is … .*	← Schreibt 5–6 wichtige Fakten aus der *Option* auf.
Part C →	***Notes:*** *Lots of dangerous … in … .*	← Lasst Platz für Notizen.

2. Wählt eine Präsentationsform, die ihr interessant findet und bei der ihr eure Talente am besten anwenden könnt. Hier ein paar Beispiele:

A display (Nützliche Talente: Zeichnen, Entwerfen)	**A demonstration** (Nützliche Talente: Dinge basteln und erklären)	**A sales talk** (Nützliche Talente: Kommunizieren, Reden)

A discussion (Nützliche Talente: Reden, im Team arbeiten)	**A performance** (Nützliche Talente: Singen, Darstellen, Schauspielern)	**A computer presentation** (Nützliche Talente: mit Geräten umgehen, Tippen)

Weitere Präsentationsformen, die ihr in diesem Buch findet, sind: *an advert, an interview, a PowerPoint presentation, a reading, a quiz, a summary, a report, a talk, a gallery walk, a survey.*

3. Tipps für eine PowerPoint-Präsentation:

1. Plan your presentation on paper first.
2. Write down a title.
3. Write down the aspects of the topic as a list.
4. Write a few key words on each aspect.
5. Start your PowerPoint programme.
6. Type the title on to one 'page' and your key words on to the other 'pages'. Use your key words in sentences during your presentation.
7. Use pictures and diagrams to improve your presentation.

4. Überprüft, ob eure Mitschüler / innen alles verstanden haben, was ihr ihnen gezeigt bzw. erzählt habt.

Schriftlich	Das können z. B. Fragen, ein Lückentext, ein beschriftetes Diagramm, ein Quiz, ein Kreuzworträtsel, ein Fehlertext bzw. ein Fehlerbild sein.
Mündlich	Spiele aller Art – Rollenspiele, Ratespiele, Nacherzählungen, Interviews, Zusammenfassungen, …, z. B.: 1. Ein Kartenspiel: Schreibe Fragen auf Kärtchen. Die anderen ziehen eine Karte und beantworten die Frage. 2. Ein „Käfig mit Haien": Eure Gruppe im „Käfig" stellt den „Haien" draußen Fragen zu eurer *Option*. Wer die Frage richtig beantwortet, ersetzt den Fragenden im „Käfig". Gewonnen haben die Schüler / innen, die nach 10 Minuten noch im „Käfig" sind.

19 Eine Diskussion durchführen

Es gibt viele verschiedene Arten einer Diskussion.
Folgende Tipps und Redewendungen können euch helfen:

	Tipps	Ausdrücke
1	Einigt euch auf eine Aussage *(statement)*.	*I think … is a good statement.* *Let's vote on it. Who's for / against the statement …?*
2	Schreibt sie an die Tafel.	*Statement: The School of the Air is … .*
3	Wer macht den Vorsitz? Er / Sie muss die Diskussion mithilfe der Sätze rechts leiten.	*Good morning / afternoon.* *Our statement is: … .* *Speakers for / against the statement are … .* *Each speaker has got … minutes.* *The first speaker for / against the statement is … .* *…, it's your turn. You may speak now.* *Thank you … . Your time is up.*
4	Die Sprecher sammeln Argumente für und gegen die Aussage.	*I agree / don't agree with the statement.* *In my opinion … .* *I think it is wrong / important to say that … .*
5	Der / Die Vorsitzende fragt, ob andere ihre Meinung äußern möchten.	*Yes, …, what would you like to say?*
6	Der / Die Vorsitzende beendet die Diskussion und fordert zur Abstimmung auf.	*Who is for / against the statement?* *The results of the vote are … for and … against the statement.*

Mediation and communication

Topic 1

COMMUNICATION SKILLS

Hören und Lesen

- Achte auf Überschriften, Eigennamen und die Aufmachung des Textes.
- Auch die Abbildungen können dir wichtige Informationen liefern.
- Neue Wörter, z.B. aus den Bereichen „Technik", „Mode" und „Umwelt", sind in vielen Sprachen sehr ähnlich und deshalb leicht zu erschließen.
- Unbekannte Wörter kann man häufig bestimmten Sachgruppen zuordnen, z.B. Cola, Tee, Wasser gehören zur Gruppe der Getränke. Dies hilft dir beispielsweise bei Speisekarten.
- Konzentriere dich auf Schlüsselwörter wie Namen, Zeit- und Ortsangaben und Zahlen.
- Beim Hören wird die Hauptinformation häufig mit anderen Worten nochmals wiederholt. Hör deshalb konzentriert bis zum Schluss zu.

Übertragen

- Es ist wichtig, den Inhalt sinngemäß zu übertragen. Erfasse den Kern der Aussage.
- Aus Broschüren benötigt man oft nur bestimmte Fakten, z.B. Preise, Öffnungszeiten usw. Ein Stichwortzettel mit den Fakten, nach denen man sucht, kann hier sehr hilfreich sein.
- Gebrauchsanweisungen zu technischen Geräten sind häufig auf Englisch geschrieben, aber viele technische Wörter sind auf Deutsch und Englisch ähnlich.

Situation 1

Du liest einen Urlaubsprospekt von Australien. Dein jüngerer Bruder sieht die Bilder und stellt dir Fragen zu dem Text.

AUSTIKI HOLIDAYS FOR FREE & EASY ADVENTURE!

Austiki is an Australian company which offers tours for all young people between 18 and 25. Holidays the way you love them: "Free and easy adventure" is our motto! Because we are an international group, we use one language – English. So you'll need to understand simple English and to speak a little.
Our modern coaches travel to many interesting places on different routes. You'll sleep in hotels, in lodges or on farms. We offer a great events programme with lots of exciting activities. So we're sure you'll find something to interest you! Of course, there'll also be some free time – when you can each do your own thing.

Along the Great Ocean Road ...

Have a 'walkabout' ...

Melbourne night life ...

And sea life, too!

1. Was ist Austiki?
2. Willst du an der Tour teilnehmen?
3. Sind nur Deutsche in der Gruppe?
4. Fährt man überall mit dem Zug hin?
5. Wo übernachtet man? In Zelten?
6. Muss man immer in der Gruppe bleiben?

Situation 2

Du wirst an einem Schüleraustausch nach Australien teilnehmen. Im Internet bist du auf die folgende Internetseite gestoßen. Du willst die anderen Schüler und Schülerinnen eurer Schule an der Reise teilhaben lassen.

Übertrage die Informationen ins Deutsche und gestalte damit in Deutsch ein Poster für sie.

Unusual facts about Australia

Koalas sleep about 21 hours a day.

Australia is the driest and flattest continent on earth.

When they are born, baby kangaroos are only about 2cm long.

The hottest temperature they've ever recorded in Australia was 50.7°C.

Australia has about 2,000 different sorts of spiders.

Australia's first policemen were 12 convicts.

At the end of the 19th century an Australian weatherman started to give women's names to tropical storms.

Storm warning
Melanie will reach coast in the next hour!

Melbourne has, after Athens, the largest Greek population in the world.

The Great Barrier Reef is the largest living thing on earth.

Australia was once called New Holland (= *Nova Hollandia*)!

There are more than two kangaroos and six sheep for every person in Australia.

Topic 2

Situation 1

Im Englischunterricht arbeitet ihr gemeinsam mit dem Fach Deutsch an einem Projekt zum Thema „Was sind gute Freunde?" Dazu habt ihr persönliche Erfahrungen gesammelt und viel gelesen und recherchiert.
Ihr erarbeitet gerade einen Kriterien-Katalog zu diesem Thema. Bei deinen Recherchen bist du auf dieses Gedicht gestoßen.

Friends

You know those days when everything is black or brown or grey
Your parents argue all the time; don't hear a word you say
Well, don't be sad and don't go mad
You aren't alone, just grab your phone
And we'll be there, because we care
The gang is on its way!

If in the middle of the night, you have an awful dream
You've lost your way, or met a ghost, or fallen in a stream!
We'll help you through, for we're your crew
We'll be your guide[1], we're on your side
So why not try it, we're your diet
Of chocolate cake with cream.

[1]guide [gaɪd] – *Führer/in*

Finde mithilfe des Gedichts noch weitere Kriterien, die du zu deiner deutschen Liste „Was sind gute Freunde?" hinzufügen kannst.

1, 35 **Situation 2**

Du hörst dir „SafeSpace", eine Sendung für Jugendliche eines englischen Radiosenders an. In der Sendung gibt es ein Sorgentelefon für junge Leute mit Problemen.
Du hörst eines der Telefongespräche an und gibst deiner Familie, die nicht alles verstanden hat, Auskunft auf ihre Fragen.

1. Handelt es sich bei dem Überfall um einen Fahrraddiebstahl oder was ist passiert?
2. Warum musste der Junge ins Krankenhaus?
3. Ist der Junge ins Koma gefallen oder warum sagt er: „I was dead."?
4. Welchen Rat gibt die Moderatorin?
5. Habe ich richtig verstanden, dass der Radiosender den Anrufern auch hilft? Was genau können die tun?

Topic 3

Situation

Ihr besucht ein Berufsberatungszentrum. Während ihr auf den Veranstaltungsbeginn wartet, schaut ihr euch dort um und findet neben vielen deutschen Broschüren auch Werbung englischer Firmen. Dabei ist dir ein Bewerbungswegweiser aufgefallen, der Tipps für ein Bewerbungsgespräch enthält. Du willst zu Hause mit deiner Familie darüber sprechen.
Informiere sie über die folgenden zehn Punkte.

Top 10 Rules for a job interview!

1. Don't be late! Leave from home early enough.
2. Maybe there are still other people waiting for a job interview. Be friendly and polite when you talk to them but don't tell them any details.

3. Learn as much as you can about the company before you go to the interview. You may be asked questions on this.
4. Speak slowly in the job interview.

5. When talking, look into your partners' eyes. Don't show that you are nervous. Try to be relaxed.

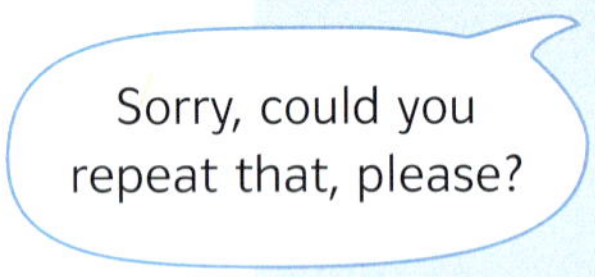

6. Be honest! If you don't understand a question or know an answer, tell the interviewer or ask him or her to repeat it in other words.
7. Be prepared to talk about your future plans. Think about this carefully at home a few days before the interview.
8. Prepare a list of questions you would like to ask the interviewer. This shows your interest in the job and the company.

9. Smile a lot and show that you are very interested in the job.
10. Be friendly and show that you can be a good team worker, too.

Topic 4

Situation

Eure englische Partnerschule berichtet euch in einer E-Mail über ein Umweltprojekt zum Klimaschutz, das sie abgeschlossen hat. Ein Bereich dieses Projektes war die Frage, welchen Beitrag jeder Einzelne von ihnen dazu leisten kann. Als Ergebnis sind einige Poster entstanden, auf denen die Arbeitsgruppen ihre wichtigsten Positionen dargestellt haben.
Ihr habt die Poster in der Schule ausgehängt. Übertrage die Texte sinngemäß ins Deutsche, damit sich alle, auch Besucher eurer Schule, gut informieren können.

Switch off your computer, CD-player or video player when you have finished your work!

Switch off the light when you leave the room!

Don't waste energy at home! Keep the doors and windows closed when it's cold outside.

Use energy-saving electronic devices[1]!

Spend as much time as possible in fresh air! This can help to save energy, too.

Spend one day per week meat-free! Breeding[2] animals needs much more water than growing vegetables.

Be careful about what you eat. Buy food from the region to avoid[3] long-distance transport.

Recycle your rubbish!

Learn about different energy-saving cars and talk about this problem with your family!

Before you go somewhere, decide if you must ask your parents to take you there by car or if you could walk, ride on your bike or skate there.

You could also think about public transport!

Plant a tree!

[1]device [dɪˈvaɪs] – *Gerät*, [2]to breed [bri:d] – *züchten*, [3]to avoid [əˈvɔɪd] – *vermeiden*

Inhalt

Grammatikbegriffe *Grammatical terms*

(Lateinisch) / Deutsch	Englisch	Englisches Beispiel
Adjektiv / Eigenschaftswort **Ov5**	adjective	quick, small, nice, old
Adverb / Umstandswort	adverb	always, often, quickly, loudly
Aktiv **G2, Ov1**	active voice	The program switches the lights off.
Bedingungssätze Typ I **G4** (*If*-Sätze + Präsens)	conditional clauses (present)	If it's sunny, we'll go swimming.
Bedingungssätze Typ II **G5** (*If*-Sätze + Präteritum)	conditional clauses (past)	If I had money, I would buy new clothes.
Demonstrativpronomen / hinweisendes Fürwort	demonstrative pronoun	this, that, these, those
Gerundium **G6**	Gerund	We enjoy going to parties.
Häufigkeitsadverb	adverb of frequency	always, often, sometimes, never
Hauptsatz	main clause	She will buy a key.
Hilfsverb **G1, Ov2**	auxiliary	be, have got, do
Imperativ/Befehlsform	imperative	Don't talk! Listen, please!
Indirekte Rede mit Zeitverschiebung **G8**	reported speech (later)	He said that he wasn't jealous.
Indirekte Rede ohne Zeitverschiebung **G7**	reported speech (immediate)	She says she's ill.
Infinitiv / Grundform des Verbs	infinitive	to do, to go, to see
Mengenangaben	expressions of quantity	some, any, a lot of, much, many
modales Hilfsverb, Modalverb **G3**	modal verb	may, must/n't, need/n't, should/n't, can/'t
Nebensatz	sub-clause	If she arrives late, …

(Lateinisch) / Deutsch	Englisch	Englisches Beispiel
Objektpronomen	object pronoun	me, you, him, her, it, us, them
Passiv in der einfachen Gegenwart G2, Ov1	passive voice: simple present	Everything is done by remote control.
Passiv in der einfachen Vergangenheit Ov1	passive voice: simple past	The car was stolen yesterday.
Perfekt	present perfect	Tom has painted the walls.
Personalpronomen / persönliches Fürwort	personal pronoun	I, you, she, he, it, we, you, they
Plural / Mehrzahl	plural	girls, children, babies
Possessivbegleiter / besitzanzeigendes Fürwort	possessive pronoun	my, your, his, her, its, our, their
Präposition	preposition	in, on, at, about, over
Präsens / einfache Gegenwart Ov1–Ov4	simple present	I live in Greenwich.
Präteritum / einfache Vergangenheit Ov1–Ov4	simple past	I watched TV yesterday.
Relativpronomen	relative pronoun	Sam is the boy who I like.
Relativsatz	relative clause	Everyone who lives here can speak English.
Signalwort Ov1	signal word	last, ago, yesterday, ever, yet
Singular/Einzahl	singular	a girl, a boy, an apple
Steigerung von Adjektiven Ov5	comparison of adjectives	old – older – the oldest, good – better – the best
2. Stammform, 3. Stammform Ov1	perfect participle, past participle	ate, eaten; did, done; went, gone
Stützwort 'one'/'ones'	prop word 'one'/'ones'	Which one do you like best?
Substantiv / Hauptwort	noun	book, dog, sandwich
Verb / Tätigkeitswort G1	verb	to be, to go, to do, to write
Verlaufsform der Gegenwart Ov3	present progressive	We are having a party.
Vollverb G1	verb	to go, to do, to write
will-Futur Ov1–Ov4	'will'-future	I hope it will be warm tomorrow.
Zusammensetzungen mit *some* und *any*	compounds of 'some' and 'any'	somebody, anybody, someone, anyone, something, anything, somewhere, anywhere

G1 Verben — *Verbs*

1. Vollverben

Mit **Vollverben** kannst du ausdrücken, was jemand tut. Um Vergangenes auszudrücken, wird im *simple past* in allen Personen *-(e)d* an das Vollverb angehängt *(used)* bzw. die zweite Stammform bei unregelmäßigen Verben verwendet (*ate, saw, wrote, read)*.

▶ Im *simple present* nach *he, she, it*
da wissen wir: Das **-s** muss mit.

Auf einen Blick

Simple present

I	**use**	a computer.
You	**use**	a computer.
He / She	**uses**	a computer.
We	**use**	a computer.
You	**use**	a computer.
They	**use**	a computer.

Why **do** you/we/they **use** a computer?
Why **does** he/she **use** a computer?

Simple past

I	**used**	a computer.
You	**used**	a computer.
He / She	**used**	a computer.
We	**used**	a computer.
You	**used**	a computer.
They	**used**	a computer.

When **did** you/we/they **use** a computer?
When **did** he/she **use** a computer?

2. Hilfsverben

Neben Vollverben gibt es auch **Hilfsverben**. Man benötigt sie z.B., um einen Satz zu verneinen oder eine Frage zu bilden (siehe auch Ov3–Ov4).

Verneinung im *Simple present*

I	**don't use**	a computer.
You	**don't use**	a computer.
He / She	**doesn't use**	a computer.
We	**don't use**	a computer.
You	**don't use**	a computer.
They	**don't use**	a computer.

Don't you/we/they **use** a computer?
Doesn't he/she **use** a computer?

Verneinung im *Simple past*

I	**didn't use**	a computer.
You	**didn't use**	a computer.
He / She	**didn't use**	a computer.
We	**didn't use**	a computer.
You	**didn't use**	a computer.
They	**didn't use**	a computer.

Didn't you/we/they **use** a computer?
Didn't he/she **use** a computer?

▶ *Do, don't* und *doesn't* vor das Verb
im Deutschen ist es umgekehrt!
Auch *did* und *didn't* setz dorthin.
Erst dann macht es auf Englisch Sinn.

G 2 Das Passiv im *simple present* — *The passive voice: 'simple present'*

1. Aktiv

Das Subjekt (der / die Handelnde) in einem Satz ist aktiv. Deshalb nennt man diese Betrachtungsweise auch Aktiv.

Bank robbers often steal money.
Subject — Verb — Object

Bankräuber stehlen oft Geld.

2. Passiv

Wer hier das Geld gestohlen hat, ist unwichtig oder manchmal auch nicht bekannt. Weil das Geld selbst (nämlich das Objekt aus dem Aktivsatz) jetzt im Blickpunkt steht, wird es zum neuen Subjekt im Passivsatz. Die Form im *simple present* wird oft für Feststellungen bzw. Fakten verwendet. Man findet sie häufig auf **Hinweisschildern.**

Money is often stolen.

Geld wird oft gestohlen.

3. „by" + Handelnde

Möchte der Sprecher / die Sprecherin das Subjekt aus dem Aktivsatz (die Bankräuber) aber doch gern nennen, kann er / sie dieses mit der Präposition *by* am Satzende anfügen. Ob eine Situation aktiv oder passiv ist, hängt vom Sprecher ab, d.h. was er / sie besonders betonen will – die Handelnden oder die Handlung selbst (siehe auch Ov1).

active	Bank robbers often steal money	*Bankräuber stehlen oft Geld.*
passive	Money is often stolen by bank robbers.	*Geld wird oft von Bankräubern gestohlen.*

Bildung

am / is / are (not)	**+ Verb-*ed* / 3. Stammform**	**+ by …**

Beispielsätze:

This shop **is closed** for the summer.
These toilets **are cleaned by** students.
This book **isn't sold** in the US.
Visitors **are asked** to wait outside.

G 3 Modale Hilfsverben *Modals*

Mit den modalen Hilfsverben kannst du Folgendes ausdrücken:
was jemand tun **kann** oder nicht tun kann → **can (can't)**
was jemand tun **muss** oder nicht tun muss → **must (needn't)**
was jemand tun **darf** oder nicht tun darf → **may (mustn't)**
was jemand tun **sollte** oder nicht tun sollte → **should (shouldn't)**

Dies musst du dir merken:
- *Modals* stehen nur im *simple present*, bilden also **keine Vergangenheit** (außer bei *can* – *could*).
- Sie erhalten **kein -s** nach *he/she/it*.
- Bei **Verneinungen** kannst du einfach ***not*** an das *modal* **anhängen**.
- Bei **Fragen** steht das **modale Hilfsverb am Satzanfang**.

You **can** fly to Australia. But you **can't** travel there by train.	*Du kannst nach Australien fliegen, aber du kannst nicht mit dem Zug dort hinfahren.*
Before you leave, you **must** get a visa. But you **needn't** buy Australian dollars.	*Bevor du abfliegst, musst du ein Visum holen, aber du musst keine australischen Dollars kaufen.*
You **may** bring presents into the country. But you **mustn't** bring any food.	*Du darfst Geschenke ins Land bringen, aber du darfst keine Lebensmittel einführen.*
You **should** drink a lot on the flight. But you **shouldn't** drink any alcohol.	*Auf dem Flug solltest du viel trinken, aber du solltest keinen Alkohol trinken.*

Beachte!
must = *müssen*, needn't = *nicht müssen/brauchen*, must not/mustn't = *nicht dürfen*!

▶ Das ist easy – *must* heißt „müssen"
und das musst du sonst noch wissen:
„muss nicht" – *needn't*, „darf nicht" – *mustn't*,
dann sind alle *modals* passend.

YOU MUSTN'T DRIVE FAST HERE!

Auf einen Blick

can	*können*	I **can** play the drums.	*Ich kann Schlagzeug spielen.*
can't	*nicht können*	My friend **can't** speak French.	*Mein Freund kann nicht / kann kein Französisch sprechen.*
must	*müssen*	You **must** learn the new words!	*Ihr müsst die neuen Wörter lernen.*
needn't	*nicht müssen / brauchen*	You **needn't** do this exercise.	*Ihr müsst diese Aufgabe nicht machen.*
mustn't	*nicht dürfen*	You **mustn't** drink alcohol!	*Ihr dürft keinen Alkohol trinken.*
may	*dürfen*	You **may** use a dictionary.	*Ihr dürft ein Wörterbuch benutzen.*
should	*sollte/t/st*	You **should** take an umbrella with you.	*Ihr solltet einen Regenschirm mitnehmen.*
shouldn't	*sollte/t/st nicht*	You **shouldn't** forget your homework.	*Ihr solltet eure Hausaufgaben nicht vergessen.*

G 4 Bedingungssätze (*if*-Sätze) Typ I *if-clauses (present)*

Erinnere dich: Bedingungssätze bestehen aus zwei Teilen: dem Nebensatz mit *if* und dem Hauptsatz. Mit dem *if*-Satz drückst du eine **erfüllbare Bedingung** aus. Der Hauptsatz sagt, was passiert, wenn diese Bedingung erfüllt wird.

- Der ***if*-Satz** steht dabei im ***simple present*** und im **Hauptsatz** wird meist das ***will-future*** verwendet.
- Der ***if*-Satz** kann am Anfang oder Ende des Satzes stehen. Steht er am **Anfang,** wird er **durch Komma abgetrennt**. In der deutschen Übersetzung verwenden wir häufig für diese Sätze die Gegenwart.

Erfüllbare Bedingung

if-Satz (simple present)	Hauptsatz (will-future)	
If it **rains**,	we'**ll stay** at home.	*Wenn es regnet, bleiben wir zu Hause / werden wir zu Hause bleiben.*
If it **doesn't rain**,	we **won't stay** at home.	*Wenn es nicht regnet, bleiben wir nicht zu Hause.*
If it **doesn't rain**,	we'**ll go** swimming.	*Wenn es nicht regnet, gehen wir schwimmen.*

Beachte!
Verneinungen müssen **nicht** in beiden Satzteilen gleichzeitig vorkommen.

Bildung

If … verb(s),
If … don't / doesn't + verb, … will + verb … / … won't + verb …

▶ *Will* oder *won't* im Satz? Dann ist für *if* kein Platz!

Beispielsätze

1. If you fly to Australia, you'll need a visa.	1. *Wenn du nach Australien fliegst, brauchst du ein Visum.*
2. If you work hard, you'll get a good mark.	2. *Wenn du fleißig arbeitest, bekommst du eine gute Note.*
3. I'll be very happy if our team wins this time.	3. *Ich freue mich, wenn unser Team diesmal gewinnt.*
4. Promise you'll call me if you need me.	4. *Versprich mir, dass du mich anrufst, wenn du mich brauchst.*
5. If you don't learn the rules, you won't pass the test.	5. *Wenn du die Regeln nicht lernst, bestehst du den Test nicht.*
6. Jackie won't be happy if we don't visit her.	6. *Jackie ist traurig (freut sich nicht), wenn wir sie nicht besuchen.*
7. Will you stay at home if it rains?	7. *Bleibst du zu Hause, wenn es regnet?*
8. What will you do then?	8. *Was machst du dann?*

G 5 Bedingungssätze (*if*-Sätze) Typ II — *if-clauses (past)*

Bedingungssätze bestehen aus zwei Teilen, dem **Nebensatz mit *if*** und dem **Hauptsatz** (siehe G 4).
Bei Bedingungssätzen vom **Typ II** wird mit dem Nebensatz eine **offene Bedingung** ausgedrückt, d.h. die Bedingung kann zwar erfüllt werden, aber es ist relativ unwahrscheinlich.

- Der ***if*-Satz** steht dabei im ***simple past*** und im **Hauptsatz** wird ***would*** verwendet.
- Der ***if*-Satz** kann am Anfang oder Ende des Satzes stehen. Steht er am **Anfang,** wird er **durch ein Komma abgetrennt**.
- In der **deutschen Übersetzung** wird im *if*-Satz oft anstelle der Möglichkeitsform des Verbs eine **Umschreibung mit „würde"** verwendet.

Aussagen

If I **went** there, *Wenn ich dorthin fahren würde/führe,*	I **would take** photos of the coral reef. *würde ich Fotos vom Korallenriff machen.*

Verneinung

If I **went** there, *Wenn ich dorthin fahren würde/führe,*	I **wouldn't take** photos of new hotels. *würde ich keine Fotos von neuen Hotels machen.*
If I **didn't go** to Australia this year, *Wenn ich in diesem Jahr nicht nach Australien fahren würde,*	I **would travel** to the Maldives. *würde ich auf die Malediven reisen.*

Bildung

	If-Satz	Hauptsatz
Aussage	if … **simple past**	… **would / wouldn't** + verb
Verneinung	if … **didn't** + verb	… **would / wouldn't** + verb

Beachte!
Verneinungen müssen nicht in beiden Satzteilen gleichzeitig vorkommen.

Beispielsätze

1. If I had holidays, I would stay in bed.	1. *Wenn ich Ferien hätte, würde ich im Bett bleiben.*
2. If you were here, I wouldn't be so alone.	2. *Wenn du hier wärst, wäre ich nicht so allein.*
3. If I didn't live in Germany, I would live in Canada.	3 *Wenn ich nicht in Deutschland lebte, würde ich in Kanada leben.*
4. If I had lots of money, I'd buy a space shuttle.	4. *Wenn ich viel Geld hätte, würde ich eine Raumfähre kaufen.*
5. We would save time if you helped me.	5. *Wir würden Zeit sparen, wenn du mir helfen würdest.*
6. If I didn't have a broken leg, I'd play football.	6. *Wenn ich kein gebrochenes Bein hätte, würde ich Fußball spielen.*

G 6 Gerundium — *Gerund*

Ein *gerund* verhält sich wie ein Nomen und wird aus einem Verb *+ing* gebildet. Das gibt es auch im Deutschen, z. B. aus **schwimmen** wird **das Schwimmen**.
Es kann **Subjekt oder Objekt** eines Satzes sein und steht auch **oft nach einer Präposition**.

- Ist ein *gerund* **Subjekt des Satzes**, steht es am **Satzanfang**. Meistens verwendet man *gerunds*, um etwas über Hobbys oder Aktivitäten auszudrücken.
- Ins Deutsche werden sie häufig mit einem Verb oder einem Infinitiv mit „zu" übertragen.

Als Subjekt

Swimming is my hobby.	*Schwimmen ist mein Hobby.*
Reading is fun.	*Lesen macht Spaß.*
Riding a bike keeps you fit.	*Rad fahren hält fit.*

Als Objekt

I like **watching** TV and **going** to parties.	*Ich sehe gern fern und liebe es, auf Partys zu gehen.*
I don't like **playing** ball games.	*Ich spiele nicht gern Ballspiele.*
Stop **talking,** please!	*Hör(t) bitte auf zu reden.*

Mit Präposition

I'm worried about not **finding** friends.	*Ich mache mir Sorgen, dass ich keine Freunde finde.*
I'm interested in **reading** books.	*Ich interessiere mich für (das Lesen von) Bücher(n).*
I'm good at **swimming.**	*Ich kann gut schwimmen.*

Bildung

Verb + ing

▶ Kurzer Mitlaut wird verdoppelt,
stummes ***-e*** wird abgekoppelt,
y das wird zu ***i***, präg es ein, vergiss es nie!

Verwendung	Beispielsätze	
als Subjekt	**Laughing** is healthy.	*Lachen ist gesund.*
als Objekt love, like, enjoy, don't like, hate, start, stop	What **do** you **like doing**?	*Was macht ihr gern?*
	We **like / enjoy swimming**.	*Wir schwimmen gern.*
	We **don't like / hate reading**.	*Wir lesen nicht gerne. / Wir hassen es zu lesen.*
	When **did** you **start jogging**?	*Wann habt ihr mit dem Joggen angefangen?*
	Stop asking questions, please!	*Hört bitte auf, Fragen zu stellen!*
mit Präposition be fed up with, be worried about, be afraid of, be frightened of, be good at, look forward to, be no sense in	Are you **fed up with answering** them?	*Habt ihr keine Lust mehr, sie zu beantworten?*
	I'm worried about missing the bus.	*Ich habe Angst, meinen Bus zu verpassen.*
	She's **afraid of flying**.	*Sie hat Angst vor dem Fliegen.*
	Why **is** she **frightened of flying**?	*Warum hat sie Angst vor dem Fliegen?*
	Thereis **no sense in shouting**.	*Es ist nicht sinnvoll zu schreien.*

G7 Indirekte Rede (sofort) — *Reported speech (immadiate)*

1 Direkte Rede

Rede kann direkt oder indirekt sein. Direkte Rede wird häufig in **Dialogtexten** verwendet, z. B. in **Theaterstücken,** bei der Wiedergabe von **Rollenspielen, Telefonaten**, aber auch in manchen Erzählformen, z. B. in **Geschichten.** (Hier setzt man sie oft in Anführungszeichen.)

Old man: Hello! I'm from Greenwich.
Young man: No, I wouldn't like a sandwich.
Old man: Do you come from Germany?
Young man: No, I didn't hurt my knee. I hurt my left arm.
Old man: Oh, you can't hear very well.
Young man: Yes, I have lots of interesting things to tell.

2 Indirekte Rede

Verben wie *to say, to think, to explain, to tell, to ask,* … leiten die **indirekte Rede** ein. Die wörtliche Rede wird einfach mit einem Nebensatz, der mit dass – ***that***, ob – ***if*** oder einem **Fragewort** beginnt, angefügt.

Indirekte Rede – sofort berichtet

Direkte Rede ***simple present***	**Einleitung** ***simple present***	**Indirekte Rede** ***simple present***
"He **must have** a nice smile." *„Er muss ein süßes Lächeln haben."*	The girl **says** *Das Mädchen sagt,*	(that) he **must have** a nice smile. *dass er ein süßes Lächeln haben muss.*
"Such girls **don't have** a chance." *„Solche Mädchen haben keine Chance."*	The boy **explains** *Der Junge erklärt,*	(that) such girls **don't have** a chance. *dass solche Mädchen keine Chance haben.*
"What **do** you **find** attractive?" *„Was findet ihr attraktiv?"*	The reporter **asks** *Der Reporter fragt,*	what they **find** attractive. *was sie attraktiv finden.*
"**Are** you interested?" *„Seid ihr interessiert?"*	He **wants to know** *Er will wissen,*	if they **are** interested. *ob sie interessiert sind.*

Beachte!

- Wie im Deutschen wechselt die 1. Person zur 3. Person:

  I – ich → *he/she* – er / sie
  we – wir → *they* – sie
  my – mein → *his/her* – sein / ihr
  our – unser → *their* – ihr (Pl.)

- Bei Fragen entfällt das *do* als Umschreibung und das Verb übernimmt die Zeitform.
  "**Do** you **come** from Germany?" – He wants to know **if he comes** from Germany.

G 8 Indirekte Rede (später) — *Reported speech (later)*

Wenn direkte Rede erst später berichtet wird, steht das einleitende Verb im *simple past*. Im Folgesatz gibt es eine **Zeitverschiebung**. Solche Erzählformen findest du auch oft in der Literatur, z. B. in **Erzählungen, Geschichten**, aber auch in **Berichten** usw.

Indirekte Rede – später berichtet

Direkte Rede *simple present*	**Einleitung** *simple past*	**Indirekte Rede** *simple past*
"He **has** a nice smile." *„Er hat ein süßes Lächeln."*	The girl **said** *Das Mädchen sagte,*	(that) he **had** a nice smile. *dass er ein süßes Lächeln hat.*
"Such girls **don't have** a chance." *„Solche Mädchen haben keine Chance."*	The boy **explained** *Der Junge erklärte,*	(that) such girls **didn't have** a chance. *dass solche Mädchen keine Chance haben.*
"What **do** you **find** attractive?" *„Was findet ihr attraktiv?"*	The reporter **asked** *Der Reporter fragte,*	what they **found** attractive. *was sie attraktiv finden.*
"**Are** you interested?" *„Seid ihr interessiert?"*	He **wanted to know** *Er wollte wissen,*	if they **were** interested. *ob sie interessiert sind.*

PRESENT → **PAST**

Beachte!

- Manche Verben ändern im *simple past* ihre Form nicht.
  "It **should** be OK!" → He **told** me it **should** be OK.
- Bei Fragen entfällt das *do* als Umschreibung und das Verb übernimmt die Zeitform.
  "What **do** you **find** attractive?" → He wanted to know what they **found** attractive.

Ov1 Aktiv und Passiv *Active and passive voice*

ACTIVE			
Beispiel	They **built** Canberra in 1908.	We **switch on** our computers every morning.	I hope my friends **will take** some good photos of me at the zoo.
Bildung	**verb-ed / 2. Stammform**	**verb (s)**	**will + verb**
(AKTIV) ↑ Zeitform ↓ (PASSIV)	→ **Simple past** • Berichten über Vergangenes	→ **Simple present** • regelmäßige Handlungen • Tatsachen • Fakten	→ **Will-future** • Voraussagen • spontane Entscheidungen • Versprechen, Hilfe
Signalwörter	ago, yesterday, last …, in (year)	always, often, sometimes, every …	I hope / think / …, in (year), tomorrow, next (Wochentag),
Bildung	**was / were + verb-ed / 3. Stammform** (+**by**)	**is / are + verb-ed / 3. Stammform** (+**by**)	**will be + verb-ed / 3. Stammform** (+**by**)
Beispiel	Canberra **was built** in 1908.	Our computers **are switched on** every morning (**by** us).	I hope some good photos of me **will be taken** (**by** my friends).
PASSIVE			

Beachte!
- Ob ein Satz im Aktiv oder Passiv verwendet wird, hängt von der Absicht des Sprechers / der Sprecherin ab.
- Will er / sie ausdrücken, wer etwas tut, getan hat oder tun wird, verwendet er / sie das Aktiv.
- Soll aber mehr betont werden, was mit wem geschieht, verwendet er / sie eine Passivkonstruktion. Hier ist also die Handlung wichtig.
- Falls der / die Handelnde bekannt ist, kann er / sie mit *by* hinzugefügt werden.

Ov 2 Formen von *be* in den einzelnen Zeiten: Aussagen und Verneinung

The verb *'to be' in different tenses: statements and negations*

Aussagen – Langformen / Kurzformen

Pronouns	simple present	simple past	will-future
I	I'm (am)	I was	I'll (will) be
You	You're (are)	You were	You 'll (will) be
He/She/It	He's/She's/It's (is)	He/She/It was	He'll/She'll/It'll (will) be
We	We're (are)	We were	We'll (will) be
You	You're (are)	You were	You'll (will) be
They	They're (are)	They were	They'll (will) be

Verneinungen

Pronouns	simple present	simple past	will-future
I	I'm not	I wasn't	I won't be
You	You aren't	You weren't	You won't be
He/She/It	He/She/It isn't	He/She/It wasn't	He/She/It won't be
We	We aren't	We weren't	We won't be
You	You aren't	You weren't	You won't be
They	They aren't	They weren't	They won't be

Yes / No-Fragen

Pronouns	simple present	simple past	will-future
I	Am I …?	Was I …?	Will I be …?
You	Are you …?	Were you …?	Will you be …?
He/She/It	Is he/she/it …?	Was he/she/it …?	Will he/she/it be …?
We	Are we …?	Were we …?	Will we be …?
You	Are you …?	Were you …?	Will you be …?
They	Are they …?	Were they …?	Will they be …?

Wh-Fragen

Pronouns	simple present	simple past	will-future
I	Who am I …?	Who was I …?	Who will I be …?
You	Where are you …?	Where were you …?	Where will you be …?
He/She/It	How is he/she/it …?	How was he/she/it …?	How will he/she it be …?
We	When are we …?	When were we …?	When will we be …?
You	Why are you …?	Why were you …?	Why will you be …?
They	What are they …?	What were they …?	What will they be …?

Beachte!

- Nach Personalpronomen verwendet man in der Regel die Kurzform von *be*.
- Die Langform benötigst du aber nach Substantiven und bei Fragen und Verneinungen:
  *The weather **is** good today. **Am** I …? **Were** you …? You **aren't** … . **Will** they …?*

Ov3 Vollverben (regelmäßige) in den einzelnen Zeiten

Regular verbs in different tenses

Infinitiv: to live

Aussagen

Pronouns	simple past	present progressive	simple present	will-future
	verb-*ed*	*am/is/are* + verb-*ing*	verb (+s)	*will* + verb
I	I lived	I'm (am) living	I live	I will live
You	You lived	You're (are) living	You live	You will live
He/She/It	He/She/It lived	He's/She's/It's (is) living	He/She/It lives	He/She/It will live
We	We lived	We're (are) living	We live	We will live
You	You lived	You're (are) living	You live	You will live
They	They lived	They're (are) living	They live	They will live

Verneinungen

Pronouns	simple past	present progressive	simple present	will-future
I	I didn't live	I'm not living	I don't live	I won't live
You	You didn't live	You aren't living	You don't live	You won't live
He/She/It	He/She/It didn't live	He/She/It isn't living	He/She/It doesn't live	He/She/It won't live
We	We didn't live	We aren't living	We don't live	We won't live
You	You didn't live	You aren't living	You don't live	You won't live
They	They didn't live	They aren't living	They don't live	They won't live

Fragen

Pronouns	simple past	present progressive	simple present	will-future
I	Did I live …?	Am I living …?	Do I live …?	Will I live …?
You	Did you live …?	Are you living …?	Do you live …?	Will you live …?
He/She/It	Did he/she/it live …?	Is he/she/it living …?	Does he/she/it live …?	Will he/she/it live …?
We	Did we live …?	Are we living …?	Do we live …?	Will we live …?
You	Did you live …?	Are you living …?	Do you live …?	Will you live …?
They	Did they live …?	Are they living …?	Do they live …?	Will they live …?

Examples:

I **live** in Germany.
I **lived** in England 10 years ago.
When I'm 18, I hope I'**ll live** in my own flat.
Look at this photo. I'**m living** here at the moment with my grandparents.

Ov4 Vollverben (unregelmäßige) in den einzelnen Zeiten

Irregular verbs in different tenses

Infinitiv: to drive (a car)

Aussagen

Pronouns	simple past	present progressive	simple present	will-future
	2. Form	*am/is/are* + verb-*ing*	verb + (s)	*will* + verb
I	I drove	I'm (am) driving	I drive	I'll (will) drive
You	You drove	You're (are) driving	You drive	You'll (will) drive
He/She/It	He/She/It drove	He's/She's/It's (is) driving	He/She/It drives	He'll/She'll/It'll (will) drive
We	We drove	We're (are) driving	We drive	We'll (will) drive
You	You drove	You're (are) driving	You drive	You'll (will) drive
They	They drove	They're (are) driving	They drive	They'll (will) drive

Verneinungen

Pronouns	simple past	present progressive	simple present	will-future
I	I didn't drive	I'm not driving	I don't drive	I won't drive
You	You didn't drive	You aren't driving	You don't drive	You won't drive
He/She/It	He/She/It didn't drive	He/She/It isn't driving	He/She/It doesn't drive	He/She/It won't drive
We	We didn't drive	We aren't driving	We don't drive	We won't drive
You	You didn't drive	You aren't driving	You don't drive	You won't drive
They	They didn't drive	They aren't driving	They don't drive	They won't drive

Fragen

Pronouns	simple past	present progressive	simple present	will-future
I	Did I drive …?	Am I driving …?	Do I drive …?	Will I drive …?
You	Did you drive …?	Are you driving …?	Do you drive …?	Will you drive …?
He/She/It	Did he drive …?	Is he driving …?	Does he drive …?	Will he drive …?
We	Did we drive …?	Are we driving …?	Do we drive …?	Will we drive …?
You	Did you drive …?	Are you driving …?	Do you drive …?	Will you drive …?
They	Did they drive …?	Are they driving …?	Do they drive …?	Will they drive …?

Examples:

I **don't drive** to school – I always **go** by bus!
We **drove** to France last September.
I'm sure I'**ll drive** to school in my own car next year.
Where's Dad? – He'**s driving** Mum to the station.

Ov 5 Die Steigerung der Adjektive — *The comparison of adjectives*

1. Die Steigerung auf *-er/-est*

Einsilbige Adjektive:

1. Form	2. Form	3. Form	
long	long**er**	(the) long**est**	*lang – länger – am längsten*
big	big**ger**	(the) big**gest**	*groß – größer – am größten*
safe	saf**er**	(the) saf**est**	*sicher – sicherer – am sichersten*

Einige zweisilbige Adjektive (z. B. auf -y)**:**

1. Form	2. Form	3. Form	
healthy	health**ier**	(the) health**iest**	*gesund – gesünder – am gesündesten*
pretty	prett**ier**	(the) prett**iest**	*schön – schöner – am schönsten*

2. Die Steigerung mit *more/most*

Zwei- und mehrsilbige Adjektive

1. Form	2. Form	3. Form	
exciting	**more** exciting	(the) **most** exciting	*aufregend – aufregender – am aufregendsten*
famous	**more** famous	(the) **most** famous	*berühmt – berühmter – am berühmtesten*
expensive	**more** expensive	(the) **most** expensive	*teuer – teurer – am teuersten*

Auf einen Blick

Ein- und einige zweisilbige Adjektive, z. B. auf *-y*	**Zwei- und mehrsilbige Adjektive**
Adjective + -er/est	***more/most + Adjective***

Beachte!
In der 2. Steigerungsform kann die Vergleichsgröße mit ***than*** (im Deutschen ‚als') angefügt werden.
He's old**er than** my brother. — *Er ist älter als mein Bruder.*
The red T-shirt is **more** expensive **than** the white one. — *Das rote T-Shirt ist teurer als das weiße.*

3. Besonderheiten

Diese Besonderheiten musst du dir einprägen.

nice	nic**er**	the nic**est**
big	big**ger**	the big**gest**
healthy	health**ier**	the health**iest**

Kurzer Mitlaut wird verdoppelt,
stummes ***-e*** wird abgekoppelt,
y das wird zu ***i***, präg es ein, vergiss es nie!

Beachte!
- Einige Adjektive werden unregelmäßig gesteigert.
  good – better – (the) best — *gut – besser – am besten*
  bad – worse – (the) worst — *schlecht – schlechter – am schlechtesten*
  little – less – (the) least — *wenig – weniger – am wenigsten*
- Einige Adjektive kann man nicht steigern: sie sind schon am Ende einer Skala, z. B. *superb, wrong, …*

G1 Vollverben und Hilfsverben (→ pp. 54–56)

1 All on one trip!

a) *Put each verb in the simple present and find out about a teenager's trip to Australia.*

Jeff's aunt (*to live*) in Australia and (*to work*) at the airport in Sydney. Every year she (*to send*) a ticket to Jeff and he (*to fly*) to Sydney. After about a week in the city he and his cousin Lance (*to travel*) to a cattle station[1] in the north. They both (*to work*) there for about a month. They (*to find*) farm life really hard but they (*to love*) the wide open spaces out there. Jeff and Lance (*to save*) all their money and when their job (*to end*), they (*to spend*) a week on a diving holiday together. Jeff (*to feel*) very happy when he (*to be*) in Australia!

[1]cattle station ['kætl ˌsteɪʃn] – *Rinderfarm*

b) *Read your text from a) and then correct the following sentences. Use 'doesn't' or 'don't'.*
Example: 1. Jeff's aunt **has** a job at the bank. No, she **doesn't have** a job … . She has … .

1. Jeff's aunt has a job at the bank.
2. Jeff lives in Australia.
3. Jeff visits his aunt in Perth.
4. He stays in the city for about a month.
5. Then he goes to the south with his cousin.
6. There they help on a cattle drive.
7. Jeff and Lance think the work is easy.
8. They both enjoy wide open doors.
9. They spend a week on a riding holiday.
10. Jeff's trips to Australia make him very tired.

c) *A reporter wants to do an interview with Jeff. Make up some questions. Use 'do' or 'does'.*

1.	Do/Does +	… you want to fly to Australia again	?
2.		… your cousin Lance go to school in Sydney	
3.		… Lance visit you in London sometimes	
4.		… you like life in the city or in the country better	
5.		… your holiday job on the station pay well	
6.		… you both go diving every year	
7.		… you plan to live in Australia one day	

d) *Now complete Jeff's answers to the reporter's questions in Ex. 1 c).*

1. Yes, I really (*to think*) that it's a great country!
2. No, he and a friend (*to be*) on a dive instructor's course at the moment.
3. Yes, he usually (*to come*) over here in spring.
4. Well, I (*to like*) both, in fact. But the ocean (*to be*) the best of all!
5. Yes, it (*to pay*) enough for us to have a great holiday after all that hard work!
6. No, not always. Sometimes we (*to help*) on nature projects on the Great Barrier Reef.
7. Well, I (*to think*) it's too early to make plans. But maybe when I (*to finish*) school …

2 A report

Look at Ex. 1a) again. Put the verbs in the simple past and write a report about Jeff's last visit to Australia.
Start like this: Jeff's aunt sent him a ticket and he … . After about a week in the city … .

G 2 Das Passiv im *simple present* (→ p. 57)

1 The American way

a) *How are these things done in the US? Complete each sentence with a word from the boxes.*

1. Usually the word 'colour' … without a 'u'.
2. Football … with a round ball.
3. Spanish … in some states in the South.
4. Often cream cheese … on bagels.
5. A map of the world … with America in the middle.
6. The toilet … the toilet. People say, "Excuse me. Where's the bathroom?"

is drawn | isn't called | is written | is served | isn't played | is spoken

b) *Match each of the things with a passive form.* Example: Mistakes are made.

mistakes ✓ • presents • questions • words • songs • letters • photos • autographs • prizes

are sung • are spoken • are won • are given • are taken • are signed • are asked • are written • are made ✓

2 Out in nature

Look at the pairs of pictures. Decide which one is correct and write sentences in the passive.

Example: 1. Wild animals **aren't protected** in the School of the Air! They**'re protected** in zoos.
2. The forest … by … . It's … by … .

G 3 Modale Hilfsverben (→ p. 63)

1 Sayings

a) *Write the sayings into your exercise book and underline the modals.*

b) *Match the sayings with the meanings.*

Sayings:	What the sayings mean:
1. You can lead a horse to water but you can't make him drink. 2. All good things must come to an end. 3. You should let sleeping dogs lie. 4. People who live in glass houses shouldn't throw stones. 5. A cat may look at a king.	a. A poor person can do things that a rich person can do. b Don't talk about a problem. Keep quiet about it. c. You can help a person to do something, but he / she must want to do it, too. d. Nothing lasts forever. e. Don't talk about other peoples' mistakes. Everyone makes mistakes!

2 A big difference!

a) *Look at the four photos and match each one with the right caption.*

1

2

3

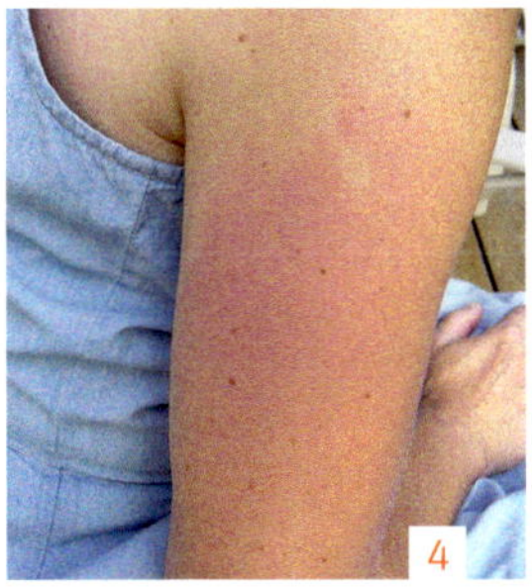
4

D Keep out!

A Cycling is healthy!

B Oh, that hurts!

C Perfect weather!

b) *Choose 'mustn't' or 'needn't' and complete the sentences which go with the above photos.*

1. So we … pack our anoraks.
2. You … go into the water!
3. Thanks, but you … pick me up, Dad!
4. You really … stay out in the sun so long.

3 A tourist brochure

Use modals to complete these sentences from a tourist brochure.

1. You (*must / can't*) ride our cows but you (*may / mustn't*) ride our horses if you want to.
2. Tourists (*shouldn't / can't*) go walking without any water. They (*may / should*) always take some bottles with them.
3. You (*should / mustn't*) wear a hat on the beach but you (*must / needn't*) wear a coat.
4. Visitors (*must / may*) take photos of the crocodiles but they (*mustn't / can*) get too close.
5. Parents (*needn't / must*) tell their kids not to play with snakes and they (*can't / should*) know what to do in an emergency.
6. No one (*should / can't*) swim where there are crocodiles. They (*can / mustn't*) be dangerous.

G 4 Bedingungssätze (*if*-Sätze) Typ I (→ p. 65)

1 What if?

a) *Find the dialogue pairs.*
Example: A: Let's go swimming in the lake – B: Yes, but what **if it rains**?

A:
1. Let's go swimming in the lake. ✓
2. I'd like to stay at the disco longer.
3. What about visiting our mate Jake?
4. Let's buy takeaway pizzas.
5. Why don't we get some DVDs?
6. Concert tickets are a good present for Jo.
7. Those jeans are really wicked!

B:
a. But what if they're cold when we get home?
b. OK, but what if they're too expensive?
c. Yes, but what if it rains? ✓
d. But what if we miss the last bus?
e. But what can we do if he's not at home?
f. Yeah, cool! But what if they don't fit you?
g. But it's late. What if the shops are already closed?

b) *Write A's answers to B's questions. Use the ideas from the box.*
Example: A: Let's go swimming … . – B: Yes, but what **if it rains**? – A: Well, **if it rains**, we'**ll get** wet!

I / to ask for some larger ones • we / to buy a CD • we / to get wet! ✓ • I / to pay for a taxi • brother / to lend us his DVDs • I / to put in our microwave • we / to go to the park

G 5 Bedingungssätze (*if*-Sätze) Typ II (→ p. 66)

1 What would happen …?

These people could still do these things. What would happen if they decided to do them?
Example: 1. Ella – learn Spanish: If Ella **learnt** Spanish, it **would be** helpful in her job.

1. Ella – learn Spanish: If Ella …, it (*to be*) helpful in her job.
2. Marley – work in a bank: If Marley …, she (*to feel*) very bored.
3. Ali and Shahid – visit Australia: If Ali and Shahid …, they (*not to come*) back.
4. Doug – call 'TalkLine': If Doug …, he (*to get*) some good advice.
5. Jane – try a new sport: If Jane …, she (*to enjoy*) it much more.
6. Tom – become a mechanic: If Tom …, he (*not to need*) anyone to fix his car!

2 Winning the lottery

Your grandad is dreaming of winning the lottery! But he often forgets things, so help him to find the right words. Use the ones below (you can use each one more than once).

1. If I … the lottery, I … rich. I … on the sofa. I … round the world!
2. If I … round the world, I … my girlfriend with me.
3. If I … my girlfriend with me, we … Las Vegas and we … to a casino.
4. If we … to the casino, I … lots of money.
5. Oh, I FORGOT!!! If I … the lottery, I … to win money in a casino!

to visit | to come | to travel | not / to sit | to be | to win | to go | to take | not / to need

G 6 Gerundium (→ p. 59)

1 A dating profile

Kai is looking for a girlfriend. Finish his dating profile. Use the verbs in the boxes to make gerunds.

hear | listen | talk | play | spend | watch | shop | have ✓ | dance | do | swim

Hi, I'm Kai!

I'm looking for a girl who enjoys **having** a good time!
I've got lots of different hobbies: I love … films in the cinema, so it would be good if you loved that, too! Of course, … in clubs is also really cool and I'm crazy about hip-hop and rap music.

… football or … most kinds of sports is not my thing, I'm afraid. I enjoy … but only in the sea and when it's warm. I really like … to music.

Girls who just can't stop … about other nice guys are not for me! And if they only want to spend the weekend … in town then they needn't apply. ; -)

So if you think we have similar interests and think that we would enjoy … time together, just send me a message!

I look forward to[1] … from you!
Kai xxxx

[1] to look forward to ['fɔːwəd] – *sich freuen auf*

2 The driving test

You show your dad this cartoon. He looks surprised. Complete the sentences using a gerund.

Passing your driving test is easy if …

Well done! Now do this once more after drinking this and you'll get a driving license

You: Hey, look at this comic, Dad! Now you can see why I'm looking forward to (*do*) my driving test.
Dad: Oh my God! Don't they know that (*sleep*) on the streets is dangerous?
You: Oh, you're right! (*Lie*) on the streets is not a good idea! How can people be so stupid!
Dad: And (*give*) alcohol to drivers is even worse!
You: Why? I think (*drink*) and (*drive*) at the same time is really cool! I enjoy (*have*) a drink before I drive.
Dad: WHAT?? Oh no! I'll be frightened of (*go*) out on the streets when you get your license!
You: Dad, there is no sense in (*worry*)! Stop (*be*) silly. I'm joking! You know how I love (*make*) jokes. And I only wanted to see what you'd say.
Dad: I just hope that you are as good at (*drive*) as you are at joking!

G7 Indirekte Rede (sofort berichtet) (→ p. 60)

1 Things famous singers say …

You're having a fun afternoon with friends and you're just reading "Hello!" magazine together. Talk about what some of your favourite singers say in it.

Examples:
1. "Katie says **that** no one is interested in what happens to singers who don't make it."
2. "Melanie and Geri say **that they**'re old enough to take care of **their** own lives."

1. Katie: *No one is interested in what happens to singers who don't make it!*

2. Melanie & Geri: *We're old enough to take care of our own lives!*

3. Elton: *The great thing about rock 'n' roll is that almost anyone can become a star.*

4. Natasha: *It's a terrible article! They should call their newspaper The Daily Disaster!*

5. Orville: *Sometimes having more is really less …*

6. Stevie: *My fans are important, but I can't live my life for them.*

7. Sean: *I would love to get an Oscar this time!*

G8 Indirekte Rede (später berichtet) (→ p. 61)

1 An interview

Greg comes home from an interview and tells his mum what the manager asked him and said to him. Complete the sentences. Use the information from the boxes below.

Hi, Greg. How was your interview? Tell me about it!

The manager asked me lots of questions and she told me a lot about the company …
1. First of all she asked me how old **I was**.
2. Then she wanted to know which school … .
3. After that she asked me if … .
4. Then she wanted to know why … .
5. Later she told me that they … .
6. Then she added that … .
7. After that she warned me that … .
8. Last of all she advised me that I should … .

Manager's questions:	**Info on company**
• How old are you? ✓	• 150 workers
• Which school do you go to?	• working hours: 8 am – 4 pm
• Do you do any sports?	• people don't smoke in building
• Why do you want to work here?	• should wear a suit to work

VOCABULARY

SKILLS

Diese Checkliste kann dir helfen, Fehler zu vermeiden und deine Rechtschreibung zu verbessern. Prüfe alle deine Texte damit.

- Schreibung:
  - ☑ ‚gh' wird meist nicht gesprochen. Vergiss es beim Schreiben nicht.
  - ☑ ‚k' kommt vor ‚t' so gut wie nie vor, z.B. action – Aktion, October – Oktober
- Gleiche Aussprache, unterschiedliche Schreibung:
  - ☑ [i:] z.B. t**ea**cher, m**ee**ting, m**e**dia, magaz**i**ne, p**eo**ple, f**ie**ld
  - ☑ [u:] z.B. f**oo**d, r**ou**te, to d**o**, swims**ui**t, s**u**permarket, tr**ue**, cr**ew**
- Gleiche Aussprache, unterschiedliche Schreibung und Bedeutung:
  - ☑ [i:] z.B. s**ee** – sehen, s**ea** – Meer; m**ee**t – treffen, m**ea**t – Fleisch
  - ☑ [u:] z.B. **two** – zwei, **too** – auch
- Verdoppelung der Endkonsonanten:
  - ☑ to sto**p** – sto**pp**ing, sto**pp**ed
  - ☑ to pla**n** – pla**nn**ing, pla**nn**ed
- ‚y' wird zu ‚ie':
  - ☑ in der 3. Person Singular: z.B. to carr**y** – he carr**ie**s; to cr**y** – she cr**ie**s; **aber**: to bu**y** – she bu**ys**
  - ☑ im Plural: z.B. cit**y** – cit**ie**s, part**y** – part**ie**s; **aber**: bo**y** – bo**ys**
  - ☑ bei der Steigerung von Adjektiven: z.B. happ**y** – happ**ier** – (the) happ**iest**; eas**y** – eas**ier** – (the) eas**iest**
- Ähnlich und doch anders:
  - ☑ Wortendung ‚le': z.B. *engl.* simp**le** – *dt.* simp**el**; *engl.* tit**le** – *dt.* Tit**el**; *engl.* midd**le** – *dt.* Mitt**el**
  - ☑ ‚ph' statt ‚f': z.B. *engl.* **ph**one – *dt.* Telefon; *engl.* **ph**oto – *dt.* **F**oto
- Großschreibung:
  - ☑ Monatsnamen: z.B. January, July, December
  - ☑ Wochentage: z.B. Monday, Wednesday, Saturday
  - ☑ Eigennamen: z.B. Tom, Lisa, the Brooks, the London Eye, the Thames
  - ☑ geografische Namen: Bristol, Greenwich, Germany, Italy
- Plural:
  - ☑ Der Plural bekommt normalerweise ein -s: z.B. friend – friend**s**, chair – chair**s**, film – film**s**
  - ☑ Endet ein Wort auf s oder x, wird -es angehängt: z.B. bus – bus**es**, box – box**es**
  - ☑ Manche Wörter haben einen unregelmäßigen Plural: z.B. man – men, child – children, shelf – shelves, mouse – mice
- Apostroph:
  - ☑ bei Kurzformen: z.B. she is → she's; they are → they're
  - ☑ beim Genitiv-s: z.B. Sam's bike, Emma's family, the Jacksons' house, the children's games
- Wörterbuch:
  - ☑ Prüfe die Schreibung aller Wörter, bei denen du dir nicht ganz sicher bist, indem du sie im Wörterbuch nachschlägst.

Vocabulary

Auf den folgenden Seiten findest du alle neuen englischen Wörter und Ausdrücke. Sie stehen in der Reihenfolge, wie sie im Buch vorkommen.
Diese Wortliste ist in drei Spalten aufgeteilt:

- Links stehen die englischen Wörter und Sätze.
- In der Mitte werden sie übersetzt.
- Rechts findest du Beispiele, Erklärungen und Tipps, die dir beim Lernen helfen.

Die fett gedruckten Wörter musst du lernen. Normal gedruckte Wörter solltest du wiedererkennen, wenn du sie hörst oder liest.
Gleich nach jedem neuen englischen Wort steht die Lautschrift in eckigen Klammern. Sie zeigt dir, wie das neue Wort ausgesprochen wird. Wie du diese Lautzeichen liest, siehst du unten.

Englische Laute

Mitlaute				Selbstlaute		Doppellaute	
[b]	**b**ed	[p]	**p**icture	[ɑː]	c**ar**	[aɪ]	**I**, m**y**
[d]	**d**ay	[r]	**r**ed	[æ]	**a**pple	[aʊ]	n**ow**, m**ou**se
[ð]	**th**e	[s]	**s**ix	[e]	p**e**n	[eɪ]	n**a**me, th**ey**
[f]	**f**amily	[ʃ]	**sh**e	[ə]	**a**gain	[eə]	th**ere**, p**air**
[g]	**g**o	[t]	**t**en	[ɜː]	g**ir**l	[ɪə]	h**ere**, id**ea**
[ŋ]	morni**ng**	[tʃ]	lun**ch**	[ʌ]	b**u**t	[əʊ]	hell**o**
[h]	**h**ouse	[v]	**v**ideo	[ɪ]	**i**t	[ɔɪ]	b**oy**
[j]	**y**ou	[w]	**w**e, **o**ne	[i]	happ**y**	[ʊə]	s**ure**
[k]	**c**an, mil**k**	[z]	ea**s**y	[iː]	t**ea**cher		
[l]	**l**etter	[ʒ]	revi**s**ion	[ɒ]	d**o**g		
[m]	**m**an	[dʒ]	pa**g**e	[ɔː]	b**a**ll		
[n]	**n**o	[θ]	**th**ank you	[ʊ]	b**oo**k		
				[u]	Jan**u**ary		
				[uː]	t**oo**, tw**o**		

[ː] der vorangehende Laut ist lang, z. B. *you* [juː]

[ˈ] die folgende Silbe wird betont, z. B. *hello* [həˈləʊ]

In jeder *Topic* findest du Übungen zum Vokabellernen sowie einen Kasten mit *Useful phrases*, die dir helfen, dich auf Englisch zu verständigen.

Außerdem gibt es zu jeder *Topic* einen Kasten, in dem du Interessantes zur Landeskunde erfährst.

Auf das *Vocabulary* folgt das *Dictionary*, eine alphabetische Wortliste aller englischen Wörter im Buch. Wenn du ein Wort nicht verstehst, kannst du es hier nachschlagen

Abkürzungen und Zeichen

pl	Plural, Mehrzahl
sg	Singular, Einzahl
infml	umgangssprachlich
10	Auf dieser Seite kommen die Wörter vor.

!	Achtung!
↔	ist das Gegenteil von
→	ist verwandt mit
=	entspricht

! *Information* hat keine Mehrzahl.
permanent ↔ temporary
drive → driver
Dear Jenny = Liebe Jenny

Topic 1 Oz 4 us!

Australien

Australien ist flächenmäßig der sechstgrößte Staat der Erde, außerdem der kleinste Kontinent und die größte Insel der Welt. Australien wird auch als *Oz* oder *Down Under* bezeichnet. Mit nur zwei Einwohnern pro km² hat Australien die niedrigste Bevölkerungsdichte der Welt. 90 % der Einwohner stammen aus Europa. Einen kleinen Teil der Gesamtbevölkerung machen die australischen Ureinwohner, die Aborigines, aus.

Seit der australische Kontinent von England besiedelt wurde, wird dort Englisch gesprochen, und es herrscht Linksverkehr wie in England. Die australische Flagge besteht aus einer kleinen britischen Flagge und sechs Sternen. Der große Stern steht für die Bundesstaaten und Territorien Australiens, während die fünf kleineren Sterne das Sternbild *Kreuz des Südens* darstellen.
Ungefähr drei Viertel der Fläche Australiens sind kaum oder gar nicht besiedelt. Diese Regionen bezeichnet man als *Outback*, weil sie fernab der Zivilisation liegen. Ein großer Teil des Outbacks besteht aus Wüste, in der manchmal jahrelang kein Regen fällt. Im Outback befinden sich auch riesige Rinder- und Schaffarmen. Einige dieser Farmen sind mit über 30.000 km² so groß wie Nordrhein-Westfalen.
Der australische Kontinent trennte sich vor rund 50 Millionen Jahren von den anderen Kontinenten der Erde ab. Deshalb konnte sich dort eine besondere Tierwelt entwickeln. Dazu zählen die Beuteltiere, wie z. B. Kängurus und Koalas, oder das Schnabeltier. Es ist das einzige Säugetier der Erde, das Eier legt.
Eine Attraktion an der australischen Küste ist das Great Barrier Reef. Es ist mit einer Fläche von über 340.000 km² das größte Korallenriff der Erde. Das Riff bietet Lebensraum für eine Vielzahl von Korallen- und Fischarten, darunter Delfine, Haie und Rochen, sowie Schildkröten und Wale.

Wie groß ist eigentlich Deutschland? Gibt es hier auch besondere Tier- oder Pflanzenarten? Wie groß sind deutsche Farmen oder Bauernhöfe? Würdest du gerne weit abgelegen im Outback leben?

Check-in

9	**kangaroo** [ˌkæŋgr'u:]	Känguru →	A *kangaroo* is an Australian animal.
	the Outback ['aʊtbæk]	das Outback *(australisches Hinterland)* →	the wild, empty country away from Australia's towns and cities
	opera ['ɒprə]	Oper →	concert – play – musical – *opera*
	diver ['daɪvə]	Taucher/Taucherin	

Aspects

10	**aspect** ['æspekt]	Aspekt, Gesichtspunkt, Seite	
	Aborigine [ˌæbə'rɪdʒni]	Ureinwohner/Ureinwohnerin Australiens, Aborigine →	The *Aborigines* were the first people who lived in Australia.
	continent ['kɒntɪnənt]	Kontinent, Erdteil →	country – *continent*

to **claim** [kleɪm]	beanspruchen, (ein)fordern; behaupten →	to take sth (e.g. land) and call it your own
convict ['kɒnvɪkt]	Sträfling →	somebody who is in prison
First Fleet [ˌfɜːst 'fliːt]	First Fleet *(erste Flotte von Schiffen, die Sträflinge nach Australien brachte)*	
had escaped [ˌhæd‿ɪ'skeɪpt]	waren geflüchtet, waren entkommen	
jail [dʒeɪl]	Gefängnis →	*jail* = prison
death [deθ]	Tod, Todesfall →	dead → *death* life ↔ *death*
sentence ['sentənts]	Verurteilung, Urteil, Strafe	
colony ['kɒləni]	Kolonie	
No. ['nʌmbə]	Nummer →	short for 'number'
creature ['kriːtʃə]	Kreatur, Geschöpf, Lebewesen	
Down Under [ˌdaʊn‿'ʌndə]	Down Under *(Spitzname für Australien)*; in Australien	
koala [kəʊ'ɑːlə]	Koala →	A *koala* is an Australian animal.
cute [kjuːt]	niedlich, süß	
to **threaten** ['θretn]	(be)drohen	
crocodile ['krɒkədaɪl]	Krokodil	
snake [sneɪk]	Schlange →	A lof of people are afraid of *snakes*.
to **cut down** [kʌt 'daʊn]	abholzen, fällen →	This tree is ill. We have to *cut* it *down*.
to **cut**, **cut**, **cut** [kʌt; kʌt; kʌt]	(ab)schneiden	
eucalyptus [ˌjuːk'lɪptəs]	Eukalyptus →	A *eucalyptus* is an Australian tree.
to **protect** [prə'tekt]	(be)schützen	
law [lɔː]	Gesetz(gebung), Recht	
jelly bean ['dʒeli biːn]	*engl. Süßigkeit* →	*Jelly beans* are sweets.
option ['ɒpʃn]	Auswahlmöglichkeit, Option	
reef [riːf]	Riff →	The Great Barrier Reef is a famous *reef* in Australia.
urgent ['ɜːdʒnt]	dringend	
applicant ['æplɪkənt]	Bewerber/Bewerberin, Antragsteller/ Antragstellerin →	somebody who applies for a job
to **damage** ['dæmɪdʒ]	beschädigen	
11 School of the Air [ˌskuːl‿əv ði 'eə]	School of the Air *(Fernunterricht per Internet)*	
the **Olympics** *(Olympic Games)* [əʊ'lɪmpɪks; əʊˌlɪmpɪk 'geɪmz]	Olympiade, Olympische Spiele →	There are summer and winter *Olympics*.
barbecue ['bɑːbɪkjuː]	Grill(party)	
guide [gaɪd]	Führer/Führerin; Handbuch	
typically ['tɪpɪkli]	typisch →	type → *typically*

Animals

Mache einen Cluster zum Thema *Animals*. Welche Tiere kennst du schon? Welche hast du neu dazu gelernt? Teile die Tiere in verschiedene Gruppen ein *(pets, farm animals, Australian animals, dangerous animals etc.)*. Finde so viele Wörter wie möglich!

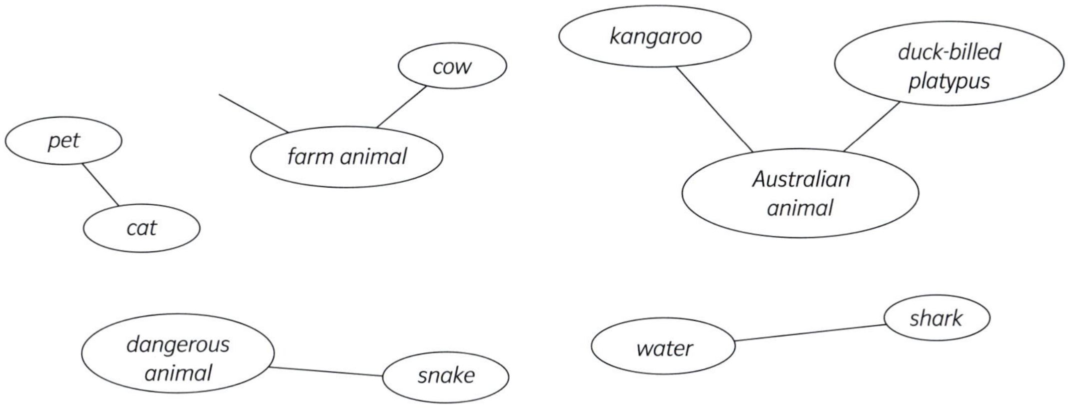

Option 1

12 **deadly** ['dedli]	tödlich, tod- →	death → dead → *deadly*
Sydney Funnel Web Spider ['sɪdni ˌfʌnl web 'spaɪdə]	australische Trichternetzspinne	
spider ['spaɪdə]	Spinne	
to **bite, bit, bitten** [baɪt; bɪt; 'bɪtn]	beißen →	If a funnel web spider *bites* you, you can die very fast.
unless [ən'les]	es sei denn, (dass) …	
anti ['æntɪ]	gegen-, anti-	
venom ['venəm]	Gift *(z. B. von Schlangen und Insekten)*; Bosheit →	*venom* ↔ anti venom
advice [əd'vaɪs]	Rat(schlag)	
to **leave sb alone** [ˌli:v‿ə'ləʊn]	jmdn. in Ruhe lassen →	*Leave me alone!*
Blue Ring Octopus [ˌblu: rɪŋ 'ɒktəpəs]	blaugeringelter Krake	
octopus ['ɒktəpəs]	Oktopus, Krake	
Aussie *(Aus)* ['ɒzi]	Australier/Australierin	
to **sting, stung, stung** [stɪŋ; stʌŋ; stʌŋ]	stechen, beißen	
to **disturb** [dɪ'stɜ:b]	stören, belästigen →	Don't *disturb* this animal!
saltie *(Aus)* ['sɔ:lti]	Salzwasserkrokodil	
salt [sɔ:lt]	Salz →	Yukky! There's too much *salt* in the pudding.
saltwater ['sɔ:ltˌwɔ:tə]	Salzwasser	
sea wasp ['si: ˌwɒsp]	Seewespe →	*Sea wasps* are very dangerous creatures.
jellyfish, jellyfish *(pl)* ['dʒelifɪʃ]	Qualle →	A sea wasp is a *jellyfish*.
surfer ['sɜ:fə]	Surfer/Surferin →	to surf → surfing → *surfer*

	tights *(pl)* [taɪts]	Strumpfhose	
	vinegar ['vɪnɪgə]	Essig	
	stinger suit [ˌstɪŋə 'su:t]	Quallen-Schutzanzug	
	to **survive** [sə'vaɪv]	überleben, bestehen, durchstehen →	If you want to *survive* in the sea around Australia, you should wear a stinger suit.
	Brown Snake [ˌbraʊn 'sneɪk]	Braunschlange, Braunotter	
	bite [baɪt]	Biss, Stich; Bissen	
	remote [rɪ'məʊt]	fern, abgelegen →	far away
	to **keep away** [ki:p‿ə'weɪ]	sich fernhalten, wegbleiben →	If you *keep away* from sth, you don't go near it.
	Great White Shark [ˌgreɪt waɪt 'ʃɑ:k]	Weißer Hai	
	shark [ʃɑ:k]	Hai	
	seal [si:l]	Seehund, Robbe →	The *seals* at the zoo get their food at 3 o'clock: you can watch them.
13	to display [dɪ'spleɪ]	ausstellen, (an)zeigen	

What animals do

Ordne den Tieren die passenden Verben zu.

kangaroo – fish – sea wasp – snake – dog – crocodile – bird

to swim – to sting – to sing – to bark – to jump – to attack – to bite

Option 2

14	**dive centre** ['daɪv ˌsentə]	Tauchzentrum	
	diving ['daɪvɪŋ]	Tauch-, Tauchen	
	instructor [ɪn'strʌktə]	Lehrer/Lehrerin, Ausbilder/Ausbilderin →	somebody who teaches something
	to **apply (for)** [ə'plaɪ]	sich bewerben (um), sich anmelden (zu) →	*to apply* → applicant
	certificate [sə'tɪfɪkət]	Zertifikat, Bescheinigung, Urkunde, Zeugnis →	When you've passed an exam, you get a *certificate*.
	insurance [ɪn'ʃʊərns]	Versicherung	
	valid ['vælɪd]	gültig, zulässig	
	working visa ['wɜ:kɪŋ ˌvi:zə]	Arbeitserlaubnis	
	driving licence *(BE)* ['draɪvɪŋ ˌlaɪsnts]	Führerschein →	When you have passed your driving test, you are given a *driving licence*.
	full-time (F/T) [ˌfʊl'taɪm]	Vollzeit-	
	temporary ['temprəri]	vorübergehend, temporär, befristet →	*temporary* ↔ permanent
	permanent ['pɜ:mnənt]	permanent, dauerhaft →	for a very long time or for ever
	contract ['kɒntrækt]	Vertrag, Abkommen	
	pay [peɪ]	Lohn, Gehalt, Bezahlung →	to pay → *pay*
	further ['fɜ:ðə]	weiter	
	reference ['refrns]	Referenz; Bezug, Verweis	

vacancy ['veɪknsi]	Stellenangebot, offene Stelle; freies Zimmer →	There's a *vacancy* in our company.
surfboard ['sɜ:fbɔ:d]	Surfbrett	
experience [ɪk'spɪəriənts]	Erfahrung, Erlebnis	
part-time (P/T) [ˌpɑ:t'taɪm]	Teilzeit- →	*part-time* ↔ full-time
weekday ['wi:kdeɪ]	Wochentag, Werktag	
closing ['kləʊzɪŋ]	(Ab-)Schluss, Schließung	
seeker [si:kə]	Suchender/Suchende	
detail ['di:teɪl]	Detail, Einzelheit	
provider [prə'vaɪdə]	Anbieter/Anbieterin, Lieferant/Lieferantin; Provider	
helper ['helpə]	Helfer/Helferin →	to help → *helper*
government ['gʌvnmənt]	Regierung →	a group of people whose job it is to 'look after' a country
successful [sək'sesfl]	erfolgreich	
professional [prə'feʃnl]	professionell, beruflich, Berufs- →	If you do sth in a *professional* way, you do it very well.
course [kɔ:s]	Kurs →	If you want to learn sth, you can do a *course*.
historical [hɪ'stɒrɪkl]	geschichtlich, historisch →	history → *historical*
disability [ˌdɪsə'bɪləti]	Behinderung; Unfähigkeit	
online [ˌɒn'laɪn]	online, im Internet	
link [lɪŋk]	Link; Verknüpfung	
to **link** [lɪŋk]	verbinden, verknüpfen	
career [kə'rɪə]	Beruf; Laufbahn, Karriere	
contact ['kɒntækt]	Kontakt, Verbindung	
15 application [ˌæplɪ'keɪʃn]	Bewerbung, Antrag; Anwendung	
ad [æd]	Anzeige; Werbespot →	short for 'advert'
to **require** [rɪ'kwaɪə]	benötigen, brauchen; anfordern	
title ['taɪtl]	Bezeichnung	
curriculum vitae (CV) [kə'rɪkjələm 'vi:taɪ]	Lebenslauf →	If you apply for a job, you should send your *CV*.
Advanced Lifesaving Certificate [ədˌvɑ:nst 'laɪfˌseɪvɪŋ səˌtɪfɪkət]	Rettungsschwimm-abzeichen	
Beginners Diving Certificate [bɪˌgɪnəz 'daɪvɪŋ səˌtɪfɪkət]	Grundtauchschein	
interest ['ɪntrəst]	Interesse	
referee [ˌrefr'i:]	Referenz *(Person)* →	somebody who gives a reference
to hang up [hæŋ‿'ʌp]	aufhängen	

Words in action

16 to replace [rɪ'pleɪs]	ersetzen	
typical ['tɪpɪkl]	typisch, kennzeichnend →	type → *typical*

Applying for a job

Die folgenden Wörter sind nützlich, wenn du dich auf Englisch bewerben willst.

to apply	sich bewerben	*part-time*	Teilzeit
applicant	Bewerber/Bewerberin	*pay*	Lohn
application	Bewerbung	*permanent*	permanent, dauerhaft
career	Beruf, Laufbahn	*professional*	professionell
certificate	Zertifikat, Bescheinigung, Urkunde, Zeugnis	*referee*	Referenz *(Person)*
		reference	Referenz
contract	Vertrag	*shift*	Schicht
curriculum vitae (CV)	Lebenslauf	*temporary*	vorübergehend, temporär
full-time	Vollzeit	*vacancy*	Stellenangebot
insurance	Versicherung	*working visa*	Arbeitserlaubnis
job ad	Stellenanzeige		

Füge die passenden Wörter ein.

1. *Applicants are given … training.*
2. *For … information, please contact our manager.*
3. *This job is …, 10 hours a week.*
4. *If you want to work in another country, you need a … .*
5. *Please send your … via e-mail to jobs@davyjones.com.au.*
6. *… must be interested in the environment.*

Everyday English: Travelling

Die folgenden *phrases* helfen dir, wenn du in einem englischsprachigen Land auf Reisen bist.

Could you tell me the time of the next train/bus to …, please?	Könnten Sie mir die Abfahrtszeit des nächsten Zuges/Busses nach … sagen?
Do I have to change trains?	Muss ich umsteigen?
What platform does it leave from?	An welchem Bahnsteig fährt er ab?
What time does it arrive ?	Wann kommt er an?
How long is the journey?	Wie lange dauert die Reise?
Is there a flight to …, please?	Gibt es einen Flug nach … ?
Is there a bus to the airport?	Gibt es einen Bus zum Flughafen?
Does this train/bus go to … ?	Fährt dieser Zug/Bus nach … ?
How much is a one-way ticket to … ?	Was kostet eine einfache Fahrkarte nach … ?
How much is a return ticket to … ?	Was kostet eine Rückfahrkarte nach … ?
How long is the flight/train ride/bus ride?	Wie lange dauert der Flug/die Bahnfahrt/die Busfahrt?
When does the plane/train/bus leave?	Wann fliegt das Flugzeug ab? Wann fährt der Zug/Bus ab?
Where can I buy a ticket?	Wo kann ich eine Fahrkarte kaufen?
Where's the dining car?	Wo ist der Speisewagen?
Where's the non-smoking car?	Wo ist der Nichtraucherwagen?
Where can I catch a taxi?	Wo finde ich ein Taxi?

Arbeite mit einem Partner. Einer von euch ist der Reisende, der andere gibt Auskunft. Übt englische Dialoge und verwendet dafür die oben stehenden *phrases*.

Topic 2 Chilling-out time

Schulabschlüsse und berufliche Ausbildung in Großbritannien

Die meisten Schüler in Großbritannien besuchen eine *Comprehensive School*. Diese ist vergleichbar mit einer deutschen Gesamtschule. Im Alter von 15-16 machen die Schüler Abschlussprüfungen, die sogenannten *GCSEs (General Certificate of Secondary Education)*. Die Schüler entscheiden mit Hilfe der Lehrer, in welchen und in wie vielen Fächern sie die Prüfung ablegen möchten. Die meisten entscheiden sich für Englisch, Mathematik und Naturwissenschaften. Viele wählen auch noch Englische Literatur, eine moderne Fremdsprache und Technik oder Design. Die Benotung erfolgt statt mit Zahlen durch die Buchstaben A – G, wobei A die beste Note ist. Nur in den Fächern, in denen man die Note A, B oder C erhalten hat, kann man einen *A-level*-Kurs *(Advanced Levels)* erwerben. Die *A-level*-Prüfungen entsprechen dem deutschen Abitur und sind Voraussetzung, wenn man an einer Universität studieren möchte.

Für handwerkliche und technische Berufe ist ein sogenanntes *NVQ (National Vocational Qualification)* von Vorteil. Dies ist ein praxisorientierter Leistungsnachweis, den man in Verbindung mit einem Ausbildungs- oder Arbeitsplatz erwirbt. Das *NVQ* bestätigt, dass man die nötigen Kenntnisse und Fähigkeiten für einen bestimmten Beruf besitzt. Außerdem kann man am *City and Guilds of London Institute* weitere berufliche Qualifikationen erwerben, indem man Kurse besucht und eine Prüfung ablegt. Diese *City & Guilds* sind Voraussetzung für bestimmte Berufe wie z. B. Mechatroniker.

NVQs und *City & Guilds* gibt es in verschiedenen Schwierigkeitsstufen, die aufeinander aufbauen. Für alle Abschlüsse und Kurse, die man gemacht oder besucht hat, erhält man Punkte. Daraus kann ein zukünftiger Arbeitgeber ersehen, wie geeignet man für einen bestimmten Beruf ist.

Welche Schulabschlüsse gibt es in Deutschland? Welche Voraussetzungen braucht man in Deutschland, wenn man eine Berufsausbildung machen will? Wo kann man sich darüber informieren?

Check-in

26	to pretend [prɪ'tend]	vorgeben, tun als ob	
	to **mess around** [ˌmes‿ə'raʊnd]	herumalbern	

Aspects

28	**aspect** ['æspekt]	Aspekt, Gesichtspunkt, Seite	
	to **hang around** [ˌhæŋ‿ə'raʊnd]	rumhängen, herumlungern →	to hang out
	in [ɪn]	von, aus →	Only 2 *in* 10 of the pupils in my class like Maths.
	member ['membə]	Mitglied →	If you belong to a gang, you are a *member* of it.
	peer [pɪə]	Gleichaltriger/Gleichaltrige	
	to **belong (to)** [bɪ'lɒŋ]	gehören (zu) →	Who does this bag *belong to?* = Whose bag is this?

	crime [kraɪm]	Verbrechen; Kriminalität	
	greeting [ˈgriːtɪŋ]	Gruß, Begrüßung	
	six-pack [ˈsɪkspæk]	Waschbrettbauch	
	odour [ˈəʊdə]	Geruch, Duft →	you can smell it
	to **be a turn-off** [ˈtɜːnɒf]	abtörnend sein, zum Abgewöhnen sein →	If something *is a turn-off*, you don't like it or hate it.
	need [niːd]	Bedürfnis, Bedarf; Erfordernis →	Your *needs* are what you need.
	option [ˈɒpʃn]	Auswahlmöglichkeit, Option	
29	**mural** [ˈmjʊərl]	Graffiti, Wandmalerei →	A *mural* is a painting on a wall.
	volunteer [ˌvɒlənˈtɪə]	Freiwilliger/Freiwillige; freiwillig	
	artist [ˈɑːtɪst]	KünstlerKünstlerin →	art → *artist*
	to **e-mail** [ˈiːmeɪl]	mailen, per E-Mail schicken →	an e-mail → to *e-mail*
	to **complete** [kəmˈpliːt]	ausfüllen, erledigen, fertigstellen, vervollständigen	
	application [ˌæplɪˈkeɪʃn]	Bewerbung, Antrag; Anwendung →	If you want a job, you first have to send in an *application*.
	to **film** [fɪlm]	filmen →	a film → *to film*
	to **get in the way** (of) [ˌget‿ɪn‿ðə‿ˈweɪ]	etw. verhindern; im Weg stehen	
	experience [ɪkˈspɪəriənts]	Erfahrung, Erlebnis	
	telephone [ˈtelɪfəʊn]	Telefon →	Phone is the short form of *'telephone'*.

Revision: American English – British English

AE	***BE***	***AE***	***BE***
apartment	*flat*	*neighb**o**r*	*neighb**ou**r*
*col**o**r*	*col**ou**r*	*progra**m***	*progra**mme***
French fries	*chips*	*vacation*	*holidays*
*harb**o**r*	*harb**ou**r*		

Relationships

Ordne die folgenden Wörter in die Tabelle ein.

angry – to love – to like – careful – to hate – to kiss – friendly – helpful

careful …	angry …

Finde noch mehr Wörter und füge sie in die Tabelle ein.

Option 1

30 **torn** [tɔ:n]	hin- und hergerissen, zerrissen →	If you are *torn* between two things, you don't know which to choose.
competition [ˌkɒmpəˈtɪʃn]	Wettbewerb, Turnier →	In a *competition* the person or team who is the best wins.
council [ˈkaʊnsl]	Gemeinderat	
to **waste** [weɪst]	verschwenden →	Don't *waste* my time!
waste [weɪst]	Verschwendung; Abfall →	Let's stop! It's a *waste* of time.
That sucks! [ðæt ˈsʌks]	Das ist ätzend!	
to **let sb down** [let ˈdaʊn]	jmdn. im Stich lassen, jmdn. enttäuschen →	You didn't help me, you *let me down*.
31 quality [ˈkwɒləti]	Qualität; Eigenschaft	
advice [ədˈvaɪs]	Rat(schlag) →	I don't know what to do. Is there any *advice* you can give me?
remixed [ˈri:mɪkst]	neu gemischt	

Verben und Nomen mit gleicher Form

Im Englischen gibt es viele Nomen, die dieselbe Form haben wie das dazugehörige Verb, z. B.

to drink	trinken	→	*drink*	Getränk
to help	helfen	→	*help*	Hilfe
to interview	interviewen	→	*interview*	Interview
to rain	regnen	→	*rain*	Regen
...	...	→	...	...

Ergänze die Liste und finde so viele Beispiele wie möglich.

reading [ˈri:dɪŋ]	Lesung; Lektüre	
to read out [ri:d‿ˈaʊt]	etw. laut vorlesen	

Option 2

32 **perfect** [ˈpɜ:fɪkt]	perfekt, vollkommen	
talent [ˈtælənt]	Talent →	If you have *talent*, you are – or can become – very good at something.
adult [ˈædʌlt]	Erwachsener/Erwachsene →	child ↔ *adult*
close [kləʊs]	nahe	
voluntary [ˈvɒləntri]	freiwillig; ehrenamtlich →	When you do *voluntary* work, you aren't paid for what you do.
part-time (P/T) [ˌpɑ:tˈtaɪm]	Teilzeit-	
cage [keɪdʒ]	Käfig →	A lot of birds in zoos are kept in *cages*.
to **stink, stank, stunk** [stɪŋk; stæŋk; stʌŋk]	stinken	
keeper [ˈki:pə]	Wärter/Wärterin, Aufseher/Aufseherin; Inhaber/Inhaberin →	to keep → *keeper*
health [helθ]	Gesundheit →	healthy → *health*

check [tʃek]	(Über-)Prüfung, Kontrolle →	to check → a *check*
sea lion ['siː ˌlaɪən]	Seelöwe	
studies *(pl)* ['stʌdiz]	Studium; Lernen →	student → to study → *studies*
cameraman, cameramen *(pl)* ['kæmrəmæn; 'kæmrəmen]	Kameramann	
qualification [ˌkwɒlɪfɪ'keɪʃn]	Qualifikation, Befähigung	
to **apply (for)** [ə'plaɪ]	sich bewerben (um), sich anmelden (zu) →	*to apply* → applicant
apprenticeship [ə'prentɪʃɪp]	Lehre, Ausbildung →	You can do an *apprenticeship* after school.
technical ['teknɪkl]	technisch; handwerklich, fachlich	
photography [fə'tɒɡrəfi]	Fotografie →	a photo → *photography*

Verben der Bewegung

to come down	herunterkommen	*to go up*	hinaufgehen
to come in	hereinkommen	*to jump about*	herumspringen
to come over	herüberkommen	*to jump up*	hochspringen
to fall off	herunterfallen	*to lie down*	(sich) hinlegen
to get into	einsteigen	*to run away*	wegrennen
to get off	aussteigen	*to run into*	gegenlaufen
to get on	aufsteigen	*to run out*	hinausrennen
to get onto	einsteigen	*to turn around*	sich umdrehen
to get out	aussteigen/entkommen	*to turn back*	umkehren
to get up	aufstehen	*to turn over*	umdrehen
to go down	hinuntergehen	*to set off*	aufbrechen, sich auf den Weg machen
to go in	hineingehen		
to go out	(hin-)ausgehen	*to sit down*	sich hinsetzen
to go over	hinübergehen		

Schreibe zu jedem dieser Verben einen Beispielsatz.

	chef [ʃef]	Koch/Köchin, Küchenchef/-chefin →	der Chef = the boss; der Koch = the *chef*
	full-time (F/T) [ˌfʊl'taɪm]	Vollzeit- →	part-time ↔ *full-time*
	to **prepare** [prɪ'peə]	vorbereiten, zubereiten →	to get something ready
	NVQ (National Vocational Qualification) [ˌenviː'kjuː]	Berufsqualifikation in England	
	nutrition [njuː'trɪʃn]	Ernährung(slehre)	
	course [kɔːs]	Kurs →	If you want to learn sth, you can do a *course*.
	to **train** [treɪn]	eine Ausbildung machen →	I'm *training* to be a teacher.
33	suitable ['suːtəbl]	geeignet, passend →	Food without fish or meat in it is *suitable* for vegetarians.
	career [kə'rɪə]	Beruf; Laufbahn, Karriere	
	to agree [ə'ɡriː]	zustimmen, einer Meinung sein →	I *agree* with you. = I think what you say is right.
	to **realise** ['rɪəlaɪz]	erkennen, sich klar werden →	Suddenly I *realised* … = Plötzlich wurde mir klar …

	likes *(pl)* [laɪks]	Vorlieben
	dislikes *(pl)* [dɪ'slaɪks]	Abneigungen
	to inform [ɪn'fɔ:m]	informieren, benachrichtigen
	to suit [su:t]	passen (zu)

Words in action

34	hyphen ['haɪfn]	Bindestrich	
	to **shop** [ʃɒp]	einkaufen →	Jade *shops* with her friends every day.

Everyday English: Friends and enemies

Die folgenden *phrases* helfen dir, wenn du einen Streit schlichten willst.

You look angry. What's wrong?	Du siehst wütend aus. Was ist los?
Is there anything I can do?	Kann ich irgendwas tun?
Please stop arguing.	Bitte hört auf zu streiten.
Let's talk it over.	Lass/Lasst uns darüber reden.
Give him/her a chance to explain it.	Gib ihm/ihr eine Chance, das zu erklären.
I'm upset.	Ich habe mich aufgeregt.
Please leave him/her alone.	Bitte lass ihn/sie in Ruhe.
Please stop bullying this person.	Bitte hör/hört auf, ihn/sie zu tyrannisieren.
It's not OK to	Es ist nicht in Ordnung zu ... .
What's your problem?	Was ist dein/euer Problem.

Arbeitet in einer Gruppe. Einige von euch streiten und einer aus eurer Gruppe versucht zu schlichten. Verwendet dafür die oben stehenden *phrases*.

Topic 3 Freedom's just another word for ...

Rassentrennung

Die US-amerikanische Bürgerrechtsbewegung (*Civil Rights Movement*, kurz *CRM*) kämpfte dafür, dass die Schwarzen in den USA die gleichen Bürgerrechte bekamen wie die Weißen. Unter Bürgerrechten versteht man die Grundrechte (Freiheit, Gleichheit, Unverletzlichkeit von Leben und Eigentum etc.) sowie das Wahlrecht.

Als die Sklaverei 1865 abgeschafft wurde, erhielten die Schwarzen in den USA zwar offiziell die vollen Bürgerrechte, wurden aber weiterhin diskriminiert. Viele Weiße sahen die Schwarzen als Menschen „zweiter Klasse" und wollten keinen Kontakt mit ihnen. Deshalb führten einige südliche Bundesstaaten der USA (z. B. Alabama und Tennessee) Gesetze zur Rassentrennung (*Segregation*) ein. Es gab nun extra Schulen, Hotels und Restaurants nur für Schwarze, auf öffentlichen Toiletten gab es getrennte Waschbecken und im Bus waren bestimmte Plätze für Weiße und Schwarze reserviert. Angeblich sollte die Rassentrennung nur das Zusammenleben von Schwarzen und Weißen regeln. In Wirklichkeit war die Rassentrennung aber eine Diskriminierung der Schwarzen, denn die Einrichtungen für Schwarze waren immer schlechter als die für Weiße, Schwarze durften kein Land kaufen und die Ehe zwischen Schwarzen und Weißen war verboten.

In den 1950er-Jahren begannen die Schwarzen allmählich, sich gegen die Diskriminierungen zu wehren. Durch öffentliche Proteste, Boykotts und Berichte in Zeitungen, Radio und Fernsehen machten sie die Bevölkerung auf die Diskriminierungen aufmerksam. Es kam zu Gerichtsverhandlungen, und schließlich wurde die Rassentrennung in Schulen und öffentlichen Verkehrsmitteln aufgehoben. Am 2. Juli 1964 trat der *Civil Rights Act* in Kraft, ein Bürgerrechtsgesetz, das die politische, rechtliche und soziale Rassendiskriminierung für unrechtmäßig erklärte.

Hast du selbst schon Diskriminierung erlebt? Bei dir selbst, bei Freunden oder einfach irgendwo auf der Straße? Was glaubst du, warum manche Menschen andere diskriminieren? Und wie sollte man sich am besten dagegen wehren?

Check-in

40	**on one's own** [ɒn wʌnz‿ˈəʊn]	(ganz) allein →	Her friends didn't want to go to the cinema, so she went *on her own*.
	fall [fɔːl]	Fall, Sturz →	to fall → a *fall*
	to **protest** [prəʊˈtest]	protestieren →	! Achte auf die Betonung: [-ˈ-]
	equal [ˈiːkwəl]	gleich(wertig), Gleich- →	*equal* = the same
	parachuting [ˈpærəˌʃuːtɪŋ]	Fallschirmspringen	
	paragliding [ˈpærəˌglaɪdɪŋ]	Paragliding, Gleitschirmfliegen	
	advertising *(no pl.)* [ˈædvətaɪzɪŋ]	Werbung, Reklame; Werbe-	
	product [ˈprɒdʌkt]	Produkt, Artikel, Ware	
41	**tenant** [ˈtenənt]	Mieter/Mieterin	

snowboarding ['snəʊbɔ:dɪŋ]	Snowboarden →	Some people say *snowboarding* is a bit like surfing in the snow.
anti ['æntɪ]	gegen-, anti-	
protest ['prəʊtest]	Protest	
racial ['reɪʃl]	Rassen-	
discrimination [dɪˌskrɪmɪ'neɪʃn]	Diskriminierung; Unterscheidung →	There is still racial *discrimination* in the US.
fence [fens]	Zaun	

Aspects

42 **aspect** ['æspekt]	Aspekt, Gesichtspunkt, Seite	
right [raɪt]	Recht →	In Germany, people over 18 have the *right* to vote.
religion [rɪ'lɪdʒn]	Religion →	*religion* → religious
option ['ɒpʃn]	Auswahlmöglichkeit, Option	
Black [blæk]	Schwarzer/Schwarze	
opinion [ə'pɪnjən]	Meinung →	I think … = In my *opinion* …
violence ['vaɪələnts]	Gewalt(tätigkeit) →	When there is *violence*, people try to hurt or even kill others.
demo ['deməʊ]	Demonstration, Demo; Darstellung	
media *(pl)* ['mi:diə]	Medien →	Books, e-mails and the cinema are all *media*.
pride [praɪd]	Stolz; Hochmut →	proud → *pride*
murder ['mɜ:də]	Mord, Ermordung	
to **ring out** [ˌrɪŋ‿'aʊt]	erklingen, ertönen	
at last [ət 'lɑ:st]	endlich, schließlich →	David is in a shop: he looks at all the shoes, and *at last* a shop assistant says, "Can I help you?"
death [deθ]	Tod, Todesfall →	dead → *death* life ↔ *death*
to **rest** [rest]	rasten, ausruhen; liegen	
rest [rest]	Rast, Ruhe	
reaction [ri'ækʃn]	Reaktion, Resonanz	
killer ['kɪlə]	Mörder/Mörderin →	to kill → *killer*
43 to **owe** [əʊ]	verdanken, schulden →	We *owe* our freedom to people who fought for it.
career [kə'rɪə]	Beruf; Laufbahn, Karriere	
to **go it alone** [ˌgeʊ‿ɪt‿ə'leʊn]	einen Alleingang starten, es allein schaffen →	to go solo
aid [eɪd]	Hilfe, Beistand, Förderung →	help
including [ɪn'klu:dɪŋ]	einschließlich, inklusive	
advice [əd'vaɪs]	Rat(schlag)	
experience [ɪk'spɪəriənts]	Erfahrung, Erlebnis	
profile ['prəʊfaɪl]	Profil; Porträt; Steckbrief	
to **give up** [gɪv‿'ʌp]	aufgeben →	They didn't *give up* their dream.

fighting ['faɪtɪŋ]	Kampf(-) →	to fight → *fighting*
spirit ['spɪrɪt]	Geist; Stimmung	
success [sək'ses]	Erfolg	
pioneer [ˌpaɪə'nɪə]	Pionier/Pionierin, Wegbereiter/ Wegbereiterin →	The first immigrants in the US were real *pioneers*.
adaptable [ə'dæptəbl]	anpassungsfähig	
attempt [ə'tempt]	Versuch; Anschlag	
solo ['səʊləʊ]	allein, Allein-, solo, Solo- →	alone
non-stop [ˌnɒn'stɒp]	non-stop, durchgehend, ohne Unterbrechung →	without a stop
balloon [bə'lu:n]	(Heiß-)Luftballon →	Yesterday I went on a *balloon* flight.
successful [sək'sesfl]	erfolgreich →	success → *successful*
several ['sevrl]	mehrere, verschiedene	
enterprising ['entəpraɪzɪŋ]	geschäftstüchtig, unternehmungslustig	
had tried [hæd 'traɪd]	hatte versucht	

Englische Wörter im Deutschen

Viele englische Wörter verwenden wir auch im Deutschen, wie z. B.

computer, download, killer, laptop, sandwich

Solche Wörter kannst du dir besonders gut merken. Mache eine Liste und sammle so viele dieser Wörter, wie dir einfallen.

Option 1

44 **milestone** ['maɪlstəʊn]	Meilenstein →	A historical *milestone* is an important event in history.
slavery ['sleɪvri]	Sklaverei →	In 1865 the US abolished *slavery*.
citizen ['sɪtɪzn]	(Staats-)Bürger/Bürgerin	
slave [sleɪv]	Sklave/Sklavin	
pay [peɪ]	Lohn, Gehalt, Bezahlung →	to pay → *pay*
policy ['pɒlɪsi]	Politik, politische Linie; Grundsatz	
segregation *(no pl)* [ˌsegrɪ'geɪʃn]	(Rassen-)Trennung →	In 1954 *segregation* in schools and universities ended.
to **mix** [mɪks]	mixen, mischen →	If you *mix* blue and yellow, you get green.
officially [ə'fɪʃli]	offiziell	
Civil Rights Movement (CRM) [ˌsɪvl 'raɪts ˌmu:vmənt]	Bürgerrechtsbewegung	
movement ['mu:vmənt]	Bewegung →	to move → *movement*
colored *(AE)* ['kʌləd]	bunt, farbig; Farbiger/ Farbige →	colo(u)r → *colo(u)red*
nobody ['nəʊbədi]	niemand	
non-violent [ˌnɒn'vaɪəlnt]	gewaltfrei →	without violence

to **accept** [ək'sept]	akzeptieren, hinnehmen; annehmen →	If you *accept* sth, you don't have anything against it.
law [lɔ:]	Gesetz(gebung), Recht →	If you break the *law*, you may get into trouble.
such [sʌtʃ]	solch →	It was *such* a good party that nobody wanted to go home.
National Guard [ˌnæʃnl 'gɑ:d]	Nationalgarde	
protester [prə'testə]	Protestierender/ Protestierende, Demonstrant/ Demonstrantin →	protest → *protester* → to protest
to **march** [mɑ:tʃ]	marschieren →	When people walk together as a group, they *march*.
march [mɑ:tʃ]	Marsch	
speech [spi:tʃ]	(An-)Sprache, Rede; Sprechen →	to speak → *speech*
weapon ['wepən]	Waffe	
race [reɪs]	Rasse →	There are lots of people of different *races* in New York.
riot [raɪət]	Aufruhr, Ausschreitung, Unruhe	
to **break out** [ˌbreɪk‿'aʊt]	ausbrechen	
to **shoot, shot, shot** [ʃu:t; ʃɒt; ʃɒt]	(ab)schießen, erschießen	
government ['gʌvnmənt]	Regierung →	a group of people whose job it is to 'look after' a country
to **ban** [bæn]	verbieten, ausschließen; (ver)bannen	
ban [bæn]	Verbot, Sperre; Bann	
society [sə'saɪəti]	Gesellschaft; Verein →	social → *society*
position [pə'zɪʃn]	Position	
firm [fɜ:m]	Firma, Unternehmen, Gesellschaft →	a company that sells goods or services
45 **civil rights** *(pl)* [ˌsɪvl 'raɪts]	Bürgerrechte →	Martin Luther King was the American *civil rights* leader.
civil ['sɪvl]	bürgerlich, zivil, Bürger-, Staats-	
peaceful ['pi:sfl]	friedlich →	peace → *peaceful*
unfair [ʌn'feə]	ungerecht, unfair	
treatment ['tri:tmənt]	Behandlung	
to **make sb do sth** [meɪk]	jmdn. veranlassen, etw. zu tun; jmdn. dafür gewinnen, etw. zu tun →	I wish I could *make my dad understand*.
in turn [ɪn 'tɜ:n]	abwechselnd, der Reihe nach	
gallery ['gælri]	Galerie	

False friends

Viele englische Wörter verwenden wir auch im Deutschen, wie z. B. *computer*. Es gibt aber auch *False friends* – englische Wörter, die den deutschen sehr ähnlich sind, aber eine ganz andere Bedeutung haben. Bei diesen Wörtern musst du aufpassen wie z. B. bei

to become	!	werden
brave	!	mutig, tapfer
to mean	!	bedeuten
…	!	…

Finde noch mehr solcher *False friends* und schreibe sie auf.

Option 2

46	**careers advice** [kəˈrɪəz ədˌvaɪs]	Berufsberatung	
	supreme [suːˈpriːm]	höchster/höchste/höchstes, oberster/oberste/oberstes →	highest
	ruler [ˈruːlə]	Herrscher/Herrscherin	
	universe [ˈjuːnɪvɜːs]	Universum, Weltraum	
	reason [ˈriːzn]	Grund →	Why did you do it? What was the *reason*?
	third [θɜːd]	Drittel →	A *third* of 9 is 3.
	to **fulfill** *(AE)* [fʊlˈfɪl]	erfüllen, genügen	
	reader [ˈriːdə]	Leser/Leserin →	to read → *reader*
	bistro bar [ˌbiːstrəʊ ˈbɑː]	Bistro	
	snack bar [ˈsnæk ˌbɑː]	Café, Imbissstube	
	catering [ˈkeɪtrɪŋ]	Gastronomie, Verpflegung, Catering	
	course [kɔːs]	Kurs →	I did a catering *course* because I want to open a restaurant.
	chef [ʃef]	Koch/Köchin, Küchenchef/-chefin →	der Chef = the boss; der Koch = the *chef*
	to **quit**, **quit**, **quit** [kwɪt; kwɪt; kwɪt]	aufgeben, mit etw. aufhören; kündigen	
	to **earn** [ɜːn]	verdienen →	She has got a good job and *earns* a lot of money.
	employer [ɪmˈplɔɪə]	Arbeitgeber/Arbeitgeberin →	the person that you work for; your boss
	mood [muːd]	Stimmung, Laune	
	to **rent** [rent]	mieten, pachten →	to pay money for sth you use, for example an apartment or a car
	rent [rent]	Miete, Pacht	
	loan [ləʊn]	Darlehen, Kredit →	money which a bank gives you and which you have to pay back later
	to **loan** [ləʊn]	ausleihen, verleihen →	to *loan* money *(AE)*, to *loan* a picture to a museum *(BE)*

to **have a day off** [ˌhæv‿ə ˈdeɪ‿ɒf]	einen Tag frei haben	
regular [ˈregjələ]	regelmäßig, regulär	

Wörter mit mehreren Bedeutungen

Viele englische Wörter haben mehr als eine Bedeutung. Oft kennst du ein Wort schon, lernst aber später eine neue Bedeutung dazu. Dann musst du beim Lesen des Satzes entscheiden, welche Bedeutung richtig ist, z. B.

*Turn **right**.*	Biege **rechts** ab.
*That's **right**.*	Das ist **richtig**.
*People over eighteen have the **right** to vote.*	Menschen über achtzehn haben das **Recht** zu wählen.
*I'd like fish and chips for the main **course**, please.*	Ich hätte gerne Fisch und Chips als Haupt**gang**.
*I'm doing an English **course**.*	Ich mache einen Englisch**kurs**.

Finde noch mehr solcher Wörter mit mehreren Bedeutungen. Mache eine Liste und schreibe zu jeder Bedeutung einen englischen Beispielsatz mit der deutschen Übersetzung.

employee [ɪmˈplɔɪiː]	Angestellte/Angestellter, Mitarbeiter/Mitarbeiterin →	Someone who works for you is your *employee*.
47 self-employment [ˌselfɪmˈplɔɪmənt]	Selbstständigkeit	
pros and cons [ˌprəʊz‿ənd ˈkɒnz]	Für und Wider, Pro und Kontra, Vor- und Nachteile	
order [ˈɔːdə]	Befehl, Anweisung →	If you give *orders*, you tell others what to do.
baguette [bæɡˈet]	Baguette →	a kind of bread
slug [slʌɡ]	Nacktschnecke →	Most people don't like *slugs*.
temporary [ˈtemprəri]	vorübergehend, temporär, befristet	
creature [ˈkriːtʃə]	Kreatur, Geschöpf, Lebewesen	
importance [ɪmˈpɔːtnts]	Bedeutung, Wichtigkeit	
sense [sens]	Sinn, Bedeutung	
record [ˈrekɔːd]	Aufnahme, Aufzeichnung; Beleg; Akte →	! Achtung Aussprache! to record → *record*
to **train** [treɪn]	ausbilden, lernen; trainieren →	to *train* → training
to **act** [ækt]	sich verhalten, handeln, agieren	
limit [ˈlɪmɪt]	Limit, Grenze, Beschränkung	
outgoing [ˈaʊtɡəʊɪŋ]	aufgeschlossen, kontaktfreudig →	if you like meeting other people

Check-out

49 to recognise [ˈrekəgnaɪz] erkennen

Everyday English: On the phone

Die folgenden *phrases* helfen dir, wenn du in einem englischsprachigen Land anrufen möchtest.

Hello, this is … .	Hallo, hier spricht … .
I'm calling from Germany.	Ich rufe aus Deutschland an.
Could I speak to … please?	Könnte ich bitte mit … sprechen?
Could I have extension …, please?	Könnten Sie mich bitte zur Durchwahl … durchstellen?
Will you try extension … instead?	Möchten Sie es stattdessen bei der Durchwahl … probieren?
Could you put me through to …, please?	Könnten Sie mich bitte zu … durchstellen?
I'm sorry, … is not here right now.	Es tut mir leid, … ist zur Zeit nicht da.
Could you take a message, please?	Könnten Sie bitte etwas ausrichten?
Can I take a message?	Kann ich etwas ausrichten?
I'll call again later.	Ich rufe später noch einmal an.
Thank you. Bye.	Danke. Auf Wiederhören.

Arbeite mit einem Partner. Einer von euch ist der Anrufer, der andere beantwortet den Anruf. Übt englische Dialoge und verwendet dafür die oben stehenden *phrases*.

Topic 4 Global matters

Globalisierung

Unter „Globalisierung" versteht man den Prozess, bei dem die Welt immer weiter vereinheitlicht wird. Die Kontinente und Länder der Erde bilden dabei ein immer enger werdendes Netzwerk. Dies geschieht in verschiedenen Bereichen: Wirtschaft, Politik, Kultur, Umwelt, Kommunikation etc.

Sehr viele Produkte wie z. B. Handys, Fernseher, Markenkleidung oder Autos kann man heutzutage überall auf der Welt kaufen. Meist werden sie in Asien hergestellt und dann in die ganze Welt verschickt. Fast-Food- und Restaurantketten wie z. B. McDonalds, Pizza Hut oder Starbucks gibt es in fast allen Ländern der Erde und exotische Obst- und Gemüsesorten, die es früher nur in fernen Ländern gab, kann man heute das ganze Jahr über in Deutschland finden.

Durch Fernsehen, Internet und andere Kommunikationsmittel ist man heute überall auf der Welt erreichbar und mit dem Flugzeug in wenigen Stunden auf einem anderen Kontinent. Auch die Kultur unterliegt der Globalisierung. Filme, Fernsehserien, Musik und Mode sind überall auf der Welt bekannt. Dadurch breitet sich auch die englische Sprache immer weiter aus, da sie weltweit als Handelssprache verwendet wird.

Das alles hat auch Nachteile. Viele Unternehmen verlagern ihre Fabriken ins Ausland, in sogenannte Billiglohnländer, so dass im Heimatland Arbeitsplätze verloren gehen. In den Billiglohnländern dagegen müssen die Menschen in den Fabriken sehr viel für sehr wenig Geld arbeiten. Wenn die Produkte dann in weit entfernte Länder verschickt werden, belastet dies die Umwelt. Die Verbreitung von Film und Musik oder Mode wird ebenfalls kritisch gesehen. Wenn alle Menschen auf der Welt dasselbe sehen und kaufen, wird mit der Zeit alles eintönig und die Vielfalt geht verloren.

Globalisierung ist ein schwieriges Thema. Man kann jederzeit alles kaufen und überall hin reisen, vorausgesetzt, man hat genug Geld. Ist das gut oder schlecht?

Wo begegnet dir die Globalisierung im Alltag? Wenn du das nächste Mal einkaufen gehst, prüfe doch beim Obst und Gemüse nach, aus welchem Land es stammt. Oder schau auf die Etiketten in deiner Kleidung. Wo wurde sie hergestellt? Was war der letzte tolle Film, den du gesehen hast? In welchem Land wurde er gedreht?

Viele Menschen sind gegen die Globalisierung. Sie verlangen beispielsweise, dass wir wieder mehr Produkte kaufen, die im eigenen Land hergestellt wurden. Wie denkst du darüber?

Check-in

58	**global** ['gləʊbl]	global, Erd- →	A *global* problem is one that the whole world shares.
	dirt [dɜːt]	Schmutz, Dreck	
	chemical ['kemɪkl]	Chemikalie; chemisch	
	trade [treɪd]	Handel	
	opportunity [ˌɒpə'tjuːnəti]	Gelegenheit; Möglichkeit →	sth that is possible

	energy ['enədʒi]	Energie; Kraft →	We should use more alternative sorts of *energy*.
	climate ['klaɪmət]	Klima →	what the weather in a place is like
	inter-cultural [ˌɪntə'kʌltʃrl]	interkulturell	
	headline ['hedlaɪn]	Überschrift, Schlagzeile	
	death [deθ]	Tod, Todesfall →	dead → *death* life ↔ *death*
	oil [ɔɪl]	Öl	
	cocoa ['kəʊkəʊ]	Kakao →	Without *cocoa* there would be no chocolate.
59	**communication** [kəˌmju:nɪ'keɪʃn]	Kommunikation, Verständigung	
	alternative [ɔ:l'tɜ:nətɪv]	alternativ; Alternative →	What *alternative* forms of energy do you know?
	solar panel [ˌsəʊlə 'pænl]	Sonnenkollektor	
	panel ['pænl]	Tafel, Platte; Element	
	windmill ['wɪnmɪl]	Windmühle; Windrad, Windkraftanlage	

Bildung von Nomen I

Aus vielen Verben kannst du ein Nomen bilden, indem du die Endung *-ing* anhängst, z. B.

to cook	→	*cooking*	kochen	→	das Kochen
to dive	→	*diving*	tauchen	→	das Tauchen
to fish	→	*fishing*	fischen, angeln	→	das Fischen, Angeln
to learn	→	*learning*	lernen	→	das Lernen
…	→	…	…	→	…

Finde noch mehr solcher Beispiele und füge sie in die Liste ein.

Aspects

60	**aspect** ['æspekt]	Aspekt, Gesichtspunkt, Seite	
	product ['prɒdʌkt]	Produkt, Artikel, Ware	
	globalisation [ˌgləʊblaɪ'zeɪʃn]	Globalisierung →	We talk about *globalisation* when big companies are found in lots of different countries, or when you can buy the same things all over the world.
	airline ['eəlaɪn]	Fluggesellschaft, Fluglinie	
	pros and cons [ˌprəʊz‿ənd 'kɒnz]	Für und Wider, Pro und Kontra, Vor- und Nachteile	
	multinational [ˌmʌlti'næʃnl]	multinational →	national → *multinational*
	shipping ['ʃɪpɪŋ]	Schifffahrt, Verschiffung	
	caution *(no pl)* ['kɔ:ʃn]	Vorsicht, Warnung	

	criminal ['krɪmɪnl]	Krimineller/Kriminelle, Verbrecher/Verbrecherin; kriminell →	crime → *criminal*
	to **cause** [kɔ:z]	verursachen, hervorrufen →	If you *cause* sth, you make it happen.
	to **dump sth** [dʌmp]	abladen, auskippen, verklappen →	dump → *to dump*
	greenhouse gas [ˌgri:nhaʊs 'gæs]	Treibhausgas →	*Greenhouse gases* are bad for the environment.
	gas [gæs]	Gas *(BE)*; Benzin *(AE)* →	Most people in Europe use either *gas* or electricity for cooking.
	option ['ɒpʃn]	Auswahlmöglichkeit, Option	
	to **agree** [ə'gri:]	einer Meinung sein →	I *agree* with you. = I think what you say is right.
	government ['gʌvnmənt]	Regierung →	a group of people whose job it is to 'look after' a country
	worldwide [ˌwɜ:ld'waɪd]	weltweit →	world → *worldwide*
	future ['fju:tʃə]	Zukunft	
	talk [tɔ:k]	Vortrag; Rede, Gespräch →	to talk → *a talk*
	situation [ˌsɪtju'eɪʃn]	Situation	
	slave [sleɪv]	Sklave/Sklavin	
	environmental [ɪnˌvaɪərn'mentl]	Umwelt-, die Umwelt betreffend, umweltbedingt →	environment → *environmental*
	to **offer** ['ɒfə]	anbieten →	Can I *offer* you a drink? = Would you like a drink?
61	**nightmare** ['naɪtmeə]	Albtraum →	a terrible dream
	coral ['kɒrəl]	Koralle; Korallen- →	There are a lot of pieces of *coral* on the beach.
	reef [ri:f]	Riff →	The Great Barrier Reef is a famous *reef* in Australia.
	centimetre (cm) ['sentɪˌmi:tə]	Zentimeter	
	to **warn** [wɔ:n]	warnen, ermahnen	
	(global) warming [ˌgləʊbl 'wɔ:mɪŋ]	(Erd-)Erwärmung →	*Global warming* is dangerous because the sea level is rising.
	to **continue** [kən'tɪnju:]	fortfahren, andauern, weitergehen, weitermachen →	to go on
	eco [i:kəʊ]	Öko-, Umwelt- →	Our car is *eco*-friendly.
	to **launch** [lɔ:nʃ]	einführen, herausbringen; starten, abschießen	
	launch [lɔ:nʃ]	Einführung, Start; Abschuss	
	to **run on** ['rʌn‿ɒn]	laufen mit *(Auto)* →	An eco car *runs on* electricity.
	fossil fuel ['fɒsl ˌfju:əl]	fossiler Brennstoff →	Oil is a *fossil fuel.*
	fossil ['fɒsl]	Fossil; fossil, versteinert	
	fuel ['fju:əl]	Treibstoff; Brennmaterial →	Cars need *fuel.*
	to **test** [test]	testen, prüfen →	to check
	light [laɪt]	leicht; hell	

Bildung von Nomen II

Aus Verben oder Adjektiven kannst du ein Nomen bilden, indem du eine bestimmte Endung anhängst. Dafür gibt es verschiedene Möglichkeiten, z. B.

- die Endung ***-ion***:
  - *to act* → *act**ion***
- die Endung ***-ment***:
  - *to move* → *move**ment***
  - *to advertise* → *advertise**ment***
- die Endung ***-er***:
  - *to lead* → *lead**er***
  - *to teach* → *teach**er***
- die Endung ***-ation***:
  - *to inform* → *inform**ation***
  - *to apply* → *applic**ation***
- die Endung ***-ity***:
  - *electric* → *electric**ity***
  - *national* → *national**ity***

Finde für jede Endung weitere Beispiele für Nomen. Aus welchen Verben oder Adjektiven kannst du sie bilden?

Option 1

62	to **guarantee** [ˌgærn'tiː]	garantieren, sicherstellen, bürgen	
	deal [diːl]	Handel; Abmachung, Übereinkunft	
	producer [prə'djuːsə]	Produzent/Produzentin, Erzeuger/Erzeugerin →	To produce a film, you need a director, actors, a *producer*, and lots of other people.
	condition [kən'dɪʃn]	Kondition; Bedingung	
	label ['leɪbl]	Etikett; Beschriftung; Siegel →	a piece of paper on a bottle, box etc. that tells you what it is and what's in it
	to **label** ['leɪbl]	beschriften, benennen, etikettieren →	to put a piece of paper on a bottle, box etc. that tells you what it is and what's in it
	logo ['ləʊgəʊ]	Logo; Firmenzeichen →	a design or symbol that a company uses for its products
	pay [peɪ]	Lohn, Gehalt, Bezahlung →	to pay → *pay*
	community [kə'mjuːnəti]	Gemeinde; Gemeinschaft →	We don't live in a big city, our village is just a small *community*.
	bar [bɑː]	Tafel, Riegel, Stück; Stange →	Mrs Dixon is buying two *bars* of soap and a *bar* of chocolate.
	co-operative [kəʊ'ɒprətɪv]	Kooperative →	When farmers work together and sell the products together, they form a *co-operative*.
	export ['ekspɔːt]	Export; Ausfuhr	
	to **export** [ɪk'spɔːt]	exportieren, ausführen	
	to **realise** ['rɪəlaɪz]	erkennen, sich klar werden →	Suddenly I *realised* … = Plötzlich wurde mir klar …
	organisation [ˌɔːgnaɪ'zeɪʃn]	Organisation, Unternehmen →	to organize → *organisation*
	divine [dɪ'vaɪn]	göttlich	
	turnover ['tɜːnˌəʊvə]	Umsatz, Absatz →	The company's *turnover* is more than 20 million pounds.
	mission ['mɪʃn]	Mission, Auftrag, Aufgabe →	something that sb very much wants to do, usually to help other people in some way

	successful [sək'sesfl]	erfolgreich →	success → *successful*
	classic ['klæsɪk]	klassisch	
	source [sɔ:s]	Quelle; Grund	
63	to **grow, grew, grown** [grəʊ; gru:; grəʊn]	wachsen (lassen); anbauen; zunehmen →	We *grow* vegetables in our garden.
	stand [stænd]	(Messe-)Stand	
	sales talk ['seɪlz tɔ:k]	Verkaufsgespräch	
	to design [dɪ'zaɪn]	entwerfen; zeichnen	
	crunchy ['krʌntʃi]	knusprig	
	yummy ['jʌmi]	lecker →	This cake is *yummy*! = This cake tastes fantastic!
	nutty ['nʌti]	nussig; schmackhaft	
	smooth [smu:θ]	weich, geschmeidig, glatt →	Feel this T-shirt – it's really *smooth*.
	milky ['mɪlki]	milchig	

Wortfamilien

Viele neue Wörter, die du lernst, sind mit Wörtern verwandt, die du bereits kennst. Sie gehören dann zur selben Wortfamilie, z. B.

to apply → *applicant* → *application*
to act → *action* → *active* → *activity* → *actor* → *actress*
farm → *farmer* → *farming*

Bilde Wortfamilien für die folgenden Wörter:

attract – camp – cook – dive – electric – help – dead – office – paint – scare – science – skate – swim

Option 2

64	**danger** ['deɪndʒə]	Gefahr →	*danger* → dangerous
	adapted [ə'dæptɪd]	adaptiert, angepasst	
	deadly ['dedli]	tödlich, tod-	
	islander ['aɪləndə]	Inselbewohner/ Inselbewohnerin →	someone who lives on an island
	fisherman, fishermen *(pl)* ['fɪʃəmən; 'fɪʃəmen]	Fischer; Angler	
	local ['ləʊkl]	einheimisch, ortsansässig	
	spa [spɑ:]	Wellness-Center, Spa →	A lof of hotels have their own *spa*.
	diving ['daɪvɪŋ]	Tauch-, Tauchen →	to dive → *diving*
	instructor [ɪn'strʌktə]	Lehrer/Lehrerin, Ausbilder/ Ausbilderin →	somebody who teaches something
	underwater [ˌʌndə'wɔ:tə]	Unterwasser- →	an *underwater* camera
	experience [ɪk'spɪəriənts]	Erfahrung, Erlebnis	
	to **turn** [tɜ:n]	werden →	The situation *turned* dangerous.
	wetsuit ['wetsu:t]	Taucheranzug, Neoprenanzug	
	dive [daɪv]	Tauch-; Tauchgang	

	cleaning station ['kli:nɪŋ ˌsteɪʃn]	Putzerstation →	a place in the sea where small fish clean bigger fish
	manta ray ['mænta ˌreɪ]	Mantarochen →	A *manta ray* is a large sea creature.
	current ['kʌrnt]	Strömung; Strom →	Be careful, the *current* here is very strong.
	up current ['ʌp ˌkʌrnt]	Strömung, die nach oben zieht	
	crash [kræʃ]	Unfall, Aufprall; Absturz	
	to **drop** [drɒp]	sinken *(beim Tauchen)*	
	to **carry along** [ˌkæri‿ə'lɒŋ]	mitführen, mitreißen	
65	**decompression** [ˌdi:kəm'preʃn]	Dekompression, Druckverminderung	
	buddy *(infml)* ['bʌdi]	Tauchbegleiter/ Tauchbegleiterin; Kumpel, Kamerad/ Kameradin →	You should always dive with a *buddy.*
	a couple of [ə 'kʌpl‿əv]	ein paar, einige →	I need to buy *a couple of* new T-shirts.
	shot [ʃɒt]	Aufnahme, Foto; Einstellung	
	creature ['kri:tʃə]	Kreatur, Geschöpf, Lebewesen	
	fin [fɪn]	(Schwimm-)Flosse →	Fish and divers have *fins.*
	wing [wɪŋ]	Flügel →	Birds and planes have *wings.*
	no ... at all [ˌnəʊ ... ət‿'ɔ:l]	überhaupt kein/keine →	When we went surfing, there was *no* wind *at all.*
	diver ['daɪvə]	Taucher/Taucherin →	to dive → *diver* → diving
66	had gone [hæd 'gɒn]	waren gegangen	
	logbook ['lɒgbʊk]	Logbuch →	a book where you write down what you have done on a ship
	entry ['entri]	Eintrag, Eintragung	
	wasn't feeling [ˌwɒznt 'fi:lɪŋ]	fühlte sich nicht	
	to **itch** [ɪtʃ]	jucken	
	heart [hɑ:t]	Herz	
	base [beɪs]	Station, Basis; Fuß	
	to **assure** [ə'ʃʊə]	etw. zusichern, versichern, sicherstellen →	They *assured* her that he'd be OK.
	dot [dɒt]	Punkt, Pünktchen	
	bit [bɪt]	Stückchen; Auszug, Teil	
	tear [tɪə]	Träne →	When you cry, you have *tears* in your eyes.
	shade [ʃeɪd]	Schatten, Schattierung →	Keep in the *shade* if you sit in the garden.
	reader ['ri:də]	Lesebuch, Leseheft, Lektüre	
67	to retell [ri:'tel]	nacherzählen, nochmals erzählen	
	had seen [hæd 'si:n]	hatte gesehen	
	to sum up [ˌsʌm‿'ʌp]	zusammenfassen	
	low [ləʊ]	niedrig, tief →	high ↔ *low*
	messy ['mesi]	unordentlich, chaotisch, durcheinander	
	to read out [ri:d‿'aʊt]	etw. laut vorlesen	

Everyday English: Shopping

Die folgenden *phrases* helfen dir, wenn du in einem englischsprachigen Land etwas kaufen willst.

May I help you?	Kann ich Ihnen helfen?/Was darf es sein?
I'd like …, please.	Ich hätte gerne … .
I'm looking for … .	Ich suche … .
Do you sell …?	Verkaufen Sie … ?
How much is/are this/these … ?	Wieviel kostet/kosten der/die/das … ?
That's … .	Es kostet … .
I'd like to buy a … .	Ich möchte gerne ein/eine/einen … kaufen.
Where's the shoe department?	Wo ist die Schuhabteilung?
Where's the men's/women's department?	Wo ist die Herrenabteilung/Damenabteilung?
Where can I try it on?	Wo kann ich das anprobieren?
The changing room is over there.	Die Umkleidekabine ist da drüben.
Do you have a larger/smaller size?	Haben Sie das in einer größeren/kleineren Größe?
It's too big/small/tight/wide/short/long.	Das ist zu groß/klein/eng/weit/kurz/lang.
Yes, of course. What size are you?	Ja, natürlich. Welche Größe brauchen Sie?
It fits well.	Es passt gut.
It doesn't fit.	Es passt nicht.
I'll take it.	Ich nehme es.
Do you take credit cards?	Nehmen Sie Kreditkarten?
Can you fix/repair this?	Können Sie das reparieren?
Do you have any German newspapers/magazines?	Haben Sie deutsche Zeitungen/Zeitschriften?

Arbeite mit einem Partner. Einer von euch ist der Kunde, der andere der Verkäufer. Übt englische Dialoge und verwendet dafür die oben stehenden *phrases*.

Dictionary

In dieser alphabetischen Liste ist das Vokabular von *Orange Line 1* bis *5* enthalten. Namen werden in einer gesonderten Liste am Ende des Vokabulars aufgelistet.
Das Zeichen ° bei einem Eintrag weist darauf hin, dass das Wort zum rezeptiven Wortschatz zählt.
Die mit * gekennzeichneten Verben sind unregelmäßig.
Wendungen, die aus mehreren Wörtern bestehen, werden meist unter mehreren Stichwörtern aufgeführt.
So ist z. B. *at home* unter *at* und *home* zu finden.
Die Fundstellen verweisen auf das erstmalige Vorkommen der Wörter, z. B.
about [ə'baʊt] über **I U3**, 40 kommt zum ersten Mal vor in Band I, Unit 3, Seite 40.
dirty ['dɜ:ti] schmutzig **II U1**, 10 kommt zum ersten Mal vor in Band II, Unit 1, Seite 10.
U = Unit, T = Topic, LU = Link-up, FA = Fakultativer Anhang (nur Namen)

A

a, an [ə; ən] ein/eine **I U1,** 10
a bit [ə 'bɪt] ein bisschen **I U2,** 35
a couple of [ə 'kʌpl‿əv] ein paar, einige **V T4,** 65
a few [ə 'fju:] einige, ein paar **II U4,** 52
a lot [ə 'lɒt] viel **II U1,** 15
a lot of [ə 'lɒt‿əv] viel/viele, eine Menge **I U2,** 30
a week [ə 'wi:k] pro Woche, in der Woche **II U4,** 52
Aborigine [ˌæbə'rɪdʒni] Ureinwohner/Ureinwohnerin Australiens, Aborigine **V T1,** 10
about [ə'baʊt] über **I U3,** 40; ungefähr, circa, etwa **III U1,** 11
out and about ['aʊt‿nd‿ə'baʊt] unterwegs °**I U4,** 54
to jump about [ˌdʒʌmp‿ə'baʊt] herumspringen **III U4,** 58
What about …? [wɒt‿ə'baʊt] Was ist mit …? Wie wäre es mit …? **I U2,** 30
What's the film about? [wɒts ðə 'fɪlm‿əˌbaʊt] Wovon handelt der Film? °**II U3,** 43
above [ə'bʌv] oben, über, oberhalb **II U5,** 70
abroad [ə'brɔ:d] im/ins Ausland **III U4,** 57
absence ['æbsns] Abwesenheit **IV U2,** 25
accent ['æksnt] Akzent **II U3,** 36
to **accept** [ək'sept] akzeptieren, hinnehmen; annehmen **V T3,** 44
access ['ækses] Zugang **IV U4,** 65
accident ['æksɪdnt] Unfall **II U3,** 41
acre ['eɪkə] Morgen *(Flächenmaß: 40,47 Ar)* **IV U4,** 58
across [ə'krɒs] waagerecht *(im Kreuzworträtsel)* °**II U3,** 42; über, hinüber, quer durch/darüber **III U1,** 10; breit, im Durchmesser **IV U3,** 49
to **act** [ækt] spielen *(Theater)* **I U7,** 90; sich verhalten, handeln, agieren **V T3,** 47
action ['ækʃn] Handlung, Aktion **III U1,** 9
activity [æk'tɪvəti] Aktivität **III U3,** 47
actor ['æktə] Schauspieler **I U7,** 96
actress ['æktrəs] Schauspielerin **III U2,** 25
ad [æd] Anzeige; Werbespot **V T1,** 15
adaptable [ə'dæptəbl] anpassungsfähig **V T3,** 43
adapted [ə'dæptɪd] adaptiert, angepasst °**V T4,** 64
adaptor [ə'dæptə] Adapter **IV U3,** 44
to **add** [æd] hinzufügen, addieren **III U4,** 60
address [ə'dres] Adresse **I U5,** 70
adjective ['ædʒəktɪv] Adjektiv, Eigenschaftswort °**I U1,** 22
adult ['ædʌlt] Erwachsener/Erwachsene **V T2,** 32
advanced [əd'vɑ:nst] fortgeschritten **III U4,** 57
adventure [əd'ventʃə] Abenteuer **II U6,** 80
adverb ['ædvɜ:b] Adverb °**II U7,** 90
adverb of manner [ˌædvɜ:b‿əv 'mænə] Adverb der Art und Weise °**II U7,** 90
advert ['ædvɜ:t] Anzeige, Werbespot **IV U2,** 25
advertising *(no pl.)* ['ædvətaɪzɪŋ] Werbung, Reklame; Werbe- °**V T3,** 40
advice [əd'vaɪs] Rat(schlag) **V T1,** 12; **V T2,** 31; **V T3,** 43
careers advice [kə'rɪəz ədˌvaɪs] Berufsberatung **V T3,** 46
to **advise** [əd'vaɪz] raten **III U4,** 59
*to be **afraid (of)** [bi:‿ə'freɪd] Angst haben (vor), sich fürchten (vor) **III U4,** 56
after ['ɑ:ftə] nach *(zeitlich)* **I LUB,** 39
afternoon [ˌɑ:ftə'nu:n] Nachmittag **I U2,** 34
afternoon tea [ˌɑ:ftənu:n 'ti:] Nachmittagstee **I U7,** 94
in the afternoon [ˌɪn ði ˌɑ:ftə'nu:n] nachmittags, am Nachmittag **I U3,** 47
aftershave ['ɑ:ftəʃeɪv] Aftershave, Rasierwasser **III U3,** 46
again [ə'gen] wieder **I U3,** 48
against [ə'genst] gegen **III U1,** 9
age [eɪdʒ] Alter; Zeitalter **III U3,** 40
agency ['eɪdʒnsi] Agentur, Behörde **IV U3,** 48
agent ['eɪdʒnt] Agent/Agentin, Vertreter/Vertreterin **IV U3,** 48
ago [ə'gəʊ] vor *(zeitlich)* **II U2,** 26
to **agree** [ə'gri:] zustimmen, einer Meinung sein °**V T2,** 33; **V T4,** 60
aid [eɪd] Hilfe, Beistand, Förderung **V T3,** 43
air [eə] Luft **II U4,** 55
on the air [ˌɒn ði‿'eə] auf Sendung **II U4,** 55

airline ['eəlaɪn] Fluggesellschaft, Fluglinie **VT4,** 60
airport ['eəpɔ:t] Flughafen **II U7,** 89
alarm [ə'lɑ:m] Alarm **II U7,** 90
alarm clock [ə'lɑ:m ˌklɒk] Wecker **I U5,** 75
album ['ælbəm] Album **IV U5,** 73
alcohol ['ælkəhɒl] Alkohol **IV U2,** 25
A-levels *(pl)* ['eɪlevlz] brit. Abitur **III U4,** 57
alien ['eɪliən] Fremder/Fremde, Außerirdischer/Außerirdische **III U5,** 70
alien ['eɪliən] fremd, ausländisch **IV U3,** 48
alive [ə'laɪv] am Leben, lebendig **III U4,** 60
all [ɔ:l] alle/alles; ganz **I U3,** 50
all over [ˌɔ:l‿'əʊvə] überall **IV U1,** 10
all right [ɔ:l 'raɪt] in Ordnung **IV U4,** 64
in all [ɪn‿'ɔ:l] im Ganzen **III U4,** 53
no … at all [ˌnəʊ … ət‿'ɔ:l] überhaupt kein/keine **VT4,** 65
allegiance [ə'li:dʒns] Treue **IV U2,** 23
almost ['ɔ:lməʊst] fast, beinahe **III U3,** 39
alone [ə'ləʊn] allein **III U3,** 41
to go it alone [ˌgəʊ‿ɪt‿ə'ləʊn] **VT3,** 43
to leave sb alone [ˌli:v‿ə'ləʊn] jmdn. in Ruhe lassen **VT1,** 12
along [ə'lɒŋ] entlang **I U7,** 91
to carry along [ˌkæri‿ə'lɒŋ] mitführen, mitreißen **VT4,** 64
alphabet ['ælfəbet] Alphabet, Abc **I U1,** 15
alphabetical [ˌælfə'betɪkl] alphabetisch **I U6,** 88
already [ɔ:l'redi] schon **I U2,** 34
also ['ɔ:lsəʊ] auch **I U5,** 68
alternative [ɔ:l'tɜ:nətɪv] Alternative *(Musikrichtung)* **IV U5,** 76; alternativ; Alternative **VT4,** 59
although [ɔ:l'ðəʊ] obwohl **III U3,** 46
always ['ɔ:lweɪz] immer, ständig **I U1,** 16
a.m. [ˌeɪ'em] vormittags *(Uhrzeit)* **III U4,** 57
ambulance ['æmbjələns] Krankenwagen **III U1,** 9
American [ə'merɪkən] amerikanisch; Amerikaner/Amerikanerin **II U4,** 50
American football [əˌmerɪkən 'fʊtbɔ:l] Football **III U1,** 8
Native American [ˌneɪtɪv‿ə'merɪkən] Ureinwohner/Ureinwohnerin Amerikas, Indianer/Indianerin **IV U1,** 10
ancient ['eɪnʃnt] alt, antik **III U3,** 39
and [ænd] und **I U1,** 11
angry ['æŋgri] verärgert, böse **II U1,** 18
to be angry with [bi: 'æŋgri wɪð] böse sein auf **II U2,** 26
animal ['ænɪml] Tier **I U6,** 82
announcement [ə'naʊntsmənt] Ankündigung; Durchsage **IV U2,** 29
anorak ['ænəræk] Anorak **II U6,** 82
another [ə'nʌðə] noch ein/eine, ein anderer/eine andere/ein anderes **II U3,** 44
answer ['ɑ:ntsə] Antwort **I U4,** 58
to **answer** ['ɑ:ntsə] antworten, beantworten °**I LUA,** 24
answerphone ['ɑ:nsəfəʊn] Anrufbeantworter **III U4,** 59
anti ['æntɪ] gegen-, anti- **VT1,** 12; **VT3,** 41
any ['eni] einige; etwas **II U4,** 54
anybody ['eniˌbɒdi] jeder (beliebige) **III U5,** 71
anything ['eniθɪŋ] etwas, irgendetwas **I U5,** 66
anywhere ['eniweə] überall; irgendwo **III U3,** 39
apartment *(AE)* [ə'pɑ:tmənt] Wohnung, Apartment **IV U3,** 42
apple ['æpl] Apfel **I U1,** 14
applicant ['æplɪkənt] Bewerber/Bewerberin, Antragsteller/Antragstellerin **VT1,** 10
application [ˌæplɪ'keɪʃn] Bewerbung, Antrag; Anwendung **VT2,** 29
to **apply (for)** [ə'plaɪ] sich bewerben (um), sich anmelden (zu) **VT1,** 14; **VT2,** 32
apprenticeship [ə'prentɪʃɪp] Lehre, Ausbildung **VT2,** 32
April ['eɪprl] April **I U5,** 70
area ['eəriə] Gebiet; Fläche **II U7,** 94
rest area ['rest ˌeəriə] Rastplatz **IV U4,** 61
arena [ə'ri:nə] Arena, Stadion **II U2,** 22
to **argue** ['ɑ:gju:] streiten, argumentieren **III U2,** 30
to have an **argument** [ˌhæv‿ən‿'ɑ:gjəmənt] sich streiten **III U4,** 52
arm [ɑ:m] Arm **II U3,** 40; Ärmel **IV U2,** 31
around [ə'raʊnd] (um …) herum, umher **II U6,** 78; ungefähr, zirka, etwa **IV U3,** 49
to hang around [ˌhæŋ‿ə'raʊnd] rumhängen, herumlungern **VT2,** 28
See you around! [ˌsi: jə ə'raʊnd] Bis dann!, Bis … **IV U2,** 26
to **arrest** [ə'rest] festnehmen, verhaften **III U5,** 78
to **arrive** [ə'raɪv] ankommen **I U6,** 86
Art [ɑ:t] Kunst **II U1,** 10
article ['ɑ:tɪkl] Artikel °**IV U2,** 27
artist ['ɑ:tɪst] Künstler/Künstlerin **VT2,** 29
as [æz; əz] als, wie **II U4,** 52; während **IV U3,** 46
as … as [æz … æz; əz … əz] so … wie … **II U4,** 52
as long as [əz 'lɒŋ‿əz] solange wie **I U7,** 94
as well as [əz 'wel‿əz] sowohl … als auch **III U4,** 57
to **ask** [ɑ:sk] fragen **I U3,** 44
to ask (for) ['ɑ:sk fə] fragen (nach), bitten (um) **I U4,** 60
*to be **asleep** [ˌbi:‿ə'sli:p] schlafen **II U7,** 94
aspect ['æspekt] Aspekt, Gesichtspunkt, Seite **VT1,** 10; **VT2,** 28; **VT3,** 42; **VT4,** 60
ass *(AE)* [æs] Hintern, Arsch **IV U5,** 80
assembly [ə'sembli] Versammlung, Morgenappell **II U1,** 10
assistant [ə'sɪstnt] Assistent/Assistentin **III U5,** 75
shop assistant ['ʃɒp‿əˌsɪstnt] Verkäufer/Verkäuferin **II U5,** 67
to **assure** [ə'ʃʊə] etw. zusichern, versichern, sicherstellen **VT4,** 66
astronaut ['æstrənɔ:t] Astronaut/Astronautin **IV U3,** 40
at [æt; ət] in, auf, bei, an **I U1,** 10
at any time [æt‿eni 'taɪm] jederzeit **IV U2,** 25
at first [ət 'fɜ:st] zuerst, zunächst **II U6,** 80
at home [ət 'həʊm] zu Hause **I U2,** 26
at last [ət 'lɑ:st] endlich, schließlich **VT3,** 42
at least [ət 'li:st] wenigstens, mindestens **I U6,** 87
at night [ət 'naɪt] nachts **II U3,** 47
at once [ət 'wʌnts] sofort, plötzlich **II U7,** 94
at the back [ət ðə 'bæk] hinten, im hinteren Teil °**II U7,** 96

at the bottom [ət ðə 'bɒtəm] im unteren Teil **III U1,** 14
at the front [ət ðə 'frʌnt] im vorderen Teil, vorne **IV U1,** 9
at the moment [ət ðə 'məʊmənt] im Augenblick, momentan **I U7,** 90
at the top [ət ðə 'tɒp] oben, im oberen Teil **III U1,** 14
to **attack** [ə'tæk] angreifen **III U5,** 74
attempt [ə'tempt] Versuch; Anschlag **V T3,** 43
Attention! [ə'tenʃn] Achtung! °**IV U2,** 29
to **attract** [ə'trækt] anziehen **IV U4,** 65
attractive [ə'træktɪv] attraktiv **IV U2,** 26
audience ['ɔ:diəns] Publikum **III U4,** 53
audition [ɔ:'dɪʃn] Vorsprechen, Vorsingen, Vortanzen **II U5,** 64
August ['ɔ:gəst] August **I U5,** 70
aunt [ɑ:nt] Tante **I U2,** 28
Aussie *(Aus)* ['ɒzi] Australier/Australierin °**V T1,** 12
Australian [ɒs'treɪliən] australisch; Australier/Australierin **II U4,** 50
autograph ['ɔ:təgrɑ:f] Autogramm **I U7,** 96
autumn ['ɔ:təm] Herbst **I U6,** 79
average ['ævrɪdʒ] durchschnittlich **III U5,** 68
award [ə'wɔ:d] Auszeichnung, Preis **IV U5,** 72
away [ə'weɪ] weg **I U3,** 48
to run away [rʌn‿ə'weɪ] wegrennen **I U3,** 48
awesome ['ɔ:səm] toll **IV U2,** 26
awful ['ɔ:fl] schrecklich, furchtbar **III U5,** 72

B

baby, babies *(pl)* ['beɪbi; 'beɪbiz] Baby, Säugling **I U6,** 82
back [bæk] Rücken **II U3,** 41
at the back [ət ðə 'bæk] hinten, im hinteren Teil °**II U7,** 96
like the back of my hand ['bæk‿əv maɪ ˌhænd] wie meine Westentasche **III U2,** 30
back [bæk] Hinter-, rückwärtig **II U4,** 56
back line [ˌbæk 'laɪn] Grundlinie **III U1,** 10
back [bæk] zurück **I U3,** 42
to sit back [ˌsɪt 'bæk] sich zurücklehnen **IV U1,** 16
background ['bækgraʊnd] Hintergrund **IV U1,** 8
backless ['bækləs] rückenfrei **IV U5,** 72
bacon ['beɪkn] Schinkenspeck **IV U1,** 12
bad [bæd] schlecht **I U5,** 74
bad luck [ˌbæd 'lʌk] Pech **I U4,** 63
badminton ['bædmɪntən] Badminton, Federball **I U3,** 40
bag [bæg] Tasche, Tüte **I U1,** 14
school bag ['sku:l bæg] Schultasche, Schulranzen **I U1,** 14
sleeping bag ['sli:pɪŋ ˌbæg] Schlafsack **I U6,** 84
bagel ['beɪgl] Bagel **IV U1,** 12
baguette [bæg'et] Baguette **V T3,** 47
baker ['beɪkə] Bäcker/Bäckerin **III U2,** 28
ball [bɔ:l] Ball **I U1,** 20
balloon [bə'lu:n] (Heiß-)Luftballon **V T3,** 43
ballroom ['bɔ:lrʊm] Ballsaal **IV U2,** 23
ballroom dancing [ˌbɔ:lrʊm 'dɑ:ntsɪŋ] Gesellschaftstanz **IV U2,** 23
ban [bæn] Verbot, Sperre; Bann **V T3,** 44
to **ban** [bæn] verbieten, ausschließen; (ver)bannen **V T3,** 44
banana [bə'nɑ:nə] Banane **II U1,** 15
to go bananas [ˌgəʊ bə'nɑ:nəz] verrückt werden, durchdrehen **II U5,** 66
band [bænd] Bande; Band, Kapelle **IV U3,** 48
steel band [ˌsti:l 'bænd] Steelband *(Band, deren Instrumente aus leeren Ölfässern bestehen)* **III U4,** 54
to **bang** [bæŋ] fest klopfen **II U7,** 94
bank [bæŋk] Bank **IV U5,** 80
piggy bank ['pɪgi bæŋk] Sparschwein **II U2,** 23
bar [bɑ:] Bar, Kneipe **IV U2,** 30; Tafel, Riegel, Stück; Stange **V T4,** 62
bistro bar [ˌbi:strəʊ 'bɑ:] Bistro **V T3,** 46
burger bar ['bɜ:gə ˌbɑ:] Fastfood-Restaurant **I U5,** 68
snack bar ['snæk ˌbɑ:] Café, Imbissstube **V T3,** 46
barbecue ['bɑ:bɪkju:] Grill(party) **V T1,** 11
bark [bɑ:k] Bellen **III U5,** 78
to **bark** [bɑ:k] bellen **I U3,** 48
barking ['bɑ:kɪŋ] Bellen **IV U4,** 65
barman, barmen *(pl)* ['bɑ:mən, 'bɑ:men] Barmann, Barkeeper **IV U4,** 64
barn [bɑ:n] Scheune **II U7,** 88
barn owl ['bɑ:n‿aʊl] Schleiereule **II U7,** 94
base [beɪs] Base **III U1,** 14; Station, Basis; Fuß **V T4,** 66
baseball ['beɪsbɔ:l] Baseball **III U1,** 9
basement ['beɪsmənt] Kellergeschoss, Untergeschoss **III U3,** 46
basketball ['bɑ:skɪtbɔ:l] Basketball **I U3,** 40
bass [beɪs] Bass **IV U5,** 76
bat [bæt] Schläger **III U1,** 8
to **bat** [bæt] schlagen **III U1,** 8
bathroom ['bɑ:θrʊm] Bad, Badezimmer **I LUA,** 24
bathtub ['bɑ:θtʌb] Badewanne **IV U3,** 42
batter ['bætə] Schlagmann/Schlagfrau **III U1,** 9
battery ['bætri] Batterie, Akku **II U7,** 95
BC (= before Christ) [bi:'si:] vor Christus **III U1,** 13
*to **be** [bi:] sein **I U1,** 23
It's a draw. [ˌɪts‿ə 'drɔ:] Es steht unentschieden. **III U1,** 12
to be afraid (of) [bi:‿ə'freɪd] Angst haben (vor), sich fürchten (vor) **III U4,** 56
to be angry with [bi: 'æŋgri wɪð] böse sein auf **II U2,** 26
to be asleep [ˌbi:‿ə'sli:p] schlafen **II U7,** 94
to be a turn-off ['tɜ:nɒf] abtörnend sein, zum Abgewöhnen sein **V T2,** 28
to be called [bi: 'kɔ:ld] heißen, genannt werden **III U4,** 59
to be cold [bi: 'kəʊld] frieren **II U2,** 24
to be fed up [bi: ˌfed‿'ʌp] die Nase voll haben **I U2,** 34
to be frightened (of) [bi: 'fraɪtnd] Angst haben (vor) **II U6,** 83
to be fun [bi: 'fʌn] Spaß machen **I U3,** 43
to be good with … [bi: 'gʊd wɪð] gut mit … umgehen können **I U2,** 34
to be in a hurry [bi:‿ɪn‿ə 'hʌri] es eilig haben **I U2,** 30
to be into [bi:‿'ɪntə] interessiert sein an **IV U5,** 76
to be lost [bi: 'lɒst] sich verirrt haben **III U3,** 40
to be missing [bi: 'mɪsɪŋ] fehlen **III U1,** 14

to be nuts about [bi: ˌnʌtsˬə'baʊt] verrückt nach … sein **II U1,** 18
to be on [bi:ˬ'ɒn] an der Reihe sein; im Gange sein, laufen **II U5,** 70; an sein, brennen *(Licht)* **II U7,** 94
to be pleased with [bi: 'pli:zd wɪð] zufrieden sein mit **I U6,** 87
to be right [bi: 'raɪt] Recht haben **II U4,** 56
to be sorry [bi: 'sɒri] Leid tun **III U3,** 44
to be trapped [bi: 'træpt] in der Falle sitzen **II U6,** 83
to be upset [bi: ʌp'set] aufgeregt sein, bestürzt sein **II U3,** 44
to be welcome to do [bi: 'welkəm] gerne etwas tun können **III U4,** 56
to be worried [bi: 'wʌrid] besorgt sein, beunruhigt sein **I U6,** 87
to be wrong [bi: 'rɒŋ] Unrecht haben **III U3,** 47
beach [bi:tʃ] Strand **III U1,** 10
bean [bi:n] Bohne **II U4,** 54
bear [beə] Bär/Bärin **IV U4,** 65
beard [bɪəd] Bart **III U5,** 76
beautiful ['bju:tɪfl] schön, wunderschön **I U6,** 78
because [bɪ'kɒz] weil **I U2,** 30
*to **become** [bɪ'kʌm] werden **III U2,** 25
bed [bed] Bett **I LUA,** 25
to get out of bed [ˌgetˬaʊtˬəv 'bed] aufstehen **II U7,** 94
bedroom ['bedrʊm] Schlafzimmer **I LUA,** 24
before [bɪ'fɔ:] vor; bevor **I LUB,** 39
*to **begin** [bɪ'gɪn] beginnen, anfangen **II U3,** 47
beginning [bɪ'gɪnɪŋ] Anfang, Beginn **IV U1,** 14
behind [bɪ'haɪnd] hinter **I U1,** 18
Belgian ['beldʒən] belgisch; Belgier/Belgierin **IV U1,** 10
to **believe** [bɪ'li:v] glauben **II U1,** 18
bell [bel] Glocke, Klingel **II U2,** 24
The bell rings. [ðə 'bel rɪŋz] Es klingelt. **II U4,** 50
to **belong (to)** [bɪ'lɒŋ] gehören (zu) **V T2,** 28
below [bɪ'ləʊ] unterhalb, unten **IV U1,** 18
beside [bɪ'saɪd] neben, außer **II U1,** 18
best [best] beste/bester/bestes **II U1,** 14; am besten **III U1,** 10
*to **bet** [bet] wetten **II U1,** 14
better ['betə] besser **II U4,** 50
between [bɪ'twi:n] zwischen **I U7,** 90
big [bɪg] groß **I U1,** 12
bike [baɪk] Fahrrad **I LUB,** 38
by bike [baɪ 'baɪk] mit dem Fahrrad **I U4,** 57
bill [bɪl] Rechnung **II U4,** 55
bin [bɪn] Mülleimer, Mülltonne **III U3,** 40
bird [bɜ:d] Vogel **II U4,** 59
birth [bɜ:θ] Geburt **III U1,** 11
birthday ['bɜ:θdeɪ] Geburtstag **I U5,** 68
biscuit ['bɪskɪt] Keks **I U5,** 68
bistro bar [ˌbi:strəʊ 'bɑ:] Bistro **V T3,** 46
bit [bɪt] Stück, Stückchen °**III U5,** 69; Stückchen; Auszug, Teil **V T4,** 66
a bit [ə 'bɪt] ein bisschen **I U2,** 35
bite [baɪt] Biss, Stich; Bissen **V T1,** 12
*to **bite** [baɪt] beißen **V T1,** 12
black [blæk] schwarz **I LUA,** 24
Black [blæk] Schwarzer/Schwarze **V T3,** 42
blackout *(AE)* ['blækaʊt] Stromausfall **IV U3,** 42
blanket ['blæŋkɪt] (Woll-)Decke **II U6,** 74
wet blanket [wet 'blæŋkɪt] Miesmacher/Miesmacherin **II U6,** 74
blind [blaɪnd] blind **III U3,** 46
bling bling *(slang)* [ˌblɪŋ 'blɪŋ] Klunker **IV U5,** 76
bloke [bləʊk] Typ, Kerl **I U7,** 96
blond [blɒnd] blond **II U2,** 28
blond(e)-haired ['blɒnd ˌheəd] blond **III U2,** 25
blood [blʌd] Blut **III U5,** 74
bloody ['blʌdi] blutig; *hier:* verdammt **III U1,** 12
*to **blow** [bləʊ] blasen **III U2,** 28
to blow up [bləʊˬ'ʌp] aufblasen °**I U5,** 71
blue [blu:] blau **I LUA,** 24
board [bɔ:d] Tafel, Wandtafel **I U1,** 18
notice board ['nəʊtɪs bɔ:d] schwarzes Brett **III U4,** 57
boat [bəʊt] Boot, Schiff **III U2,** 28
body ['bɒdi] Körper **III U5,** 78
bomb [bɒm] Bombe **IV U3,** 41
boogie ['bu:gi] Boogie *(Tanzstil)* °**IV U5,** 80
book [bʊk] Buch **I U1,** 14
exercise book ['eksəsaɪz ˌbʊk] Heft, Übungsheft **I U1,** 14
to **book** [bʊk] buchen, reservieren **III U5,** 73
boot [bu:t] Stiefel **III U5,** 76
rubber boots *(pl)* [ˌrʌbə 'bu:ts] Gummistiefel **II U6,** 74
rugby boot ['rʌgbi bu:t] Rugbyschuh, Stollenschuh **III U1,** 8
border ['bɔ:də] Grenze **IV U4,** 64
bored [bɔ:d] gelangweilt **II U2,** 24
boring ['bɔ:rɪŋ] langweilig **I U1,** 20
*was/were/is/are **born** [bɔ:n] wurde(n)/wird/werden geboren **III U1,** 11
borough ['bʌrə] Bezirk, Stadtteil **IV U1,** 9
to **borrow** ['bɒrəʊ] borgen, leihen **I U2,** 34
boss [bɒs] Boss, Chef/Chefin **IV U3,** 48
both [bəʊθ] beide **III U3,** 46
It's no **bother.** ['bɒðə] Kein Problem. **III U5,** 72
to **bother** ['bɒðə] stören, belästigen °**III U3,** 44
bottle ['bɒtl] Flasche **I U5,** 68
at the **bottom** [ət ðə 'bɒtəm] im unteren Teil **III U1,** 14
boulevard ['bu:ləvɑ:d] Boulevard, Prachtstraße **IV U5,** 78
bowl [bəʊl] Schüssel **II U4,** 50
box, boxes *(pl)* [bɒks; 'bɒksɪz] Kiste, Schachtel, Kasten **I U5,** 68
fact box ['fækt bɒks] Infokasten **III U1,** 8
phone box ['fəʊn ˌbɒks] Telefonzelle **III U3,** 44
boy [bɔɪ] Junge **I U1,** 16
boyfriend ['bɔɪfrend] Freund *(in einer Paarbeziehung)* **III U4,** 53
brand [brænd] brand- **IV U2,** 23
brave [breɪv] tapfer, mutig **III U5,** 74
bread [bred] Brot **II U4,** 49
break [breɪk] Pause **II U1,** 12
*to **break** [breɪk] (zer)brechen, kaputtmachen **II U5,** 68
to break out [ˌbreɪkˬ'aʊt] ausbrechen **V T3,** 44
to **break-dance** ['breɪkdɑ:nts] Breakdance tanzen **I LUB,** 38
breakdown ['breɪkdaʊn] Autopanne; Zusammenbruch **IV U4,** 61
breakfast ['brekfəst] Frühstück **I U3,** 44
to have breakfast [hæv 'brekfəst] frühstücken **III U2,** 23
bridge [brɪdʒ] Brücke **I LUC,** 52
fire **brigade** ['faɪə brɪˌgeɪd] Feuerwehr **III U2,** 28
brilliant ['brɪljənt] toll, prima; leuchtend **II U5,** 70

*to **bring** [brɪŋ] bringen, mitbringen **I U3,** 43
to bring in [brɪŋ‿'ɪn] hereinbringen, mitbringen °**I U7,** 93
British ['brɪtɪʃ] britisch **III U1,** 15
brochure ['brəʊʃə] Broschüre, Prospekt °**III U2,** 27
broke [brəʊk] pleite, abgebrannt **IV U5,** 80
broken ['brəʊkn] kaputt, zerbrochen, gebrochen **I U6,** 84
brother ['brʌðə] Bruder **I LUA,** 25
brown [braʊn] braun **I LUA,** 24
to **brush** [brʌʃ] putzen, bürsten **IV U3,** 46
speech **bubble** ['spi:tʃ ˌbʌbl] Sprechblase °**III U3,** 41
buddy *(infml)* ['bʌdi] Tauchbegleiter/Tauchbegleiterin; Kumpel, Kamerad/Kameradin **VT4,** 65
*to **build** [bɪld] bauen **III U2,** 22
building ['bɪldɪŋ] Gebäude **III U1,** 9
light **bulb** ['laɪt bʌlb] Glühbirne **IV U3,** 44
bully ['bʊli] jemand, der andere tyrannisiert **II U3,** 47
to **bully** ['bʊli] tyrannisieren °**II U3,** 47
*to go **bump** [gəʊ 'bʌmp] rumsen °**II U7,** 94
burger ['bɜ:gə] Hamburger **I U5,** 68
burger bar ['bɜ:gə ˌbɑ:] Fastfood-Restaurant **I U5,** 68
burglar ['bɜ:glə] Einbrecher/Einbrecherin **II U7,** 90
*to **burn** [bɜ:n] (ver)brennen **III U2,** 28
to **bury** ['beri] begraben, beerdigen **III U5,** 74
bus, buses *(pl)* [bʌs; 'bʌsɪz] Bus **I LUC,** 52
bus stop ['bʌs ˌstɒp] Bushaltestelle **I LUC,** 52
on the bus [ˌɒn ðə 'bʌs] im Bus **II U1,** 18
to take a bus tour [ˌteɪk‿ə 'bʌs tʊə] eine Busfahrt machen **IV U4,** 58
bush [bʊʃ] Busch, Strauch **I U6,** 86
business ['bɪznɪs] Geschäft, Branche **IV U1,** 14
businessman ['bɪznɪsmən] Geschäftsmann **III U2,** 24
busy ['bɪzi] beschäftigt, ausgefüllt **I U2,** 34; belebt **III U2,** 24
but [bʌt] aber **I U2,** 26; außer **IV U5,** 80
butter ['bʌtə] Butter **I U7,** 94
button ['bʌtn] Auslöser; Knopf **II U7,** 95
*to **buy** [baɪ] kaufen **I U5,** 66
by [baɪ] bis **II U6,** 78; von **IV U5,** 80
by bike [baɪ 'baɪk] mit dem Fahrrad **I U4,** 57
by the way [ˌbaɪ ðə 'weɪ] übrigens **IV U4,** 61
bye [baɪ] tschüss **I U1,** 16

C

café ['kæfeɪ] Café **I U3,** 48
cafeteria [ˌkæfə'tɪəriə] Cafeteria **I U1,** 20
cage [keɪdʒ] Käfig **VT2,** 32
cake [keɪk] Kuchen **I U5,** 68
calendar ['kæləndə] Kalender **I U5,** 71
call [kɔ:l] Anruf °**I U6,** 83
phone call ['fəʊn ˌkɔ:l] (Telefon-)Anruf °**II U4,** 57
to **call** [kɔ:l] rufen, anrufen, nennen **I U3,** 48
That's what I call .... [ˌðæts wɒt‿'aɪ ˌkɔ:l] Das nenne ich .... **II U1,** 14
to be called [bi: 'kɔ:ld] heißen, genannt werden **III U4,** 59
caller ['kɔ:lə] Anrufer/Anruferin °**III U4,** 59
calm [kɑ:m] ruhig **II U6,** 80
camera ['kæmrə] Kamera, Fotoapparat **II U5,** 62
cameraman, cameramen *(pl)* ['kæmrəmæn; 'kæmrəmen] Kameramann **VT2,** 32
camp [kæmp] Camp, Lager **IV U4,** 62
campfire ['kæmpfaɪə] Lagerfeuer **IV U4,** 58
camping ['kæmpɪŋ] Camping, Zelten **I U6,** 84
***can** [kæn] können, dürfen **I U1,** 19
to **canoe** [kə'nu:] Kanu fahren **III U3,** 40
canyon ['kænjən] Schlucht, Canyon **IV U4,** 56
cap [kæp] Kappe, Mütze **I U5,** 66
capital city [ˌkæpɪtl 'sɪti] Hauptstadt °**III U2,** 27
capital letter [ˌkæpɪtl 'letə] Großbuchstabe °**II U3,** 37
capsule ['kæpsju:l] Kapsel **III U2,** 22
captain ['kæptɪn] Kapitän **IV U2,** 23
caption ['kæpʃn] Untertitel; Bildunterschrift °**III U2,** 22
car [kɑ:] Auto **I U3,** 49
card [kɑ:d] Karte **I LUB,** 38
day travel card [ˌdeɪ 'trævl ˌkɑ:d] Tagesfahrkarte **III U2,** 27
*to take **care** [teɪk 'keə] aufpassen; sich kümmern **IV U2,** 29
to **care** [keə] sich kümmern, sich interessieren, wichtig nehmen **III U4,** 60
I don't care. [aɪ dəʊnt 'keə] Es ist mir egal. **II U4,** 58
career [kə'rɪə] Beruf; Laufbahn, Karriere °**VT1,** 14; °**VT2,** 33; **VT3,** 43
careers advice [kə'rɪəz ədˌvaɪs] Berufsberatung **VT3,** 46
careful ['keəfl] vorsichtig; sorgfältig **II U6,** 80
caretaker ['keəteɪkə] Hausmeister/Hausmeisterin **I U1,** 12
carpet ['kɑ:pɪt] Teppichboden **IV U5,** 73
carrot ['kærət] Karotte, Mohrrübe **II U1,** 15
to **carry** ['kæri] tragen **I U6,** 80; befördern **III U2,** 30
to carry along [ˌkæri‿ə'lɒŋ] mitführen, mitreißen **VT4,** 64
cartoon [kɑ:'tu:n] Cartoon, Zeichentrickfilm **III U5,** 68
pencil **case** ['pensl ˌkeɪs] Federmäppchen **I U1,** 14
casino [kə'si:nəʊ] Casino **IV U4,** 57
castle ['kɑ:sl] Schloss, Burg **II U7,** 88
cat [kæt] Katze **I U2,** 26
*to **catch** [kætʃ] fangen °**II U3,** 45; fangen, erreichen **III U1,** 8
catcher ['kætʃə] Fänger/Fängerin **III U1,** 14
catering ['keɪtrɪŋ] Gastronomie, Verpflegung, Catering **VT3,** 46
cathedral [kə'θi:drl] Kathedrale, Dom **III U2,** 24
cattle *(pl. only)* ['kætl] (Rind-)Vieh **IV U4,** 58
cattle drive ['kætl ˌdraɪv] Viehtrieb **IV U4,** 58
to **cause** [kɔ:z] verursachen, hervorrufen **VT4,** 60
caution *(no pl)* ['kɔ:ʃn] Vorsicht, Warnung °**VT4,** 60
caviar ['kæviɑ:] Kaviar **IV U5,** 80
CD [ˌsi:'di:] CD **I U5,** 69
CD player [ˌsi:'di: ˌpleɪə] CD-Player **II U4,** 56
cell phone *(AE)* ['sel ˌfəʊn] Handy, Mobiltelefon **IV U3,** 42
Celsius (C) ['selsiəs] Celsius **II U6,** 78

cent [sent] Cent *(Währung)* **IV U1,** 13
centimetre (cm) ['sentɪˌmiːtə] Zentimeter **VT4,** 61
centre ['sentə] Zentrum, Mittelpunkt **I LUC,** 52
dive centre ['daɪv ˌsentə] Tauchzentrum **VT1,** 14
information centre [ɪnfə'meɪʃn ˌsentə] Informationszentrum **I LUC,** 52
century ['sentʃri] Jahrhundert **III U1,** 8
ceremony ['serɪməni] Zeremonie **IV U5,** 73
certainly ['sɜːtnli] sicher, gewiss **III U5,** 72
certificate [sə'tɪfɪkət] Zertifikat, Bescheinigung, Urkunde, Zeugnis **VT1,** 14
Advanced Lifesaving Certificate [əd'vɑːnst 'laɪfˌseɪvɪŋ sə'tɪfɪkət] Rettungsschwimmabzeichen °**VT1,** 15
Beginners Diving Certificate [bɪ'gɪnəz daɪvɪŋ sə'tɪfɪkət] Grundtauchschein °**VT1,** 15
chain [tʃeɪn] Kette **II U3,** 40
chair [tʃeə] Stuhl **I U1,** 18
champagne [ʃæm'peɪn] Champagner **IV U5,** 80
*to take your **chance** [ˌteɪk jɔː 'tʃɑːns] etw. wagen, etw. riskieren **III U3,** 47
change [tʃeɪndʒ] Wechselgeld; Änderung **II U4,** 55
change of place [ˌtʃeɪndʒ‿əv 'pleɪs] Ortswechsel °**III U4,** 55
to **change** [tʃeɪndʒ] (ver)ändern, tauschen, wechseln **II U3,** 42; umsteigen **III U2,** 24
channel ['tʃænl] Kanal; Programm **III U3,** 39
chant [tʃɑːnt] Sprechgesang °**IV U2,** 29
to **chant** [tʃɑːnt] rhythmisch rufen; singen **IV U2,** 23
chaos ['keɪɒs] Chaos, Durcheinander **IV U4,** 61
chaperon ['ʃæprəʊn] Begleitperson, Anstandswauwau **IV U5,** 80
character ['kærəktə] Charakter; Figur °**IV U2,** 31
charity ['tʃærɪti] Wohltätigkeit, Wohltätigkeitsverein **I U7,** 90
chart [tʃɑːt] Schaubild, Diagramm °**II U4,** 51
charts *(pl)* [tʃɑːts] Charts, Hitparade **III U5,** 70
chat [tʃæt] Geplauder, Unterhaltung **I U2,** 33
chat room ['tʃæt rʊm] Chatroom *(Internetforum, wo man sich online unterhalten kann)* **IV U5,** 76
to **chat** [tʃæt] sich unterhalten **I U2,** 33
cheap [tʃiːp] billig **I U5,** 68
check [tʃek] (Über-)Prüfung, Kontrolle **VT2,** 32
to **check** [tʃek] überprüfen **I U6,** 82; untersuchen; kontrollieren **II U3,** 40
to check out [tʃek‿'aʊt] sich etwas ansehen **IV U5,** 76
cheerleader ['tʃɪəˌliːdə] Cheerleader *(Mädchen, das in einer Gruppe eine Sportmannschaft anfeuert)* **IV U2,** 22
cheese [tʃiːz] Käse **I U5,** 68
cream cheese [ˌkriːm 'tʃiːz] Frischkäse **IV U1,** 12
chef [ʃef] Koch/Köchin, Küchenchef/-chefin **VT2,** 32; **VT3,** 46
chemical ['kemɪkl] Chemikalie; chemisch **VT4,** 58
cherry ['tʃeri] Kirsche **IV U1,** 12
chicken ['tʃɪkɪn] Huhn, Hähnchen **II U4,** 49
child, children *(pl)* [tʃaɪld; 'tʃɪldrɪn] Kind **I U2,** 26
only child ['əʊnli ˌtʃaɪld] Einzelkind **I U2,** 26
to **chill out** [tʃɪl‿'aʊt] sich entspannen, chillen **IV U5,** 76
Chinese [tʃaɪ'niːz] chinesisch **II U4,** 49
chip *(AE)* [tʃɪp] Chip °**IV U4,** 63
chips *(pl)* [tʃɪps] Pommes frites **II U1,** 14
chocolate ['tʃɒklət] Schokolade **I U1,** 18
choice [tʃɔɪs] Auswahl, Wahl **IV U3,** 46
to **choke** [tʃəʊk] ersticken, keine Luft bekommen **III U4,** 60
*to **choose** [tʃuːz] wählen, auswählen **I U4,** 54
chorus ['kɔːrəs] Refrain **IV U5,** 80
church [tʃɜːtʃ] Kirche **I LUC,** 52
cigarette [ˌsɪgr'et] Zigarette **IV U2,** 25
cinema ['sɪnəmə] Kino **II U1,** 18
circle ['sɜːkl] Kreis **III U3,** 39
citizen ['sɪtɪzn] (Staats-)Bürger/ Bürgerin **VT3,** 44
city ['sɪti] Stadt, Großstadt **II U7,** 89
capital city [ˌkæpɪtl 'sɪti] Hauptstadt °**III U2,** 27
civil ['sɪvl] bürgerlich, zivil, Bürger-, Staats- **VT3,** 45
civil rights *(pl)* [ˌsɪvl 'raɪts] Bürgerrechte **VT3,** 45
Civil Rights Movement (CRM) [ˌsɪvl 'raɪts ˌmuːvmənt] Bürgerrechtsbewegung **VT3,** 44
to **claim** [kleɪm] beanspruchen, (ein)fordern, behaupten **VT1,** 10
to **clap** [klæp] klatschen **I U1,** 15
class [klɑːs] Schulklasse, Klasse **I U1,** 16; Kurs, Unterricht **II U1,** 18
classic ['klæsɪk] klassisch **VT4,** 62
classroom ['klɑːsrʊm] Klassenzimmer **I U1,** 16
if-**clause** ['ɪfklɔːz] if-Satz °**IV U4,** 59
to **clean** [kliːn] säubern, reinigen **II U3,** 40
cleaning station ['kliːnɪŋ ˌsteɪʃn] Putzerstation **VT4,** 64
clean [kliːn] sauber **III U3,** 40
cleaner ['kliːnə] Raumpfleger/ Raumpflegerin, Putzkraft **IV U4,** 63
clear [klɪə] klar **II U7,** 90
to **click** [klɪk] klicken **II U5,** 64
cliff [klɪf] Klippe **II U7,** 93
climate ['klaɪmət] Klima **VT4,** 58
to **climb** ['klaɪm] klettern, steigen, besteigen **II U2,** 30
clock [klɒk] Uhr **I U4,** 54
alarm clock [ə'lɑːm ˌklɒk] Wecker **I U5,** 75
o'clock [ə'klɒk] Uhr *(Zeitangabe)* **I U3,** 40
to **close** [kləʊz] schließen, zumachen **I LUC,** 53
close [kləʊs] nahe **VT2,** 32
closed [kləʊzd] zu, geschlossen °**I U2,** 32
closing ['kləʊzɪŋ] (Ab-)Schluss, Schließung **VT1,** 14
clothes *(pl)* [kləʊðz] Kleider, Kleidung **II U2,** 23
cloud [klaʊd] Wolke **II U7,** 94
cloudy ['klaʊdi] wolkig **II U6,** 78
club [klʌb] Klub, Verein, Arbeitsgemeinschaft **I LUB,** 39
clue [kluː] Hinweis **II U1,** 13
to have no clue [ˌhæv nəʊ 'kluː] keine Ahnung haben **IV U5,** 80
clumsy ['klʌmzi] ungeschickt, tollpatschig **IV U2,** 31
Hey, clumsy! ['klʌmzi] He, du Tollpatsch! **IV U2,** 31
cluster ['klʌstə] Cluster °**IV U2,** 23
coach [kəʊtʃ] Reisebus **III U2,** 26

coast [kəʊst] Küste **II U7,** 88
coastline ['kəʊstˌlaɪn] Küstenlinie **III U3,** 38
coat [kəʊt] Mantel **II U7,** 90
cocoa ['kəʊkəʊ] Kakao **VT4,** 58
code [kəʊd] Verschlüsselung, Code **IV U3,** 46
coffee ['kɒfi:] Kaffee **III U2,** 26
coke [kəʊk] Cola **II U4,** 49
cold [kəʊld] kalt **I U4,** 62
to be cold [bi: 'kəʊld] frieren **II U2,** 24
collage [kɒl'ɑ:ʒ] Collage °**IV U5,** 81
to **collect** [kə'lekt] sammeln **I LUB,** 38; abholen **II U5,** 71
college ['kɒlɪdʒ] College; Institut **III U4,** 57
colony ['kɒləni] Kolonie **VT1,** 10
colored *(AE)* ['kʌləd] bunt, farbig; Farbiger/Farbige **VT3,** 44
colorful *(AE)* ['kʌləfl] bunt, farbig **IV U2,** 23
colour ['kʌlə] Farbe **I LUA,** 24
*to **come** [kʌm] kommen **I U2,** 33
Come on. [kʌm‿'ɒn] Komm./Kommt. **I U2,** 35
to come down [kʌm 'daʊn] herunterkommen, sich legen **III U1,** 16
to come in [kʌm‿'ɪn] hereinkommen **I U3,** 48
to come over [kʌm‿'əʊvə] herüberkommen **I U2,** 27
to come true [kʌm 'tru:] wahr werden °**II U7,** 91
comedy ['kɒmədi] Komödie **III U5,** 68
comfortable ['kʌmpftəbl] komfortabel, bequem **IV U4,** 61
comic ['kɒmɪk] Comic(heft) **I LUB,** 38
communication [kəˌmju:nɪ'keɪʃn] Kommunikation, Verständigung **VT4,** 59
community [kə'mju:nəti] Gemeinde; Gemeinschaft **VT4,** 62
company ['kʌmpəni] Gesellschaft, Firma; Kompanie **III U2,** 30
comparative [kəm'pærətɪv] Komparativ **II U4,** 50
to **compare** [kəm'peə] vergleichen **III U4,** 57
competition [ˌkɒmpə'tɪʃn] Wettbewerb, Turnier **VT2,** 30
to **complete** [kəm'pli:t] ausfüllen, erledigen, fertigstellen, vervollständigen **VT2,** 29
complete [kəm'pli:t] vollständig °**III U1,** 11
comprehensive school [kɒmprɪ'hensɪv ˌsku:l] Gesamtschule **III U4,** 56
compulsory [kəm'pʌlsri] obligatorisch, zwingend **III U4,** 57
computer [ˌkəm'pju:tə] Computer **I LUA,** 25
concert ['kɒnsət] Konzert **II U2,** 23
condition [kən'dɪʃn] Kondition; Bedingung **VT4,** 62
conqueror ['kɒŋkrə] Eroberer °**III U2,** 28
contact ['kɒntækt] Kontakt, Verbindung °**VT1,** 14
to **contact** ['kɒntækt] kontaktieren, sich in Verbindung setzen **IV U2,** 25
content ['kɒntent] Inhalt **III U4,** 53
continent ['kɒntɪnənt] Kontinent, Erdteil **VT1,** 10
to **continue** [kən'tɪnju:] fortfahren, andauern, weitergehen, weitermachen **VT4,** 61
contract ['kɒntrækt] Vertrag, Abkommen **VT1,** 14
remote **control** [rɪˌməʊt kən'trəʊl] Fernbedienung, Fernsteuerung **IV U3,** 41
to **control** [kən'trəʊl] kontrollieren, beherrschen **IV U3,** 42
conversation [ˌkɒnvə'seɪʃn] Unterhaltung °**III U3,** 45
convict ['kɒnvɪkt] Sträfling **VT1,** 10
cook [kʊk] Koch/Köchin **III U5,** 70
to **cook** [kʊk] kochen **IV U3,** 44
cooking ['kʊkɪŋ] Kochen, Koch- **I U3,** 40
cool [ku:l] cool, prima **I U1,** 20; kühl **IV U1,** 16
co-operative [kəʊ'ɒprətɪv] Kooperative **VT4,** 62
cop *(AE)* [kɒp] Polizist/Polizistin **IV U1,** 16
to **copy** ['kɒpi] abschreiben, kopieren **II U5,** 63
Cor! [kɔ:] Mann! **III U1,** 12
coral ['kɒrəl] Koralle; Korallen- **VT4,** 61
corner ['kɔ:nə] Ecke **III U2,** 26
cornflakes ['kɔ:nfleɪks] Cornflakes **I U5,** 68
Cornish ['kɔ:nɪʃ] kornisch; aus Cornwall **III U3,** 42
to **correct** [kə'rekt] korrigieren, verbessern °**I LUB,** 38
correct [kə'rekt] richtig, korrekt **II U1,** 10
corridor ['kɒrɪdɔ:] Gang, Flur, Korridor **I U7,** 96
*to **cost** [kɒst] kosten **IV U3,** 42
cottage ['kɒtɪdʒ] kleines Landhaus, Ferienhaus **III U4,** 54
couch potato ['kaʊtʃ pəˌteɪtəʊ] Fernsehglotzer/Fernsehglotzerin, Couchpotato **III U5,** 75
***could** [kʊd] konnte/konnten **II U4,** 52; könnte/könnten **III U1,** 12
council ['kaʊnsl] Gemeinderat **VT2,** 30
countdown ['kaʊntdaʊn] Countdown **III U5,** 70
country ['kʌntri] Countrymusik **IV U5,** 73
country, countries *(pl)* ['kʌntri; 'kʌntriz] Land **I U2,** 29
in the country [ˌɪn ðə 'kʌntri] auf dem Land **I U6,** 78
couple ['kʌpl] Paar **IV U3,** 48
a couple of [ə 'kʌpl‿əv] ein paar, einige **VT4,** 65
courier ['kʊriə] Kurier **III U2,** 30
course [kɔ:s] Gang *(Menü)* **II U4,** 49; Kurs **VT1,** 14; **VT2,** 32; **VT3,** 46
of course [əv 'kɔ:s] natürlich, selbstverständlich **I U1,** 19
court [kɔ:t] Spielfeld **III U1,** 10
cousin ['kʌzn] Cousin/Cousine **I U2,** 28
cover ['kʌvə] Einband, Titelseite **II U5,** 64
cow [kaʊ] Kuh **I U6,** 82
cowboy ['kaʊbɔɪ] Rinderhirte, Cowboy **IV U4,** 57
at the **crack of dawn** [ˌkræk‿əv 'dɔ:n] im Morgengrauen **III U2,** 30
crash [kræʃ] Unfall, Aufprall; Absturz **VT4,** 64
Crash! [kræʃ] Bumm!, Krach! **III U3,** 47
to **crawl** [krɔ:l] kriechen, krabbeln; schleichen **III U3,** 47
crazy ['kreɪzi] verrückt **I U7,** 96
to drive crazy [draɪv 'kreɪzi] verrückt machen **II U5,** 71
to **creak** [kri:k] knarren, quietschen **II U7,** 94
cream [kri:m] Creme, Sahne **IV U1,** 12
cream cheese [ˌkri:m 'tʃi:z] Frischkäse **IV U1,** 12
ice-cream [aɪs 'kri:m] Eiscreme **I U7,** 92
creature ['kri:tʃə] Kreatur, Geschöpf, Lebewesen **VT1,** 10; **VT3,** 47; **VT4,** 65
crew [kru:] Crew, Besatzung, Mannschaft **III U5,** 75

cricket ['krɪkɪt] Kricket **I U7,** 92
crime [kraɪm] Verbrechen; Kriminalität **VT2,** 28
criminal ['krɪmɪnl] Krimineller/Kriminelle, Verbrecher/Verbrecherin; kriminell **VT4,** 60
crisp [krɪsp] Kartoffelchip **I U1,** 18
crocodile ['krɒkədaɪl] Krokodil **VT1,** 10
to **cross** [krɒs] überqueren, kreuzen **IV U4,** 64
crossword (puzzle) ['krɒswɜːd 'pʌzl] Kreuzworträtsel °**I U5,** 71
crowd [kraʊd] Menschenmenge **III U1,** 17
crown [kraʊn] Krone **III U2,** 22
cruise [kruːz] Kreuzfahrt **III U3,** 39
crunchy ['krʌntʃi] knusprig **VT4,** 63
cry [kraɪ] Schrei **III U5,** 74
to **cry** [kraɪ] weinen; schreien, rufen **II U3,** 36
cup [kʌp] Pokal; Tasse, Kelch **III U1,** 13
cupboard ['kʌbəd] Küchenschrank, Schrank **I U1,** 18
cupcake ['kʌpkeɪk] rundes Küchlein **IV U1,** 12
current ['kʌrnt] Strömung; Strom **VT4,** 64
up current ['ʌp ˌkʌrnt] Strömung, die nach oben zieht **VT4,** 64
curriculum [kə'rɪkjələm] Lehrplan, Stundenplan **IV U2,** 22
curriculum vitae (CV) [kə'rɪkjələm 'viːtaɪ] Lebenslauf **VT1,** 15
curry ['kʌri] Curry *(Gewürz oder Gericht)* **II U4,** 49
curtain ['kɜːtn] Vorhang **IV U3,** 44
curve [kɜːv] Kurve **III U4,** 60
customer ['kʌstəmə] Kunde/Kundin **III U2,** 30
customs *(pl)* ['kʌstəmz] Zoll **II U7,** 90
*to **cut** [kʌt] (ab)schneiden **VT1,** 10
to cut down [kʌt 'daʊn] abholzen, fällen **VT1,** 10
cute [kjuːt] niedlich, süß **VT1,** 10

D

dad [dæd] Papa, Vati **I LUA,** 25
daily ['deɪli] täglich **III U5,** 68
dairy ['deəri] Molkerei **III U2,** 30
to **damage** ['dæmɪdʒ] beschädigen **VT1,** 10
damn [dæm] verdammt **IV U5,** 80
dance [dɑːnts] Tanz **III U4,** 63
dance floor ['dɑːnts flɔː] Tanzfläche **IV U2,** 31
square dance ['skweə ˌdɑːnts] Square Dance **IV U4,** 58
to **dance** [dɑːnts] tanzen **I U3,** 40
dancehall ['dɑːntshɔːl] Dancehall *(Musikrichtung)* **IV U5,** 73
dancing ['dɑːntsɪŋ] Tanzen **IV U2,** 23
ballroom dancing [ˌbɔːlrʊm 'dɑːntsɪŋ] Gesellschaftstanz **IV U2,** 23
danger ['deɪndʒə] Gefahr **VT4,** 64
dangerous ['deɪndʒrəs] gefährlich **II U4,** 56
Danish ['deɪnɪʃ] dänisch; *hier:* Plundergebäck **IV U1,** 12
to **dare** [deə] wagen, riskieren **IV U2,** 29
dark ['dɑːk] Dunkelheit, Finsternis **III U3,** 47
dark [dɑːk] dunkel **I U2,** 34
date [deɪt] Datum **I U5,** 70; Verabredung **IV U2,** 26
to **date** [deɪt] sich verabreden **IV U2,** 24
daughter ['dɔːtə] Tochter **IV U5,** 80
dawn [dɔːn] Morgendämmerung, Tagesanbruch **III U2,** 30
at the crack of dawn [ˌkræk‿əv 'dɔːn] im Morgengrauen **III U2,** 30
day [deɪ] Tag **I LUB,** 39
Have a nice day. [ˌhæv‿ə naɪs 'deɪ] Einen schönen Tag (noch). **II U4,** 55
day travel card [ˌdeɪ 'trævl ˌkɑːd] Tagesfahrkarte **III U2,** 27
one day [wʌn 'deɪ] eines Tages **II U3,** 36
sports day ['spɔːts deɪ] Sportfest **I U7,** 90
to have a day off [ˌhæv‿ə 'deɪ‿ɒf] einen Tag frei haben **VT3,** 46
dead [ded] tot **III U5,** 74; *hier:* leer **IV U3,** 45
deadly ['dedli] tödlich, tod- **VT1,** 12; °**VT4,** 64
deal [diːl] Handel; Abmachung, Übereinkunft **VT4,** 62
dear [dɪə] Schatz *(Anrede)* **III U4,** 60
Oh dear! [əʊ 'dɪə] Oje! **III U5,** 73
dear [dɪə] lieb **I U3,** 44
Dear ... [dɪə] Liebe ... *(Anrede in Briefen)* **II U3,** 36
death [deθ] Tod, Todesfall **VT1,** 10;
December [dɪ'sembə] Dezember **I U5,** 70
to **decide** [dɪ'saɪd] entscheiden **II U5,** 64
decompression [ˌdiːkəm'preʃn] Dekompression, Druckverminderung **VT4,** 65
decoration [ˌdek'reɪʃn] Dekoration **IV U1,** 14
deep [diːp] tief **IV U4,** 58
definition [ˌdefɪ'nɪʃn] Definition **II U1,** 20
to **defuse** [ˌdiː'fjuːz] entschärfen **IV U3,** 41
degree (°) [dɪ'griː] Grad **II U6,** 78
delayed [dɪ'leɪd] verspätet, verzögert **IV U4,** 61
to **delete** [dɪ'liːt] löschen *(Text)* **II U5,** 63
deli *(AE)* ['deli] Imbissstube, Deli **IV U1,** 12
to **deliver** [dɪ'lɪvə] (aus)liefern **III U2,** 30
demo ['deməʊ] Demonstration, Demo; Darstellung **VT3,** 42
dentist ['dentɪst] Zahnarzt/Zahnärztin **IV U3,** 48
department store [dɪ'pɑːtmənt stɔː] Kaufhaus **I LUC,** 52
departure [dɪ'pɑːtʃə] Abflug, Abreise **II U7,** 90
to **describe** [dɪ'skraɪb] beschreiben **IV U4,** 61
description [dɪ'skrɪpʃn] Beschreibung °**III U1,** 15
to **deserve** [dɪ'zɜːv] verdienen **IV U5,** 80
to **design** [dɪ'zaɪn] entwerfen; zeichnen °**VT4,** 63
designer [dɪ'zaɪnə] Designer/Designerin **IV U5,** 72
desk [desk] Schreibtisch **I U1,** 18; Schalter **II U7,** 90
dessert [dɪ'zɜːt] Dessert, Nachtisch **II U4,** 49
to **destroy** [dɪ'strɔɪ] zerstören **III U2,** 28
detail ['diːteɪl] Detail, Einzelheit °**VT1,** 14
detective [dɪ'tektɪv] Detektiv/Detektivin **II U2,** 30
detective story [dɪ'tektɪv ˌstɔːri] Krimi **III U5,** 68
store detective ['stɔː dɪˌtektɪv] Kaufhausdetektiv/Kaufhausdetektivin **II U2,** 30
dialogue ['daɪəlɒg] Dialog, Gespräch **III U2,** 29
diamond ['daɪəmənd] Diamant **III U5,** 70
diary ['daɪəri] Tagebuch, Terminkalender °**III U2,** 31
dictionary ['dɪkʃnri] Wörterbuch **III U4,** 63

to **die** [daɪ] sterben **III U5,** 77
diet [daɪət] Diät **II U4,** 52
to go on a diet [ˌgəʊ‿ɒn ə 'daɪət] eine Diät machen **II U4,** 52
difference ['dɪfrns] Unterschied **III U4,** 56
different ['dɪfrnt] anders, verschieden **I U6,** 78
difficult ['dɪfɪklt] schwierig **II U1,** 13
*to **dig up** [dɪg‿'ʌp] ausgraben **III U1,** 16
digital ['dɪdʒɪtl] digital **II U5,** 62
dime [daɪm] Zehncentstück *(Währung)* **IV U1,** 13
diner *(AE)* ['daɪnə] Imbissstube **IV U4,** 57
dining room ['daɪnɪŋ rʊm] Esszimmer, Speisesaal **I LUA,** 24
dinner ['dɪnə] Abendessen, Mittagessen **IV U4,** 61
to **direct** [dɪ'rekt] leiten, anweisen; Regie führen **IV U5,** 74
direct [dɪ'rekt] direkt **III U4,** 53
director [dɪ'rektə] Direktor/Direktorin, Regisseur/Regisseurin **III U5,** 75
dirt [dɜːt] Schmutz, Dreck **VT4,** 58
dirty ['dɜːti] schmutzig **II U1,** 10
disability [ˌdɪsə'bɪləti] Behinderung; Unfähigkeit **VT1,** 14
to **disappear** [ˌdɪsə'pɪə] verschwinden **II U6,** 83
disappointed [ˌdɪsə'pɔɪntɪd] enttäuscht **III U4,** 52
disaster [dɪ'zɑːstə] Desaster, Katastrophe **III U4,** 54
disco ['dɪskəʊ] Disko **I U5,** 74
to **discover** [dɪ'skʌvə] entdecken **IV U4,** 64
discrimination [dɪˌskrɪmɪ'neɪʃn] Diskriminierung; Unterscheidung **VT3,** 41
to **discuss** [dɪ'skʌs] diskutieren °**III U1,** 14
dislikes *(pl)* [dɪ'slaɪks] Abneigungen °**VT2,** 33
to **display** [dɪ'spleɪ] ausstellen, (an)zeigen °**VT1,** 13
disrespect [ˌdɪsrɪ'spekt] Respektlosigkeit, Verachtung **IV U5,** 76
to **diss** *(slang)* [dɪs] beleidigen; schneiden **IV U5,** 76
distance ['dɪstns] Distanz, Entfernung **III U3,** 42
to **disturb** [dɪ'stɜːb] stören, belästigen **VT1,** 12

dive [daɪv] Tauch-; Tauchgang **VT4,** 64
dive centre ['daɪv ˌsentə] Tauchzentrum **VT1,** 14
to **dive** [daɪv] tauchen **III U3,** 41
diver ['daɪvə] Taucher/Taucherin **VT1,** 9; **VT4,** 65
divine [dɪ'vaɪn] göttlich °**VT4,** 62
diving ['daɪvɪŋ] Tauch-, Tauchen **VT1,** 14; **VT4,** 64
divorced from [dɪ'vɔːst frɒm] geschieden von **I U2,** 28
dizzy ['dɪzi] schwindlig **IV U1,** 16
DJ [ˌdiː'dʒeɪ] DJ **I U2,** 33
*to **do** [duː] machen, tun **I U1,** 15
to do sports [duː 'spɔːts] Sport treiben **I U7,** 92
doctor ['dɒktə] Arzt/Ärztin **II U3,** 40
to see a doctor [siː‿ə 'dɒktə] zum Arzt gehen **II U4,** 52
docu soap ['dɒkju ˌsəʊp] Dokusoap **III U5,** 68
documentary [ˌdɒkjə'mentri] Dokumentarfilm **III U5,** 68
dog [dɒg] Hund **I U2,** 27
dog-tired [ˌdɒg 'taɪəd] hundemüde **I U3,** 49
to walk the dog [wɔːk ðə 'dɒg] mit dem Hund spazieren gehen **I U3,** 42
doll [dɒl] Puppe °**IV U3,** 47
dollar ['dɒlə] Dollar *(Währung)* **IV U1,** 12
domino ['dɒmɪnəʊ] Dominospiel °**II U2,** 26
door [dɔː] Tür **I U1,** 18
next door [ˌnekst 'dɔː] nebenan **III U1,** 16
doorbell ['dɔːbel] Türklingel **II U5,** 66
doorstep ['dɔːstep] Türstufe **III U1,** 16
dope *(slang)* [dəʊp] *hier:* toll °**IV U5,** 80
dot [dɒt] Punkt, Pünktchen **VT4,** 66
double ['dʌbl] Doppelgänger; das Doppelte **I U7,** 97
down [daʊn] (nach) unten, herunter, hinunter, nieder **II U2,** 30; senkrecht *(im Kreuzworträtsel)* °**II U3,** 42
Down Under [ˌdaʊn‿'ʌndə] Down Under *(Spitzname für Australien)*; in Australien **VT1,** 10
Go down .... ['gəʊ daʊn] Geh ... entlang. **I LUC,** 53
to come down [kʌm 'daʊn] herunterkommen, sich legen **III U1,** 16
to go down [gəʊ 'daʊn] hinuntergehen, entlanggehen **II U2,** 30

to lie down [laɪ 'daʊn] (sich) hinlegen, niederlegen **III U3,** 46
to sit down [sɪt 'daʊn] sich (hin)setzen **I U1,** 19
to **download** [ˌdaʊn'ləʊd] herunterladen **II U5,** 63
downstairs [daʊn'steəz] unten, im unteren Stock **I U2,** 27
dragon ['drægn] Drache **IV U1,** 14
drama ['drɑːmə] Theater, Drama **I U3,** 40
dramatic [drə'mætɪk] dramatisch **III U5,** 68
It's a **draw.** [ˌɪts‿ə 'drɔː] Es steht unentschieden. **III U1,** 12
*to **draw** [drɔː] zeichnen **I LUB,** 38
dream [driːm] Traum **I LUA,** 25
to **dream** [driːm] träumen **IV U5,** 80
dress [dres] Kleid, Kleidung **IV U2,** 23
evening dress ['iːvnɪŋ ˌdres] Abendkleid **IV U5,** 72
to **dress** [dres] sich anziehen **I U3,** 44
drill [drɪl] Bohrer, Bohrmaschine **IV U1,** 17
drink [drɪŋk] Getränk **I U7,** 95
*to **drink** [drɪŋk] trinken **I U5,** 75
to **drip** [drɪp] tropfen (lassen), tröpfeln **IV U3,** 42
cattle **drive** ['kætl ˌdraɪv] Viehtrieb **IV U4,** 58
*to **drive** [draɪv] fahren **I U6,** 86
to drive crazy [draɪv 'kreɪzi] verrückt machen **II U5,** 71
driving licence *(BE)* ['draɪvɪŋ ˌlaɪsnts] Führerschein **VT1,** 14
driver ['draɪvə] Fahrer/Fahrerin **I U4,** 54
driver's license (AE) ['draɪvəz ˌlaɪsnts] Führerschein **IV U4,** 64
to **drop** [drɒp] fallen, fallen lassen **II U1,** 18; sinken *(beim Tauchen)* **VT4,** 64
drug [drʌg] Droge; Medikament *(AE)* **IV U2,** 25
drummer ['drʌmə] Schlagzeuger/Schlagzeugerin **IV U5,** 76
drums *(pl)* [drʌmz] Schlagzeug **I U2,** 26
to **dry** [draɪ] trocknen **IV U3,** 42
dump [dʌmp] Dreckloch, Müllkippe **II U7,** 88
to **dump sth** [dʌmp] abladen, auskippen, verklappen **VT4,** 60
during *(+ noun)* ['djʊərɪŋ] während *(+ Nomen)* **III U1,** 8
dusty ['dʌsti] staubig **IV U4,** 58

Dutch [dʌtʃ] niederländisch; Niederländer/Niederländerinnen **IV U1,** 10
DVD [di:vi:'di:] DVD **II U5,** 62
DVD player [ˌdi:vi:'di: ˌpleɪə] DVD-Player **II U5,** 62
to **dye** [daɪ] färben **II U2,** 28

E

each [i:tʃ] jede/jeder/jedes **III U1,** 8; je, jeweils **III U4,** 53
each other [ˌi:tʃ‿'ʌðə] sich gegenseitig **II U1,** 19
ear [ɪə] Ohr **II U3,** 40
early ['ɜ:li] früh **I U3,** 46
to **earn** [ɜ:n] verdienen **V T3,** 46
earth [ɜ:θ] Erde **IV U3,** 40
east [i:st] Osten **I U4,** 54
easy ['i:zi] einfach, leicht **I U1,** 20
*to **eat** [i:t] essen, fressen **I U3,** 44
to **echo** ['ekəʊ] widerhallen **III U5,** 78
eco [i:kəʊ] Öko-, Umwelt- **V T4,** 61
edge [edʒ] Rand, Kante **IV U5,** 78
education [edʒʊ'keɪʃn] Erziehung, Bildung **II U1,** 10
Physical Education (PE) [ˌfɪzɪkl‿edʒʊ'keɪʃn] Sport *(Schulfach)* **II U1,** 10
Religious Education (RE) [rɪˌlɪdʒəs‿edʒʊ'keɪʃn] Religionsunterricht **II U1,** 12
egg [eg] Ei **I U5,** 68
not … **either** [ˌnɒt … 'aɪðə] auch nicht **IV U3,** 48
elbow ['elbəʊ] Ellbogen **II U3,** 41
electric [ɪ'lektrɪk] elektrisch **IV U1,** 17
electricity [ˌelɪk'trɪsəti] Elektrizität, Strom **IV U3,** 42
elementary school *(AE)* [elɪ'mentri ˌsku:l] Grundschule **IV U2,** 28
elephant ['elɪfənt] Elefant **I U7,** 96
else [els] sonst, noch **I U5,** 66
e-mail ['i:meɪl] E-Mail **I U3,** 44
to **e-mail** ['i:meɪl] E-Mail schreiben **IV U5,** 76; mailen, per E-Mail schicken **V T2,** 29
embarrassing [ɪm'bærəsɪŋ] peinlich **II U2,** 26
emergency [ɪ'mɜ:dʒnsi] Notfall, Notlage **III U5,** 70
to **emigrate** ['emɪgreɪt] emigrieren, auswandern **IV U1,** 10
employee [ɪm'plɔɪi:] Angestellte/Angestellter, Mitarbeiter/Mitarbeiterin **V T3,** 46
employer [ɪm'plɔɪə] Arbeitgeber/Arbeitgeberin **V T3,** 46
empty ['empti] leer **II U1,** 18
end [end] Ende, Schluss **II U6,** 84
in the end [ɪn ði:‿'end] schließlich, zum Schluss **II U6,** 80
to **end** [end] enden **I U5,** 76; beenden, abschließen **IV U2,** 26
to end in ['end‿ɪn] enden auf °**II U7,** 90
to end up [ˌend‿'ʌp] enden, landen **IV U4,** 64
ending ['endɪŋ] Ende, Schluss *(einer Geschichte)* °**II U1,** 19
enemy ['enəmi] Feind/Feindin **II U3,** 43
energy ['enədʒi] Energie; Kraft **V T4,** 58
engine ['endʒɪn] Motor **IV U1,** 16
English ['ɪŋglɪʃ] englisch **I U1,** 11; Engländer/Engländerinnen **IV U1,** 10
to **enjoy** [ɪn'dʒɔɪ] sich erfreuen, genießen **II U6,** 80
enough [ɪ'nʌf] genug, genügend **III U1,** 14
to **enter** ['entə] sich beteiligen; eintreten, betreten **III U4,** 53
enterprising ['entəpraɪzɪŋ] geschäftstüchtig, unternehmungslustig **V T3,** 43
entry ['entri] Eintrag, Eintragung **V T4,** 66
envelope ['envələʊp] Briefumschlag, Umschlag **II U7,** 90
environment [ɪn'vaɪərnmənt] Umwelt, Umgebung **II U6,** 74
environmental [ɪnˌvaɪərn'mentl] Umwelt- die Umwelt betreffend, umweltbedingt **V T4,** 60
equal ['i:kwəl] gleich(wertig), Gleich- **V T3,** 40
equipment [ɪ'kwɪpmənt] Ausrüstung, Ausstattung **IV U3,** 41
er [ɜ:] äh °**I U1,** 12
erm [ɜ:m] äh °**II U3,** 38
to **escape** [ɪ'skeɪp] flüchten, entkommen **II U6,** 78
had escaped [ˌhæd‿ɪ'skeɪpt] waren geflüchtet, waren entkommen °**V T1,** 10
especially [ɪ'speʃli] besonders **III U2,** 30
etc. [ɪt'setrə] usw., et cetera **II U1,** 10
eucalyptus [ˌju:k'lɪptəs] Eukalyptus **V T1,** 10
euro ['jʊərəʊ] Euro *(Währung)* **I U5,** 73
European [ˌjʊərə'pi:ən] europäisch °**II U6,** 85
even ['i:vn] selbst, sogar **I U7,** 90
not even [nɒt‿'i:vn] nicht einmal **III U4,** 54
evening ['i:vnɪŋ] Abend **I U3,** 47
evening dress ['i:vnɪŋ ˌdres] Abendkleid **IV U5,** 72
in the evening [ˌɪn ði: 'i:vnɪŋ] abends, am Abend **I U3,** 47
that evening [ˌdæt‿'i:vnɪŋ] an diesem Abend **II U1,** 19
this evening [ðɪs 'i:vnɪŋ] heute Abend **III U3,** 46
event [ɪ'vent] Veranstaltung, Ereignis **I U7,** 90
ever ['evə] jemals **II U5,** 66
every ['evri] jede/jeder/jedes **I U3,** 40
everybody ['evribɒdi] jeder; alle **IV U2,** 23
everyday ['evrideɪ] alltäglich °**III U1,** 12
everything ['evriθɪŋ] alles **II U4,** 50
everywhere ['evriweə] überall **II U5,** 71
evidence ['evɪdnts] Beweis °**II U6,** 83
exact [ɪg'zækt] genau, exakt **IV U3,** 46
exam [ɪg'zæm] Examen, Prüfung **III U4,** 57
example ['ɪgzɑ:mpl] Beispiel °**I U1,** 13
for example [fər‿ɪg'zɑ:mpl] zum Beispiel **III U4,** 53
except [ɪk'sept] außer **IV U5,** 76
exchange [ɪks'tʃeɪndʒ] Austausch, Tausch **I U7,** 94
excited [ɪk'saɪtɪd] aufgeregt **I U5,** 74
exciting [ɪk'saɪtɪŋ] spannend, aufregend **II U4,** 51
Excuse me! [ɪk'skju:z mi] Entschuldigung! **I U3,** 42
exercise ['eksəsaɪz] Übung, Aufgabe **I U1,** 19
exercise book ['eksəsaɪz ˌbʊk] Heft, Übungsheft **I U1,** 14
to **exercise** ['eksəsaɪz] üben, Sport treiben **II U4,** 52
to **exist** [ɪg'zɪst] existieren **IV U3,** 41
exit ['eksɪt] Ausgang, Abgang, Ausfahrt **IV U4,** 61
to **expect** [ɪk'spekt] erwarten **III U2,** 30
expensive [ɪk'spensɪv] teuer **I U5,** 68
experience [ɪk'spɪəriənts] Erfahrung, Erlebnis **V T1,** 14; **V T2,** 29; **V T3,** 43; **V T4,** 64

experiment [ɪk'sperɪmənt] Experiment, Versuch **II U1,** 13
expert ['ekspɜ:t] Experte/Expertin °**IV U3,** 49
to **explain** [ɪk'spleɪn] erklären, erläutern **II U5,** 64
to **explore** [ɪk'splɔ:] erkunden, erforschen **IV U3,** 41
export ['ekspɔ:t] Export; Ausfuhr **V T4,** 62
to **export** [ɪk'spɔ:t] exportieren, ausführen **V T4,** 62
extra ['ekstrə] zusätzlich; Zusatz **III U4,** 58
eye [aɪ] Auge **I U2,** 35
eyebrow ['aɪbraʊ] Augenbraue **III U4,** 52

F

fabulous ['fæbjələs] fabelhaft, fantastisch **IV U4,** 57
face [feɪs] Gesicht **I U3,** 48
fact [fækt] Fakt, Tatsache **II U2,** 32
fact box ['fækt bɒks] Infokasten **III U1,** 8
fact file (on) ['fækt faɪl] Ordner mit Informationen (über) **III U2,** 27
in fact [ɪn 'fækt] in der Tat, genau genommen **II U7,** 94
factory ['fæktri] Fabrik, Werk **IV U3,** 48
factual ['fæktʃʊəl] Sach-, sachlich °**IV U1,** 14
Fahrenheit (F) ['færnhaɪt] Fahrenheit **IV U1,** 16
to **faint** [feɪnt] ohnmächtig werden **IV U1,** 17
fair [feə] Messe, Jahrmarkt **I U7,** 90
summer fair ['sʌmə ˌfeə] Sommerfest **I U7,** 90
fair [feə] gerecht, fair **III U1,** 12; blond, hell **III U5,** 68
fall [fɔ:l] Fall, Sturz **V T3,** 40
*to **fall** [fɔ:l] fallen, herunterfallen, hinfallen **II U2,** 26
to fall off [fɔ:l‿'ɒf] herunterfallen **II U3,** 40
family ['fæmli] Familie **I LUA,** 25
family tree ['fæmli tri:] Familienstammbaum °**I U2,** 28
famine ['fæmɪn] Hungersnot **IV U1,** 10
famous ['feɪməs] berühmt **I U4,** 54
fan [fæn] Fan **II U5,** 66
fantastic [fæn'tæstɪk] fantastisch, großartig **I U7,** 94
FAQ (frequently asked question) ['fri:kwəntli ˌɑ:skt 'kwestʃən] FAQ (häufig gestellte Frage) °**III U4,** 56
far [fɑ:] weit **II U6,** 78
so far ['səʊ fɑ:] bis jetzt °**III U5,** 77
to go far [gəʊ 'fɑ:] weit kommen, es weit bringen **III U2,** 22
farm [fɑ:m] Bauernhof, Farm **I U6,** 78
farmer ['fɑ:mə] Bauer/Bäuerin, Landwirt/Landwirtin **I U6,** 82
farmhouse ['fɑ:mhaʊs] Bauernhaus **II U7,** 88
fashion ['fæʃn] Mode **II U6,** 82
fast [fɑ:st] schnell **II U4,** 50
fast food [ˌfɑ:st 'fu:d] Schnellimbiss °**II U4,** 50
father ['fɑ:ðə] Vater **III U3,** 46
faucet *(AE)* ['fɔ:sɪt] Wasserhahn **IV U3,** 44
favourite ['feɪvrɪt] Lieblings- **I U1,** 12
February ['februəri] Februar **I U5,** 70
*to **feed** [fi:d] füttern **I U6,** 80
to be fed up [bi: ˌfed‿'ʌp] die Nase voll haben **I U2,** 34
*to **feel** [fi:l] fühlen, sich fühlen **II U3,** 40
to feel for ['fi:l fə] tasten nach **III U3,** 46
to feel homesick [ˌfi:l 'həʊmsɪk] Heimweh haben **IV U4,** 64
to feel sick [fi:l 'sɪk] Übelkeit verspüren **II U3,** 46
to feel sorry for [fi:l 'sɒri] Mitleid haben mit, bedauern **III U1,** 16
feeling ['fi:lɪŋ] Gefühl **III U4,** 54
fence [fens] Zaun **V T3,** 41
ferry ['feri] Fähre **III U3,** 39
festival ['festɪvl] Festival, Fest **IV U1,** 14
fetish ['fetɪʃ] Fetisch °**IV U5,** 80
few [fju:] wenige **II U5,** 71
a few [ə 'fju:] einige, ein paar **II U4,** 52
fiction ['fɪkʃn] Erfindung, Fiktion **III U5,** 68
science fiction [ˌsaɪəns 'fɪkʃn] Sciencefiction **III U5,** 68
field [fi:ld] Feld, Acker **I U6,** 88
sports field ['spɔ:ts fi:ld] Sportplatz **I U7,** 92
fierce [fɪəs] bösartig **II U5,** 70
fight [faɪt] Kampf **III U1,** 16
*to **fight** [faɪt] streiten, kämpfen **III U4,** 59
fighting ['faɪtɪŋ] Kampf(-) **V T3,** 43
figure ['fɪgə] Figur, Gestalt **II U7,** 94; Zahl, Ziffer °**III U1,** 13
fact **file (on)** [ˌfækt 'faɪl] Ordner mit Informationen (über) **III U2,** 27
to **fill** [fɪl] füllen **IV U2,** 31
to fill in [fɪl‿'ɪn] ausfüllen, einsetzen **II U5,** 64
film [fɪlm] Film **II U3,** 43
to **film** [fɪlm] filmen **V T2,** 29
fin [fɪn] (Schwimm-)Flosse **V T4,** 65
final ['faɪnl] letzte/letzter/letztes **III U5,** 70
finally ['faɪnli] endlich **III U2,** 24
*to **find** [faɪnd] finden **I U3,** 48
to find out [faɪnd‿'aʊt] herausfinden **I U4,** 62
fine [faɪn] Geldbuße, Geldstrafe **III U2,** 24
fine [faɪn] gut, in Ordnung, fein, schön **I U7,** 94
finger ['fɪŋgə] Finger **II U3,** 41
to **finish** ['fɪnɪʃ] beenden, erledigen, aufhören **I U2,** 34
fire [faɪə] Feuer, Brand **I U7,** 96; Feuerstelle, Kaminfeuer **III U2,** 28
fire brigade ['faɪə brɪˌgeɪd] Feuerwehr **III U2,** 28
Where's the fire? [ˌweəz ðə 'faɪə] Wo brennt's denn? **I U7,** 96
firestorm ['faɪəstɔ:m] Feuersturm °**III U2,** 28
firework ['faɪəwɜ:k] Feuerwerkskörper, *Plural:* Feuerwerk **IV U1,** 14
firm [fɜ:m] Firma, Unternehmen, Gesellschaft **V T3,** 44
first [fɜ:st] zuerst; erster/erste/erstes **I U4,** 54
at first [ət 'fɜ:st] zuerst, zunächst **II U6,** 80
first of all [ˌfɜ:st‿ɒf‿'ɔ:l] zuerst, zuallererst, zunächst **IV U4,** 62
fish, fish *(pl)* [fɪʃ] Fisch **I U6,** 78
to **fish** [fɪʃ] fischen, angeln **I U6,** 82
fisherman, fishermen *(pl)* ['fɪʃəmən; 'fɪʃəmen] Fischer; Angler **V T4,** 64
fishing ['fɪʃɪŋ] Angeln, Fischen **I U6,** 78
*to have a **fit** [ˌhæv‿ə 'fɪt] einen Anfall bekommen, Zustände kriegen **III U4,** 60
to **fit** [fɪt] passen **II U6,** 76
fit [fɪt] fit **II U4,** 52

to fix [fɪks] manipulieren **IV U2,** 31; reparieren; befestigen, anbringen **IV U3,** 41
flag [flæg] Flagge, Fahne **I U2,** 29
flame [fleɪm] Flamme **III U2,** 28
flare [fleə] Leuchtfeuer; Lichtschein **IV U3,** 49
flash [flæʃ] Aufblinken, Blitzen **II U7,** 95
flash flood ['flæʃˌflʌd] flutartige Überschwemmung, Sintflut **II U6,** 74
to **flash** [flæʃ] blitzen, blinken **IV U1,** 16
flat [flæt] Wohnung **I U2,** 26
flat [flæt] flach, platt **IV U1,** 16
flight [flaɪt] Flug **II U2,** 23
flood [flʌd] Überschwemmung, Hochwasser **II U6,** 74
flash flood ['flæʃˌflʌd] flutartige Überschwemmung, Sintflut **II U6,** 74
floor [flɔ:] Fußboden **II U5,** 71
dance floor ['dɑ:nts flɔ:] Tanzfläche **IV U2,** 31
flossy *(slang)* ['flɒsi] aufgemotzt °**IV U5,** 80
flower ['flaʊə] Blume **I U6,** 78
*to **fly** [flaɪ] fliegen **II U7,** 88; wehen **III U3,** 40
fog [fɒg] Nebel **II U6,** 78
foggy ['fɒgi] neblig **I U6,** 79
folder ['fəʊldə] Ordner, Mappe **I U4,** 60
folk [fəʊk] Volksmusik **IV U5,** 73
folks *(Anrede)* [fəʊks] Leute **IV U1,** 16
to **follow** ['fɒləʊ] hinterhergehen, folgen, befolgen **I U7,** 96
following ['fɒləʊɪŋ] folgend/folgender/folgende/folgendes **III U4,** 57
food [fu:d] Essen, Nahrung, Lebensmittel **I U7,** 95
fast food [ˌfɑ:st 'fu:d] Schnellimbiss °**II U4,** 50
foot, feet *(pl)* [fʊt; fi:t] Fuß **I U4,** 54; Fuß *(Längenmaß: 30,48 cm)* **III U1,** 11
on foot [ɒn 'fʊt] zu Fuß **I U4,** 57
football ['fʊtbɔ:l] Fußball **I U1,** 12
American football [əˌmerɪkən 'fʊtbɔ:l] Football **III U1,** 8
footstep ['fʊtstep] Schritt **III U3,** 46
for [fɔ:; fə] für **I U1,** 11; seit **II U5,** 69
for example [fər‿ɪg'zɑ:mpl] zum Beispiel **III U4,** 53
for hours [fər‿'aʊəz] stundenlang **II U4,** 52
for miles [fə‿'maɪlz] meilenweit **IV U4,** 65
for supper [fə 'sʌpə] zum Abendessen **II U3,** 38
forecast ['fɔ:kɑ:st] Vorhersage *(Wetter)* **II U6,** 78
*to **forecast** ['fɔ:kɑ:st] vorhersagen *(Wetter)* **IV U3,** 41
foreground ['fɔ:graʊnd] Vordergrund **IV U1,** 8
foreign ['fɒrɪn] fremd, ausländisch **II U1,** 10
*to **forget** [fə'get] vergessen **I U4,** 60
fork [fɔ:k] Gabel **II U4,** 50
form [fɔ:m] Formular, Form **II U5,** 64
long form ['lɒŋ fɔ:m] Langform °**I U1,** 16
to **form** [fɔ:m] formen, bilden **IV U5,** 76
formal ['fɔ:ml] formal, formell, förmlich **IV U2,** 23
forum ['fɔ:rəm] Forum **IV U5,** 76
fossil ['fɒsl] Fossil; fossil, versteinert **V T4,** 61
fossil fuel ['fɒslˌfju:əl] fossiler Brennstoff **V T4,** 61
foul [faʊl] Foul **III U1,** 12
to **found** [faʊnd] gründen **IV U1,** 10
free [fri:] frei **I U3,** 40; kostenlos, umsonst **IV U1,** 12
freedom ['fri:dəm] Freiheit **IV U1,** 9
to **freestyle** *(slang)* ['fri:staɪl] improvisieren **IV U5,** 76
French [frentʃ] französisch **II U1,** 18
French fries *(AE)* ['frentʃˌfraɪz] Pommes frites **IV U1,** 12
frequent ['fri:kwənt] häufig °**III U4,** 56
fresh [freʃ] frisch **II U4,** 54
Friday ['fraɪdeɪ] Freitag **I LUB,** 39
friend [frend] Freund/Freundin **I U1,** 16
to make friends (with) [ˌmeɪk 'frendz] Freundschaft schließen (mit) **IV U4,** 64
friendly ['frendli] freundlich, nett **IV U1,** 14
to **frighten away** [ˌfraɪtn‿ə'weɪ] abschrecken **II U7,** 88
*to be **frightened** (of) [bi: 'fraɪtnd] Angst haben (vor) **II U6,** 83
frightening ['fraɪtnɪŋ] schrecklich, furchtbar **II U6,** 80
from [frɒm] aus, von **I U1,** 10
divorced from [dɪ'vɔ:st frɒm] geschieden von **I U2,** 28
Where are you from? [ˌweər‿ə jə 'frɒm] Woher kommst du? **I U1,** 11
front [frʌnt] Vorderseite **IV U2,** 31
at the front [ət ðə 'frʌnt] im vorderen Teil, vorne **IV U1,** 9
in front of [ɪn 'frʌnt‿əv] vor **I U3,** 49
fruit [fru:t] Obst, Frucht **II U1,** 15
frustrated [frʌs'treɪtɪd] frustriert **III U4,** 52
fuel ['fju:əl] Treibstoff; Brennmaterial **V T4,** 61
fossil fuel ['fɒslˌfju:əl] fossiler Brennstoff **V T4,** 61
to **fulfill** *(AE)* [fʊl'fɪl] erfüllen, genügen **V T3,** 46
full (of) [fʊl] ganz, voll (von/mit) **III U1,** 11
full-time (F/T) [ˌfʊl'taɪm] Vollzeit- **V T1,** 14; **V T2,** 32
fun [fʌn] Spaß **I U3,** 41
Have fun! [ˌhæv 'fʌn] Viel Spaß! **I U6,** 82
to be fun [bi: 'fʌn] Spaß machen **I U3,** 43
to have fun [ˌhæv 'fʌn] Spaß haben, sich amüsieren **I U6,** 82
funeral ['fju:nrəl] Beerdigung **II U6,** 76
funk [fʌŋk] Funk *(Musikrichtung)* **IV U5,** 76
funny ['fʌni] komisch, lustig **I LUA,** 25
furious ['fjʊəriəs] wütend **III U3,** 47
furniture ['fɜ:nɪtʃə] Möbel **I LUA,** 25
further ['fɜ:ðə] weiter **V T1,** 14
fuse-box ['fju:zbɒks] Sicherungskasten **III U3,** 47
future ['fju:tʃə] Zukunft, Futur **V T4,** 60

G

gallery ['gæləri] Galerie °**V T3,** 45
game [geɪm] Spiel **I U2,** 26
miming game ['maɪmɪŋ geɪm] Pantomime °**I U6,** 81
gang [gæŋ] Gang, Bande **IV U2,** 25
gangster ['gæŋkstə] Gangster/Gangsterin, Verbrecher/Verbrecherin **IV U5,** 76
garden ['gɑ:dn] Garten **I U2,** 26
gas [gæs] Gas *(BE)*; Benzin *(AE)* **V T4,** 60
greenhouse gas [ˌgri:nhaʊs 'gæs] Treibhausgas **V T4,** 60
gate [geɪt] Tor, Pforte; Gate **II U7,** 90
GCSE [ˌdʒi:si:es'i:] Prüfung zum Abschluss der Sekundarstufe **III U4,** 57

g'day [gəˈdeɪ] Tag, hallo *(australische Begrüßung)* °**II U1,** 14
Geography [dʒiˈɒgrəfi] Geografie, Erdkunde **II U1,** 10
German [ˈdʒɜːmən] deutsch; Deutscher/Deutsche **I U1,** 17
*to **get** [get] besorgen, kommen, bekommen **I U3,** 44; holen **II U2,** 26; werden **II U6,** 83
to get hungry [get ˈhʌŋgri] Hunger bekommen **II U4,** 56
to get interested [get ˈɪntrəstɪd] sich interessieren **III U2,** 31
to get in the way (of) [ˌget‿ɪn‿ðə‿ˈweɪ] etw. verhindern; im Weg stehen **VT2,** 29
to get into [get‿ˈɪntə] einsteigen in *(Auto)* **I U5,** 75
to get into such a state [get‿ˌɪntə sʌtʃ‿ə ˈsteɪt] durchdrehen, (sich) verrückt machen **III U4,** 60
to get it [ˈget‿ɪt] etwas verstehen, begreifen **IV U3,** 48
to get lost [get ˈlɒst] verloren gehen, sich verirren **I U3,** 48
to get off [get‿ˈɒf] aussteigen aus **I U4,** 59
to get on [get‿ˈɒn] einsteigen *(in Zug, Bus ...)* **III U2,** 29; aufsteigen **III U5,** 74
to get onto [get‿ˈɒntə] einsteigen *(Bus)* **II U1,** 19
to get out [get‿ˈaʊt] aussteigen **I U6,** 86; entkommen **III U3,** 47
to get out of bed [ˌget‿aʊt‿əv ˈbed] aufstehen **II U7,** 94
to get ready [get ˈredi] sich vorbereiten **II U5,** 68
to get ... right/wrong [get ... ˈraɪt/ˈrɒŋ] richtig/falsch machen **II U3,** 44
to get to [ˈget tə] kommen zu, kommen nach, erreichen **III U2,** 26
to get up [get‿ˈʌp] aufstehen **I U3,** 44
to get ... wrong [get ... ˈrɒŋ] falsch verstehen °**II U3,** 47
ghost [gəʊst] Geist, Gespenst **I U2,** 34
girl [gɜːl] Mädchen **I U1,** 16
girlfriend [ˈgɜːlfrend] Freundin *(in einer Paarbeziehung)* **II U3,** 39
*to **give** [gɪv] geben, schenken **I U4,** 60
to give ... a dirty look [ˌgɪv‿ə dɜːti ˈlʊk] einen vernichtenden Blick zuwerfen **II U1,** 10
to give up [gɪv‿ˈʌp] aufgeben **VT3,** 43
glad [glæd] froh **III U4,** 58
glamorous [ˈglæmrəs] glamourös **IV U5,** 72
glass [glɑːs] Glas **II U4,** 50
glasses *(pl)* [ˈglɑːsɪz] Brille **IV U3,** 48
glee [gliː] Entzücken **III U4,** 60
global [ˈgləʊbl] global, Erd- **VT4,** 58
(global) warming [ˌgləʊbl ˈwɔːmɪŋ] (Erd-)Erwärmung **VT4,** 61
globalisation [ˌgləʊblaɪˈzeɪʃn] Globalisierung **VT4,** 60
glove [glʌv] Handschuh **III U1,** 8
to **glow** [gləʊ] leuchten **III U5,** 76
*to **go** [gəʊ] gehen **I U1,** 19
Go down .... [ˈgəʊ daʊn] Geh ... entlang. **I LUC,** 53
Go left. [gəʊ ˈleft] Biege nach links ab. **I LUC,** 52
Go right. [gəʊ ˈraɪt] Biege nach rechts ab. **I LUC,** 52
had gone [hæd ˈgɒn] waren gegangen °**VT4,** 66
to go bananas [ˌgəʊ bəˈnɑːnəz] verrückt werden, durchdrehen **II U5,** 66
to go bump [gəʊ ˈbʌmp] rumsen °**II U7,** 94
to go down [gəʊ ˈdaʊn] hinuntergehen, entlanggehen **II U2,** 30
to go far [gəʊ ˈfɑː] weit kommen, es weit bringen **III U2,** 22
to go for a walk [ˌgəʊ fər‿ə ˈwɔːk] spazieren gehen **III U5,** 76
to go in [gəʊ‿ˈɪn] hineingehen **II U2,** 26
to go + -ing [gəʊ] ... gehen **II U4,** 52
to go it alone [ˌgeʊ‿ɪt‿əˈleʊn] einen Alleingang starten, es allein schaffen **VT3,** 43
to go off [gəʊ‿ˈɒf] losgehen *(Alarm)* **II U7,** 95
to go on [gəʊ‿ˈɒn] andauern; weitermachen **IV U1,** 14
to go on a diet [ˌgəʊ‿ɒn ə ˈdaɪət] eine Diät machen **II U4,** 52
to go out [gəʊ‿ˈaʊt] (hin)ausgehen, erlöschen **II U3,** 38
to go over [gəʊ‿ˈəʊvə] hinübergehen **II U3,** 38
to go places [ˌgəʊ ˈpleɪsɪz] herumreisen **IV U4,** 64
to go red [gəʊ ˈred] rot werden **II U1,** 11
to go up [gəʊ‿ˈʌp] hinaufgehen °**I U4,** 61
to go weak [gəʊ ˈwiːk] schwach werden **III U4,** 60
to go with [ˈgəʊ‿wɪð] passen zu **III U1,** 9
to go without [ˌgəʊ wɪˈðaʊt] ohne ... auskommen **II U4,** 52
to go wrong [gəʊ ˈrɒŋ] schief gehen **II U6,** 85
to go [tə‿ˈgəʊ] zum Mitnehmen **IV U1,** 12
goal [gəʊl] Tor, Ziel **I U1,** 12
winning goal [ˈwɪnɪŋ gəʊl] Siegtreffer **III U4,** 58
goalkeeper [ˈgəʊlˌkiːpə] Torwart **III U1,** 10
goblin [ˈgɒblɪn] Kobold **II U7,** 90
My **God!** [maɪ ˈgɒd] Mein Gott! **II U6,** 82
gold [gəʊld] Gold **II U7,** 90
good [gʊd] gut **I U1,** 16
Good grief! [gʊd ˈgriːf] Du liebe Zeit! **II U2,** 28
Good luck! [ˌgʊd ˈlʌk] Viel Glück! **I U4,** 63
Good morning! [ˈgʊd ˈmɔːnɪŋ] Guten Morgen! **I U1,** 16
I'm good at ... [aɪm ˈgʊd‿ət] ich bin gut in ... **I U1,** 20
to be good with ... [biː ˈgʊd wɪð] gut mit ... umgehen können **I U2,** 34
to have a good time [ˌhæv‿ə gʊd ˈtaɪm] sich amüsieren **I U5,** 75
goodbye [gʊdˈbaɪ] auf Wiedersehen **I U1,** 19
goods *(pl)* [gʊdz] Güter, Waren **IV U4,** 57
government [ˈgʌvnmənt] Regierung **VT1,** 14; **VT3,** 44; **VT4,** 60
to **grab** [græb] greifen, schnappen **III U3,** 47
grade *(AE)* [greɪd] Klasse, Note **IV U2,** 22
to **graduate** [ˈgrædjueɪt] den Schulabschluss machen **IV U2,** 28
grammar [ˈgræmə] Grammatik °**II U1,** 16
grammar school [ˈgræmə ˌskuːl] Gymnasium **III U4,** 57
gramme [græm] Gramm **III U1,** 11
grandad [ˈgrændæd] Opa **I LUA,** 25
grandma [ˈgrændmɑː] Oma **I LUA,** 25
grass [grɑːs] Gras, Rasen **III U1,** 8
grave [greɪv] Grab **III U5,** 69
gravestone [ˈgreɪvstəʊn] Grabstein **III U5,** 74

great [greɪt] großartig, toll **I U2,** 26; groß **III U2,** 22
Greek [gri:k] griechisch; Grieche/Griechin **I U2,** 29
green [gri:n] grün **I LUA,** 24
greenhouse ['gri:nhaʊs] Gewächshaus **II U6,** 81
greenhouse gas [ˌgri:nhaʊs 'gæs] Treibhausgas **VT4,** 60
greeting ['gri:tɪŋ] Gruß, Begrüßung °**VT2,** 28
grey [greɪ] grau **III U5,** 77
grid [grɪd] Gitter, Tabelle **III U4,** 57
Good **grief!** [gʊd 'gri:f] Du liebe Zeit! **II U2,** 28
ground [graʊnd] Boden **II U2,** 26
group [gru:p] Gruppe **I U4,** 54
*to **grow** [grəʊ] wachsen (lassen); anbauen; zunehmen **VT4,** 63
to **guarantee** [ˌgærn'ti:] garantieren, sicherstellen, bürgen **VT4,** 62
national **guard** [ˌnæʃnl 'gɑ:d] Nationalgarde °**VT3,** 44
to **guard** [gɑ:d] bewachen **II U7,** 90
to **guess** [ges] raten, vermuten **III U4,** 57
guest [gest] Gast **III U5,** 72
guide [gaɪd] Führer/Führerin; Handbuch °**VT1,** 11
guitar [gɪ'tɑ:] Gitarre **IV U5,** 76
gun [gʌn] Schusswaffe **III U5,** 78
gunshot ['gʌnʃɒt] Schuss **III U5,** 78
guy [gaɪ] Typ, Kerl; *Plural:* Leute **IV U5,** 79
gym [dʒɪm] Turnhalle **I U3,** 40

H

Ha! [hɑ:] Ha! **III U4,** 58
hair [heə] Haar, Haare **II U2,** 28
hairdresser ['heəˌdresə] Friseur/Friseurin **II U2,** 28
hairdryer ['heəˌdraɪə] Fön **IV U3,** 44
half [hɑ:f] Hälfte **IV U4,** 62
half [hɑ:f] halb **II U6,** 83
half an hour [ˌhɑ:f‿ən‿'aʊə] eine halbe Stunde **II U2,** 26
half past (two) ['hɑ:f pɑ:st] halb (drei) **I U3,** 40
half-price [ˌhɑ:f'praɪs] zum halben Preis **III U1,** 12
half-sister ['hɑ:fˌsɪstə] Halbschwester **I U2,** 26
hall [hɔ:l] Halle, Saal, Flur **I U3,** 40
ham [hæm] Schinken **II U4,** 49
hand [hænd] Hand **II U3,** 41
Hands off! [hændz‿'ɒf] Hände weg! **II U4,** 50
handbag ['hænbæg] Handtasche **III U2,** 24
*to **hang** around [ˌhæŋ‿ə'raʊnd] rumhängen, herumlungern **VT2,** 28
to hang out [hæŋ‿'aʊt] sich herumtreiben **III U4,** 54
to hang up [hæŋ‿'ʌp] aufhängen °**VT1,** 15
Hang on! ['hæŋ‿ɒn] Moment mal! Warte mal! **I U6,** 82
to **happen** ['hæpn] geschehen, passieren **I U6,** 86
happy ['hæpi] glücklich, froh **I U2,** 33
harbor *(AE)* ['hɑ:bə] Hafen **IV U1,** 9
hard [hɑ:d] hart; schwierig, stark **II U6,** 82
harm [hɑ:m] Schaden, Verletzung **III U4,** 60
hat [hæt] Hut **II U2,** 26
hate [heɪt] Hass **II U1,** 10
to **hate** [heɪt] hassen **II U1,** 10
*to **have** [hæv] haben **I U5,** 68
Have a nice day. [ˌhæv‿ə naɪs 'deɪ] Einen schönen Tag (noch). **II U4,** 55
Have fun! [ˌhæv 'fʌn] Viel Spaß! **I U6,** 82
to have a day off [ˌhæv‿ə 'deɪ‿ɒf] einen Tag frei haben **VT3,** 46
to have a fit [ˌhæv‿ə 'fɪt] einen Anfall bekommen, Zustände kriegen **III U4,** 60
to have a good time [ˌhæv‿ə gʊd 'taɪm] sich amüsieren **I U5,** 75
to have a look [ˌhæv‿ə 'lʊk] (an)schauen, nachschauen **III U5,** 72
to have an argument [ˌhæv‿ən‿'ɑ:gjəmənt] sich streiten **III U4,** 52
to have a party [ˌhæv‿ə 'pɑ:ti] eine Party feiern **I U5,** 68
to have breakfast [hæv 'brekfəst] frühstücken **III U2,** 23
to have fun [ˌhæv 'fʌn] Spaß haben, sich amüsieren **I U6,** 82
to have got [hæv 'gɒt] besitzen, haben **I U2,** 30
to have no clue [ˌhæv nəʊ 'klu:] keine Ahnung haben **IV U5,** 80
to have supper [hæv 'sʌpə] zu Abend essen **I U3,** 44
to have to ['hæv tə] müssen **II U5,** 64
he [hi:] er **I U1,** 12
head [hed] Kopf **II U3,** 36
heading ['hedɪŋ] Überschrift °**IV U2,** 32
headline ['hedlaɪn] Überschrift, Schlagzeile °**VT4,** 58
headphones *(pl)* ['hedfəʊnz] Kopfhörer **II U4,** 56
health [helθ] Gesundheit **VT2,** 32
healthy ['helθi] gesund **II U4,** 50
*to **hear** [hɪə] hören **I U6,** 78
heart [hɑ:t] Herz **VT4,** 66
heat [hi:t] Hitze **IV U1,** 17
heating ['hi:tɪŋ] Heizung **II U6,** 78
heavy ['hevi] schwer **II U4,** 51
heavy metal [ˌhevi 'metl] Heavy Metal **IV U5,** 76
height [haɪt] Höhe, Größe **III U1,** 11
helicopter ['helɪˌkɒptə] Helikopter, Hubschrauber **II U6,** 83
hell [hel] Hölle **IV U5,** 80
Hello! [he'ləʊ] Hallo! **I U1,** 10
helmet ['helmət] Helm **III U1,** 8
help [help] Hilfe **I U2,** 34
to **help** [help] helfen **I U2,** 34
helper ['helpə] Helfer/Helferin **VT1,** 14
helpful ['helpfəl] hilfreich **II U5,** 71
helpless ['helpləs] hilflos **III U3,** 46
helpline ['helplaɪn] telefonischer Beratungsdienst, Notruf °**III U4,** 59
her [hɜ:] ihr/ihre; sie **I U2,** 26
Her Majesty [hə 'mædʒəsti] Ihre Majestät °**III U5,** 78
here [hɪə] hier **I U1,** 12
Here you are! ['hɪə ju:‿ɑ:] Bitte schön! **I U1,** 20
hero, heroes *(pl)* ['hɪərəʊ; 'hɪərəʊz] Held **II U3,** 43
heroine ['herəʊɪn] Heldin **III U5,** 68
hey [heɪ] he °**I U1,** 16
Hi! [haɪ] Hi! **I U1,** 10
Hi, there! ['haɪ ðeə] Hallo! **IV U2,** 26
*to **hide** [haɪd] (sich) verstecken **I U6,** 86
high [haɪ] hoch, groß **II U2,** 30
high-tech [ˌhaɪ'tek] high-tech **IV U3,** 42
high school ['haɪ ˌsku:l] High School *(weiterführende Schule in den USA, Oberstufe)* **IV U2,** 22
to **highlight** ['haɪlaɪt] hervorheben, markieren °**IV U2,** 28
highway *(AE)* ['haɪweɪ] Bundesstraße, Highway **IV U4,** 57

hill [hɪl] Berg, Hügel **IV U4,** 58
him [hɪm] ihn, ihm **I U4,** 60
himself [hɪm'self] sich (selbst) **III U1,** 17
hip hop ['hɪp hɒp] Hip-Hop **III U4,** 53
his [hɪz] sein/seine **I LUA,** 25
Hispanic [hɪ'spænɪk] hispanisch, lateinamerikanisch; Hispano-Amerikaner/-Amerikanerin **IV U4,** 64
historical [hɪ'stɒrɪkl] geschichtlich, historisch **VT1,** 14
History ['hɪstəri] Geschichte **II U1,** 10
hit [hɪt] Hit **III U5,** 70
*to **hit** [hɪt] schlagen, treffen **II U3,** 36
hobby, hobbies *(pl)* ['hɒbi; 'hɒbiz] Hobby **I LUB,** 38
hockey ['hɒki] Hockey **II U1,** 16
ice hockey ['aɪs ˌhɒki] Eishockey **II U2,** 23
holiday ['hɒlədeɪ] Feiertag **IV U4,** 60
holiday(s) ['hɒlədeɪ(z)] Urlaub, Ferien **II U7,** 88
home [həʊm] Zuhause, Heim; nach Hause **I U1,** 11; Heimat(-) **III U1,** 8
at home [ət 'həʊm] zu Hause **I U2,** 26
home plate ['həʊm ˌpleɪt] Home Plate **III U1,** 14
to take home [ˌteɪk 'həʊm] nach Hause bringen **I U2,** 35
homecoming ['həʊmkʌmɪŋ] Homecoming *(Schulfest an amerikanischen High Schools)* **IV U2,** 22
homecoming queen [ˌhəʊmkʌmɪŋ 'kwi:n] Ballkönigin **IV U2,** 23
*to feel **homesick** [ˌfi:l 'həʊmsɪk] Heimweh haben **IV U4,** 64
homework ['həʊmwɜ:k] Hausaufgabe(n) **I U1,** 19
homie *(slang)* ['həʊmi] Kumpel **IV U5,** 76
honest ['ɒnɪst] ehrlich **IV U2,** 31
to **hoot** [hu:t] schreien, rufen *(Eule)* **II U7,** 94
to **hope** [həʊp] hoffen **I U5,** 72
horoscope ['hɒrəskəʊp] Horoskop **II U6,** 80
horrible ['hɒrəbl] schrecklich, furchtbar **II U2,** 24
horse [hɔ:s] Pferd **I LUB,** 38
hospital ['hɒspɪtl] Krankenhaus **II U3,** 36
host [həʊst] Gastgeber; Talkmaster **III U5,** 70
hot [hɒt] heiß **I U6,** 79; toll; scharf **IV U2,** 26
hotel [həʊ'tel] Hotel **III U2,** 27
hotel suite [həʊ'tel ˌswi:t] Hotelsuite **III U2,** 27
hotline ['hɒtlaɪn] Hotline **IV U4,** 61
hound [haʊnd] Jagdhund **III U5,** 70
hour ['aʊə] Stunde **I U2,** 34
hours *(pl)* ['aʊəz] Öffnungszeiten **I U4,** 62
for hours [fər‿'aʊəz] stundenlang **II U4,** 52
half an hour [ˌhɑ:f‿ən‿'aʊə] eine halbe Stunde **II U2,** 26
house [haʊs] Haus **I LUA,** 25
house-sitter [ˌhaʊs'sɪtə] Haussitter/Haussitterin °**IV U1,** 15
how [haʊ] wie **I U1,** 11
How are you? [ˌhaʊ‿'ɑ: ju:] Wie geht es dir/Ihnen/euch? **I U6,** 83
how many [haʊ 'meni] wie viele **I U5,** 68
How much is/are … ? [ˌhaʊ 'mʌtʃ‿ɪz/ɑ:] Wie viel kostet/kosten … ? **I U5,** 66
How old are you? [haʊ‿'əʊld‿ɑ: ju:] Wie alt bist du? **I U1,** 11
how to … ['haʊ tə] wie man … °**II U3,** 37
huge [hju:dʒ] riesig, gewaltig **IV U1,** 14
human ['hju:mən] Mensch; menschlich **IV U3,** 41
hundred ['hʌndrəd] hundert **II U2,** 23
hungry ['hʌŋgri] hungrig **II U1,** 14
to get hungry [get 'hʌŋgri] Hunger bekommen **II U4,** 56
hunting ['hʌntɪŋ] Jagen **III U5,** 74
*to be in a **hurry** [bi:‿ɪn‿ə 'hʌri] es eilig haben **I U2,** 30
Hurry up! [ˌhʌri‿'ʌp] Beeil dich! **I U2,** 30
*to **hurt** [hɜ:t] verletzen, weh tun **II U3,** 40
hurt [hɜ:t] verletzt **III U5,** 74
hurtful ['hɜ:tfl] verletzend °**IV U2,** 27
hyphen ['haɪfn] Bindestrich °**VT2,** 34

I

I [aɪ] ich **I U1,** 10
I'd like to [ˌaɪd 'laɪk tə] ich würde gern **II U2,** 22
I don't care. [aɪ dəʊnt 'keə] Es ist mir egal. **II U4,** 58
I'd rather [aɪd 'rɑ:ðə] ich würde lieber **II U2,** 22
I'm having … . [aɪm 'hævɪŋ] Ich nehme … . **II U1,** 14
I'm scared. [aɪm 'skeəd] Ich habe Angst. **II U3,** 44
I want my … pierced. [aɪ 'wɒnt maɪ … 'pɪəst] Ich möchte mein/e … piercen lassen. **III U4,** 52
ice [aɪs] Eis **II U2,** 23
ice-cream [aɪs 'kri:m] Eiscreme **I U7,** 92
ice hockey ['aɪs ˌhɒki] Eishockey **II U2,** 23
ice rink ['aɪs rɪŋk] Eis-/Schlittschuhbahn **II U2,** 23
icon ['aɪkɒn] Ikone **III U3,** 47
idea [aɪ'dɪə] Idee, Einfall **I LUB,** 38
no idea [ˌnəʊ‿aɪ'dɪə] keine Ahnung **III U3,** 46
idiot ['ɪdɪət] Idiot, Dummkopf **I U1,** 21
if [ɪf] wenn, falls; ob **II U7,** 90
if-clause ['ɪfklɔ:z] if-Satz °**IV U4,** 59
ill [ɪl] krank; schlecht **IV U2,** 25
illegal [ɪ'li:gl] illegal, unrechtmäßig, rechtswidrig **IV U3,** 48
image ['ɪmɪdʒ] Bild, Image, Abbild, Vorstellung °**IV U4,** 57
to **imagine** [ɪ'mædʒɪn] sich (etwas) vorstellen **III U4,** 57
immigrant ['ɪmɪgrənt] Immigrant/Immigrantin, Einwanderer/Einwanderin **IV U1,** 9
to **immigrate** ['ɪmɪgreɪt] immigrieren, einwandern **IV U1,** 10
immigration [ˌɪmɪ'greɪʃn] Immigration, Einwanderung **IV U1,** 10
importance [ɪm'pɔ:tnts] Bedeutung, Wichtigkeit °**VT3,** 47
important [ɪm'pɔ:tnt] wichtig; einflussreich **II U6,** 74
impression [ɪm'preʃn] Eindruck °**II U4,** 57
in [ɪn] in; herein **I U1,** 10; von, aus **VT2,** 28
in all [ɪn‿'ɔ:l] im Ganzen **III U4,** 53
in fact [ɪn 'fækt] in der Tat, genau genommen **II U7,** 94
in front of [ɪn 'frʌnt‿əv] vor **I U3,** 49
in the end [ɪn ði:‿'end] schließlich, zum Schluss **II U6,** 80
in turn [ɪn 'tɜ:n] abwechselnd, der Reihe nach °**VT3,** 45

inch [ɪnʃ] Zoll *(Längenmaß: 2,54cm)* **III U1,** 11
including [ɪn'klu:dɪŋ] einschließlich, inklusive **V T3,** 43
independent [ˌɪndɪ'pendənt] unabhängig **III U3,** 46; Independent *(Musikrichtung)* **IV U5,** 76
Indian ['ɪndiən] indisch **II U4,** 49
indie ['ɪndi] Indie *(Musikrichtung)* **IV U5,** 76
industry ['ɪndəstri] Industrie **III U5,** 68
info ['ɪnfəʊ] Info °**III U4,** 58
to **inform** [ɪn'fɔ:m] informieren, benachrichtigen °**V T2,** 33
information [ˌɪnfə'meɪʃn] Information/Informationen **I LUC,** 52
information centre [ɪnfə'meɪʃn ˌsentə] Informationszentrum **I LUC,** 52
inheritor [ɪn'herɪtə] Erbe/Erbin **III U5,** 76
inside [ɪn'saɪd] innen, drin, nach drinnen **I U5,** 75
instruction [ɪn'strʌkʃn] Instruktion, Anweisung °**II U4,** 59
instructor [ɪn'strʌktə] Lehrer/Lehrerin, Ausbilder/Ausbilderin **V T1,** 14; **V T4,** 64
insurance [ɪn'ʃʊərns] Versicherung **V T1,** 14
intelligent [ɪn'telɪdʒnt] intelligent, klug; vernünftig **IV U3,** 42
inter-cultural [ˌɪntə'kʌltʃrl] interkulturell **V T4,** 58
interest ['ɪntrəst] Interesse **V T1,** 15
interested ['ɪntrəstɪd] interessiert **II U1,** 18
to get interested [get 'ɪntrəstɪd] sich interessieren **III U2,** 31
interesting ['ɪntrəstɪŋ] interessant **II U4,** 51
international [ˌɪntə'næʃnl] international **III U3,** 39
Internet ['ɪntənet] Internet **II U1,** 14
to surf the Internet [ˌsɜ:f ði‿'ɪntənet] im Internet surfen **II U1,** 14
Interstate *(AE)* [ˌɪntə'steɪt] Autobahn **IV U4,** 57
interview ['ɪntəvju:] Interview **II U1,** 17
to **interview** ['ɪntəvju:] interviewen **II U1,** 17
into ['ɪntə] in; in … hinein **I U3,** 44
to get into [get‿'ɪntə] einsteigen in *(Auto)* **I U5,** 75
to run into [rʌn‿'ɪntə] laufen gegen, stoßen gegen **III U1,** 17
introduction [ˌɪntrə'dʌkʃn] Einleitung °**II U4,** 55
to **invent** [ɪn'vent] erfinden **III U4,** 53
invention [ɪn'ventʃn] Erfindung **IV U3,** 41
inventor [ɪn'ventə] Erfinder/Erfinderin **IV U5,** 74
invitation [ˌɪnvɪ'teɪʃn] Einladung **I U5,** 70
to **invite** [ɪn'vaɪt] einladen **I U5,** 68
IQ [ˌaɪ'kju:] IQ *(Intelligenzquotient)* **IV U3,** 43
Irish ['aɪrɪʃ] irisch **II U7,** 90; Iren/Irinnen **IV U1,** 10
to **iron** [aɪən] bügeln **II U7,** 90
irregular [ɪ'regjələ] unregelmäßig °**II U2,** 26
island ['aɪlənd] Insel **II U6,** 82
islander ['aɪləndə] Inselbewohner/Inselbewohnerin **V T4,** 64
it [ɪt] es **I U1,** 12
It said … . [ɪt 'sed] Es lautete … . **II U2,** 30
Italian [ɪ'tæliən] italienisch; Italiener/Italienerin **I U2,** 29
to **itch** [ɪtʃ] jucken **V T4,** 66
item ['aɪtəm] Punkt, Gegenstand, Thema °**IV U1,** 17
its [ɪts] sein/seine; ihr/ihre **III U1,** 8

J

jacket ['dʒækɪt] Jacke **I U6,** 86
jail [dʒeɪl] Gefängnis **V T1,** 10
jam [dʒæm] Marmelade **I U7,** 94
traffic jam ['træfɪk ˌdʒæm] Stau **III U2,** 22
January ['dʒænjuəri] Januar **I U5,** 70
jazz [dʒæz] Jazz **II U3,** 45
jealous (of) ['dʒeləs] eifersüchtig, neidisch (auf) **II U3,** 45
jeans *(pl)* [dʒi:nz] Jeans **IV U2,** 23
jelly bean ['dʒeli bi:n] *engl. Süßigkeit* **V T1,** 10
jellyfish, **jellyfish** *(pl)* ['dʒelifɪʃ] Qualle **V T1,** 12
jerk *(slang)* [dʒɜ:k] Trottel **IV U2,** 26
jewel ['dʒu:əl] Juwel **III U2,** 22
jewellery ['dʒu:əlri] Schmuck **III U5,** 70
job [dʒɒb] Arbeitsstelle, Job **II U6,** 80
on the job [ˌɒn ðə 'dʒɒb] bei der Arbeit **III U5,** 70
to **jog** [dʒɒg] joggen **II U4,** 52
jogger [dʒɒgə] Jogger/Joggerin **IV U1,** 9
to **join** [dʒɔɪn] beitreten, sich anschließen; verbinden **IV U4,** 58
joke [dʒəʊk] Witz **I U1,** 20
to **joke** [dʒəʊk] scherzen, Witze machen **I U6,** 82
journey ['dʒɜ:ni] Reise, Fahrt **II U7,** 90
judge [dʒʌdʒ] Kampfrichter **II U5,** 70
juice [dʒu:s] Saft **IV U2,** 30
July [dʒʊ'laɪ] Juli **I U5,** 70
long **jump** ['lɒŋ ˌdʒʌmp] Weitsprung **I U7,** 90
to **jump** [dʒʌmp] springen **II U2,** 30
to jump about [ˌdʒʌmp‿ə'baʊt] herumspringen **III U4,** 58
to jump up [dʒʌmp‿'ʌp] hochspringen, aufspringen **II U6,** 82
June [dʒu:n] Juni **I U5,** 70
just [dʒʌst] nur, gerade, einfach **I U2,** 30

K

kangaroo [ˌkæŋgr'u:] Känguru **V T1,** 9
*to **keep** [ki:p] (be)halten **II U4,** 55; *hier:* aufbewahren **IV U3,** 44
Keep out! [ki:p‿'aʊt] Eintritt verboten! **I U2,** 26
to keep away [ki:p‿ə'weɪ] sich fernhalten, wegbleiben **V T1,** 12
keeper ['ki:pə] Wärter/Wärterin, Aufseher/Aufseherin; Inhaber/Inhaberin **V T2,** 32
key [ki:] Schlüssel **II U5,** 67
to **kick** [kɪk] treten **I U5,** 74
kickboard ['kɪkbɔ:d] Kickboard, Roller **IV U1,** 9
kid [kɪd] Kind **I U3,** 44
to **kill** [kɪl] tot machen **III U1,** 10
killer ['kɪlə] Mörder/Mörderin **V T3,** 42
kilo (kg) ['kɪləʊ] Kilo(gramm) **II U4,** 54
kilometre ['kɪləʊˌmi:tə; kɪ'lɒmɪtə] Kilometer **III U2,** 27
kind [kaɪnd] Art, Sorte **III U2,** 30
Kinetoscope [kɪ'netəskəʊp] Kinetoskop °**IV U5,** 74
king [kɪŋ] König **III U2,** 22
kiss [kɪs] Kuss **IV U2,** 26
to **kiss** [kɪs] küssen **III U5,** 68
PE **kit** [ˌpi:‿'i: kɪt] Sportzeug **II U1,** 10
kitchen ['kɪtʃɪn] Küche **I LUA,** 24
knee [ni:] Knie **II U3,** 41

knife, knives *(pl)* [naɪf; naɪvz] Messer **II U4,** 50
knight [naɪt] Ritter **II U2,** 22
knock [nɒk] Klopfen, Schlag **I U2,** 34
to **knock** [nɒk] klopfen; stoßen, schlagen **III U5,** 78
to knock out [nɒk‿'aʊt] k.o. schlagen, umhauen **III U1,** 17
*to **know** [nəʊ] wissen, kennen **I U4,** 58
koala [kəʊ'ɑ:lə] Koala **VT1,** 10

L

lab(oratory) [læb; lə'bɒrətri] Labor **II U2,** 23
label ['leɪbl] Etikett; Beschriftung; Siegel **VT4,** 62
to **label** ['leɪbl] beschriften, benennen, etikettieren **VT4,** 62
lad [læd] Junge **III U1,** 12
lake [leɪk] See **III U3,** 42
lamb [læm] Lamm, Lammfleisch **II U4,** 49
lamp [læmp] Lampe, Leuchte **IV U3,** 44
land [lænd] Land **I LUB,** 38
to **land** [lænd] landen **III U3,** 39
lane [leɪn] Fahrspur, Gasse **IV U5,** 80
language ['læŋgwɪdʒ] Sprache **I U2,** 29
lantern ['læntən] Laterne **I U7,** 90
laptop ['læptɒp] Laptop **I U2,** 34
large [lɑ:dʒ] groß, riesig **I U5,** 66
lassi ['lasɪ] Lassi *(Jogurtgetränk)* **II U4,** 49
to **last** [lɑ:st] dauern, anhalten **IV U4,** 64
last [lɑ:st] letzter/letzte/letztes **I U7,** 90
at last [ət 'lɑ:st] endlich, schließlich **VT3,** 42
last night [lɑ:st 'naɪt] gestern Abend/Nacht **II U3,** 37
late [leɪt] (zu) spät, verspätet **I U1,** 16
Latino [lə'ti:nəʊ] Latinomusik; Latino **IV U5,** 73
to **laugh** [lɑ:f] lachen **I U5,** 74
to laugh at ['lɑ:f‿ət] auslachen, sich lustig machen über **II U3,** 36
launch [lɔ:nʃ] Einführung, Start; Abschuss **VT4,** 61
to **launch** [lɔ:nʃ] einführen, herausbringen; starten, abschießen **VT4,** 61
law [lɔ:] Gesetz(gebung), Recht **VT1,** 10; **VT3,** 44
lead [led] Blei **IV U2,** 31
leader ['li:də] Führer/Führerin, Anführer/Anführerin **II U6,** 80
leaf, leaves *(pl)* [li:f; li:vz] Blatt **III U4,** 60
to **lean out** [li:n‿'aʊt] (sich) hinauslehnen **II U7,** 94
*to **learn** [lɜ:n] lernen **I U3,** 40; erfahren **III U1,** 8
least [li:st] am wenigsten **IV U5,** 76
at least [ət 'li:st] wenigstens, mindestens **I U6,** 87
*to **leave** [li:v] lassen, verlassen, abfahren **I U3,** 43; (weg)gehen **II U1,** 18
to leave sb alone [ˌli:v‿ə'ləʊn] jmdn. in Ruhe lassen **VT1,** 12
left [left] linker/linke/linkes; links **I U4,** 55
Go left. [gəʊ 'left] Biege nach links ab. **I LUC,** 52
on the left [ɒn ðə 'left] links **I U2,** 28
to turn left [tɜ:n 'left] links abbiegen **II U7,** 97
left [left] übrig **II U4,** 54
leg [leg] Bein **II U3,** 41
legal ['li:gl] legal, rechtlich, Rechts- **IV U3,** 48
lemonade [ˌlemə'neɪd] Limonade **I U5,** 68
*to **lend** [lend] leihen **II U7,** 90
leprechaun ['leprəkɔ:n] Gnom, Kobold °**II U7,** 90
less [les] weniger **IV U2,** 29
lesson ['lesn] Unterrichtsstunde **I U1,** 15
*to **let** [let] lassen **III U4,** 52
Let's .... [lets] Lasst uns .... **I U1,** 10
to let sb down [let 'daʊn] jmdn. im Stich lassen, jmdn. enttäuschen **VT2,** 30
letter ['letə] Buchstabe; Brief **I U1,** 15
capital letter [ˌkæpɪtl 'letə] Großbuchstabe °**II U3,** 37
lettuce ['letɪs] Kopfsalat **II U4,** 54; *(slang)* Geld °**IV U5,** 80
level ['levl] Ebene, Niveau **III U4,** 57
library ['laɪbri] Bibliothek, Bücherei **III U4,** 56
driving **licence** *(BE)* ['draɪvɪŋ ˌlaɪsnts] Führerschein **VT1,** 14
driver's **license** *(AE)* ['draɪvəz ˌlaɪsnts] Führerschein **IV U4,** 64
to **lie** [laɪ] lügen **IV U2,** 31
*to **lie** [laɪ] liegen **III U3,** 46
to lie down [laɪ 'daʊn] (sich) hinlegen, niederlegen **III U3,** 46
life, lives *(pl)* [laɪf; laɪvz] Leben **II U3,** 42
lifeguard ['laɪfgɑ:d] Rettungsschwimmer/ Rettungsschwimmerin **III U3,** 40
lifestyle ['laɪfstaɪl] Lebensart **IV U5,** 80
light [laɪt] Licht **II U7,** 94
light bulb ['laɪt bʌlb] Glühbirne **IV U3,** 44
light [laɪt] leicht; hell **VT4,** 61
to **like** [laɪk] mögen, gern haben **I U3,** 44
I'd like to [ˌaɪd 'laɪk tə] ich würde gern **II U2,** 22
would like [wʊd 'laɪk] hätte(n) gern, möchte(n) gern **II U4,** 52
like [laɪk] wie *(Vergleich)* **I U6,** 86
like the back of my hand ['bæk‿əv maɪ ˌhænd] wie meine Westentasche **III U2,** 30
likes *(pl)* [laɪks] Vorlieben °**VT2,** 33
limit ['lɪmɪt] Limit, Grenze, Beschränkung **VT3,** 47
limousine [ˌlɪmə'zi:n] Limousine **IV U5,** 80
line [laɪn] Zeile, Text, Linie **I U3,** 43
back line [ˌbæk 'laɪn] Grundlinie **III U1,** 10
ocean **liner** ['əʊʃn ˌlaɪnə] Ozeandampfer **III U3,** 39
link [lɪŋk] Verbindung, Bindeglied **III U5,** 70; Link; Verknüpfung **VT1,** 14
to **link** [lɪŋk] verbinden, verknüpfen **VT1,** 14
lion ['laɪən] Löwe **II U5,** 68
sea lion ['si: ˌlaɪən] Seelöwe **VT2,** 32
lip balm ['lɪp bɑ:m] Lippenpflegestift **II U6,** 82
list [lɪst] Liste **I U5,** 68
to **listen** ['lɪsn] zuhören, anhören **I U1,** 11
little ['lɪtl] klein **I U6,** 82; wenig **IV U3,** 48
to **live** [lɪv] wohnen, leben **I U3,** 45
live [laɪv] live **III U4,** 53
living room ['lɪvɪŋ rʊm] Wohnzimmer **I LUA,** 24
loan [ləʊn] Darlehen, Kredit **VT3,** 46
to **loan** [ləʊn] ausleihen, verleihen **VT3,** 46
local ['ləʊkl] lokal, örtlich **III U2,** 24; einheimisch, ortsansässig **VT4,** 64

to **lock** [lɒk] abschließen **III U3,** 47
locker ['lɒkə] Schließfach **II U1,** 10
logbook ['lɒgbʊk] Logbuch **VT4,** 66
logo ['ləʊgəʊ] Logo; Firmenzeichen **VT4,** 62
lonely ['ləʊnli] einsam **III U1,** 16
long [lɒŋ] lang **I U3,** 44
as long as [əz 'lɒŋ‿əz] solange wie **I U7,** 94
long form ['lɒŋ fɔ:m] Langform °**I U1,** 16
long jump ['lɒŋ ˌdʒʌmp] Weitsprung **I U7,** 90
look [lʊk] Blick, Aussehen **II U1,** 10
to give … a dirty look [ˌgɪv‿ə dɜ:ti 'lʊk] einen vernichtenden Blick zuwerfen **II U1,** 10
to have a look [ˌhæv‿ə 'lʊk] (an)schauen, nachschauen **III U5,** 72
to **look** [lʊk] sehen, schauen, aussehen **I U1,** 12
to look after [lʊk‿'ɑ:ftə] sich kümmern um, aufpassen auf **II U1,** 14
to look at ['lʊk‿ət] (sich) ansehen **I U6,** 82
to look for ['lʊk fə] suchen nach **I U6,** 81
to look round [lʊk 'raʊnd] sich umsehen **II U1,** 18
to look up [lʊk‿'ʌp] (hin)aufschauen; nachschlagen **II U2,** 30
*to **lose** [lu:z] verlieren **II U4,** 52
Lost and Found ['lɒst ˌənd 'faʊnd] Fundbüro **III U4,** 56
to be lost [bi: 'lɒst] sich verirrt haben **III U3,** 40
to get lost [get 'lɒst] verloren gehen, sich verirren **I U3,** 48
a **lot** [ə 'lɒt] viel **II U1,** 15
a lot of [ə 'lɒt‿əv] viel/viele, eine Menge **I U2,** 30
lots (of) ['lɒts‿əv] viel/viele **II U7,** 88
lots of love [ˌlɒts‿əv 'lʌv] viele Grüße *(am Briefende)* **III U4,** 58
loud [laʊd] laut **II U7,** 91
love [lʌv] Herzliche Grüße *(am Briefende)*; Liebe **I U6,** 78
lots of love [ˌlɒts‿əv 'lʌv] viele Grüße *(am Briefende)* **III U4,** 58
to **love** [lʌv] lieben, gern mögen **I U3,** 44
low [ləʊ] niedrig, tief **VT4,** 67
low-cut ['ləʊkʌt] tief ausgeschnitten **IV U5,** 72
luck [lʌk] Glück **I U4,** 63
bad luck [ˌbæd 'lʌk] Pech **I U4,** 63
Good luck! [ˌgʊd 'lʌk] Viel Glück! **I U4,** 63
lucky ['lʌki] glücklich **I U1,** 16
luckily ['lʌkɪli] glücklicherweise **IV U2,** 24
you're lucky [jʊə 'lʌki] du hast Glück **I U1,** 16
luggage ['lʌgɪdʒ] Gepäck **II U7,** 90
lunch [lʌntʃ] Mittagessen **I U1,** 18
lunchtime ['lʌntʃtaɪm] Mittag, Mittagszeit **I U1,** 19
lyrics ['lɪrɪks] Liedtext **IV U5,** 81

M

machine [mə'ʃi:n] Maschine, Apparat **IV U5,** 80
mad [mæd] verrückt; wütend **II U1,** 18
magazine [mægə'zi:n] Zeitschrift, Magazin **I U2,** 33
main [meɪn] Haupt- **II U4,** 49
Her **Majesty** [hə 'mædʒəsti] Ihre Majestät °**III U5,** 78
*to **make** [meɪk] machen, tun **I U1,** 11
to make friends (with) [ˌmeɪk 'frendz] Freundschaft schließen (mit) **IV U4,** 64
to make it ['meɪk‿ɪt] es schaffen **III U4,** 58
to make sb do sth [meɪk] jmdn. veranlassen, etw. zu tun; jmdn. dafür gewinnen, etw. zu tun **VT3,** 45
to make sure [meɪk 'ʃʊə] sichergehen **II U6,** 82
to make up [meɪk‿'ʌp] erfinden, sich ausdenken **I U4,** 62
make-up ['meɪkʌp] Make-up, Schminke **I U7,** 90
man, men *(pl)* [mæn; men] Mann **I U4,** 62
manager ['mænɪdʒə] Manager/Managerin **I U2,** 26
adverb of **manner** [ˌædvɜ:b‿əv 'mænə] Adverb der Art und Weise °**II U7,** 90
mansion ['mænʃn] Villa °**IV U1,** 15
manta ray ['mænta ˌreɪ] Mantarochen **VT4,** 64
many ['meni] viele, etliche **I U5,** 68
how many [haʊ 'meni] wie viele **I U5,** 68
map [mæp] Stadtplan, Landkarte **I LUC,** 52
mind map ['maɪnd mæp] Wörternetz *(eine Art Schaubild)* °**III U1,** 19
maple ['meɪpl] Ahorn **IV U1,** 12
march [mɑ:tʃ] Marsch **VT3,** 44
to **march** [mɑ:tʃ] marschieren **VT3,** 44
March [mɑ:tʃ] März **I U5,** 70
mark [mɑ:k] Fleck **I U2,** 30; Note *(in der Schule)* **II U3,** 44
to **mark** [mɑ:k] markieren **IV U1,** 14
market ['mɑ:kɪt] Markt **II U2,** 22
married to ['mærid tə] verheiratet mit **I U2,** 28
to **marry** ['mæri] heiraten **III U2,** 32
match [mætʃ] Spiel, Wettkampf **II U2,** 24
to **match** [mætʃ] passen zu; zuordnen, zusammenfügen **IV U2,** 30
to match up ['mætʃ‿ʌp] zusammenfügen °**II U4,** 52
mate [meɪt] Kamerad/Kameradin, Kumpel **III U4,** 60
material [mə'tɪəriəl] Material; Stoff **IV U2,** 24
Maths [mæθs] Mathematik **II U1,** 10
matter ['mætə] Angelegenheit, Frage **IV U5,** 76
no matter [nəʊ 'mætə] egal **IV U5,** 80
What's the matter? [ˌwɒts ðə 'mætə] Was ist los? **III U5,** 76
to **matter** ['mætə] von Bedeutung sein, ausmachen **IV U5,** 76
***may** [meɪ] kann/könnte(n) vielleicht **II U4,** 55; *hier:* dürfen **IV U2,** 28
May [meɪ] Mai **I U5,** 70
maybe ['meɪbi] vielleicht **I U7,** 96
me [mi:] mich, mir **I LUB,** 38
meal [mi:l] Mahlzeit **II U4,** 52
*to **mean** [mi:n] bedeuten, meinen **I U4,** 55
mean [mi:n] gemein **IV U2,** 31
meaning ['mi:nɪŋ] Bedeutung °**I U7,** 98
measurement ['meʒəmənt] Maßeinheit, Maß °**III U3,** 43
meat [mi:t] Fleisch **III U3,** 44
mechanic [mə'kænɪk] Mechaniker/Mechanikerin **IV U4,** 64
media *(pl)* ['mi:diə] Medien **VT3,** 42
mediation [ˌmi:di'eɪʃn] Sprachmittlung °**III U1,** 13
medium ['mi:diəm] mittel **I U5,** 66
*to **meet** [mi:t] (sich) treffen **I U3,** 45
meeting ['mi:tɪŋ] Treffen, Besprechung **II U1,** 12
member ['membə] Mitglied **VT2,** 28

menu ['menju:] Speisekarte, Menü **II U1,** 14
Meow! [mi:'aʊ] Miau! °**I U2,** 35
mess [mes] Durcheinander, Unordnung **III U2,** 31
to **mess around** [ˌmes‿ə'raʊnd] herumalbern **VT2,** 26
message ['mesɪdʒ] Nachricht **II U3,** 38
text message ['tekst ˌmesɪdʒ] SMS **I U6,** 80
messy ['mesi] unordentlich, chaotisch, durcheinander **VT4,** 67
metal ['metl] Metal *(Musikrichtung)*; Metall **IV U5,** 76
heavy metal [ˌhevi 'metl] Heavy Metal **IV U5,** 76
metre ['mi:tə] Meter **III U2,** 27
Mexican ['meksɪkən] mexikanisch; Mexikaner/Mexikanerin **IV U4,** 64
mice *(pl)* [maɪs] Mäuse **I U3,** 45
microphone ['maɪkrəfəʊn] Mikrofon **II U5,** 71
microwave ['maɪkrəʊweɪv] Mikrowelle **IV U3,** 44
middle ['mɪdl] Mitte; Mittel- **IV U4,** 65
middle school *(AE)* ['mɪdl ˌsku:l] Mittelschule *(weiterführende Schule in den USA, Mittelstufe)* **IV U2,** 28
midnight ['mɪdnaɪt] Mitternacht **II U6,** 78
*__might__ [maɪt] könnte/könnten **IV U4,** 64
mile [maɪl] Meile **II U6,** 74
for miles [fə‿'maɪlz] meilenweit **IV U4,** 65
milestone ['maɪlstəʊn] Meilenstein **VT3,** 44
milk [mɪlk] Milch **I U5,** 68
milkman, milkmen *(pl)* ['mɪlkmən; 'mɪlkmen] Milchmann **III U2,** 30
milkshake ['mɪlkʃeɪk] Milchshake **IV U1,** 12
milky ['mɪlki] milchig **VT4,** 63
million ['mɪlɪən] Million **II U2,** 23
to **mime** [maɪm] pantomimisch darstellen °**I U6,** 81
miming game ['maɪmɪŋ geɪm] Pantomime °**I U6,** 81
mind [maɪnd] Geist, Verstand **III U5,** 71
He had something on his mind. [maɪnd] Ihn beschäftigte etwas. **III U5,** 71
mind map ['maɪnd mæp] Wörternetz °**III U1,** 19
*Would you **mind ... ?** [ˌwʊd jə 'maɪnd] Hätten Sie/Hättest du etwas dagegen ... ? **III U4,** 56
mineral ['mɪnərəl] Mineral- **II U4,** 49
minute ['mɪnɪt] Minute **I U4,** 64
to **miss** [mɪs] vermissen, fehlen; verpassen **II U6,** 76; verfehlen **III U4,** 56
to miss a turn [mɪs ə 'tɜ:n] einmal aussetzen °**II U6,** 79
Miss [mɪs] Frau *(Anrede)* **I U7,** 94
missing ['mɪsɪŋ] fehlend °**I U4,** 64
to be missing [bi: 'mɪsɪŋ] fehlen **III U1,** 14
mission ['mɪʃn] Mission, Auftrag, Aufgabe **VT4,** 62
mistake [mɪ'steɪk] Fehler **IV U2,** 26
mister ['mɪstə] *hier:* Sie *(Anrede)* **IV U1,** 17
to **mix** [mɪks] mixen, mischen **VT3,** 44
to **moan** [məʊn] (sich) (be)klagen, stöhnen **III U1,** 16
mobile ['məʊbaɪl] Handy, Mobiltelefon **I U1,** 11
model ['mɒdl] Modell **III U2,** 25
modern ['mɒdn] modern **IV U3,** 41
moment ['məʊmənt] Moment, Augenblick **I U7,** 90
at the moment [ət ðə 'məʊmənt] im Augenblick, momentan **I U7,** 90
Monday ['mʌndeɪ] Montag **I LUB,** 39
on Mondays [ɒn 'mʌndeɪz] montags **I LUB,** 39
money ['mʌni] Geld **I U5,** 67
pocket money ['pɒkɪt ˌmʌni] Taschengeld **II U2,** 22
to **monitor** ['mɒnɪtə] überwachen **IV U3,** 41
monster ['mɒnstə] Monster **IV U1,** 12
month [mʌnθ] Monat **I U5,** 70
mood [mu:d] Stimmung, Laune **VT3,** 46
moon [mu:n] Mond **II U7,** 94
moor [mɔ:] Hochmoor **II U6,** 74
more [mɔ:] mehr **I U2,** 29
morning ['mɔ:nɪŋ] Morgen, Vormittag **I U1,** 16
Good morning! ['gʊd 'mɔ:nɪŋ] Guten Morgen! **I U1,** 16
in the morning [ˌɪn ðə 'mɔ:nɪŋ] morgens, am Morgen, vormittags **I U3,** 47
(the) next morning [ˌnekst 'mɔ:nɪŋ] am nächsten Morgen **II U1,** 18
most [məʊst] das meiste, die meisten **I U3,** 44
motel [məʊ'tel] Motel **IV U3,** 44
mother ['mʌðə] Mutter **III U3,** 46
motion ['məʊʃn] Bewegung **IV U5,** 74
motor ['məʊtə] Motor **IV U5,** 74
motorbike ['məʊtəbaɪk] Motorrad **IV U4,** 57
mountain ['maʊntɪn] Berg **IV U3,** 48
mouse [maʊs] Maus **I U1,** 10
mouth [maʊθ] Mund **II U3,** 41
move [mu:v] Schritt, Bewegung **IV U2,** 27
to **move** [mu:v] (sich) bewegen; umziehen **II U6,** 78
movement ['mu:vmənt] Bewegung **VT3,** 44
Civil Rights Movement (CRM) [ˌsɪvl 'raɪts ˌmu:vmənt] Bürgerrechtsbewegung **VT3,** 44
movie *(AE)* ['mu:vi] Film **IV U2,** 26
silent movie [ˌsaɪlənt 'mu:vi] Stummfilm **IV U5,** 74
movies *(AE)* ['mu:viz] Kino **IV U2,** 26
MP3 [empi:'θri:] MP3 **II U5,** 62
MP3 player [empi:'θri: ˌpleɪə] MP3-Player **II U5,** 62
Mr ['mɪstə] Herr *(Anrede)* **I U1,** 12
Mrs ['mɪsɪz] Frau *(Anrede)* **I U1,** 12
much [mʌtʃ] viel **I U5,** 66
How much are ... ? [ˌhaʊ 'mʌtʃ‿ɑ:] Wie viel kosten ... ? **I U5,** 66
How much is ... ? [ˌhaʊ 'mʌtʃ‿ɪz] Wie viel kostet ... ? **I U5,** 66
muddle ['mʌdl] Durcheinander °**III U3,** 42
mule [mju:l] Maultier **IV U4,** 58
multinational [ˌmʌlti'næʃnl] multinational **VT4,** 60
mum [mʌm] Mama, Mutti **I LUA,** 25
mural ['mjʊərl] Graffiti, Wandmalerei **VT2,** 29
murder ['mɜ:də] Mord, Ermordung **VT3,** 42
museum [mju:'zi:əm] Museum **I LUC,** 52
music ['mju:zɪk] Musik **I U2,** 34
musical ['mju:zɪkl] Musical **III U5,** 68
musician [mju:'zɪʃn] Musiker/Musikerin **IV U5,** 76
*__must__ [mʌst] müssen **I U7,** 94
my [maɪ] mein/meine **I U1,** 10
My God! [maɪ 'gɒd] Mein Gott! **II U6,** 82

My name is … . [maɪ 'neɪm‿ɪz] Ich heiße … . **I U1,** 10
myself [maɪ'self] (ich) selbst; mich (selbst) **III U5,** 78
mystery ['mɪstəri] Geheimnis, Rätsel **III U5,** 76
myth [mɪθ] Mythos **III U5,** 69

N

name [neɪm] Name **I U1,** 10
My name is … . [maɪ 'neɪm‿ɪz] Ich heiße … . **I U1,** 10
What's your name? [ˌwɒts jə 'neɪm] Wie heißt du? **I U1,** 11
to **name** [neɪm] (be)nennen **IV U1,** 10
national ['næʃnl] national **II U6,** 82; National-, landesweit **III U1,** 10
national guard [ˌnæʃnl 'gɑ:d] Nationalgarde °**V T3,** 44
national park [ˌnæʃnl 'pɑ:k] Nationalpark **IV U4,** 56
native ['neɪtɪv] eingeboren, einheimisch, gebürtig **IV U1,** 10
Native American [ˌneɪtɪv‿ə'merɪkən] Ureinwohner/Ureinwohnerin Amerikas, Indianer/Indianerin **IV U1,** 10
near [nɪə] in der Nähe von, nahe **I LUC,** 53
nearly ['nɪəli] fast, annähernd **III U1,** 16
need [ni:d] Bedürfnis, Bedarf; Erfordernis **V T2,** 28
to **need** [ni:d] brauchen, benötigen, müssen **II U1,** 21
negative ['negətɪv] Verneinung °**III U5,** 71; negativ, verneint °**IV U5,** 83
neighborhood *(AE)* ['neɪbəhʊd] Viertel; Nachbarschaft **IV U1,** 9
neighbour ['neɪbə] Nachbar/Nachbarin **II U7,** 90
neon ['ni:ɒn] neonfarben **IV U1,** 9
nephew ['nefju:] Neffe **III U5,** 76
nervous ['nɜ:vəs] nervös, aufgeregt **II U5,** 71
net [net] Netz **III U1,** 10
never ['nevə] niemals **I U3,** 44
new [nju:] neu **I U1,** 10
news *(sg.)* [nju:z] Nachricht(en), Neuigkeit(en) **III U4,** 58
breaking news [ˌbreɪkɪŋ 'nju:z] neueste Nachrichten **IV U2,** 22
newsagent ['nju:sˌeɪdʒənt] Zeitschriftenhändler/ Zeitschriftenhändlerin **I LUC,** 52
newspaper ['nju:sˌpeɪpə] Zeitung **III U2,** 24
next [nekst] nächster/nächste/ nächstes **I U5,** 69; als Nächstes °**II U1,** 19
next door [ˌnekst 'dɔ:] nebenan **III U1,** 16
(the) next morning [ˌnekst 'mɔ:nɪŋ] am nächsten Morgen **II U1,** 18
next to ['nekst tə] neben **I U2,** 28
nice [naɪs] nett **I U1,** 12; schön **II U4,** 54
nickel ['nɪkl] Nickel *(Währung)* **IV U1,** 13
nickname ['nɪkneɪm] Spitzname **IV U5,** 73
night [naɪt] Nacht, Abend **I U3,** 44
at night [ət 'naɪt] nachts **II U3,** 47
last night [lɑ:st 'naɪt] gestern Abend/ Nacht **II U3,** 37
night nurse ['naɪt nɜ:s] Nachtschwester **I U3,** 47
nightmare ['naɪtmeə] Albtraum **V T4,** 61
no [nəʊ] nein, nicht; kein/keine **I U1,** 12
no … at all [ˌnəʊ … ət‿'ɔ:l] überhaupt kein/keine **V T4,** 65
no idea [ˌnəʊ‿aɪ'dɪə] keine Ahnung **III U3,** 46
no one ['nəʊwʌn] niemand **II U2,** 30
No. ['nʌmbə] Nummer **V T1,** 10
nobody ['nəʊbədi] niemand **V T3,** 44
noise [nɔɪz] Geräusch, Lärm **I U2,** 35
none [nʌn] keiner/keine **II U7,** 88
non-stop [ˌnɒn'stɒp] non-stop, durchgehend, ohne Unterbrechung **V T3,** 43
non-violent [ˌnɒn'vaɪələnt] gewaltfrei **V T3,** 44
normal ['nɔ:ml] normal **I U3,** 44
north [nɔ:θ] Norden **I U4,** 55
nose [nəʊz] Nase **II U3,** 41
not [nɒt] nicht **I U1,** 16
not … either [ˌnɒt … 'aɪðə] auch nicht **IV U3,** 48
not even [nɒt‿'i:vn] nicht einmal **III U4,** 54
not … yet [jet] noch nicht **II U5,** 66
note [nəʊt] Notiz, Anmerkung **II U1,** 11
sick note ['sɪk ˌnəʊt] Krankmeldung **II U2,** 28
to take notes [teɪk 'nəʊts] sich Notizen machen °**II U4,** 55
nothing ['nʌθɪŋ] nichts **II U4,** 50
notice ['nəʊtɪs] Anschlag, Notiz **III U4,** 57
notice board ['nəʊtɪs bɔ:d] schwarzes Brett **III U4,** 57
to **notice** ['nəʊtɪs] bemerken **III U3,** 46
noun [naʊn] Nomen °**III U1,** 19
November [nəʊ'vembə] November **I U5,** 70
now [naʊ] jetzt, nun **I U1,** 20
right now [ˌraɪt 'naʊ] jetzt gleich, in diesem Augenblick **I U7,** 92
nowhere ['nəʊweə] nirgendwo(hin) **IV U4,** 65
number ['nʌmbə] Nummer, Zahl **I U1,** 11
phone number ['fəʊn ˌnʌmbə] Telefonnummer **I U1,** 11
nurse [nɜ:s] Krankenschwester, Krankenpfleger **I U3,** 47
night nurse ['naɪt nɜ:s] Nachtschwester **I U3,** 47
nutrition [nju:'trɪʃn] Ernährung(slehre) **V T2,** 32
*to be **nuts about** [bi: ˌnʌts‿ə'baʊt] verrückt nach … sein **II U1,** 18
nutty ['nʌti] nussig; schmackhaft **V T4,** 63

O

object ['ɒbdʒɪkt] Objekt, Gegenstand °**IV U3,** 44
observatory [əb'zɜ:vətri] Observatorium, Sternwarte **I U5,** 73
ocean ['əʊʃn] Ozean **III U3,** 39
ocean liner ['əʊʃn ˌlaɪnə] Ozeandampfer **III U3,** 39
October [ɒk'təʊbə] Oktober **I U5,** 70
octopus ['ɒktəpəs] Oktopus, Krake **V T1,** 12
Blue Ring Octopus [ˌblu: rɪŋ 'ɒktəpəs] blaugeringelter Krake °**V T1,** 12
odd one out [ɒd wʌn‿'aʊt] das nicht dazu passende (Wort) **II U5,** 72
odour ['əʊdə] Geruch, Duft **V T2,** 28
of [ɒv; əv] von **I U2,** 26
of course [əv 'kɔ:s] natürlich, selbstverständlich **I U1,** 19
off [ɒf] herunter, ab, weg von **II U3,** 36
to get off [get‿'ɒf] aussteigen aus **I U4,** 59
to have a day off [ˌhæv‿ə deɪ‿'ɒf] einen Tag frei haben **V T3,** 46
to send off [send‿'ɒf] vom Platz verweisen **III U1,** 12

to switch off [ˌswɪtʃ‿ˈɒf] ausschalten **IV U1,** 17
to take off [ˌteɪk‿ˈɒf] abheben, starten, abfliegen **IV U1,** 16
offer [ˈɒfə] Angebot **IV U5,** 77
to **offer** [ˈɒfə] anbieten **V T4,** 60
office [ˈɒfɪs] Büro **II U2,** 31
post office [ˈpəʊst‿ˌɒfɪs] Postamt **III U2,** 26
officer [ˈɒfɪsə] Beamter/Beamtin **III U3,** 39
official [əˈfɪʃl] Beamter/Beamtin **IV U1,** 10
officially [əˈfɪʃli] offiziell **V T3,** 44
often [ˈɒfn] oft **I U3,** 44
oh [əʊ] oh °**I U1,** 12
Oh dear! [əʊ ˈdɪə] Oje! **III U5,** 73
oil [ɔɪl] Öl **V T4,** 58
Oink-oink! [ɔɪŋk‿ɔɪŋk] Grunz! °**I U6,** 82
OK [əʊˈkeɪ] o.k. **I U1,** 12
is OK with us [ɪz‿əʊˈkeɪ wɪð‿ʌs] ist uns recht **I U6,** 78
We're OK. [ˌwɪər‿əʊˈkeɪ] Es geht uns gut. **I U6,** 83
old [əʊld] alt **I U1,** 11
How old are you? [haʊ‿ˈəʊld‿ɑː juː] Wie alt bist du? **I U1,** 11
on [ɒn] auf, an **I U1,** 14
to … on [ɒn] weiter- **IV U3,** 48
on foot [ɒn ˈfʊt] zu Fuß **I U4,** 57
on Mondays [ɒn ˈmʌndeɪz] montags **I LUB,** 39
on one's own [ɒn wʌnz‿ˈəʊn] (ganz) allein **V T3,** 40
on record [ɒn ˈrekɔːd] verzeichnet, dokumentiert **III U3,** 40
on the air [ˌɒn ði‿ˈeə] auf Sendung **II U4,** 55
on the bus [ˌɒn ðə ˈbʌs] im Bus **II U1,** 18
on the job [ˌɒn ðə ˈdʒɒb] bei der Arbeit **III U5,** 70
on the left [ɒn ðə ˈleft] links **I U2,** 28
on the right [ɒn ðə ˈraɪt] rechts **I U2,** 28
on time [ɒn ˈtaɪm] pünktlich **IV U3,** 46
to be on [biː‿ˈɒn] an der Reihe sein; im Gange sein, laufen **II U5,** 70; an sein, brennen *(Licht)* **II U7,** 94
once [wʌnts] einmal, einst **II U3,** 36
at once [ət ˈwʌnts] sofort, plötzlich **II U7,** 94
one day [wʌn ˈdeɪ] eines Tages **II U3,** 36
one(s) [wʌn(z)] *(Platzhalter für ein Nomen)* **III U2,** 25
online [ˌɒnˈlaɪn] online, im Internet **V T1,** 14
only [ˈəʊnli] nur, bloß, erst **I U2,** 26; einziger/einzige/einziges **III U5,** 76
only child [ˈəʊnli ˌtʃaɪld] Einzelkind **I U2,** 26
onto [ˈɒntuː; ˈɒntə] (auf …) hinauf, auf **II U1,** 19
Oops! [uːps] Hoppla! Huch! °**I U1,** 20
to **open** [ˈəʊpn] öffnen, aufmachen **I U1,** 19; sich öffnen, aufgehen **III U5,** 74
open [ˈəʊpn] offen, geöffnet **II U2,** 23
opera [ˈɒprə] Oper **V T1,** 9
to **operate** [ˈɒpəreɪt] bedienen; operieren **IV U3,** 41
opinion [əˈpɪnjən] Meinung **V T3,** 42
opportunity [ˌɒpəˈtjuːnəti] Gelegenheit; Möglichkeit **V T4,** 58
opposite [ˈɒpəzɪt] gegenüber °**II U4,** 49; Gegenteil °**IV U1,** 18
oppression [əˈpreʃn] Unterdrückung **IV U1,** 10
option [ˈɒpʃn] Auswahlmöglichkeit, Option **V T1,** 10; **V T2,** 28; **V T3,** 42; **V T4,** 60
or [ɔː] oder **I U1,** 11
orange [ˈɒrɪndʒ] Orange **II U4,** 54
order [ˈɔːdə] Reihenfolge, Ordnung **IV U3,** 46; Befehl, Anweisung **V T3,** 47
to **order** [ˈɔːdə] bestellen **II U4,** 49
organisation [ˌɔːgnaɪˈzeɪʃn] Organisation, Unternehmen **V T4,** 62
to **organize** [ˈɔːgənaɪz] organisieren **I U7,** 90
organizer [ˈɔːgənaɪzə] Organisator/ Organisatorin, Veranstalter/ Veranstalterin **III U4,** 53
other [ˈʌðə] anderer/andere/anderes **I U7,** 91
each other [ˌiːtʃ‿ˈʌðə] sich gegenseitig **II U1,** 19
our [ˈaʊə] unser/unsere **I U2,** 26
out [aʊt] heraus, hinaus, draußen, außerhalb **I U3,** 42
Keep out! [kiːp‿ˈaʊt] Eintritt verboten! **I U2,** 26
out and about [ˈaʊt‿nd‿əˈbaʊt] unterwegs °**I U4,** 54
out of [ˈaʊt‿əv] aus … heraus **I U3,** 49
to get out [get‿ˈaʊt] aussteigen **I U6,** 86
to knock out [nɒk‿ˈaʊt] k.o. schlagen, umhauen **III U1,** 17
to sort out [sɔːt‿ˈaʊt] klären, regeln *(ein Problem)* **I U2,** 30
to take out [teɪk‿ˈaʊt] herausnehmen **I U3,** 42
to work out [wɜːk‿ˈaʊt] herausfinden; ausarbeiten °**III U3,** 43
the Outback [ˈaʊtbæk] das Outback *(australisches Hinterland)* **V T1,** 9
outgoing [ˈaʊtgəʊɪŋ] aufgeschlossen, kontaktfreudig **V T3,** 47
outrageous [aʊtˈreɪdʒəs] gewagt; empörend **IV U5,** 72
outside [aʊtˈsaɪd] außerhalb, draußen, nach draußen **I U2,** 30
oven [ˈʌvn] Backofen **I U3,** 42
over [ˈəʊvə] vorbei, vorüber **II U5,** 70
over [ˈəʊvə] über **I U2,** 26
all over [ˌɔːl‿ˈəʊvə] überall **IV U1,** 10
over easy [ˌəʊvər‿ˈiːzi] beidseitig gebraten *(Ei)* **IV U4,** 61
over there [ˌəʊvə ˈðeə] da drüben **I U5,** 66
to come over [kʌm‿ˈəʊvə] herüberkommen **I U2,** 27
to run over [rʌn‿ˈəʊvə] hinüberrennen **IV U1,** 17
*to **overdo** [ˌəʊvəˈduː] übertreiben **IV U2,** 26
overheard [ˌəʊvəˈhɜːd] zufällig mitgehört °**III U1,** 14
to **owe** [əʊ] verdanken, schulden **V T3,** 43
barn **owl** [ˈbɑːn‿aʊl] Schleiereule **II U7,** 94
to **own** [əʊn] besitzen **IV U4,** 58
own [əʊn] eigener/eigene/eigenes **II U6,** 76
on one's own [ɒn wʌnz‿ˈəʊn] (ganz) allein **V T3,** 40
owner [ˈəʊnə] Besitzer/Besitzerin **II U5,** 71

P

pacemaker [ˈpeɪsˌmeɪkə] Herzschrittmacher **IV U3,** 41
to **pack** [pæk] packen **I U6,** 80
packet [ˈpækɪt] Päckchen, Paket **I U5,** 68
page [peɪdʒ] Seite **I U1,** 19
pain [peɪn] Schmerz **IV U3,** 48
paint [peɪnt] Farbe **II U3,** 40

to **paint** [peɪnt] (an)malen, (an)streichen **I U7,** 90
painter ['peɪntə] Maler/Malerin °**IV U1,** 15
pair [peə] Paar °**I U1,** 22
palace ['pælɪs] Palast **III U2,** 22
pancake ['pænkeɪk] Pfannkuchen **IV U1,** 12
panel ['pænl] Tafel, Platte; Element **VT4,** 59
solar panel [ˌsəʊlə 'pænl] Sonnenkollektor **VT4,** 59
to **panic** ['pænɪk] sich aufregen, in Panik geraten **II U5,** 70
panther ['pæntθə] Panter **II U2,** 25
paper ['peɪpə] Papier; Zeitung; Dokument **IV U1,** 14
parachuting ['pærəˌʃu:tɪŋ] Fallschirmspringen **VT3,** 40
parade [pə'reɪd] Parade, Umzug **IV U1,** 14
paradise ['pærəˌdaɪs] Paradies **III U3,** 40
paragliding ['pærəˌglaɪdɪŋ] Paragliding, Gleitschirmfliegen **VT3,** 40
parents *(pl)* ['peərənts] Eltern **I U2,** 26
park [pɑ:k] Park **I U3,** 40
national park [ˌnæʃnl 'pɑ:k] Nationalpark **IV U4,** 56
(park) ranger [ˌpɑ:k 'reɪndʒə] Parkaufseher/Parkaufseherin, Ranger **IV U4,** 58
theme park ['θi:m ˌpɑ:k] Freizeitpark **IV U2,** 22
part [pɑ:t] Teil **II U3,** 47; Rolle **II U5,** 70
to take part in [teɪk 'pɑ:t‿ɪn] teilnehmen an **III U4,** 53
partner ['pɑ:tnə] Partner/Partnerin **I U1,** 15
part-time (P/T) [ˌpɑ:t'taɪm] Teilzeit- **VT1,** 14; **VT2,** 32
party ['pɑ:ti] Party, Feier **I U5,** 68
to have a party [ˌhæv‿ə 'pɑ:ti] eine Party feiern **I U5,** 68
to **pass** [pɑ:s] weitergeben, herüberreichen **II U1,** 18; bestehen **IV U2,** 28; vorübergehen **IV U3,** 48
passenger ['pæsndʒə] Passagier/Passagierin, Beifahrer/Beifahrerin **III U3,** 39
passport ['pɑ:spɔ:t] (Reise-)Pass **III U3,** 44
passports *(pl)* ['pɑ:spɔ:ts] Passkontrolle **III U3,** 44
past [pɑ:st] Vergangenheit **II U1,** 13
past [pɑ:st] vorbei, vorüber **I U7,** 97; nach *(Uhrzeit)* **II U1,** 12
half past (two) ['hɑ:f pɑ:st] halb (drei) **I U3,** 40
pastrami [pəs'trɑ:mi] Pastrami **IV U1,** 12
path [pɑ:θ] Pfad, Weg **II U4,** 56
patient ['peɪʃnt] Patient/Patientin **III U5,** 70
pause [pɔ:z] Pause °**III U5,** 74
pay [peɪ] Lohn, Gehalt, Bezahlung **VT1,** 14; **VT3,** 55; **VT4,** 62
*to **pay (for)** [peɪ] (be)zahlen **IV U2,** 30
PC [ˌpi:'si:] PC **II U5,** 63; Polizeibeamter/Polizeibeamtin °**III U5,** 71
pea [pi:] Erbse **II U4,** 54
peace [pi:s] Friede **II U7,** 88
peaceful ['pi:sfl] friedlich **VT3,** 45
pear [peə] Birne **II U4,** 54
peer [pɪə] Gleichaltriger/Gleichaltrige **VT2,** 28
pen [pen] Füller **I U1,** 14
pence *(pl)* [pents] Pence *(Währung)* **I U5,** 67
pencil ['pensl] Bleistift **I U1,** 14
pencil case ['pensl ˌkeɪs] Federmäppchen **I U1,** 14
penknife, **penknives** *(pl)* ['pennaɪf; 'pennaɪvz] Taschenmesser **I U6,** 84
people ['pi:pl] Leute, Menschen **I U2,** 29
per [pɜ:] pro **III U2,** 27
per cent (%) [pə 'sent] Prozent **IV U1,** 10
perfect ['pɜ:fɪkt] perfekt, vollkommen **VT2,** 32
to **perform** [pə'fɔ:m] aufführen, auftreten **III U4,** 53
performance [pə'fɔ:məns] Aufführung, Vorstellung **III U4,** 53
perhaps [pə'hæps] vielleicht °**IV U1,** 8
period *(AE)* ['pɪəriəd] Unterrichtsstunde; Periode, Zeitabschnitt **IV U2,** 29
permanent ['pɜ:mnənt] permanent, dauerhaft **VT1,** 14
permission [pə'mɪʃn] Erlaubnis **IV U2,** 25
person ['pɜ:sn] Person **II U3,** 42
personal ['pɜ:snl] persönlich °**III U1,** 11
pet [pet] Haustier, Liebling **III U5,** 70
phone [fəʊn] Telefon **I U1,** 11
cell phone *(AE)* ['sel ˌfəʊn] Handy, Mobiltelefon **IV U3,** 42
phone box ['fəʊn ˌbɒks] Telefonzelle **III U3,** 44
phone call ['fəʊn ˌkɔ:l] (Telefon-)Anruf °**II U4,** 57
phone number ['fəʊn ˌnʌmbə] Telefonnummer **I U1,** 11
to **phone** [fəʊn] anrufen, telefonieren **I U2,** 33
phonetic [fə'netɪk] phonetisch °**III U5,** 75
photo ['fəʊtəʊ] Foto, Fotografie **II U5,** 64
photographer [fə'tɒgrəfə] Fotograf/Fotografin **IV U5,** 73
photography [fə'tɒgrəfi] Fotografie **VT2,** 32
phrase [freɪz] Redewendung, Ausdruck °**I U1,** 19
physical ['fɪzɪkl] physisch, körperlich **II U1,** 10
Physical Education (PE) [ˌfɪzɪkl‿edʒʊ'keɪʃn] Sport *(Schulfach)* **II U1,** 10
to **pick** [pɪk] pflücken; auswählen **I U6,** 78
to pick up [pɪk‿'ʌp] aufheben, abholen **II U1,** 18
picker ['pɪkə] Pflücker/Pflückerin **IV U4,** 64
pickpocket ['pɪkˌpɒkɪt] Taschendieb/Taschendiebin **III U2,** 24
picture ['pɪktʃə] Bild **I U1,** 14; Film **IV U5,** 73
to take pictures [teɪk 'pɪktʃəz] fotografieren, Fotos machen **II U5,** 62
piece [pi:s] Stück **IV U3,** 48
pier [pɪə] Pier, Landungssteg **III U2,** 26
I want my … **pierced.** [aɪ 'wɒnt maɪ … 'pɪəst] Ich möchte mein/e … piercen lassen. **III U4,** 52
pig [pɪg] Schwein **I U6,** 82
piggy bank ['pɪgi bæŋk] Sparschwein **II U2,** 23
pilot ['paɪlət] Pilot/Pilotin **IV U1,** 16
pink [pɪŋk] pink, rosa **I LUA,** 24
pioneer [ˌpaɪə'nɪə] Pionier/Pionierin, Wegbereiter/Wegbereiterin **VT3,** 43
pipe [paɪp] Pfeife **III U5,** 72
pitch [pɪtʃ] Spielfeld **III U1,** 10
pitcher ['pɪtʃə] Pitcher/Pitcherin **III U1,** 14
pizza ['pi:tsə] Pizza **I U5,** 68
place [pleɪs] Platz, Stelle, Ort **I U2,** 26
change of place [ˌtʃeɪndʒ‿əv 'pleɪs] Ortswechsel °**III U4,** 55

to go places [ˌgəʊ 'pleɪsɪz] herumreisen **IV U4,** 64
to take place [teɪk 'pleɪs] stattfinden **III U4,** 53
plan [plæn] Plan **II U5,** 66
to **plan** [plæn] planen **II U4,** 52
plane [pleɪn] Flugzeug **II U2,** 23
planet ['plænɪt] Planet **IV U3,** 41
plant [plɑːnt] Pflanze **II U6,** 74
plate [pleɪt] Teller **II U4,** 50
home plate ['həʊm ˌpleɪt] Home Plate **III U1,** 14
platform ['plætfɔːm] Plattform, Tribüne, Bahnsteig **IV U4,** 56
play [pleɪ] Theaterstück, Spiel **I U7,** 90
to **play** [pleɪ] spielen **I U1,** 14
player ['pleɪə] Spieler/Spielerin, Mitspieler/Mitspielerin **III U1,** 8
CD player [ˌsiː'diː ˌpleɪə] CD-Player **II U4,** 56
DVD player [ˌdiːviː'diː ˌpleɪə] DVD-Player **II U5,** 62
playground ['pleɪgraʊnd] Schulhof, Spielplatz **I U1,** 18
please [pliːz] bitte **I U1,** 19
*to be **pleased** with [biː 'pliːzd wɪð] zufrieden sein mit **I U6,** 87
to **pledge** [pledʒ] geloben **IV U2,** 23
to **plough** [plaʊ] pflügen **IV U3,** 41
plug [plʌg] Stecker, Stöpsel **IV U3,** 44
plural ['plʊrəl] Plural, Mehrzahl **I U6,** 88
plus [plʌs] plus, zuzüglich **IV U3,** 46
p.m. [ˌpiː'em] nachmittags (*Uhrzeit*) **III U3,** 41
pocket ['pɒkɪt] Hosen-/Jackentasche **II U2,** 22
pocket money ['pɒkɪt ˌmʌni] Taschengeld **II U2,** 22
poem ['pəʊɪm] Gedicht **III U4,** 53
poet ['pəʊɪt] Dichter/Dichterin, Poet/Poetin **III U4,** 53
poetry ['pəʊətri] Lyrik **III U4,** 53
poetry slam ['pəʊətri ˌslæm] Poetry Slam (*Gedichtwettbewerb*) **III U4,** 53
point [pɔɪnt] Punkt **II U4,** 53
to **point (to)** [pɔɪnt] zeigen (auf), deuten (auf) **IV U1,** 16
police [pə'liːs] Polizei **I U6,** 87
policeman, policemen (*pl*) [pə'liːsmən; pə'liːsmen] Polizist **II U2,** 31
policy ['pɒlɪsi] Politik, politische Linie; Grundsatz **VT3,** 44
Polish ['pəʊlɪʃ] polnisch **I U2,** 29
polite [pə'laɪt] höflich **II U3,** 39
political [pə'lɪtɪkl] politisch **IV U3,** 48
pollution [pə'luːʃn] (Umwelt-) Verschmutzung **III U2,** 30
pompom ['pɒmpɒm] Pompon (*bunte Quaste der Cheerleader*) **IV U2,** 23
pony ['pəʊni] Pony **II U6,** 74
swimming **pool** ['swɪmɪŋ ˌpuːl] Schwimmbecken; Schwimmbad **III U3,** 40
poor [pɔː; pʊə] arm **III U5,** 76
pop [pɒp] Popmusik **IV U5,** 73
to **pop** [pɒp] knallen (lassen) **IV U5,** 80
popular ['pɒpjələ] populär, beliebt **II U2,** 23
population [ˌpɒpjə'leɪʃn] Bevölkerung **III U2,** 27
pork [pɔːk] Schweinefleisch **II U4,** 49
port [pɔːt] Hafen **III U3,** 39
to **pose** [pəʊz] posieren; (sich) darstellen **IV U5,** 73
position [pə'zɪʃn] Position **VT3,** 44
positive ['pɒzətɪv] positiv, bejaht °**IV U5,** 83
possible ['pɒsəbl] möglich **III U4,** 57
post [pəʊst] Pfosten, Mast **III U1,** 13
post office ['pəʊst‿ɒfɪs] Postamt **III U2,** 26
to **post** [pəʊst] aufgeben (*einen Brief*), abschicken, posten (*im Internet-forum*) **IV U5,** 76
postcard ['pəʊstkɑːd] Postkarte **I U6,** 78
poster ['pəʊstə] Poster, Plakat **I U1,** 11
pot [pɒt] Topf **II U7,** 90
potato, potatoes (*pl*) [pə'teɪtəʊ; pə'teɪtəʊz] Kartoffel **II U4,** 54
couch potato ['kaʊtʃ pəˌteɪtəʊ] Fernsehglotzer/Fernsehglotzerin, Couchpotato **III U5,** 75
pound (£) [paʊnd] Pfund (*Währung*) **I U5,** 66
pound (lb) [paʊnd] Pfund (*Gewicht*) **II U4,** 52
poverty ['pɒvəti] Armut **IV U1,** 11
powder ['paʊdə] Puder, Pulver **III U5,** 77
power ['paʊə] Kraft, Stärke, Macht **II U6,** 74
practice ['præktɪs] Training **III U1,** 16
to **practise** ['præktɪs] üben, proben, praktizieren **II U5,** 66
to **prepare** [prɪ'peə] vorbereiten, zubereiten **VT2,** 32
present ['preznt] Geschenk **I U5,** 69; Gegenwart, Präsens °**II U2,** 26
to **present** [prɪ'zent] präsentieren; verleihen **IV U5,** 73
presentation [ˌprezn'teɪʃn] Präsentation °**III U1,** 14
president ['prezɪdnt] Präsident/Präsidentin °**II U3,** 42
to **press** [pres] drücken, pressen **II U7,** 95
to **pretend** [prɪ'tend] vorgeben, tun als ob °**VT2,** 26
pretty ['prɪti] ziemlich **IV U1,** 17
price [praɪs] Preis **I U7,** 95
half-price [ˌhɑːf'praɪs] zum halben Preis **III U1,** 12
pride [praɪd] Stolz; Hochmut **VT3,** 42
primary school ['praɪməri ˌskuːl] Grundschule **III U4,** 57
prince [prɪns] Prinz **III U2,** 25
to **print** [prɪnt] drucken **II U5,** 64
pristine ['prɪstiːn] makellos, rein **IV U5,** 80
private ['praɪvɪt] privat **III U4,** 57
prize [praɪz] Preis **IV U2,** 22
probably ['prɒbəbli] wahrscheinlich **II U7,** 88
problem ['prɒbləm] Problem, Schwierigkeit **I U1,** 20
to **produce** [prə'djuːs] herstellen, produzieren **IV U5,** 74
producer [prə'djuːsə] Produzent/Produzentin, Erzeuger/Erzeugerin **VT4,** 62
product ['prɒdʌkt] Produkt, Artikel, Ware °**VT3,** 40; **VT4,** 60
production [prə'dʌkʃn] Herstellung, Produktion **IV U5,** 73
professional [prə'feʃnl] professionell, beruflich, Berufs- **VT1,** 14
profile ['prəʊfaɪl] Profil; Porträt; Steckbrief **VT3,** 43
programme ['prəʊgræm] Programm, Sendung (*TV, Radio*) **III U5,** 68
project ['prɒdʒekt] Projekt **I U2,** 34
promise ['prɒmɪs] Versprechen °**II U6,** 77
to **promise** ['prɒmɪs] versprechen **II U6,** 77
pros and cons [ˌprəʊz‿ənd 'kɒnz] Für und Wider, Pro und Kontra, Vor- und Nachteile **VT4,** 60
to **protect** [prə'tekt] (be)schützen **VT1,** 10
protest ['prəʊtest] Protest **VT3,** 41
to **protest** [prəʊ'test] protestieren **VT3,** 40

protester [prə'testə] Protestierender/ Protestierende, Demonstrant/ Demonstrantin **VT3,** 44
proud of ['praʊd‿əv] stolz auf **III U4,** 58
provider [prə'vaɪdə] Anbieter/ Anbieterin, Lieferant/Lieferantin; Provider °**VT1,** 14
public ['pʌblɪk] öffentlich **IV U1,** 9
 public school [ˌpʌblɪk 'sku:l] staatliche Schule (USA), Privatschule (GB) **IV U2,** 28
pudding ['pʊdɪŋ] Pudding; Nachtisch **II U4,** 49
to **pull** [pʊl] ziehen **II U4,** 57
punk [pʌŋk] Punk **III U2,** 31; Punkmusik **IV U5,** 76
pupil ['pju:pl] Schüler/Schülerin **I U1,** 10
purple ['pɜ:pl] lila, violett **I LUA,** 24
to **push** [pʊʃ] stoßen, schieben, drücken **II U3,** 36
*to **put** [pʊt] setzen, stellen, legen **I U3,** 42
 to put down [pʊt 'daʊn] auflegen *(Tel.)*; hinlegen, hinstellen °**II U7,** 89
 to put in [pʊt‿'ɪn] einsetzen **II U7,** 95; einschieben **III U4,** 58; hinzufügen **IV U1,** 12
 to put on [pʊt‿'ɒn] aufsetzen; anziehen **I U6,** 81; auftragen *(Make-up)* **II U5,** 71
 to put out [pʊt‿'aʊt] ausmachen; löschen **III U2,** 28; hinausstellen **III U4,** 55
 to put up [pʊt‿'ʌp] aufstellen, aufbauen **I U6,** 84
puzzle ['pʌzl] Rätsel, Puzzle **III U4,** 62
 crossword puzzle ['krɒswɜ:d 'pʌzl] Kreuzworträtsel °**I U5,** 71

Q

qualification [ˌkwɒlɪfɪ'keɪʃn] Qualifikation, Befähigung **VT2,** 32
quality ['kwɒləti] Qualität; Eigenschaft °**VT2,** 31
quarter ['kwɔ:tə] Viertel **III U3,** 42; Vierteldollar *(Währung)* **IV U1,** 13
 quarter past ['kwɔ:tə pɑ:st] Viertel nach **I U3,** 42
 quarter to ['kwɔ:tə tə] Viertel vor **I U3,** 42
queen [kwi:n] Königin **II U5,** 62
 homecoming queen [ˌhəʊmkʌmɪŋ 'kwi:n] Ballkönigin **IV U2,** 23
question ['kwestʃn] Frage **I U2,** 31
 question mark ['kwestʃən ˌmɑ:k] Fragezeichen °**IV U1,** 17
questionnaire [ˌkwestʃə'neə] Fragebogen °**II U4,** 53
queue [kju:] Warteschlange **III U2,** 22
quick [kwɪk] schnell **I U6,** 86
quiet ['kwaɪət] Ruhe, Stille **II U7,** 88
quiet ['kwaɪət] ruhig, still, leise **I U6,** 78
*to **quit** [kwɪt] aufgeben, mit etw. aufhören; kündigen **VT3,** 46
quiz [kwɪz] Quiz, Rätsel °**I U1,** 13
quota ['kwəʊtə] Quote **IV U1,** 10

R

race [reɪs] Wettlauf, Rennen **I U7,** 92; Rasse **VT3,** 44
 to run a race [ˌrʌn‿ə 'reɪs] einen Wettlauf machen **I U7,** 92
racial ['reɪʃl] Rassen- **VT3,** 41
radio ['reɪdiəʊ] Radio **I U2,** 33
 radio show ['reɪdiəʊ ˌʃəʊ] Radiosendung **I U2,** 33
raid [reɪd] Razzia; Angriff **IV U4,** 65
rain [reɪn] Regen **II U6,** 78
to **rain** [reɪn] regnen **I U4,** 62
rainy ['reɪni] regnerisch, verregnet **I U6,** 79
rally ['ræli] Jugendtreffen, Versammlung; Rallye **IV U2,** 22
ranch [ræntʃ] Ranch **IV U4,** 57
(park) **ranger** [ˌpɑ:k 'reɪndʒə] Parkaufseher/Parkaufseherin, Ranger **IV U4,** 58
rap [ræp] Rap **I U1,** 15
to **rap** [ræp] rappen **I U3,** 40
rapper ['ræpə] Rapper/Rapperin **IV U5,** 76
I'd **rather** [aɪd 'rɑ:ðə] ich würde lieber **II U2,** 22
raw [rɔ:] grob, roh **IV U5,** 80
R&B [ˌɑ:r‿n'bi:] R&B **IV U5,** 73
to **reach** [ri:tʃ] erreichen **II U6,** 78
reaction [ri'ækʃn] Reaktion, Resonanz °**VT3,** 42
*to **read** [ri:d] lesen **I LUB,** 38
 to read out [ri:d‿'aʊt] etw. laut vorlesen °**VT2,** 31; °**VT4,** 67
reader ['ri:də] Leser/Leserin **VT3,** 46; Lesebuch, Leseheft, Lektüre °**VT4,** 66
reading ['ri:dɪŋ] Lesen °**III U5,** 74; Lesung; Lektüre °**VT2,** 31
ready ['redi] fertig, bereit **II U4,** 50
 to get ready [get 'redi] sich vorbereiten **II U5,** 68
real [rɪəl] echt, richtig, wirklich **II U3,** 38
to **realise** ['rɪəlaɪz] erkennen, sich klar werden **VT2,** 33; **VT4,** 62
reality [ri'æləti] Realität, Wirklichkeit **IV U3,** 41
 reality show [ri'æləti ˌʃəʊ] Realityshow **III U5,** 68
really ['rɪəli] wirklich **I U2,** 34
reason ['ri:zn] Grund **VT3,** 46
reception [rɪ'sepʃn] Rezeption, Empfang **III U5,** 72
recipe ['resɪpi:] Rezept **I U7,** 94
to **recognise** ['rekəgnaɪz] erkennen °**VT3,** 49
record ['rekɔ:d] (Schall-)Platte **IV U3,** 43; Aufnahme, Aufzeichnung; Beleg; Akte **VT3,** 47
 on record [ɒn 'rekɔ:d] verzeichnet, dokumentiert **III U3,** 40
to **record** [rɪ'kɔ:d] aufnehmen, aufzeichnen **II U5,** 63
recording [rɪ'kɔ:dɪŋ] Aufnahme **IV U3,** 46
red [red] rot **I LUA,** 24
 to go red [gəʊ 'red] rot werden **II U1,** 11
reef [ri:f] Riff **VT1,** 10; **VT4,** 61
ref(eree) [ˌrefr'i:] Schiedsrichter/ Schiedsrichterin **III U1,** 12
 referee [ˌrefr'i:] Referenz *(Person)* **VT1,** 15
reference ['refrns] Referenz; Bezug, Verweis **VT1,** 14
refrain [rɪ'freɪn] Refrain **IV U5,** 78
refrigerator [rɪ'frɪdʒreɪtə] Kühlschrank **IV U3,** 42
reggae ['regeɪ] Reggae **IV U5,** 73
to **register** ['redʒɪstə] (sich) registrieren, (sich) anmelden **IV U5,** 76
registration [ˌredʒɪ'streɪʃn] Registrierung, Erfassung **II U1,** 10
regular ['regjələ] Stammkunde/ Stammkundin **III U2,** 31; regelmäßig, regulär **VT3,** 46
to **rehearse** [rɪ'hɜ:s] proben *(ein Theaterstück)* **I U7,** 90
religion [rɪ'lɪdʒn] Religion **VT3,** 42
religious [rɪ'lɪdʒəs] religiös **II U1,** 12

Religious Education (RE) [rɪˌlɪdʒəs‿edʒʊ'keɪʃn] Religionsunterricht **II U1,** 12
to **relive** [ˌriː'lɪv] noch einmal erleben **III U2,** 22
to **remember** [rɪ'membə] sich erinnern (an), sich merken **I U3,** 49
to **reminisce** [ˌremɪ'nɪs] zurückdenken, in Erinnerungen schwelgen **IV U5,** 80
remixed ['riːmɪkst] neu gemischt °**V T2,** 31
remote [rɪ'məʊt] fern, abgelegen **V T1,** 12
remote control [rɪˌməʊt kən'trəʊl] Fernbedienung, Fernsteuerung **IV U3,** 41
rent [rent] Miete, Pacht **V T3,** 46
to **rent** [rent] mieten, pachten **V T3,** 46
to **repair** [rɪ'peə] reparieren **IV U1,** 17
to **repeat** [rɪ'piːt] wiederholen °**III U5,** 75
to **replace** [rɪ'pleɪs] ersetzen °**V T1,** 16
report [rɪ'pɔːt] Bericht, Meldung; Zeugnis **IV U3,** 40
to **report** [rɪ'pɔːt] berichten °**II U4,** 51
reporter [rɪ'pɔːtə] Reporter/Reporterin **I U7,** 92
to **require** [rɪ'kwaɪə] benötigen, brauchen; anfordern **V T1,** 15
rescue ['reskjuː] Rettung **III U5,** 70
to **rescue** ['reskjuː] retten **II U6,** 83
research [rɪ'sɜːtʃ] Recherche, Forschung, Untersuchung **IV U3,** 41
reservation [ˌrezə'veɪʃn] Reservat; Reservierung **IV U4,** 56
respect [rɪ'spekt] Respekt **III U4,** 53
response [rɪ'spɒns] Reaktion, Antwort **III U4,** 53
rest [rest] Rest **III U1,** 17; Rast, Ruhe **V T3,** 42
rest area ['rest ˌeəriə] Rastplatz **IV U4,** 61
to **rest** [rest] sich ausruhen, sich entspannen **III U3,** 46; rasten, ausruhen; liegen **V T3,** 42
restaurant ['restrɒnt] Restaurant **II U4,** 55
result [rɪ'zʌlt] Ergebnis, Resultat **IV U4,** 62
*to **retell** [riː'tel] nacherzählen, nochmals erzählen °**V T4,** 67
review [rɪ'vjuː] Kritik **III U5,** 73
revision [rɪ'vɪʒn] Wiederholung °**I U2,** 32
*to **rewrite** [ˌriː'raɪt] noch einmal schreiben °**II U4,** 58
rhyme [raɪm] Reim °**I LUA,** 25
rhyming ['raɪmɪŋ] (sich) reimend °**II U4,** 58
rice [raɪs] Reis **II U4,** 49
rich [rɪtʃ] reich **III U2,** 25
ride [raɪd] Ritt, Fahrt; Mitfahrgelegenheit **IV U4,** 65
*to **ride** [raɪd] fahren, reiten **I LUB,** 38
riding ['raɪdɪŋ] Reiten **IV U4,** 58
horseback riding ['hɔːsbæk ˌraɪdɪŋ] Reiten **IV U4,** 58
right [raɪt] Recht **V T3,** 42
civil rights *(pl)* [ˌsɪvl 'raɪts] Bürgerrechte °**V T3,** 45
Civil Rights Movement (CRM) [ˌsɪvl 'raɪts ˌmuːvmənt] Bürgerrechts-bewegung **V T3,** 44
right [raɪt] richtig, korrekt **I U1,** 13; rechter/rechte/rechtes; rechts **I U4,** 55
all right [ɔːl 'raɪt] in Ordnung **IV U4,** 64
Go right. [gəʊ 'raɪt] Biege nach rechts ab. **I LUC,** 52
on the right [ɒn ðə 'raɪt] rechts **I U2,** 28
right away [raɪt‿ə'weɪ] sofort, gleich **II U4,** 57
right now [ˌraɪt 'naʊ] jetzt gleich, in diesem Augenblick **I U7,** 92
to be right [biː 'raɪt] Recht haben **II U4,** 56
to get … right [get … 'raɪt] richtig machen **II U3,** 44
to turn right [tɜːn 'raɪt] rechts abbiegen **II U7,** 97
ring [rɪŋ] Ring **III U3,** 41
rubber ring [ˌrʌbə 'rɪŋ] Schwimmreifen **III U3,** 41
*to **ring** [rɪŋ] klingeln **I U5,** 75
to ring out [ˌrɪŋ‿'aʊt] erklingen, ertönen **V T3,** 42
The bell rings. [ðə 'bel rɪŋz] Es klingelt. **II U4,** 50
ice **rink** ['aɪs rɪŋk] Eis-/Schlittschuh-bahn **II U2,** 23
riot [raɪət] Aufruhr, Ausschreitung, Unruhe **V T3,** 44
rise [raɪz] Aufstieg, Anstieg **IV U5,** 74
*to **rise** [raɪz] steigen, wachsen, zunehmen **II U6,** 78
rival ['raɪvl] Rivale/Rivalin, Konkurrent/Konkurrentin **IV U2,** 31
river ['rɪvə] Fluss **I LUC,** 52
road [rəʊd] Straße, Landstraße **I LUC,** 52
to **roar** [rɔː] dröhnen **IV U1,** 16
to **rob** [rɒb] rauben, ausrauben **III U2,** 24
robber ['rɒbə] Räuber/Räuberin **IV U3,** 48
robot ['rəʊbɒt] Roboter **IV U3,** 41
rock [rɒk] Rockmusik; Stein, Felsen **IV U5,** 73
to **rock** [rɒk] rocken; schaukeln **IV U5,** 80
rodeo [rəʊ'deɪəʊ; 'rəʊdiəʊ] Rodeo **IV U4,** 57
role [rəʊl] Rolle **II U1,** 10
roof [ruːf] Dach **I U2,** 26
room [ruːm; rʊm] Zimmer, Raum, Platz **I U1,** 16
chat room ['tʃæt rʊm] Chatroom *(Internetforum, wo man sich online unterhalten kann)* **IV U5,** 76
dining room ['daɪnɪŋ rʊm] Esszimmer, Speisesaal **I LUA,** 24
living room ['lɪvɪŋ rʊm] Wohnzimmer **I LUA,** 24
roping ['rəʊpɪŋ] Einfangen der Rinder mit dem Lasso **IV U4,** 58
round [raʊnd] Runde **III U4,** 53
round [raʊnd] (um …) herum **IV U1,** 17
route [ruːt; raʊt] Route °**III U2,** 24
row [rəʊ] Reihe **III U1,** 15
royal ['rɔɪəl] königlich **III U2,** 22
RSVP [ˌɑːr‿es viː 'piː] um Antwort wird gebeten °**I U5,** 70
rubber ['rʌbə] Radiergummi **I U1,** 14; Gummi; Kautschuk **III U3,** 41
rubber boots *(pl)* [ˌrʌbə 'buːts] Gummistiefel **II U6,** 74
rubber ring [ˌrʌbə 'rɪŋ] Schwimmreifen **III U3,** 41
rubbish ['rʌbɪʃ] Abfall, Abfälle, Müll **I U6,** 84; Unsinn **II U7,** 94
rucksack ['rʌksæk] Rucksack **III U2,** 24
rugby ['rʌgbi] Rugby **III U1,** 8
rugby boot ['rʌgbi buːt] Rugbyschuh, Stollenschuh **III U1,** 8
rule [ruːl] Regel, Vorschrift **I U3,** 43
ruler ['ruːlə] Lineal **I U1,** 14; Herrscher/Herrscherin **V T3,** 46
run [rʌn] Lauf **II U4,** 57; Runde **III U1,** 9
*to **run** [rʌn] rennen, laufen **I U3,** 48
to run a race [ˌrʌn‿ə 'reɪs] einen Wettlauf machen **I U7,** 92

to run away [rʌn‿ə'weɪ] wegrennen **I U3,** 48
to run into [rʌn‿'ɪntə] laufen gegen, stoßen gegen **III U1,** 17
to run on ['rʌn‿ɒn] laufen mit *(Auto)* **V T4,** 61
to run out [rʌn‿'aʊt] ausgehen *(Zeit),* ablaufen *(Zeit)* **IV U1,** 10
to run over [rʌn‿'əʊvə] hinüberrennen **IV U1,** 17
to run upstairs [ˌrʌn‿ʌp'steəz] die Treppe hinaufrennen **III U3,** 47
runaway ['rʌnəˌweɪ] Ausreißer/Ausreißerin **III U5,** 71
runner ['rʌnə] Läufer/Läuferin **I U7,** 92
Russian ['rʌʃn] russisch; Russe/Russin **I U2,** 29

S

sacred ['seɪkrɪd] heilig **IV U4,** 56
sad [sæd] traurig, bedauerlich **II U1,** 19
safe [seɪf] sicher **III U3,** 40
to **sail** [seɪl] segeln, fahren *(Schiff)* **III U3,** 39
salad ['sæləd] Salat **II U4,** 49
sales talk ['seɪlz tɔ:k] Verkaufsgespräch °**V T4,** 63
salt [sɔ:lt] Salz **V T1,** 12
saltie *(Aus)* ['sɔ:lti] Salzwasserkrokodil °**V T1,** 12
saltwater ['sɔ:ltˌwɔ:tə] Salzwasser **V T1,** 12
same [seɪm] derselbe/dieselbe/dasselbe °**II U1,** 11
the same [seɪm] derselbe/dieselbe/dasselbe; gleich **III U1,** 19
sand [sænd] Sand **III U1,** 10
sandwich ['sænwɪdʒ] Sandwich, belegtes Brot **I U1,** 14
sandy ['sændi] sandig **III U3,** 40
satellite ['sætlaɪt] Satellit **IV U3,** 41
Saturday ['sætədeɪ] Samstag **I U2,** 34
sausage ['sɒsɪdʒ] Wurst, Würstchen **II U4,** 49
to **save** [seɪv] retten; sparen **II U6,** 80
*to **say** [seɪ] sagen, sprechen **I U1,** 11
It said .... [ɪt 'sed] Es lautete .... **II U2,** 30
What does it say? [ˌwɒt dʌz‿ɪt 'seɪ] Was steht da? **II U3,** 44
to **scare** ['skeə] Angst machen **IV U3,** 49
scared [skeəd] verängstigt **I U2,** 35
I'm scared. [aɪm 'skeəd] Ich habe Angst. **II U3,** 44
scary ['skeəri] unheimlich, gruselig **II U7,** 95
scene [si:n] Szene, Schauplatz **IV U5,** 80
scenery ['si:nri] Landschaft **IV U4,** 56
school [sku:l] Schule **I U1,** 10
comprehensive school [kɒmprɪ'hensɪv ˌsku:l] Gesamtschule **III U4,** 56
elementary school *(AE)* [elɪ'mentri ˌsku:l] Grundschule **IV U2,** 28
grammar school ['græmə ˌsku:l] Gymnasium **III U4,** 57
high school ['haɪ ˌsku:l] High School *(weiterführende Schule in den USA, Oberstufe)* **IV U2,** 22
middle school *(AE)* ['mɪdl ˌsku:l] Mittelschule *(weiterführende Schule in den USA, Mittelstufe)* **IV U2,** 28
primary school ['praɪməri ˌsku:l] Grundschule **III U4,** 57
public school [ˌpʌblɪk 'sku:l] staatliche Schule (USA), Privatschule (GB) **IV U2,** 28
school bag ['sku:l bæg] Schultasche, Schulranzen **I U1,** 14
School of the Air [ˌsku:l‿əv ði 'eə] School of the Air *(Fernunterricht per Internet)* **V T1,** 11
Science ['saɪəns] Wissenschaft, Naturwissenschaft **II U1,** 10
science fiction [ˌsaɪəns 'fɪkʃn] Sciencefiction **III U5,** 68
scientist ['saɪəntɪst] Wissenschaftler/Wissenschaftlerin **III U5,** 77
scone [skɒn] Scone *(Gebäck)* **I U7,** 94
score [skɔ:] Punktestand, Spielstand **III U1,** 12
to **score** [skɔ:] punkten, ein Tor schießen **III U1,** 9
Scottish ['skɒtɪʃ] schottisch **II U3,** 36
screen [skri:n] Bildschirm, Leinwand **III U5,** 68
screen shot ['skri:n ˌʃɒt] Screenshot **III U5,** 68
script [skrɪpt] Drehbuch **III U5,** 69
sea [si:] Meer **II U7,** 88
sea lion ['si: ˌlaɪən] Seelöwe **V T2,** 32
sea wasp ['si: ˌwɒsp] Seewespe **V T1,** 12
seal [si:l] Seehund, Robbe **V T1,** 12
search [sɜ:tʃ] Suche; Such- °**IV U5,** 73
to **search** [sɜ:tʃ] (durch)suchen °**IV U3,** 46
seasick ['si:sɪk] seekrank **IV U1,** 11
seaside ['si:saɪd] Küste, Meeresküste **III U5,** 70
season ['si:zn] Jahreszeit, Saison **I U6,** 79
seat [si:t] Sitz, Sitzplatz **II U2,** 23
second ['seknd] Sekunde **I U2,** 30
secondly ['sekndli] zweitens **IV U4,** 62
secret ['si:krət] geheim, heimlich **IV U3,** 48
secretary ['sekrətri] Sekretär/Sekretärin **III U4,** 56
*to **see** [si:] sehen **I U2,** 33; besuchen **II U1,** 19
See you! ['si: jə] Bis dann!, Bis .... **I U5,** 70
See you around! [ˌsi: jə ə'raʊnd] Bis dann!, Bis .... **IV U2,** 26
to see a doctor [si:‿ə 'dɒktə] zum Arzt gehen **II U4,** 52
seeker [si:kə] Suchender/Suchende °**V T1,** 14
segregation *(no pl)* [ˌsegrɪ'geɪʃn] (Rassen-)Trennung **V T3,** 44
seldom ['seldəm] selten **III U5,** 68
self-employment [ˌselfɪm'plɔɪmənt] Selbstständigkeit °**V T3,** 47
*to **sell** [sel] verkaufen **I U7,** 90
*to **send** [send] schicken **I U6,** 80
to send in [send‿'ɪn] einschicken **II U5,** 64
to send off [send‿'ɒf] vom Platz verweisen **III U1,** 12
sense [sens] Sinn, Bedeutung **V T3,** 47
sensible ['sensɪbl] vernünftig **III U3,** 40
sentence ['sentəns] Satz °**I U1,** 13; Verurteilung, Urteil, Strafe **V T1,** 10
September [sep'tembə] September **I U5,** 70
series, series *(pl)* ['sɪəri:z] Serie **III U5,** 70
servant ['sɜ:vnt] Diener/Dienerin **III U5,** 76
service ['sɜ:vɪs] Service, Dienst **II U6,** 83
session ['seʃn] Veranstaltung **III U4,** 57
*to **set** [set] stellen, einstellen **II U7,** 90
to set off [set‿'ɒf] auslösen *(Alarm)* **II U7,** 95; aufbrechen, sich auf den Weg machen **IV U4,** 64
to set the table [ˌset ðə 'teɪbl] den Tisch decken **II U4,** 50
to set up [set‿'ʌp] einrichten, aufbauen, gründen **IV U5,** 74

several ['sevrl] mehrere, verschiedene **V T3,** 43
shade [ʃeɪd] Schatten, Schattierung **V T4,** 66
shadow ['ʃædəʊ] Schatten **IV U5,** 78
*to **shake** [ʃeɪk] schütteln, zittern **III U4,** 60
Shall we ... ? ['ʃæl‿wi:] Wollen wir ... ? **III U4,** 59
shape [ʃeɪp] Form **IV U5,** 72
to **share** [ʃeə] teilen **III U5,** 78
shark [ʃɑ:k] Hai **V T1,** 12
Great White Shark [ˌgreɪt waɪt 'ʃɑ:k] Weißer Hai °**V T1,** 12
she [ʃi:] sie **I U1,** 12
shed [ʃed] Schuppen **I U2,** 26
sheep, sheep *(pl)* [ʃi:p] Schaf/Schafe **I U6,** 78
shelf, shelves *(pl)* [ʃelf; ʃelvz] Regal, Regalbrett **I U2,** 30
ship [ʃɪp] Schiff **I U4,** 54
shipping ['ʃɪpɪŋ] Schifffahrt, Verschiffung **V T4,** 60
shirt [ʃɜ:t] Hemd **I U3,** 44
shocked [ʃɒkt] geschockt, schockiert **III U5,** 74
shoe [ʃu:] Schuh **I U1,** 12
*to **shoot** [ʃu:t] (ab)schießen, erschießen **V T3,** 44
shop [ʃɒp] Laden, Geschäft **I U2,** 26
shop assistant ['ʃɒp‿əˌsɪstnt] Verkäufer/Verkäuferin **II U5,** 67
sports shop ['spɔ:ts ʃɒp] Sportgeschäft **I U5,** 66
to **shop** [ʃɒp] einkaufen **V T2,** 34
shopping ['ʃɒpɪŋ] Einkaufen, Einkauf **I U5,** 66
short [ʃɔ:t] kurz **I U4,** 55
shorts *(pl)* [ʃɔ:ts] Shorts, kurze Hose **II U1,** 10
shot [ʃɒt] Schuss, Schlag **III U5,** 68; Aufnahme, Foto; Einstellung **V T4,** 65
screen shot ['skri:n ˌʃɒt] Screenshot **III U5,** 68
***should** [ʃʊd] sollte/sollten **II U4,** 52
shoulder ['ʃəʊldə] Schulter **IV U2,** 31
to **shout** [ʃaʊt] schreien, rufen **I U1,** 15
show [ʃəʊ] Show, Sendung, Schau **I U2,** 33
radio show ['reɪdiəʊ ˌʃəʊ] Radiosendung **I U2,** 33
reality show [ri'æləti ˌʃəʊ] Realityshow **III U5,** 68
talk show ['tɔ:k ˌʃəʊ] Talkshow **III U5,** 68
*to **show** [ʃəʊ] zeigen **I U4,** 65
shower ['ʃaʊə] Regenguss; Dusche **II U6,** 74
to **shuffle** ['ʃʌfl] mischen °**II U6,** 79
shutter ['ʃʌtə] Verschluss, Klappe, Blende **IV U5,** 74
shuttle ['ʃʌtl] Raumfähre **IV U3,** 41
shy [ʃaɪ] schüchtern **III U4,** 57
sick [sɪk] krank **II U3,** 46
sick note ['sɪk ˌnəʊt] Krankmeldung **II U2,** 28
to feel sick [fi:l 'sɪk] Übelkeit verspüren **II U3,** 46
side [saɪd] Seite **III U2,** 26
sunny side up [ˌsʌni saɪd‿'ʌp] Spiegelei **IV U4,** 61
sidewalk *(AE)* ['saɪdwɔ:k] Gehweg °**IV U1,** 15
sight [saɪt] Sehenswürdigkeit; Sicht, Anblick **IV U4,** 57
sign [saɪn] Schild, Zeichen **I U2,** 26
vital signs *(pl)* [ˌvaɪtl 'saɪnz] Lebenszeichen **IV U5,** 78
to **sign** [saɪn] unterschreiben **II U5,** 66
signal ['sɪgnl] Signal **II U2,** 26; Zeichen **III U1,** 10
silent ['saɪlənt] still, leise **IV U5,** 74
silent movie [ˌsaɪlənt 'mu:vi] Stummfilm **IV U5,** 74
silly ['sɪli] dumm; Dummkopf **II U1,** 11
similar ['sɪmɪlə] ähnlich °**III U4,** 52
since [sɪnts] seit, seitdem **III U2,** 30
*to **sing** [sɪŋ] singen **I U2,** 33
singer ['sɪŋə] Sänger/Sängerin **II U1,** 14
sink [sɪŋk] Waschbecken *(AE),* Spülbecken **IV U3,** 44
to **sip** [sɪp] schluckweise trinken **IV U5,** 80
sir [sɜ:] mein Herr *(Anrede)* **III U5,** 72
Sir [sɜ:] Sir *(Anrede für einen Ritter)* °**III U5,** 75
sister ['sɪstə] Schwester **I LUA,** 25
half-sister ['hɑ:fˌsɪstə] Halbschwester **I U2,** 26
*to **sit** [sɪt] sitzen **I U3,** 48
to sit back [ˌsɪt 'bæk] sich zurücklehnen **IV U1,** 16
to sit down [sɪt 'daʊn] sich (hin)setzen **I U1,** 19
to sit with ['sɪt wɪθ] sich setzen zu **I U5,** 74
sitcom ['sɪtkɒm] Situationskomödie **III U5,** 70
situation [ˌsɪtju'eɪʃn] Situation **V T4,** 60
six-pack ['sɪkspæk] Waschbrettbauch **V T2,** 28
to **skate** [skeɪt] Inlineskates fahren, skaten **I LUB,** 38
skateboard ['skeɪtbɔ:d] Skateboard **I U4,** 54
skates *(pl)* [skeɪts] Inlineskates **I U4,** 54
skiing ['ski:ɪŋ] Skifahren **IV U4,** 62
skill [skɪl] Fertigkeit, Geschick **IV U4,** 58
skimming ['skɪmɪŋ] Überfliegen °**III U2,** 28
skirt [skɜ:t] Rock **II U1,** 10
sky [skaɪ] Himmel **II U7,** 94
skyscraper ['skaɪˌskreɪpə] Wolkenkratzer **IV U1,** 9
poetry **slam** ['pəʊətri ˌslæm] Poetry Slam *(Gedichtwettbewerb)* **III U4,** 53
slamster ['slæmstə] Teilnehmer/Teilnehmerin an einem Poetry Slam **III U4,** 53
slang [slæŋ] Slang °**IV U5,** 76
slave [sleɪv] Sklave/Sklavin **V T3,** 44;
slavery ['sleɪvri] Sklaverei **V T3,** 44
sleep [sli:p] Schlaf **IV U3,** 46
*to **sleep** [sli:p] schlafen **I U3,** 46
sleeping bag ['sli:pɪŋ ˌbæg] Schlafsack **I U6,** 84
sleepy ['sli:pi] schläfrig, verschlafen **II U7,** 94
slice [slaɪs] Scheibe **IV U1,** 12
slip [slɪp] Beleg, Schein **IV U2,** 25
slow [sləʊ] langsam **I U2,** 34
slug [slʌg] Nacktschnecke **V T3,** 47
small [smɔ:l] klein **I U2,** 26
smart [smɑ:t] schlau, klug **IV U3,** 40
smell [smel] Geruch, Gestank **III U3,** 46
*to **smell** [smel] riechen **III U2,** 28
to **smile** [smaɪl] lächeln **I U3,** 43
smoke [sməʊk] Rauch **III U2,** 28
to **smoke** [sməʊk] rauchen **III U5,** 72
smooth [smu:θ] weich, geschmeidig, glatt **V T4,** 63
smuggler ['smʌglə] Schmuggler/Schmugglerin **III U3,** 39
snack [snæk] Imbiss, Snack **II U4,** 55
snack bar ['snæk ˌbɑ:] Café, Imbissstube **V T3,** 46
snake [sneɪk] Schlange **V T1,** 10
Brown Snake [ˌbraʊn 'sneɪk] Braunschlange, Braunotter °**V T1,** 12

snapshot ['snæpʃɒt] Schnappschuss **IV U1,** 16
to **sniff** [snɪf] schnüffeln, schnuppern **III U5,** 78
snow [snəʊ] Schnee **II U6,** 79
to **snow** [snəʊ] schneien **II U6,** 79
snowboarding ['snəʊbɔ:dɪŋ] Snowboarden **VT3,** 41
snowy ['snəʊi] verschneit **I U6,** 79
so [səʊ] so, also, deshalb **I U2,** 26
so far ['səʊ fɑ:] bis jetzt °**III U5,** 77
soap [səʊp] Seife, Seifenoper **I U7,** 97
docu soap ['dɒkju ˌsəʊp] Dokusoap **III U5,** 68
soccer *(AE)* ['sɒkə] Fußball **IV U2,** 29
society [sə'saɪəti] Gesellschaft; Verein **VT3,** 44
socket ['sɒkɪt] Steckdose **IV U3,** 44
sofa ['səʊfə] Sofa, Couch **I LUA,** 25
soft [sɒft] leise; weich, sanft **II U7,** 94
solar ['səʊlə] Sonnen-, Solar-, solar **IV U3,** 49
solar panel [ˌsəʊlə 'pænl] Sonnenkollektor **VT4,** 59
solar system ['səʊlə ˌsɪstəm] Sonnensystem **IV U3,** 49
solo ['səʊləʊ] allein, Allein-, solo, Solo- **VT3,** 43
to **solve** [sɒlv] lösen, aufklären **III U5,** 76
some [sʌm] einige; etwas **II U1,** 13
somebody ['sʌmbədi] jemand **III U5,** 71
somehow ['sʌmhaʊ] irgendwie **IV U4,** 65
someone ['sʌmwʌn] jemand **II U5,** 70
something ['sʌmθɪŋ] etwas **II U4,** 56
sometimes ['sʌmtaɪmz] manchmal **I U3,** 44
somewhere ['sʌmweə] irgendwo **II U4,** 57
son [sʌn] Sohn **III U5,** 74
song [sɒŋ] Lied **I U2,** 33
soon [su:n] bald **I U6,** 78
sorry ['sɒri] Tut mir Leid. Entschuldigung. **I U1,** 12
I'm sorry about .... [aɪm 'sɒri‿əˌbaʊt] Es tut mir leid wegen .... °**II U3,** 39
to be sorry [bi: 'sɒri] Leid tun **III U3,** 44
to feel sorry for [fi:l 'sɒri] Mitleid haben mit, bedauern **III U1,** 16
sort [sɔ:t] Art, Sorte °**III U4,** 58
to **sort** [sɔ:t] sortieren °**I U1,** 21
to sort out [sɔ:t‿'aʊt] klären, regeln *(ein Problem)* **I U2,** 30

soul [səʊl] Soulmusik; Seele **IV U5,** 73
sound [saʊnd] Ton, Geräusch, Klang **I U6,** 85
to **sound** [saʊnd] klingen, sich anhören **III U5,** 76
soup [su:p] Suppe **II U1,** 15
sour ['saʊə] sauer **II U4,** 49
source [sɔ:s] Quelle; Grund °**VT4,** 62
south [saʊθ] Süden **I U4,** 55
southwest [ˌsaʊθ'west] Südwesten **II U6,** 78
souvenir [ˌsu:və'nɪə] Souvenir, Andenken **III U2,** 25
spa [spɑ:] Wellness-Center, Spa **VT4,** 64
space [speɪs] Raum, Platz; Weltraum **IV U3,** 40
outer space [ˌaʊtə 'speɪs] Weltraum, Weltall **IV U3,** 40
space station ['speɪs ˌsteɪʃn] Weltraumstation **IV U3,** 40
spaceship ['speɪsʃɪp] Raumschiff **IV U3,** 49
spaghetti [spə'geti] Spaghetti **II U1,** 13
Spanish ['spænɪʃ] spanisch, Spanisch **IV U4,** 64
*to **speak** [spi:k] sprechen **I U4,** 62
speaking ['spi:kɪŋ] am Apparat **III U4,** 59
speaker ['spi:kə] Sprecher/Sprecherin **III U3,** 39
special ['speʃl] besonders, speziell **III U4,** 53; Spezialität **IV U1,** 12
spectacular [spek'tækjələ] spektakulär **III U2,** 22
speech [spi:tʃ] (An-)Sprache, Rede; Sprechen **VT3,** 44
speech bubble ['spi:tʃ ˌbʌbl] Sprechblase °**III U3,** 41
*to **spell** [spel] buchstabieren **I U4,** 60
spelling ['spelɪŋ] Orthographie, Rechtschreibung °**II U3,** 43
*to **spend** [spend] verbringen; ausgeben **I U6,** 83
spicy ['spaɪsi] würzig, pikant **II U4,** 49
spider ['spaɪdə] Spinne **VT1,** 12
Sydney Funnel Web Spider ['sɪdni ˌfʌnl web 'spaɪdə] australische Trichternetzspinne °**VT1,** 12
spin-off ['spɪn‿ɒf] Nebenprodukt **IV U3,** 41
spirit ['spɪrɪt] Geist; Stimmung **VT3,** 43
sponge [spʌndʒ] Schwamm **I U7,** 90
spooky ['spu:ki] unheimlich **I U2,** 35
spoon [spu:n] Löffel **II U4,** 50

sport [spɔ:t] Sport **I U1,** 12
sports day ['spɔ:ts deɪ] Sportfest **I U7,** 90
sports field ['spɔ:ts fi:ld] Sportplatz **I U7,** 92
sports shop ['spɔ:ts ʃɒp] Sportgeschäft **I U5,** 66
to do sports [du: 'spɔ:ts] Sport treiben **I U7,** 92
sporty ['spɔ:ti] sportlich **III U2,** 25
to **spray** [spreɪ] (be)sprühen, lackieren **IV U4,** 64
spring [sprɪŋ] Frühling **I U6,** 78
square dance ['skweə ˌdɑ:nts] Square Dance **IV U4,** 58
stadium ['steɪdiəm] Stadion **III U1,** 8
staff [stɑ:f] Personal; Kollegium **III U4,** 56
stage [steɪdʒ] Bühne **IV U5,** 74
stairs *(pl)* [steəz] Treppe **III U3,** 46
stall [stɔ:l] Stand, Bude **I U7,** 90
stall holder ['stɔ:l ˌhəʊldə] Standbesitzer/Standbesitzerin **II U4,** 54
white elephant stall [ˌwaɪt 'elɪfənt stɔ:l] Trödelstand **I U7,** 96
stamp [stæmp] Briefmarke **III U3,** 41
stand [stænd] Tribüne **III U1,** 9; (Messe-)Stand **VT4,** 63
*to **stand** [stænd] stehen **III U3,** 46
star [stɑ:] Star, Stern **III U5,** 70
word star ['wɜ:d stɑ:] Wortstern °**I U1,** 22
start [stɑ:t] Anfang, Beginn, Start **II U1,** 10
to **start** [stɑ:t] anfangen, starten **I U3,** 44
starter ['stɑ:tə] Vorspeise **II U4,** 49
state [steɪt] Staat, Land; staatlich **III U4,** 57
statement ['steɪtmənt] Aussage, Behauptung °**III U5,** 71
station ['steɪʃn] Wache, Station, Bahnhof **I U6,** 87
cleaning station ['kli:nɪŋ ˌsteɪʃn] Putzerstation **VT4,** 64
space station ['speɪs ˌsteɪʃn] Weltraumstation **IV U3,** 40
statistics *(pl)* [stə'tɪstɪks] Statistik °**IV U4,** 62
statue ['stætʃu:] Statue, Standbild **IV U5,** 73
to **stay** [steɪ] bleiben **I U4,** 60
to stay out [steɪ‿'aʊt] wegbleiben **III U4,** 59

to stay with ['steɪ wɪð] wohnen bei **I U6,** 78
*to **steal** [sti:l] stehlen **II U4,** 57
steel band [ˌsti:l 'bænd] Steelband *(Band, deren Instrumente aus leeren Ölfässern bestehen)* **III U4,** 54
steelworker ['sti:lˌwɜ:kə] Stahlarbeiter/ Stahlarbeiterin °**IV U1,** 15
step [step] Stufe, Schritt **IV U1,** 9
stepdad ['stepdæd] Stiefvater **I U2,** 26
stick [stɪk] Stock **II U2,** 26
still (picture) ['stɪl ˌpɪktʃə] Standfoto **IV U5,** 74
still [stɪl] noch, immer noch **II U1,** 21; *hier:* dennoch **IV U2,** 26
*to **sting** [stɪŋ] stechen, beißen **VT1,** 12
stinger suit [ˌstɪŋə 'su:t] Quallen-Schutzanzug **VT1,** 12
*to **stink** [stɪŋk] stinken **VT2,** 32
stomach ['stʌmək] Magen, Bauch **II U3,** 41
stone [stəʊn] Stein **II U6,** 82; *brit. Gewichtseinheit* (= 6,35kg) **III U3,** 43
stop [stɒp] Halt, Haltestelle **I LUC,** 52
bus stop ['bʌs ˌstɒp] Bushaltestelle **I LUC,** 52
to **stop** [stɒp] aufhören (mit), (an)halten **I U3,** 42
to stop + -ing [stɒp] aufhören etw. zu tun **II U4,** 52
store [stɔ:] Kaufhaus, Geschäft, Laden **II U2,** 30
department store [dɪ'pɑ:tmənt stɔ:] Kaufhaus **I LUC,** 52
store detective ['stɔ: dɪˌtektɪv] Kaufhausdetektiv/ Kaufhausdetektivin **II U2,** 30
storm [stɔ:m] Sturm **II U6,** 81
stormy ['stɔ:mi] stürmisch **II U6,** 78
story ['stɔ:ri] Geschichte, Erzählung **I U1,** 21
detective story [dɪ'tektɪv ˌstɔ:ri] Krimi **III U5,** 68
stranded ['strændɪd] gestrandet **IV U4,** 61
strange [streɪndʒ] merkwürdig, seltsam **I U2,** 35
stranger ['streɪndʒə] Fremder/Fremde **III U3,** 41
strawberry ['strɔ:bri] Erdbeere **IV U1,** 12
stream [stri:m] Bach **II U6,** 82
street [stri:t] Straße **I LUC,** 52
stress [stres] Stress; Betonung **IV U3,** 46
strict [strɪkt] streng, strikt **III U4,** 52
string [strɪŋ] Schnur, Kordel, Bindfaden **IV U5,** 74
strong [strɒŋ] stark **III U5,** 74
student ['stju:dnt] Student/Studentin, Schüler/Schülerin **IV U2,** 22
studies *(pl)* ['stʌdiz] Studium; Lernen **VT2,** 32
studio ['stju:diəʊ] Studio **I U2,** 33
to **study** ['stʌdi] studieren; lernen **II U6,** 74
stuff [stʌf] Zeug, Sachen **IV U4,** 64
stupid ['stju:pɪd] dumm, blöd **I U2,** 35
style [staɪl] Stil; *hier:* Frisur **III U2,** 31
subject ['sʌbdʒɪkt] Schulfach; Thema **II U1,** 13
to **substitute** ['sʌbstɪtju:t] auswechseln, ersetzen **III U1,** 17
suburb ['sʌbɜ:b] Vorort **IV U5,** 76
success [sək'ses] Erfolg **VT3,** 43
successful [sək'sesfl] erfolgreich **VT1,** 14; **VT3,** 43; **VT4,** 62
such [sʌtʃ] solch **VT3,** 44
That **sucks!** [ðæt 'sʌks] Das ist ätzend! **VT2,** 30
suddenly ['sʌdnli] plötzlich, auf einmal **I U2,** 35
suggestion [sə'dʒestʃn] Vorschlag, Anregung °**II U4,** 53
suit [su:t] Anzug **IV U2,** 31
stinger suit [ˌstɪŋə 'su:t] Quallen-Schutzanzug **VT1,** 12
to **suit** [su:t] passen (zu) °**VT2,** 33
suitable ['su:təbl] geeignet, passend °**VT2,** 33
hotel **suite** [həʊ'tel ˌswi:t] Hotelsuite **III U2,** 27
to **sum up** [ˌsʌm‿'ʌp] zusammenfassen °**VT4,** 67
summary ['sʌmri] Zusammenfassung °**III U3,** 47
summer ['sʌmə] Sommer **I U6,** 79
summer fair ['sʌmə ˌfeə] Sommerfest **I U7,** 90
sun [sʌn] Sonne **III U3,** 40
Sunday ['sʌndeɪ] Sonntag **I LUB,** 39
sunny ['sʌni] sonnig **I U6,** 79
suntan ['sʌntæn] Sonnenbräune **II U1,** 14
superlative [su:'pɜ:lətɪv] Superlativ **II U4,** 50
supermarket ['su:pəˌmɑ:kɪt] Supermarkt **I LUC,** 52
supper ['sʌpə] Abendessen **I U3,** 44
for supper [fə 'sʌpə] zum Abendessen **II U3,** 38
to have supper [hæv 'sʌpə] zu Abend essen **I U3,** 44
to **support** [sə'pɔ:t] unterstützen **IV U5,** 80
supporter [sə'pɔ:tə] Anhänger/ Anhängerin **IV U2,** 23
supreme [su:'pri:m] höchster/höchste/ höchstes, oberster/oberste/oberstes **VT3,** 46
sure [ʃʊə] sicher **I U1,** 16
to make sure [meɪk 'ʃʊə] sichergehen **II U6,** 82
to **surf** [sɜ:f] (wind)surfen **II U1,** 14
to surf the Internet [ˌsɜ:f ði‿'ɪntənet] im Internet surfen **II U1,** 14
surfboard ['sɜ:fbɔ:d] Surfbrett **VT1,** 14
surfer ['sɜ:fə] Surfer/Surferin **VT1,** 12
surfing ['sɜ:fɪŋ] Wellenreiten, Surfen **II U1,** 14
surprised [sə'praɪzd] überrascht, erstaunt **II U1,** 18
surprising [sə'praɪzɪŋ] überraschend **II U7,** 96
survey ['sɜ:veɪ] Umfrage **I U4,** 56
survival [sə'vaɪvl] Überleben **IV U2,** 26
to **survive** [sə'vaɪv] überleben, bestehen, durchstehen **VT1,** 12
suspense [sə'spents] Spannung **IV U3,** 48
swap [swɒp] Tausch **II U7,** 88
to **swap** [swɒp] tauschen **I LUB,** 38
sweatshirt ['swetʃɜ:t] Sweatshirt **II U1,** 10
sweet [swi:t] Bonbon, Süßigkeit **II U4,** 53
sweet [swi:t] süß **I LUA,** 24
to **swerve** [swɜ:v] ausweichen, ausscheren **III U4,** 60
*to **swim** [swɪm] schwimmen **I LUB,** 38
swimmer ['swɪmə] Schwimmer/ Schwimmerin **III U3,** 39
swimming pool ['swɪmɪŋ ˌpu:l] Schwimmbecken; Schwimmbad **III U3,** 40
swimsuit ['swɪmsu:t] Badeanzug **III U3,** 40
switch [swɪtʃ] Schalter **IV U3,** 44
to **switch** off [ˌswɪtʃ‿'ɒf] ausschalten **IV U1,** 17
to switch on [swɪtʃ‿'ɒn] einschalten, anmachen **IV U3,** 42

symbol ['sɪmbl] Symbol, Sinnbild, Zeichen **IV U1,** 9
synonym ['sɪnənɪm] Synonym °**IV U5,** 83
syrup ['sɪrəp] Sirup **IV U1,** 12
system ['sɪstəm] System **III U4,** 57
solar system ['səʊlə ˌsɪstəm] Sonnensystem **IV U3,** 49

T

table ['teɪbl] Tisch **I U1,** 18; Tabelle °**III U3,** 43
table-tennis ['teɪblˌtenɪs] Tischtennis **II U7,** 88
to set the table [ˌset ðə 'teɪbl] den Tisch decken **II U4,** 50
*to **take** [teɪk] nehmen, mitnehmen, wegnehmen, bringen **I U3,** 42; dauern, *(Zeit)* brauchen **III U3,** 39
to take a bus tour [ˌteɪk‿ə 'bʌs tʊə] eine Busfahrt machen **IV U4,** 58
to take care [teɪk 'keə] aufpassen; sich kümmern **IV U2,** 29
to take home [ˌteɪk 'həʊm] nach Hause bringen **I U2,** 35
to take notes [teɪk 'nəʊts] sich Notizen machen °**II U4,** 55
to take off [ˌteɪk‿'ɒf] ausziehen, abnehmen **III U3,** 46; abheben, starten, abfliegen **IV U1,** 16
to take out [teɪk‿'aʊt] herausnehmen **I U3,** 42
to take part in [teɪk 'pɑːt‿ɪn] teilnehmen an **III U4,** 53
to take pictures [teɪk 'pɪktʃəz] fotografieren, Fotos machen **II U5,** 62
to take place [teɪk 'pleɪs] stattfinden **III U4,** 53
to take your chance [ˌteɪk jɔː 'tʃɑːns] etw. wagen, etw. riskieren **III U3,** 47
takeaway ['teɪkəweɪ] Restaurant mit Straßenverkauf; Essen zum Mitnehmen **II U4,** 48
talent ['tælənt] Talent **VT2,** 32
talk [tɔːk] Vortrag; Rede, Gespräch **VT4,** 60
sales talk ['seɪlz tɔːk] Verkaufsgespräch °**VT4,** 63
talk show ['tɔːk ˌʃəʊ] Talkshow **III U5,** 68
to **talk** [tɔːk] sprechen, reden **I U1,** 10
to talk to ['tɔːk tə] sprechen mit, reden mit **II U2,** 28
talkie ['tɔːki] Tonfilm **IV U5,** 74
tall [tɔːl] groß, hoch **II U3,** 36
task [tɑːsk] Aufgabe, Auftrag **IV U3,** 46
to **taste** [teɪst] schmecken **I U7,** 94
tasty ['teɪsti] schmackhaft **II U4,** 50
Pizza is tastier. ['piːtsə ɪz ˌteɪstɪə] Pizza schmeckt besser. **II U4,** 50
tattoo [tæt'uː] Tätowierung **III U4,** 52
taxi ['tæksi] Taxi **III U2,** 30
tea [tiː] Tee, Abendessen **I U7,** 94
afternoon tea [ˌɑːftənuːn 'tiː] Nachmittagstee **I U7,** 94
*to **teach** [tiːtʃ] lehren **I LUB,** 38
teacher ['tiːtʃə] Lehrer/Lehrerin **I U1,** 12
team [tiːm] Mannschaft, Team **II U2,** 23
tear [tɪə] Träne **VT4,** 66
technical ['teknɪkl] technisch; handwerklich, fachlich **VT2,** 32
Technology [tek'nɒlədʒi] Technik **II U1,** 10
teen [tiːn] Jugendliche/Jugendlicher **II U6,** 80
teenage ['tiːneɪdʒ] jugendlich **III U4,** 53
teenager ['tiːnˌeɪdʒə] Teenager, Jugendliche/Jugendlicher **III U2,** 24
telephone ['telɪfəʊn] Telefon °**VT2,** 29
*to **tell** [tel] erzählen, sagen **I U3,** 49
temperature ['temprətʃə] Temperatur **II U6,** 78
temporary ['temprəri] vorübergehend, temporär, befristet **VT1,** 14; **VT3,** 47
tenant ['tenənt] Mieter/Mieterin °**VT3,** 41
tennis ['tenɪs] Tennis **III U1,** 15
table-tennis ['teɪblˌtenɪs] Tischtennis **II U7,** 88
tent [tent] Zelt **I U6,** 84
term [tɜːm] Trimester *(Einteilung des englischen Schuljahrs)* °**II U1,** 10
terrible ['terəbl] schrecklich, furchtbar **I U2,** 35
test [test] Test, Klassenarbeit **II U3,** 44
to **test** [test] testen, prüfen **VT4,** 61
text [tekst] Text °**I U2,** 27
text message ['tekst ˌmesɪdʒ] SMS **I U6,** 80
to **text** [tekst] Textnachricht (SMS) schicken, simsen **III U4,** 54
than [ðən] als **I U4,** 55
to **thank** [θæŋk] danken **I U4,** 60
thank you ['θæŋk‿juː] danke **I U1,** 12
thanks [θæŋks] danke **II U2,** 26
thanks to ['θæŋks tə] dank (dir/ihnen), wegen **III U2,** 24
that [ðæt] das, jenes **I U1,** 12
that (bad) ['ðæt bæd] so (schlimm) **II U2,** 24
that evening [ˌðæt‿'iːvnɪŋ] an diesem Abend **II U1,** 19
That's what I call .... [ˌðæts wɒt‿'aɪ ˌkɔːl] Das nenne ich .... **II U1,** 14
that's why ['ðæts ˌwaɪ] deshalb **II U1,** 18
the [ðə; ði] der/die/das **I U1,** 11
theater *(AE)* ['θɪətə] Theater; Kino **IV U1,** 9
their [ðeə] ihr/ihre **I U2,** 30
them [ðem] sie, ihnen **I U4,** 60
theme park ['θiːm ˌpɑːk] Freizeitpark **IV U2,** 22
then [ðen] dann **I LUB,** 38
there [ðeə] dort, da **I U2,** 26
over there [ˌəʊvə 'ðeə] da drüben **I U5,** 66
there are [ðer‿'ɑː] da sind, es gibt **I U2,** 32
there is [ðer‿'ɪz] da ist, es gibt **I U2,** 32
these [ðiːz] diese, diese hier **I U6,** 84
they [ðeɪ] sie *(Mehrzahl)* **I U1,** 16; man **III U1,** 10
thick [θɪk] dick *(nicht für Personen)*; dumm **III U1,** 16
thing [θɪŋ] Sache, Ding **I U3,** 40
*to **think** [θɪŋk] denken **I U3,** 49; glauben **II U4,** 50
to think about ['θɪŋk‿əˌbaʊt] nachdenken über, denken an °**II U7,** 95
to think of ['θɪŋk‿əv] denken an °**II U3,** 39
third [θɜːd] Drittel **VT3,** 46
third [θɜːd] dritter/dritte/drittes **I U5,** 70
this [ðɪs] dies; dieser/diese/dieses **I U1,** 12
this evening [ðɪs 'iːvnɪŋ] heute Abend **III U3,** 46
those [ðəʊz] diese dort, jene **I U6,** 84
though [ðəʊ] trotzdem, dennoch **IV U5,** 80
thoughtful ['θɔːtfl] aufmerksam, fürsorglich **IV U2,** 26
thousand ['θaʊznd] tausend **II U2,** 23
to **threaten** ['θretn] (be)drohen **VT1,** 10
thriller ['θrɪlə] Thriller **III U5,** 68
through [θruː] durch **II U4,** 57
*to **throw** [θrəʊ] werfen **I U3,** 49

Thursday ['θɜ:zdeɪ] Donnerstag **I LUB,** 39
to **tick** [tɪk] abhaken °**II U5,** 65
ticket ['tɪkɪt] Ticket, Fahrschein, Eintrittskarte **I U7,** 90
tiger ['taɪgə] Tiger **I U2,** 26
tights *(pl)* [taɪts] Strumpfhose **V T1,** 12
till [tɪl] bis **IV U4,** 64
time [taɪm] Zeit **I U2,** 30; Mal **II U1,** 18
at any time [æt‿eni 'taɪm] jederzeit **IV U2,** 25
on time [ɒn 'taɪm] pünktlich **IV U3,** 46
to have a good time [ˌhæv‿ə gʊd 'taɪm] sich amüsieren **I U5,** 75
What's the time, please? [ˌwɒts ðə 'taɪm ˌpli:z] Wie viel Uhr ist es, bitte?, Wie spät ist es, bitte? **I U3,** 42
What time ... ? [wɒt 'taɪm] (Um) wie viel Uhr ... ? **III U1,** 12
to **time** [taɪm] stoppen, die Zeit nehmen **I U7,** 92
timeline ['taɪmlaɪn] Zeitleiste °**I U4,** 63
timetable ['taɪmteɪbl] Stundenplan, Fahrplan **II U1,** 12
tin [tɪn] Büchse **III U2,** 30
tiny ['taɪni] winzig **I LUA,** 25
tip [tɪp] Tipp **II U4,** 52; Trinkgeld **IV U1,** 12
tired ['taɪəd] müde **II U3,** 38
dog-tired [ˌdɒg 'taɪəd] hundemüde **I U3,** 49
title ['taɪtl] Titel, Überschrift **II U3,** 42; Bezeichnung **V T1,** 15
to [tʊ; tə] zu, nach, bis **I U1,** 19
toast [təʊst] Toast **IV U1,** 12
tobacco [tə'bækəʊ] Tabak **IV U2,** 25
today [tə'deɪ] heute **I U2,** 29
toe [təʊ] Zeh **II U3,** 41
together [tə'geðə] zusammen, miteinander **I LUB,** 38
toilet ['tɔɪlɪt] Toilette **I U1,** 19
tomato, tomatoes *(pl)* [tə'mɑ:təʊ; tə'mɑ:təʊz] Tomate **I U5,** 68
tomorrow [tə'mɒrəʊ] morgen **II U1,** 18
tongue twister ['tʌŋ ˌtwɪstə] Zungenbrecher °**II U4,** 55
tonight [tə'naɪt] heute Abend, heute Nacht **I U6,** 84
too [tu:] zu **I U5,** 66; auch **I U1,** 10
tooth, teeth *(pl)* [tu:θ; ti:θ] Zahn **III U5,** 74
toothache ['tu:θeɪk] Zahnschmerzen **IV U3,** 48
top [tɒp] Spitze, oberer Teil **IV U1,** 8
at the top [ət ðə 'tɒp] oben, im oberen Teil **III U1,** 14
topic ['tɒpɪk] Thema **I U2,** 33
torch, torches *(pl)* [tɔ:tʃ; 'tɔ:tʃɪz] Taschenlampe, Fackel **I U6,** 84
torn [tɔ:n] hin- und hergerissen, zerrissen **V T2,** 30
to **touch** [tʌtʃ] berühren; antippen **III U3,** 47
tough [tʌf] hart, rau, zäh **III U5,** 68
tour [tʊə] Tour, Fahrt, Reise **IV U1,** 16
tourist ['tʊərɪst] Tourist/Touristin **III U2,** 24
towards [tə'wɔ:dz] in Richtung, auf ... zu, darauf zu **III U5,** 78
tower ['taʊə] Turm **III U2,** 22
town [taʊn] Stadt **I U3,** 41
toy [tɔɪ] Spielzeug **III U2,** 24
tractor ['træktə] Traktor **IV U3,** 41
trade [treɪd] Handel **V T4,** 58
tradition [trə'dɪʃn] Tradition **III U2,** 30
traffic ['træfɪk] Verkehr **III U2,** 22
traffic jam ['træfɪk ˌdʒæm] Stau **III U2,** 22
train [treɪn] Zug **I U4,** 54
to **train** [treɪn] eine Ausbildung machen **V T2,** 32; ausbilden, lernen; trainieren **V T3,** 47
trainers ['treɪnəz] Turnschuhe **III U4,** 56
training ['treɪnɪŋ] Training, Ausbildung **III U4,** 58
transport ['trænspɔ:t] Transport **I U4,** 57
transport *(no pl.)* ['trænspɔ:t] Verkehrsmittel, Beförderung **III U2,** 27
to **transport** [træn'spɔ:t] transportieren **IV U4,** 57
*to be **trapped** [bi: 'træpt] in der Falle sitzen **II U6,** 83
travel ['trævl] Reise **III U5,** 70
day travel card [ˌdeɪ 'trævl ˌkɑ:d] Tagesfahrkarte **III U2,** 27
to **travel** ['trævl] reisen **III U3,** 38
treatment ['tri:tmənt] Behandlung **V T3,** 45
tree [tri:] Baum **I U1,** 20
family tree ['fæmli tri:] Familienstammbaum °**I U2,** 28
trendy ['trendi] modisch **III U2,** 22
tribe [traɪb] (Volks-)Stamm **IV U4,** 56
trick [trɪk] Trick, Streich **I U3,** 40
trip [trɪp] Ausflug, Reise **I U6,** 80
trolley ['trɒli] Gepäckwagen, Einkaufswagen, Handkarren **III U3,** 44
trouble ['trʌbl] Schwierigkeiten, Ärger **I U2,** 30
trousers *(pl)* ['traʊzəz] Hose **II U1,** 10
truck *(AE)* [trʌk] Lastwagen, Truck **IV U4,** 57
trucker *(AE)* ['trʌkə] Lastwagenfahrer/ Lastwagenfahrerin, Trucker **IV U4,** 57
true [tru:] wahr **II U1,** 18
to come true [kʌm 'tru:] wahr werden °**II U7,** 91
to **trust** [trʌst] vertrauen **III U3,** 46
to **try** [traɪ] versuchen, probieren **II U1,** 10
tryout ['traɪaʊt] Auswahlverfahren **IV U2,** 22
T-shirt ['ti:ʃɜ:t] T-Shirt **I U2,** 30
tucker ['tʌkə] Essen *(australischer Ausdruck)* °**II U1,** 14
Tuesday ['tju:zdeɪ] Dienstag **I LUB,** 39
tug [tʌg] Ziehen, Zupfen **III U3,** 46
tunnel ['tʌnl] Tunnel, Unterführung **I U4,** 54
turkey ['tɜ:ki] Truthahn, Pute **IV U1,** 12
Turkish ['tɜ:kɪʃ] türkisch **I U2,** 29
in **turn** [ɪn 'tɜ:n] abwechselnd, der Reihe nach °**V T3,** 45
It's your turn. [ɪts jɔ: 'tɜ:n] Du bist dran. **II U1,** 13
to **turn** [tɜ:n] sich umdrehen **III U5,** 74; werden **V T4,** 64
to turn back [tɜ:n 'bæk] umkehren, zurückgehen **II U1,** 19
to turn left/right [tɜ:n 'left/'raɪt] links/ rechts abbiegen **II U7,** 97
to turn off [tɜ:n‿'ɒf] abschalten, ausschalten **I U5,** 75
to turn on [ˌtɜ:n‿'ɒn] einschalten, anmachen **IV U3,** 44
to turn over [ˌtɜ:n‿'əʊvə] (sich) umdrehen **II U7,** 94
to turn round [tɜ:n 'raʊnd] (sich) umdrehen **II U1,** 18
to be a **turn-off** ['tɜ:nɒf] abtörnend sein, zum Abgewöhnen sein **V T2,** 28
turnover ['tɜ:nˌəʊvə] Umsatz, Absatz **V T4,** 62
TV [ˌti:'vi:] Fernsehen, Fernseher **I LUA,** 25
twice [twaɪs] zweimal **III U5,** 68
type [taɪp] Typ, Art, Sorte **IV U4,** 62
typical ['tɪpɪkl] typisch, kennzeichnend **V T1,** 16
typically ['tɪpɪkli] typisch °**V T1,** 11

U

umbrella [ʌm'brelə] Regenschirm **II U6,** 81
uncle ['ʌŋkl] Onkel **I U2,** 28
under ['ʌndə] unter **I U1,** 18
underground ['ʌndəgraʊnd] U-Bahn **III U2,** 23
to **underline** [ˌʌndə'laɪn] unterstreichen **II U1,** 18
underlined [ˌʌndə'laɪnd] unterstrichen °**I U7,** 98
*to **understand** [ˌʌndə'stænd] verstehen **III U5,** 74
underwater [ˌʌndə'wɔːtə] Unterwasser- **V T4,** 64
unfair [ʌn'feə] ungerecht, unfair **V T3,** 45
unfriendly [ʌn'frendli] unfreundlich **IV U5,** 79
unhappy [ʌn'hæpi] unglücklich **I U2,** 33
unhealthy [ʌn'helθi] ungesund **II U4,** 53
uniform ['juːnɪfɔːm] Uniform **I U3,** 44
union ['juːnjən] Liga; Vereinigung, Union **III U1,** 11
unit ['juːnɪt] Kapitel, Einheit °**IV U1,** 8
universe ['juːnɪvɜːs] Universum, Weltraum **V T3,** 46
university [ˌjuːnɪ'vɜːsəti] Universität **IV U2,** 28
unless [ən'les] es sei denn, (dass) … **V T1,** 12
until [ʌn'tɪl; n'tɪl] bis **II U4,** 56
up [ʌp] auf, hinauf, oben **II U2,** 30
Hurry up! [ˌhʌri‿'ʌp] Beeil dich! **I U2,** 30
to dig up [dɪg‿'ʌp] ausgraben **III U1,** 16
to get up [get‿'ʌp] aufstehen **I U3,** 44
to go up [gəʊ‿'ʌp] hinaufgehen °**I U4,** 61
to wake up [weɪk‿'ʌp] aufwecken, aufwachen **I U3,** 48
to walk up to [wɔːk‿'ʌp tə] hingehen, zugehen auf **III U5,** 75
up current ['ʌp ˌkʌrnt] Strömung, die nach oben zieht **V T4,** 64
up to ['ʌp tə] bis zu **III U4,** 53
What's up? [ˌwɒts‿'ʌp] Was ist los? **I U1,** 16
to **update** [ʌp'deɪt] aktualisieren °**II U5,** 62
upper ['ʌpə] oberer/obere/oberes **IV U2,** 28
*to be **upset** [biː ʌp'set] aufgeregt sein, bestürzt sein **II U3,** 44
upstairs [ʌp'steəz] oben, im oberen Stock **I U2,** 27
to run upstairs [ˌrʌn‿ʌp'steəz] die Treppe hinaufrennen **III U3,** 47
urgent ['ɜːdʒnt] dringend **V T1,** 10
us [ʌs] uns **I U4,** 60
use [juːs] Verwendung, Nutzung °**II U5,** 63
to **use** [juːz] benutzen, verwenden **I U4,** 54
useful ['juːsfl] nützlich **IV U3,** 45
useless ['juːsləs] nutzlos **III U4,** 54
usually ['juːʒli] normalerweise, gewöhnlich **II U4,** 53

V

vacancy ['veɪknsi] Stellenangebot, offene Stelle; freies Zimmer **V T1,** 14
vacation *(AE)* [və'keɪʃn] Ferien, Urlaub **IV U1,** 12
valid ['vælɪd] gültig, zulässig **V T1,** 14
valuable ['væljuəbl] wertvoll **III U2,** 22
van [væn] Lieferwagen **I U6,** 86
vegetable ['vedʒtəbl] Gemüse **II U1,** 15
venom ['venəm] Gift *(z. B. von Schlangen und Insekten)*; Bosheit **V T1,** 12
verb [vɜːb] Verb °**II U1,** 20
verse [vɜːs] Vers, Strophe **IV U5,** 78
very ['veri] sehr **I U1,** 20; aller- **IV U1,** 16
video ['vɪdiəʊ] Video **I LUB,** 38
view [vjuː] Aussicht, Sicht **III U2,** 22
to **view** [vjuː] anschauen, betrachten **IV U5,** 76
viewer ['vjuːə] Zuschauer/Zuschauerin **III U5,** 68
village ['vɪlɪdʒ] Dorf **III U4,** 54
vinegar ['vɪnɪgə] Essig **V T1,** 12
violence ['vaɪəlnts] Gewalt(tätigkeit) **V T3,** 42
virtual ['vɜːtʃuəl] virtuell **IV U3,** 41
working visa ['wɜːkɪŋ ˌviːzə] Arbeitserlaubnis **V T1,** 14
visit ['vɪzɪt] Besuch **I U7,** 94
to **visit** ['vɪzɪt] besuchen, besichtigen **I U4,** 54
visitor ['vɪzɪtə] Besucher/Besucherin **I U4,** 55
vital ['vaɪtl] lebenswichtig, unerlässlich; Lebens- **IV U5,** 78
vital signs *(pl)* [ˌvaɪtl 'saɪnz] Lebenszeichen **IV U5,** 78
vocabulary [vəʊ'kæbjəlri] Wortschatz, Vokabular °**II U1,** 20
voice [vɔɪs] Stimme **II U2,** 31
volleyball ['vɒlibɔːl] Volleyball **I U3,** 40
voluntary ['vɒləntri] freiwillig; ehrenamtlich **V T2,** 32
volunteer [ˌvɒlən'tɪə] Freiwilliger/Freiwillige; freiwillig **V T2,** 29
vote [vəʊt] Abstimmung, Stimme **IV U2,** 31
to **vote** [vəʊt] abstimmen, wählen **IV U2,** 31
V-shaped ['viːˌʃeɪpt] V-förmig °**IV U3,** 49

W

to **wait** [weɪt] warten **I U5,** 69
to wait for ['weɪt fɔː] warten auf **I U6,** 86
waiter ['weɪtə] Kellner, Bedienung **II U4,** 55
*to **wake** [weɪk] (auf)wecken **II U7,** 94
to wake up [weɪk‿'ʌp] aufwecken, aufwachen **I U3,** 48
walk [wɔːk] Spaziergang **III U5,** 76
to go for a walk [ˌgəʊ fər‿ə 'wɔːk] spazieren gehen **III U5,** 76
to **walk** [wɔːk] gehen, laufen **I U4,** 54
to walk the dog [wɔːk ðə 'dɒg] mit dem Hund spazieren gehen **I U3,** 42
to walk up to [wɔːk‿'ʌp tə] hingehen, zugehen auf **III U5,** 75
wall [wɔːl] Wand, Mauer **I U1,** 18
wallet ['wɒlɪt] Brieftasche, Geldbeutel **II U4,** 56
to **want** (to) ['wɒnt tə] wollen, mögen **I U4,** 54
to want sb to do sth [wɒnt] wollen, dass jemand etwas tut **III U4,** 52
war [wɔː] Krieg **IV U1,** 10
wardrobe ['wɔːdrəʊb] Kleiderschrank, Garderobe **I U2,** 30
warm [wɔːm] warm **II U2,** 25
(global) **warming** [ˌgləʊbl 'wɔːmɪŋ] (Erd-)Erwärmung **V T4,** 61
to **warn** [wɔːn] warnen, ermahnen **V T4,** 61
warning ['wɔːnɪŋ] Warn-; Warnung **IV U3,** 46

English – German

to **wash** [wɒʃ] (sich) waschen **I U3,** 44
waste [weɪst] Verschwendung; Abfall **V T2,** 30
to **waste** [weɪst] verschwenden **V T2,** 30
to **watch** [wɒtʃ] ansehen, beobachten **I LUB,** 38; achten auf **II U2,** 31
Watch out! [wɒtʃ‿'aʊt] Achtung!, Pass(t) auf! °**IV U2,** 31
water ['wɔːtə] Wasser **I U5,** 68
wave [weɪv] Welle **III U4,** 60
to **wave** [weɪv] winken, schwenken **II U6,** 83
way [weɪ] Weg **I U3,** 42; Art, Weise °**III U3,** 39
by the way [ˌbaɪ ðə 'weɪ] übrigens **IV U4,** 61
He is on his way to .... [ˌhiː‿ɪz‿ɒn hɪz 'weɪ tə] Er ist auf dem Weg zu .... **I U3,** 42
to get in the way (of) [ˌget‿ɪn‿ðə‿'weɪ] etw. verhindern; im Weg stehen **V T2,** 29
Which way ...? [wɪtʃ 'weɪ] Auf welche Art ...?, Auf welchem Weg ...? °**III U3,** 39
we [wiː] wir **I U1,** 16
weak [wiːk] schwach **III U4,** 60
to go weak [gəʊ 'wiːk] schwach werden **III U4,** 60
weapon ['wepən] Waffe **V T3,** 44
*to **wear** [weə] anhaben, tragen **I U3,** 45
weather ['weðə] Wetter **II U1,** 14
weatherman, weathermen *(pl)* ['weðəmən; 'weðəmen] Meteorologe °**II U6,** 78
webcam ['webkæm] Webcam °**II U5,** 63
website ['websaɪt] Website, Internetauftritt **II U5,** 64
Wednesday ['wenzdeɪ] Mittwoch **I LUB,** 39
week [wiːk] Woche **I LUB,** 39
a week [ə 'wiːk] pro Woche, in der Woche **II U4,** 52
weekday ['wiːkdeɪ] Wochentag, Werktag **V T1,** 14
weekend [ˌwiːk'end] Wochenende **I U3,** 45
weight [weɪt] Gewicht **III U1,** 11
to **welcome** ['welkəm] willkommen heißen **I U7,** 90
*to be **welcome to do** [biː 'welkəm] gerne etwas tun können **III U4,** 56
Welcome (to) ... ['welkəm tə] Willkommen (in) ... **III U4,** 57
You're welcome. [jʊə 'welkəm] Bitte sehr!, Gern geschehen! **I U1,** 19
as **well** as [əz 'wel‿əz] sowohl ... als auch **III U4,** 57
well [wel] also, na ja, nun gut **I U2,** 29
Welsh [welʃ] walisisch; Waliser/Waliserin **III U3,** 42
west [west] Westen **I U4,** 54
western ['westən] Western-, Western; westlich **IV U4,** 58
wet [wet] nass **II U6,** 74
wet blanket [wet 'blæŋkɪt] Miesmacher/Miesmacherin **II U6,** 74
wetsuit ['wetsuːt] Taucheranzug, Neoprenanzug **V T4,** 64
what [wɒt] welcher/welche/welches **I LUA,** 25; was **I U1,** 11
What about ...? [wɒt‿ə'baʊt] Was ist mit ...? Wie wäre es mit ...? **I U2,** 30
What a laugh! [ˌwɒt‿ə 'lɑːf] Wie lustig! **III U1,** 17
What a week! [ˌwɒt‿ə 'wiːk] Was für eine Woche! **II U2,** 22
What does it say? [ˌwɒt dʌz‿ɪt 'seɪ] Was steht da? **II U3,** 44
What's the film about? [wɒts ðə 'fɪlm‿əˌbaʊt] Wovon handelt der Film? °**II U3,** 43
What's the matter? [ˌwɒts ðə 'mætə] Was ist los? **III U5,** 76
What's the time, please? [ˌwɒts ðə 'taɪm ˌpliːz] Wie viel Uhr ist es, bitte?, Wie spät ist es, bitte? **I U3,** 42
What's up? [ˌwɒts‿'ʌp] Was ist los? **I U1,** 16
What's your name? [ˌwɒts jə 'neɪm] Wie heißt du? **I U1,** 11
What time ...? [wɒt 'taɪm] (Um) wie viel Uhr ...? **III U1,** 12
whatever [wɒt'evə] egal welche **IV U4,** 58
when [wen] wenn, als; wann **I U2,** 33
where [weə] wo, wohin **I U1,** 11
Where are you from? [ˌweər‿ə jə 'frɒm] Woher kommst du? **I U1,** 11
Where's the fire? [ˌweəz ðə 'faɪə] Wo brennt's denn? **I U7,** 96
which [wɪtʃ] welcher/welche/welches **II U1,** 14; der/dem/den/die/das *(Relativpronomen)* **II U3,** 42
Which way ...? [wɪtʃ 'weɪ] Auf welche Art ...?, Auf welchem Weg ...? °**III U3,** 39
while [waɪl] während **IV U4,** 61
to **whisper** ['wɪspə] flüstern, zuflüstern **II U1,** 18
white [waɪt] weiß **I LUA,** 24
white elephant stall [ˌwaɪt 'elɪfənt stɔːl] Trödelstand **I U7,** 96
who [huː] wer, wem, wen **I U5,** 70
who [huː] der/dem/den/die *(Relativpronomen)* **II U3,** 42
whole [həʊl] ganz **IV U1,** 11
whom [huːm] dem/der *(Relativpronomen)* **III U3,** 46
whose [huːz] wessen **II U5,** 68
whose [huːz] dessen/deren *(Relativpronomen)* **III U3,** 47
why [waɪ] warum **I U5,** 70
wicked ['wɪkɪd] großartig **II U5,** 70
wife, wives *(pl)* [waɪf; waɪvz] Ehefrau **III U5,** 74
wig [wɪg] Perücke **II U2,** 28
wild [waɪld] wild **III U5,** 76
***will ('ll), won't** [wɪl; wəʊnt] werden, werden nicht *(futurisch)* **II U6,** 76
*to **win** [wɪn] gewinnen, siegen **II U7,** 91
wind [wɪnd] Wind **I U2,** 35
windmill ['wɪnmɪl] Windmühle; Windrad, Windkraftanlage **V T4,** 59
window ['wɪndəʊ] Fenster **I U1,** 18
to **windsurf** ['wɪnsɜːf] windsurfen **III U3,** 40
windy ['wɪndi] windig **I U6,** 79
wing [wɪŋ] Flügel **V T4,** 65
winner ['wɪnə] Gewinner/Gewinnerin, Sieger/Siegerin **III U4,** 53
winter ['wɪntə] Winter **I U6,** 79
wish [wɪʃ] Wunsch **III U4,** 53
to **wish** [wɪʃ] wünschen **III U4,** 58
I wish I had ... [wɪʃ] Ich wünschte, ich hätte ... **III U4,** 58
with [wɪð] mit **I U1,** 14; bei **II U1,** 11
within [wɪ'ðɪn] innerhalb **III U2,** 24
without [wɪ'ðaʊt] ohne **I U4,** 54
to go without [ˌgəʊ wɪ'ðaʊt] ohne ... auskommen **II U4,** 52
wizard ['wɪzəd] Zauberer **II U5,** 69
wolf, wolves *(pl)* [wʊlf; wʊlvz] Wolf **III U5,** 74
woman, women *(pl)* ['wʊmən; 'wɪmɪn] Frau **I U4,** 62
wood [wʊd] Holz **III U3,** 41
Woof! [wʊf] Wau! °**I U2,** 27
word [wɜːd] Wort **I U1,** 15
word star ['wɜːd stɑː] Wortstern °**I U1,** 22

work [wɜːk] Arbeit **I U3,** 47
to **work** [wɜːk] arbeiten, funktionieren **I U3,** 48
to work out [wɜːk‿'aʊt] herausfinden; ausarbeiten °**III U3,** 43
worker ['wɜːkə] Arbeiter/Arbeiterin, Angestellter/Angestellte **IV U3,** 48
workman, workmen *(pl)* ['wɜːkmən; 'wɜːkmen] Handwerker **IV U1,** 17
worksheet ['wɜːkʃiːt] Arbeitsblatt **I U4,** 58
workshop ['wɜːkʃɒp] Workshop; Werkstatt **III U4,** 53
world [wɜːld] Erde, Welt **III U1,** 13
worldwide [ˌwɜːld'waɪd] weltweit **VT4,** 60
*to be **worried** [biː 'wʌrid] besorgt sein, beunruhigt sein **I U6,** 87
worry ['wʌri] Sorge °**III U4,** 54
to **worry** ['wʌri] sich Sorgen machen **I U6,** 82; ängstigen, beunruhigen **II U3,** 45
worse [wɜːs] schlimmer, schlechter **II U4,** 50
worst [wɜːst] schlimmster/schlimmste/schlimmstes, schlechtester/schlechteste/schlechtestes **II U4,** 50
***would** [wʊd] würde/würden **III U3,** 47
would like [wʊd 'laɪk] hätte(n) gern, möchte(n) gern **II U4,** 52
Would you mind … ? [ˌwʊd jə 'maɪnd] Hätten Sie/Hättest du etwas dagegen … ? **III U4,** 56
wow [waʊ] toll, wow °**I U1,** 12
*to **write** [raɪt] schreiben **I U3,** 43
to write down ['raɪt ˌdaʊn] aufschreiben °**I LUB,** 38
wrong [rɒŋ] falsch **I U1,** 16
to be wrong [biː 'rɒŋ] Unrecht haben **III U3,** 47
to get … wrong [get … 'rɒŋ] falsch machen **II U3,** 44; falsch verstehen °**II U3,** 47
to go wrong [gəʊ 'rɒŋ] schief gehen **II U6,** 85

Y

yard [jɑːd] Elle *(Längenmaß: 0,914 m)* **III U3,** 43
yeah *(slang)* [jeə] ja **IV U1,** 16
year [jɪə] Jahr, Jahrgangsstufe **I U1,** 10
yearbook ['jɪəbʊk] Jahrbuch **IV U2,** 22
year-old [ˌjɪər‿'əʊld] -jährig; -Jähriger/-Jährige **III U4,** 53
yellow ['jeləʊ] gelb **I LUA,** 24
yes [jes] ja **I U1,** 12
yesterday ['jestədeɪ] gestern **II U2,** 26
not … **yet** [jet] noch nicht **II U5,** 66
you [juː; jə] du, ihr **I U1,** 11; dich, dir, Sie, Ihnen, euch **I LUB,** 38; man **III U1,** 8
Here you are! ['hɪə juː‿ɑː] Bitte schön! **I U1,** 20
thank you ['θæŋk‿juː] danke **I U1,** 12
you're lucky [ˌjʊə 'lʌki] du hast Glück **I U1,** 16
You're welcome. [jʊə 'welkəm] Bitte sehr!, Gern geschehen! **I U1,** 19
young [jʌŋ] jung **I U3,** 45
your [jɔː] dein/deine, euer/eure, Ihr/Ihre **I U1,** 11
Yours [jɔːz] Dein …/Deine …/Euer …/Eure … *(in Briefen)* **II U3,** 36
youth [juːθ] Jugend **II U3,** 38
yukky ['jʌki] ekelhaft **III U4,** 57
yummy ['jʌmi] lecker **VT4,** 63

Z

Zap! [zæp] Zapp! °**IV U3,** 48
zone [zəʊn] Zone °**IV U4,** 60
zoo [zuː] Zoo, Tierpark **II U2,** 22
zookeeper ['zuːkiːpə] Tierpfleger/Tierpflegerin, Wärter/Wärterin **II U2,** 26

Boys' names

Abu ['ɑːbuː] **VT4,** 64
Aidan ['eɪdn] **VT2,** 29
Angus ['æŋgəs] **II FA,** 103
Arthur ['ɑːθə] **III FA,** 84
Ben [ben] **I U2,** 27
Bob [bɒb] **I U6,** 78
Brad [bræd] **IV U2,** 24
Bradley ['brædli] **IV U3,** 42
Brandon ['brændən] **IV U1,** 16
Bruce [bruːs] **IV U4,** 59
Burt [bɜːt] **II U4,** 55
Cal [kæl] **IV U2,** 30
Carly ['kɑːli] **IV U5,** 76
Chandler ['tʃændlə] **II U3,** 37
Charles [ˌtʃɑːlz] **III U5,** 76
Charlie ['tʃɑːli] **I U2,** 33
Daniel ['dænjəl] **II U4,** 51
Dave [deɪv] **III U1,** 9
David ['deɪvɪd] **I U2,** 28
Davy ['deɪvi] **VT1,** 14
Derek ['derɪk] **II U4,** 51
Dicken ['dɪkn] **II FA,** 110
Diego [di'eɪgəʊ] **IV U1,** 12
Donny ['dɒni] **IV U4,** 64
Douglas ['dʌgləs] **II FA,** 102
Ector ['ektə] **III FA,** 84
Ellroy ['elrɔi] **IV U2,** 24
Emilio [ɪ'mɪliəʊ] **VT3,** 46
Eric ['erɪk] **I FA,** 102
Frank [fræŋk] **IV U1,** 16
Fred [fred] **III U3,** 41
Gelert ['gelət] **III U5,** 69
Henry ['henri] **II FA,** 114
Ian ['iːən] **III U5,** 75
Jack [dʒæk] **I FA,** 102
Jake [dʒeɪk] **II U1,** 14
James [dʒeɪmz] **I U2,** 28
Jay [dʒeɪ] **III U5,** 73
Jim [dʒɪm] **I U5,** 73
Jo [dʒəʊ] **I FA,** 105
Joel ['dʒəʊəl] **VT4,** 64
Joey ['dʒəʊi] **II U3,** 37
John [dʒɒn] **I U4,** 57
José [həʊ'zeɪ] **IV U1,** 12
Judd [dʒʌd] **VT2,** 28
Jules [dʒuːlz] **VT2,** 31
Karim [kə'rɪm] **IV U1,** 15
Kay [keɪ] **III FA,** 84
Kingsley ['kɪŋzli] **III U2,** 34
Kofi ['kəʊfi] **VT4,** 60
Leo ['lɪːəʊ] **III U1,** 16
Leon ['lɪɒn] **III U1,** 11
Leroy ['liːrɔɪ] **IV U2,** 33
Llywelyn [lə'welɪn] **III U5,** 74
Marc [mɑːk] **III U4,** 53
Mark [mɑːk] **I U4,** 61
Mat [mæt] **VT1,** 17
Matt [mæt] **II U2,** 31
Miguel [mɪ'gel] **VT2,** 30
Mike [maɪk] **III U4,** 62
Miles [maɪlz] **IV U2,** 30
Nelson ['nelsn] **I U1,** 13
Pablo ['pɑːbləʊ] **IV U4,** 63
Patrick ['pætrɪk] **II U7,** 88
Paul [pɔːl] **I U6,** 85
Pete [piːt] **II U1,** 11
Peter ['piːtə] **I U4,** 61
Phil [fɪl] **I U2,** 28
Ray [reɪ] **III U4,** 58
Reg [redʒ] **III U2,** 30

Richard ['rɪtʃəd] **I U2,** 27
Rick [rɪk] **IV U4,** 68
Rob [rɒb] **I U2,** 26
Robert ['rɒbət] **II U4,** 51
Rodger ['rʌdʒə] **III U5,** 77
Roger ['rɒdʒə] **II U3,** 36
Ross [rɒs] **II U3,** 37
Sam [sæm] **I U1,** 16
Steve [sti:v] **I U1,** 23
Ted [ted] **I U2,** 26
Terry ['teri] **I U1,** 10
Thomas ['tɒməs] **I LUA,** 25
Tim [tɪm] **I LUA,** 25
Todd [tɒd] **II U3,** 36
Tom [tɒm] **I U1,** 10
Tony ['təʊni] **I LUA,** 25
Tyler ['taɪlə] **IV U2,** 27
Uther ['ju:θə] **III FA,** 84
William ['wɪljəm] **V T1,** 11
Zach [zæk] **V T2,** 30; **V T4,** 64

Girls' names

Alison ['ælɪsən] **II U5,** 67
Alysha [ə'lɪʃə] **IV U2,** 30
Amanda [ə'mændə] **III U5,** 75
Amber ['æmbə] **V T4,** 64
Anna ['ænə] **I U3,** 47
Brenda ['brendə] **IV U2,** 33
Carrie ['kæri] **III U4,** 54
Chloé ['kləʊi] **V T2,** 30
Connie ['kɒni] **V T1,** 14
Cora ['kɔ:rə] **V T1,** 17
Daisy ['deɪzi] **III U4,** 54
Debbie ['debi] **II U3,** 36
Dinah ['daɪnə] **IV U4,** 61
Donna ['dɒnə] **IV U2,** 30
Dorothy ['dɒrəθi] **II U5,** 68
Elena ['elɪnə] **I U2,** 28
Em [em] **II FA,** 114
Emma ['emə] **I U1,** 12
Farah ['fɑ:rə] **I U2,** 26
Fiona [fi'əʊnə] **I U1,** 23
Glinda ['glɪndə] **II FA,** 114
Grace [greɪs] **I U2,** 26
Helen ['helən] **II U7,** 88
Igraine [ɪ'greɪn] **III FA,** 84
Jade [dʒeɪd] **I U2,** 27
Jaden ['dʒeɪdn] **V T2,** 30
Jane [dʒeɪn] **III U2,** 29
Jenna ['dʒenə] **III U4,** 59
Jenny ['dʒeni] **I U4,** 57
Jo [dʒəʊ] **V T3,** 46
Julie ['dʒu:li] **III U4,** 62
Kate [keɪt] **I U4,** 57
Kath [kæθ] **I U6,** 78
Kim [kɪm] **IV U1,** 16
Laura ['lɔ:rə] **II U1,** 11
Lauren ['lɔ:rən] **III U4,** 54
Laurie ['lɒri] **IV U1,** 15
Lisa ['li:sə] **I U1,** 10
Margaret ['mɑ:grət] **V T1,** 11
Maria [mə'ri:ə] **I U2,** 28
Marita [mə'ri:tə] **IV U4,** 64
Mariya [mə'ri:ə] **IV U2,** 33
Mary ['meəri] **I U4,** 57
Monika ['mɒnɪkə] **II U3,** 37
Nadine [neɪ'di:n] **I U1,** 13
Nancy ['nænsi] **III U1,** 9
Nasreen [nʌs'ri:n] **I U2,** 26
Nicola ['nɪklə] **I FA,** 100
Nicole [nɪ'kəʊl] **II U3,** 36
Nina ['ni:nə] **IV U2,** 27
Nyla ['naɪlə] **III U4,** 54
Olivia [ɒ'lɪviə] **V T2,** 32
Pat [pæt] **II U1,** 16
Paula ['pɔ:lə] **III U1,** 11
Paula-Jo [ˌpɔ:lə 'dʒəʊ] **IV U2,** 27
Phoebe ['fi:bi] **II U3,** 37
Pru [pru:] **III U2,** 31
Rachel ['reɪtʃl] **II U3,** 37
Sally ['sæli] **I U6,** 85
Sandy ['sændi] **IV U2,** 23
Sarah ['seərə] **I U2,** 28
Sharleen [ʃə'li:n] **IV U2,** 30
Sharon ['ʃærən] **V T1,** 17
Stella ['stelə] **II FA,** 104
Sue [su:] **I U2,** 27
Susan ['su:zn] **I U2,** 28
Suzanne [su:'zæn] **I U1,** 11
Tamara [tə'mɑ:rə] **I LUA,** 25
Tammy ['tæmi] **IV U2,** 24
Terri ['teri] **IV U2,** 27
Tess [tes] **I U6,** 85
Tilly ['tɪli] **I LUA,** 25
Tina ['ti:nə] **I LUA,** 25
Toni Ann [ˌtəʊni 'æn] **III U2,** 34
Tracy ['treɪsi] **I U2,** 28
Trina ['tri:nə] **III U1,** 15
Virginia [və'dʒɪnjə] **III FA,** 96
Zahra ['zɑ:rə] **V T4,** 64
Zameera [zə'mi:rə] **V T4,** 60

Surnames

Akodu [ə'kəʊdʊ] **III U4,** 58
Barnes ['bɑ:nz] **III U1,** 16
Barrymore ['bærimɔ:] **III U5,** 76
Baskerville ['bæskəvɪl] **III U5,** 70
Bell [bel] **II U4,** 52
Berry [beri] **III U1,** 9
Black [blæk] **II U1,** 11
Bland [blænd] **II FA,** 108
Brook [brʊk] **I U1,** 12
Brown [braʊn] **II U1,** 11
Buah ['bʊə] **V T4,** 63
Burns [bɜ:nz] **III U5,** 71
Cage [keɪdʒ] **III U1,** 9
Canterville ['kæntəvɪl] **III FA,** 94
Carter ['kɑ:tə] **I U1,** 12
Cartwright ['kɑ:traɪt] **III U2,** 30
Clarke [klɑ:k] **III U3,** 46
Conte ['kɒnteɪ] **V T3,** 46
Dawson ['dɔ:sn] **V T1,** 11
Delaney [də'leɪni] **V T3,** 46
Forster ['fɔ:stə] **IV U3,** 42
Fox [fɒks] **IV U3,** 50
George [dʒɔ:dʒ] **III U1,** 11
Gibbs [gɪbz] **III U4,** 56
Gruntle ['grʌntl] **II FA,** 108
Gulch [gʌltʃ] **II FA,** 114
Gusman ['gʌzmən] **IV U4,** 63
Hall [hɔ:l] **III U5,** 75
Howard [haʊəd] **II U1,** 14
Hunter [hʌntə] **I U6,** 82
Jackson ['dʒæksn] **I U1,** 10
Jones [dʒəʊnz] **III U4,** 60
Lean [li:n] **I FA,** 104
MacDonald [mək'dɒnld] **IV U2,** 23
Marco ['mɑ:kəʊ] **II U1,** 11
Martin ['mɑ:tɪn] **I FA,** 106
McArthur [mək'ɑ:θə] **II FA,** 102
Monte ['mɒnteɪ] **I U2,** 28
Morley ['mɔ:li] **III U4,** 54
Muir [mjʊə] **II FA,** 103
Newman ['nju:mən] **I U1,** 12
O'Brien [əʊ'braɪən] **II U7,** 88
Otis ['əʊtɪs] **III FA,** 94
Pilch [pɪltʃ] **I U2,** 28
Prynn [prɪn] **III U4,** 60
Reece [ri:s] **III U4,** 59
Richards ['rɪtʃədz] **II U3,** 45
Richstone ['rɪtʃsteʊn] **III U5,** 72
Robbins ['rɒbɪnz] **III U3,** 45
Rose [rəʊz] **I U4,** 60
Simpson ['sɪmpsən] **III U5,** 70
Smith [smɪθ] **III U4,** 53

Spencer ['spentsə] **I U2,** 28
Stapleton ['steɪpltən] **III U5,** 77
Stavros ['stʌvrəs] **I U2,** 28
Taylor ['teɪlə] **I U1,** 10
Tiny ['taɪni] **I LUA,** 25
Watson ['wɒtsn] **III U5,** 69
White [waɪt] **III U2,** 29
Wilkins ['wɪlkɪnz] **III U4,** 60
Willis ['wɪlɪs] **III U5,** 75

Place names

Abergavenny [ˌæbəgə'veni] **III U1,** 11
Africa ['æfrɪkə] **VT4,** 60
Alabama [ˌælə'bæmə] **VT3,** 44
America [ə'merɪkə] **II U3,** 36
Arizona [ˌærɪ'zəʊnə] **IV U3,** 49
Asia ['eɪʒə] Asien **IV U1,** 10
Atlanta [ət'læntə] **IV U5,** 76
Atlantic [ət'læntɪk] **IV U1,** 11
Austin ['ɒstɪn] **IV U5,** 76
Australia [ɒs'treɪliə] Australien **II ZI,** 8
Avondale ['eɪvndeɪl] **III U5,** 69
Ayers Rock [ˌeəz 'rɒk] **VT1,** 9
Baker Street ['beɪkə ˌstri:t] **III U5,** 76
Barcelona [ˌbɑ:sl'əʊnə] **III U1,** 13
Bath [bɑ:θ] **I U6,** 79
Belgium ['beldʒəm] Belgien **IV U1,** 10
Bondi Beach [ˌbɒndaɪ 'bi:tʃ] **VT1,** 8
Boston ['bɒstn] **III U1,** 15
Bow Church [ˌbəʊ 'tʃɜ:tʃ] **I FA,** 108
Brighton ['braɪtn] **III U3,** 38
Brisbane ['brɪzbən] **VT1,** 14
Bristol ['brɪstl] **I U1,** 12
Britain ['brɪtn] **II FA,** 102
British Isles [ˌbrɪtɪʃ 'aɪlz] Britische Inseln **II ZI,** 8
Bronx [brɒŋks] **IV U1,** 9
Brooklyn ['brʊklɪn] **IV U1,** 9
Cairns [keənz] **VT1,** 14
California [ˌkælɪ'fɔ:niə] **IV U3,** 42
Camden ['kæmdən] **II U2,** 22
Canada ['kænədə] Kanada **III U5,** 76
Canary Wharf [kən'eəri ˌwɔ:f] **III U2,** 27
Castle Garden [ˌkɑ:sl 'gɑ:dn] **IV U1,** 10
Central Park [ˌsentrl 'pɑ:k] **IV U1,** 8
the **Channel** [ðə 'tʃænl] **III U3,** 39
Chicago [ʃɪ'kɑ:gəʊ] **III U1,** 9
China ['tʃaɪnə] **III U1,** 13
Chinatown ['tʃaɪnətaʊn] **IV U1,** 9
Chunnel ['tʃʌnl] Tunnel durch den Ärmelkanal **III U3,** 39
Colorado [ˌkɒlr'ɑ:dəʊ] **IV U4,** 61
Cornwall ['kɔ:nwɔ:l] **II U6,** 78
Covent Garden [ˌkɒvnt 'gɑ:dn] **III U2,** 24
Cutty Sark Gardens [kʌti ˌsɑ:k 'gɑ:dnz] **I U4,** 54
Dartmoor ['dɑ:tmɔ:] **III U5,** 76
Darwin ['dɑ:wɪn] **VT1,** 16
Devon ['devn] **II U6,** 78
Dover ['dəʊvə] **III U3,** 38
Dublin ['dʌblɪn] **II U7,** 88
Eastbourne ['i:stbɔ:n] **III U3,** 38
Eastern Europe [ˌi:stn 'jʊərəp] Osteuropa **IV U1,** 10
Ellis Island [ˌelɪs 'aɪlənd] **IV U1,** 9
England ['ɪŋglənd] England **I U2,** 29
Europe ['jʊərəp] Europa **IV U1,** 10
Exmoor ['eksmɔ:] **II ZI,** 8
Falmouth ['fælməθ] **III U3,** 42
Fenchurch Street ['fentʃɜ:tʃ ˌstri:t] **III U2,** 26
Folkestone ['fəʊkstən] **III U3,** 38
France [frɑ:nts] **III U3,** 39
Franklin ['fræŋklɪn] **VT1,** 14
Germany ['dʒɜ:məni] Deutschland **I U2,** 29
Ghana ['gɑ:nə] **VT4,** 59
Glasgow ['glæzgəʊ] **II FA,** 102
Goldcoast ['gəʊldˌkəʊst] **VT1,** 14
Grand Canyon [ˌgrænd 'kænjən] **IV U4,** 56
Great Tower Street [ˌgreɪt 'taʊə ˌstri:t] **III U2,** 26
Great Barrier Reef [ˌgreɪt ˌbæriə 'ri:f] **VT1,** 9
Great Barrier Reef Marine Park [ˌgreɪt ˌbæriə 'ri:f mə'ri:n ˌpɑ:k] **VT1,** 10
Great Blasket Island [ˌgreɪt ˌblɑ:skɪt 'aɪlənd] **III U3,** 42
Greece [gri:s] Griechenland **I U2,** 29
Greenwich ['grenɪdʒ] **I U1,** 10
Greenwich Village [ˌgrenɪdʒ 'vɪlɪdʒ] **IV U1,** 16
Hastings ['heɪstɪŋz] **III U3,** 38
Hawaii [hə'waɪ] **IV U4,** 62
Heathrow [ˌhi:θ'rəʊ] **III U3,** 39
Hollyoaks ['hɒliəʊks] **III U5,** 70
Hollywood ['hɒliwʊd] **III U5,** 68
Houses of Parliament [ˌhaʊzɪz‿əv 'pɑ:ləmənt] **I FA,** 114
India ['ɪndiə] Indien **IV U1,** 10
Ireland ['aɪələnd] Irland **II U6,** 85
Irish Sea [ˌaɪrɪʃ 'si:] **III U3,** 38
Isle of Dogs [ˌaɪl‿əv 'dɒgz] **I U4,** 54
Isle of Wight [ˌaɪl‿əv 'waɪt] **III U3,** 38
Istanbul [ˌɪstæn'bʊl] **I U1,** 13
Italy ['ɪtəli] Italien **I U2,** 29
Kansas ['kænzəs] **II FA,** 114
Kilkenny [kɪl'keni] **II U7,** 93
King William Walk [kɪŋ 'wɪljəm ˌwɔ:k] **I U4,** 62
Las Vegas [ˌlæs 'veɪgəs] **IV U4,** 57
Limerick ['lɪmrɪk] **II ZI,** 8
Little Oyster Island [ˌlɪtl‿ɔɪstə 'aɪlənd] **IV U1,** 10
Liverpool ['lɪvəpu:l] **VT1,** 11
Loch Ness [ˌlɒx 'nes] **II ZI,** 8
London ['lʌndən] **I U1,** 10
London Bridge [ˌlʌndən 'brɪdʒ] **III U2,** 29
Los Angeles (LA) [lɒs‿'ændʒɪli:z] **IV U4,** 60
Madrid [mə'drɪd] **I U1,** 13
the **Maldives** ['mɔ:ldi:vz] die Malediven **VT4,** 60
Manhattan [mæn'hætn] **IV U1,** 8
Marble Arch ['mɑ:bl ˌɑ:tʃ] **III U2,** 24
Mark Lane ['mɑ:k ˌleɪn] **III U2,** 26
Melbourne ['melbən] **VT1,** 16
Memphis ['memfɪs] **VT3,** 42
Mexico ['meksɪkəʊ] Mexiko **IV U1,** 10
Mexico City [ˌmeksɪkəʊ 'sɪti] **IV U4,** 65
Miami [maɪ'æmi] **IV U4,** 60
Mincing Lane ['mɪnsɪŋ ˌleɪn] **III U2,** 26
Moher ['məʊhə] **II U7,** 93
Mongolia [mɒŋ'gəʊliə] die Mongolei **VT4,** 59
Montgomery [mən'gʌmri] **VT3,** 44
Moscow ['mɒskəʊ] Moskau **III U3,** 46
Nairobi [naɪ'rəʊbi] **I U1,** 13
Neston ['nestn] **I U6,** 78
Nevada [nə'vɑ:də] Nevada **IV U4,** 58
New Amsterdam [ˌnju: 'æmstədæm] **IV U1,** 10
New Mexico [ˌnju: 'meksɪkəʊ] **IV U4,** 61
New York [ˌnju: 'jɔ:k] **I U4,** 55
New York City (NYC) [ˌnju: jɔ:k 'sɪti] **IV U1,** 8
New York Harbor [ˌnju: jɔ:k 'hɑ:bə] **IV U1,** 9
Northern Europe [ˌnɔ:ðən 'jʊərəp] Nordeuropa **IV U1,** 10
Northern Ireland [ˌnɔ:ðn‿'aɪələnd] Nordirland **II U7,** 89
North Sea [ˌnɔ:θ 'si:] Nordsee **III U3,** 38
Norway ['nɔ:weɪ] Norwegen **IV U1,** 10
Nottingham ['nɒtɪŋəm] **II U2,** 25
Oz [ɒz] Oz *(Spitzname für Australien)* **VT1,** 8
Paris ['pærɪs] **I U1,** 13

Park Row [ˌpɑːk ˈrəʊ] **I U4,** 60
Perth [pɜːθ] **II ZI,** 8
Philadelphia [ˌfɪləˈdelfiə] **V T2,** 29
Philippines [ˈfɪlɪpiːnz] Philippinen **IV U1,** 10
Phoenix [ˈfiːnɪks] **IV U3,** 49
Piccadilly Circus [ˌpɪkədɪli ˈsɜːkəs] **III U2,** 24
Poland [ˈpəʊlənd] Polen **I U2,** 29
Prescott [ˈpreskət] **IV U3,** 49
Queens [kwiːnz] **IV U1,** 9
Reno [ˈriːnəʊ] **IV U4,** 58
Republic of Ireland [rɪˌpʌblɪk‿əv‿ˈaɪələnd] Republik Irland **II U7,** 88
Rockies (Rocky Mountains) [ˈrɒkiz] **V T3,** 41
Rome [rəʊm] **IV U1,** 18
Round Rock [ˌraʊnd ˈrɒk] **IV U5,** 76
Russia [ˈrʌʃə] Russland **I U2,** 29
Salisbury [ˈsɔːlzbri] **III U3,** 38
Scilly Isles [ˈsɪli ˌaɪlz] **II U6,** 78
Scotland [ˈskɒtlənd] Schottland **II ZI,** 8
Seattle [siˈætl] **IV U4,** 60
Seething Lane [ˈsiːðɪŋ ˌleɪn] **III U2,** 26
Shannon [ˈʃænən] **II U7,** 93
Sherwood Forest [ˌʃɜːwʊd ˈfɒrɪst] **II FA,** 110
Shoreditch [ʃɔːˈdɪtʃ] **III U2,** 31
Southampton [saʊˈθæmtən] **III U3,** 38
South England [ˌsaʊθ ˈɪŋglənd] **III U3,** 39
Spain [speɪn] Spanien **III U3,** 40
Staten Island [ˌstætn ˈaɪlənd] **IV U1,** 9
Stonehenge [stəʊnˈhendʒ] **III U3,** 39
Sydney [ˈsɪdni] **V T1,** 8
Sydney Cove [ˌsɪdni ˈkəʊv] **V T1,** 10
Taronga Zoo [təˌrɒŋgə ˈzuː] **V T1,** 11
Tasmania [tæzˈmeɪniə] **V T1,** 14
Tennessee [ˌtenəˈsiː] **V T3,** 44
Texas [ˈteksəs] **IV U1,** 16
the **Thames** [temz] **I U4,** 54
Tokyo [ˈtəʊkiəʊ] **I U1,** 13
Tower Hill [ˌtaʊə ˈhɪl] **III U2,** 26
Townsville [ˈtaʊnzvɪl] **V T1,** 10
Turkey [ˈtɜːki] Türkei **I U2,** 29
Twickenham [ˈtwikənəm] **III U1,** 8
Uluru [uːˈluːruː] Uluru = Ayers Rock *(heiliger Berg der Aborigines)* **V T1,** 9
United Kingdom (UK) [juːˌnaɪtɪd ˈkɪŋdəm] Vereinigtes Königreich von Großbritannien und Nordirland **III U3,** 38
Urquhart Castle [ˌɜːkət ˈkɑːsl] **II FA,** 102
US [juːˈes] USA **IV U1,** 9
Wales [weɪlz] Wales **II ZI,** 8
Washington DC [ˌwɒʃɪŋtən diːˈsiː] **V T3,** 44
Wembley Stadium [ˈwembli ˈsteɪdiəm] **III U1,** 13
Western Australia [ˌwestən ɒsˈtreɪliə] **II U1,** 14
White Hart Lane [ˌwaɪt hɑːt ˈleɪn] **III U1,** 16
Wildcroft [ˈwaɪldkrɒft] **I FA,** 100
Wiltshire [ˈwɪltʃə] **I U6,** 78
Wimbledon [ˈwɪmbldn] **III U1,** 15
Wordsworth Way [ˌwɜːdzwəθ ˈweɪ] **V T1,** 11

Other names

Academy Award [əˌkædəmi əˈwɔːd] **IV U5,** 73
Aquarius [əˈkweəriəs] Wassermann **II U6,** 80
Arsenal [ˈɑːsnl] **III U1,** 16
Bakerloo Line [ˌbeɪkəluː ˈlaɪn] **III U2,** 24
Baskerville Hall [ˈbæskəvɪl ˌhɔːl] **III U5,** 76
Batman [ˈbætmæn] **III U5,** 75
Bell Tower [ˈbel ˌtaʊə] **III U2,** 29
Big Ben [ˌbɪg ˈben] **III U2,** 22
Blue Eagles [ˌbluː ˈiːglz] **IV U2,** 22
Blue Hills Ranch [ˌbluː hɪlz ˈræntʃ] **IV U4,** 58
Blugirl [ˈbluːgɜːl] **IV U5,** 76
Bollywood [ˈbɒliwʊd] **III U5,** 68
Bono [ˈbəʊnəʊ] **V T3,** 42
Boxing Day [ˈbɒksɪŋ ˌdeɪ] **I FA,** 114
Brooklyn Bridge [ˌbrʊklɪn ˈbrɪdʒ] **IV U1,** 9
Brushstroke Gang [ˈbrʌʃstrəʊk ˌgæŋ] **V T2,** 30
Buckingham Palace [ˌbʌkɪŋəm ˈpælɪs] **III U2,** 22
Cadillac [ˈkædɪlæk] **IV U4,** 64
Chicago Cubs [ˌʃɪˈkɑːgəʊ ˈkʌbz] **III U1,** 9
Chicago Hope [ʃɪˌkɑːgeʊ ˈhəʊp] **III U5,** 75
Circle Line [ˈsɜːkl ˌlaɪn] **III U2,** 24
Cutty Sark [ˌkʌti ˈsɑːk] **I U4,** 54
Day Chocolate Company [ˌdeɪ ˈtʃɒklət ˌkʌmpəni] **V T4,** 62
Deli Chocolate Ltd. [ˌdeli ˈtʃɒklət ˌlɪmɪtɪd] **V T4,** 69
Discman [ˈdɪskmən] **I U2,** 30
Divine Chocolate Ltd. [dɪˌvaɪn ˈtʃɒklət ˌlɪmɪtɪd] **V T4,** 62
DLR [ˌdiː‿el‿ˈɑː] **I U4,** 55
Docklands Light Railway [ˈdɒkləndz ˌlaɪt ˈreɪlweɪ] **I U4,** 55
Dubble [ˈdʌbl] **V T4,** 62
Dynamo Moscow [ˈdaɪnəməʊ ˈmɒskəʊ] **III U1,** 16
Embankment [ɪmˈbæŋkmənt] **III U2,** 24
Emergency Room [ɪˈmɜːdʒntsi ˌruːm] **III U5,** 70
Emmy [ˈemi] **IV U5,** 73
Empire State Building [ˌempaɪə ˈsteɪt ˌbɪldɪŋ] **IV U1,** 8
Fairtrade [ˌfeəˈtreɪd] Fairer Handel **V T4,** 62
General Hospital [ˌdʒenrl ˈhɒspɪtl] **III U5,** 75
GMT [ˈdʒiːemˈtiː] **I U4,** 55
GPS [ˌdʒiːpiːˈes] **IV U3,** 41
Grammy Award [ˌgræmi əˈwɔːd] **IV U5,** 73
Green Corps [ˈgriːn ˌkɔː] **V T1,** 14
Greenwich Mean Time [ˌgrenɪdʒ ˈmiːn taɪm] **I U4,** 55
Guy Fawkes [ˌgaɪ ˈfɔːks] **I FA,** 114
Harrods [ˈhærədz] **II U2,** 23
Harry Potter [ˌhæri ˈpɒtə] **II U1,** 11
24-hour clock [ˌtwenti fɔːr‿aʊə ˈklɒk] **I U4,** 54
Hualapai [ˌhʊələˈpeɪ] **IV U4,** 56
IBM [ˌaɪbiːˈem] **V T3,** 43
James Bond [ˌdʒeɪmz ˈbɒnd] **I FA,** 104
Kuapo Kokoo [ˌkʊɑːpə ˈkɒkuː] **V T4,** 62
Little Rock Nine [ˌlɪtl ˌrɒk ˈnaɪn] **V T3,** 44
London Dungeon [ˌlʌndən ˈdʌndʒn] **III U2,** 22
London Eye [ˌlʌndən‿ˈaɪ] **III U2,** 22
London Knights [ˌlʌndən ˈnaɪts] **II U2,** 22
London Underground [ˌlʌndən ˈʌndəgraʊnd] **III U2,** 23
Madonna [məˈdɒnə] **III U2,** 25
Maid Marian [ˌmeɪd ˈmæriən] **II FA,** 110
Man U [ˈmæn juː] **III U5,** 70
Meridian Line [məˈrɪdiən ˈlaɪn] **I U4,** 54
Mohawk [ˈməʊhɔːk] **IV U1,** 15
Monument [ˈmɒnjəmənt] **III U2,** 24
MTV [ˌemtiːˈviː] **I U6,** 82
Mural Arts [ˌmjʊərl‿ˈɑːts] **V T2,** 29
Mustang [ˈmʌstæŋ] **IV U5,** 80
Napoleon [nəˈpəʊliən] **II U5,** 62
NASA [ˈnæsə] NASA *(US-Weltraumbehörde)* **IV U3,** 41

Nessie ['nesi] **II FA,** 103
Nobel Peace Prize [nəʊˌbel 'pi:s ˌpraɪz] **V T3,** 44
Nottingham Panthers [ˌnɒtɪŋəm 'pæntθəz] **II U2,** 25
NVQ (National Vocational Qualification) [ˌenvi:'kju:] Berufsqualifikation in England °**V T2,** 32
OC California [ˌəʊ 'si: ˌkælɪ'fɔ:niə] **III U5,** 70
the **Olympics** *(Olympic Games)* [əʊ'lɪmpɪks; əʊˌlɪmpɪk 'geɪmz] Olympiade, Olympische Spiele **V T1,** 11
Oscar ['ɒskə] **IV U5,** 73
Palace of Westminster [ˌpælɪs əv 'wesmɪnstə] **III U2,** 22
PowerPoint ['paʊəpɔɪnt] **V T2,** 33
Queen Elizabeth [ˌkwi:n‿ɪ'lɪzəbəθ] **I U5,** 73
Robin Hood [ˌrɒbɪn 'hʊd] **II FA,** 110
Route 66 [ru:t] **IV U4,** 64
Royal Family ['rɔɪəl 'fæmli] königliche Familie **III U2,** 22
Royal Observatory [ˌrɔɪəl əb'zɜ:vətri] **I U4,** 55
Shakespeare ['ʃeɪkspɪə] **II U5,** 62
Sherlock Holmes [ˌʃɜ:lɒk 'həʊmz] **III U5,** 70
Shrove Tuesday [ˌʃrəʊv 'tju:zdeɪ] **I FA,** 115
Skywalk ['skaɪwɔ:k] **IV U4,** 56
Statue of Liberty [ˌstætʃu:‿əv 'lɪbəti] **IV U1,** 9
St James's Park [snt ˌdʒeɪmzɪz 'pɑ:k] **III U2,** 24
St Paul's Cathedral [snt ˌpɔ:lz kə'θi:drl] **III U2,** 24
Suvaruge Fushi [ˌsu:vʌ'ru:ge 'fu:ʃi:] **V T4,** 66
Taco Bell [ˌtɑ:kəʊ 'bel] **IV U5,** 80
Taj Mahal [ˌtɑ:dʒ mə'hɑ:l] **II U4,** 48
Thames Festival Lantern Procession [ˌtemz 'festɪvl 'læntən prə'seʃn] **I U7,** 90
Thanksgiving [ˌθæŋks'gɪvɪŋ] **IV U4,** 60
Times Square [ˌtaɪmz 'skweə] **IV U1,** 9
Titanic [taɪ'tænɪk] **III U3,** 39
Tower of London [ˌtaʊər‿əv 'lʌndən] **III U2,** 22
Transfair ['trænsfeə] **V T4,** 62
Tube [tju:b] Londoner U-Bahn **III U2,** 22
U2 [ju'tu:] **V T3,** 42
UFO *(Unidentified Flying Object)* ['ju:ef'əʊ] **IV U3,** 49
Video Music Award [ˌvɪdiəʊ 'mu:zɪk əˌwɔ:d] **IV U5,** 73
William the Conqueror [ˌwɪljəm ðə 'kɒŋkrə] **III U2,** 28
YouTube ['ju:tju:b] **V T2,** 32

Famous names

Angelina Jolie [ændʒˌli:nə 'dʒəʊli] **III U2,** 25
Annie Moore [ˌæni 'mɔ:] **IV U1,** 10
Arthur Conan Doyle [ˌɑ:θə ˌkəʊnən 'dɔɪl] **III U5,** 75
Beyoncé [bɪ'jɒnseɪ] **IV U5,** 73
Black Eyed Peas [ˌblæk‿aɪd 'pi:z] **IV U5,** 77
B Section ['bi: ˌsekʃn] **IV U5,** 80
Champion Jack Dupree [ˌtʃæmpiən ˌdʒæk dʊ'preɪ] **V T3,** 42
Charlie Chaplin [ˌtʃɑ:li 'tʃæplɪn] **III U4,** 62
David Beckham [ˌdeɪvɪd 'bekəm] **III U2,** 25
Eadweard Muybridge [ˌedwəd 'maɪbrɪdʒ] **IV U5,** 74
Edwin Porter [ˌedwɪn 'pɔ:tə] **IV U5,** 74
Fergie ['fɜ:gi] **IV U5,** 80
Green Day ['gri:n ˌdeɪ] **IV U5,** 73
James Cook [ˌdʒeɪmz 'kʊk] **V T1,** 10
Jennifer Hudson [ˌdʒenɪfə 'hʌdsn] **IV U5,** 72
Led Zeppelin [ˌled 'zeplɪn] **IV U5,** 76
Lil Jon [ˌlɪl 'dʒɒn] **IV U5,** 76
Ludacris ['lu:dəkrɪs] **IV U5,** 73
Martin Luther King [ˌmɑ:tɪn ˌlu:θə 'kɪŋ] **V T3,** 42
Naomi Campbell [ˌneɪəmi: 'kæmbl] **III U2,** 25
Nelly Furtado [ˌneli fə'tɑ:dəʊ] **IV U5,** 73
Nicole Kidman [nɪˌkəʊl 'kɪdmən] **IV U5,** 72
Pink [pɪŋk] **IV U5,** 73
Robbie Williams [ˌrɒbi 'wɪljəmz] **II U1,** 14
Robin Leach [ˌrɒbɪn 'li:tʃ] **IV U5,** 80
Rosa Parks [ˌrəʊzə 'pɑ:ks] **V T3,** 44
Samuel Ellis [ˌsæmjʊəl‿'elɪs] **IV U1,** 10
Sean Paul [ˌʃɔ:n 'pɔ:l] **IV U5,** 73
Steve Fossett [sti:v 'fɒsət] **V T3,** 43
Thomas Edison [ˌtɒməs‿'edɪsn] **IV U5,** 74
Zandra Rhodes [ˌzændrə 'rəʊdz] **IV U5,** 72

A

ab off [ɒf]
Abc alphabet ['ælfəbet]
Abend evening ['i:vnɪŋ]; night [naɪt]
am Abend in the evening [ˌɪn ði: 'i:vnɪŋ]
an diesem Abend that evening [ˌdæt‿'i:vnɪŋ]
heute Abend this evening [ðɪs 'i:vnɪŋ]; tonight [tə'naɪt]
zu Abend essen to have supper [hæv 'sʌpə]
Abendessen dinner ['dɪnə]; supper ['sʌpə]; tea [ti:]
zum Abendessen for supper [fə 'sʌpə]
Abendkleid evening dress ['i:vnɪŋ ˌdres]
abends in the evening [ˌɪn ði: 'i:vnɪŋ]
Abenteuer adventure [əd'ventʃə]
aber but [bʌt]
abfahren to leave [li:v]
Abfall rubbish ['rʌbɪʃ]; waste [weɪst]
Abfälle rubbish ['rʌbɪʃ]
abfliegen to take off [ˌteɪk‿'ɒf]
Abflug departure [dɪ'pɑ:tʃə]
Abgang exit ['eksɪt]
abgebrannt broke [brəʊk]
abgelegen remote [rɪ'məʊt]
zum **Abgewöhnen sein** to be a turn-off ['tɜ:nɒf]
abhalten to hold [həʊld]
abheben to take off [ˌteɪk‿'ɒf]
abholen to collect [kə'lekt]; to pick up [pɪk‿'ʌp]
abholzen to cut down [kʌt 'daʊn]
Abitur A-levels *(pl)* ['eɪlevlz]
Abkommen contract ['kɒntrækt]
abladen to dump sb [dʌmp]
ablaufen *(Zeit)* to run out [rʌn‿'aʊt]
Abmachung deal [di:l]
abnehmen to take off [ˌteɪk‿'ɒf]
Aborigine Aborigine [ˌæbə'rɪdʒni]
Abreise departure [dɪ'pɑ:tʃə]
Absatz turnover ['tɜ:nˌəʊvə]
abschalten to turn off [tɜ:n‿'ɒf]
abschicken *(einen Brief)* to post [pəʊst]
abschießen to shoot [ʃu:t]
abschließen to lock [lɒk]
Abschluss closing ['kləʊzɪŋ]
abschrecken to frighten away [ˌfraɪtn‿ə'weɪ]
abschreiben to copy ['kɒpi]
Abschuss launch [lɔ:nʃ]
abstimmen to vote [vəʊt]
Abstimmung vote [vəʊt]
Absturz crash [kræʃ]
abtörnend sein to be a turn-off ['tɜ:nɒf]
Abwesenheit absence ['æbsns]
achten auf to watch [wɒtʃ]
Acker field [fi:ld]
Adapter adaptor [ə'dæptə]
addieren to add [æd]
Adresse address [ə'dres]
Aftershave aftershave ['ɑ:ftəʃeɪv]
Agent/Agentin agent ['eɪdʒnt]
Agentur agency ['eɪdʒnsi]
agieren to act [ækt]
Ahorn maple ['meɪpl]
Akku battery ['bætri]
Akte record ['rekɔ:d]
Aktion action ['ækʃn]
Aktivität activity [æk'tɪvəti]
Akzent accent ['æksnt]
akzeptieren to accept [ək'sept]
Alarm alarm [ə'lɑ:m]
Albtraum nightmare ['naɪtmeə]
Album album ['ælbəm]
Alkohol alcohol ['ælkəhɒl]
alle everybody ['evribɒdi]
alle/alles all [ɔ:l]
aller- very ['veri]
allein alone [ə'ləʊn]; solo ['səʊləʊ]
(ganz) allein on one's own [ɒn wʌnz‿'əʊn]
Allein- solo ['səʊləʊ]
einen **Alleingang starten** to go it alone [ˌgeʊ‿ɪt‿ə'leʊn]
alles everything ['evriθɪŋ]
alles klar all right [ɔ:l 'raɪt]
Alphabet alphabet ['ælfəbet]
alphabetisch alphabetical [ˌælfə'betɪkl]
als as [æz; əz]
als *(Vergleich)* than [ðən]
als *(zeitlich)* when [wen]
also so [səʊ]
alt old [əʊld]; ancient ['eɪnʃnt]
Alter age [eɪdʒ]
alternativ alternative [ɔ:l'tɜ:nətɪv]
Alternative *(Musikrichtung)* alternative [ɔ:l'tɜ:nətɪv]
Amerikaner American [ə'merɪkən]
Hispano-Amerikaner/-Amerikanerin Hispanic [hɪ'spænɪk]
amerikanisch American [ə'merɪkən]
sich **amüsieren** to have a good time [ˌhæv‿ə gʊd 'taɪm]; to have fun [ˌhæv 'fʌn]
an at [æt; ət]; on [ɒn]
an sein to be on [bi:‿'ɒn]
anbauen to grow [grəʊ]
anbieten to offer ['ɒfə]
Anbieter/Anbieterin provider [prə'vaɪdə]
Anblick sight [saɪt]
anbringen to fix [fɪks]
andauern to continue [kən'tɪnju:]; to go on [gəʊ‿'ɒn]
Andenken souvenir [ˌsu:və'nɪə]
anderer/andere/anderes other ['ʌðə]
ein anderer/eine andere/ein anderes another [ə'nʌðə]
ändern to change [tʃeɪndʒ]
anders different ['dɪfrnt]
Änderung change [tʃeɪndʒ]
Anfang beginning [bɪ'gɪnɪŋ]; start [stɑ:t]
anfangen to begin [bɪ'gɪn]; to start [stɑ:t]
anfordern to require [rɪ'kwaɪə]
Anführer/Anführerin leader ['li:də]
Angebot offer ['ɒfə]
Angelegenheit matter ['mætə]
angeln to fish [fɪʃ]
Angeln fishing ['fɪʃɪŋ]
Angestellter/Angestellte employee [ɪm'plɔɪi:]; worker ['wɜ:kə]
Angler fisherman, fishermen *(pl)* ['fɪʃəmən; 'fɪʃəmen]
angreifen to attack [ə'tæk]
Angriff raid [reɪd]
Angst haben (vor) to be afraid (of) [bi:‿ə'freɪd]; to be frightened (of) [bi: 'fraɪtnd]
Angst machen to scare [skeə]
Ich habe Angst. I'm scared. [aɪm 'skeəd]
ängstigen to worry ['wʌri]
anhaben to wear [weə]
anhalten to stop [stɒp]
Anhänger/Anhängerin supporter [sə'pɔ:tə]
anhören to listen ['lɪsn]
sich anhören to sound [saʊnd]
fest **anklopfen** to bang [bæŋ]
ankommen to arrive [ə'raɪv]
Ankündigung announcement [ə'naʊntsmənt]
anmachen to switch on [swɪtʃ‿'ɒn]; to turn on [ˌtɜ:n‿'ɒn]

anmalen to paint [peɪnt]
anmelden to register ['redʒɪstə]
sich anmelden (zu) to apply (for) [ə'plaɪ]
sich anmelden to register ['redʒɪstə]
Anmerkung note [nəʊt]
annähernd nearly ['nɪəli]
annehmen to accept [ək'sept]
Anorak anorak ['ænəræk]
Anrufbeantworter answerphone ['ɑ:nsəfəʊn]
anrufen to call [kɔ:l]; to phone [fəʊn]
anschauen to view [vju:]; to have a look [ˌhæv‿ə 'lʊk]
Anschlag attempt [ə'tempt]; notice ['nəʊtɪs]
sich **anschließen** to join [dʒɔɪn]
ansehen to look at ['lʊk‿ət]; to watch [wɒtʃ]
sich ansehen to look at ['lʊk‿ət]
sich etwas ansehen to check out [tʃek‿'aʊt]
Ansprache speech [spi:tʃ]
Anstandswauwau chaperon ['ʃæprəʊn]
Anstieg rise [raɪz]
anstreichen to paint [peɪnt]
anti- anti ['æntɪ]
antik ancient ['eɪnʃnt]
antippen to touch [tʌtʃ]
Antrag application [ˌæplɪ'keɪʃn]
Antragsteller/Antragstellerin applicant ['æplɪkənt]
Antwort answer ['ɑ:ntsə]; response [rɪ'spɒns]
anweisen to direct [dɪ'rekt]
Anweisung order ['ɔ:də]
Anwendung application [ˌæplɪ'keɪʃn]
Anzeige ad [æd]; advert ['ædvɜ:t]
anziehen to attract [ə'trækt]; to put on [pʊt‿'ɒn]
sich anziehen to dress [dres]
Anzug suit [su:t]
Apartment apartment *(AE)* [ə'pɑ:tmənt]
Apfel apple ['æpl]
Apparat machine [mə'ʃi:n]
am Apparat speaking ['spi:kɪŋ]
April April ['eɪprl]
Arbeit work [wɜ:k]
arbeiten to work [wɜ:k]
Arbeiter/Arbeiterin worker ['wɜ:kə]
Arbeitgeber/Arbeitgeberin employer [ɪm'plɔɪə]
Arbeitsblatt worksheet ['wɜ:kʃi:t]
Arbeitserlaubnis working visa ['wɜ:kɪŋ ˌvi:zə]
Arbeitsgemeinschaft club [klʌb]
Arbeitsstelle job [dʒɒb]
Arena arena [ə'ri:nə]
Ärger trouble ['trʌbl]
argumentieren to argue ['ɑ:gju:]
arm poor [pɔ:; pʊə]
Arm arm [ɑ:m]
Ärmel arm [ɑ:m]
Armut poverty ['pɒvəti]
Arsch ass *(AE)* [æs]
Art kind [kaɪnd]; type [taɪp]
Arzt/Ärztin doctor ['dɒktə]
zum Arzt gehen to see a doctor [si:‿ə 'dɒktə]
Aspekt aspect ['æspekt]
Assistent/Assistentin assistant [ə'sɪstnt]
Astronaut/Astronautin astronaut ['æstrənɔ:t]
attraktiv attractive [ə'træktɪv]
auch also ['ɔ:lsəʊ]; too [tu:]
sowohl … als auch as well as [əz 'wel‿əz]
auf at [æt; ət]; on [ɒn]; onto ['ɒntu:; 'ɒntə]; up [ʌp]
auf … zu towards [tə'wɔ:dz]
auf dem Land in the country [ˌɪn ðə 'kʌntri]
auf einmal suddenly ['sʌdnli]
auf Sendung on the air [ˌɒn ði‿'eə]
auf Wiedersehen goodbye [gʊd'baɪ]
aufbauen to put up [pʊt‿'ʌp]; to set up [set‿'ʌp]
aufbewahren to keep [ki:p]
Aufblinken flash [flæʃ]
aufbrechen to set off [set‿'ɒf]
aufführen to perform [pə'fɔ:m]
Aufführung performance [pə'fɔ:məns]
Aufgabe exercise ['eksəsaɪz]; mission ['mɪʃn]; task [tɑ:sk]
aufgeben to give up [gɪv‿'ʌp]; to quit [kwɪt]
aufgeben *(einen Brief)* to post [pəʊst]
aufgehen to open ['əʊpn]
aufgeregt excited [ɪk'saɪtɪd]; nervous ['nɜ:vəs]
aufgeregt sein to be upset [bi: ʌp'set]
aufgeschlossen outgoing ['aʊtgəʊɪŋ]
aufheben to pick up [pɪk‿'ʌp]
aufhören to finish ['fɪnɪʃ]; to stop [stɒp]
aufhören etw. zu tun to stop + -ing [stɒp]
aufhören mit to stop [stɒp]
mit etw. aufhören to quit [kwɪt]
aufklären to solve [sɒlv]
aufmachen to open ['əʊpn]
aufmerksam thoughtful ['θɔ:tfl]
Aufnahme record ['rekɔ:d]; recording [rɪ'kɔ:dɪŋ]; shot [ʃɒt]
aufnehmen to record [rɪ'kɔ:d]
aufpassen to take care [teɪk 'keə]
aufpassen auf to look after [lʊk‿'ɑ:ftə]
Aufprall crash [kræʃ]
sich **aufregen** to panic ['pænɪk]
aufregend exciting [ɪk'saɪtɪŋ]
Aufruhr riot [raɪət]
aufschauen to look up [lʊk‿'ʌp]
Aufseher/Aufseherin keeper ['ki:pə]
aufsetzen to put on [pʊt‿'ɒn]
aufspringen to jump up [dʒʌmp‿'ʌp]
aufstehen to get out of bed [ˌget‿aʊt‿əv 'bed]; to get up [get‿'ʌp]
aufsteigen to get on [get‿'ɒn]
aufstellen to put up [pʊt‿'ʌp]
Aufstieg rise [raɪz]
Auftrag mission ['mɪʃn]; task [tɑ:sk]
auftragen *(Make-up)* to put on [pʊt‿'ɒn]
auftreten to perform [pə'fɔ:m]
aufwachen to wake up [weɪk‿'ʌp]
aufwecken to wake [weɪk]; to wake up [weɪk‿'ʌp]
aufzeichnen to record [rɪ'kɔ:d]
Aufzeichnung record ['rekɔ:d]
Auge eye [aɪ]
Augenblick moment ['məʊmənt]
im Augenblick at the moment [ət ðə 'məʊmənt]
in diesem Augenblick right now [ˌraɪt 'naʊ]
Augenbraue eyebrow ['aɪbraʊ]
August August ['ɔ:gəst]
aus from [frɒm]; in [ɪn]
aus … heraus out of ['aʊt‿əv]
ausbilden to train [treɪn]
Ausbilder/Ausbilderin instructor [ɪn'strʌktə]
Ausbildung apprenticeship [ə'prentɪʃɪp]; training ['treɪnɪŋ]
eine Ausbildung machen to train [treɪn]
ausbrechen to break out [ˌbreɪk‿'aʊt]
auschecken to check out [tʃek‿'aʊt]

German – English

sich **ausdenken** to make up [meɪk‿'ʌp]
Ausfahrt exit ['eksɪt]
Ausflug trip [trɪp]
Ausfuhr export ['ekspɔ:t]
ausführen to export [ɪk'spɔ:t]
ausfüllen to complete [kəm'pli:t]; to fill in [fɪl‿'ɪn]
Ausgang exit ['eksɪt]
ausgeben to spend [spend]
ausgehen to go out [gəʊ‿'aʊt]
ausgehen *(Zeit)* to run out [rʌn‿'aʊt]
ausgraben to dig up [dɪg‿'ʌp]
auskippen to dump sb [dʌmp]
ohne … **auskommen** to go without [ˌgəʊ wɪ'ðaʊt]
auslachen to laugh at ['lɑ:f‿ət]
im **Ausland** abroad [ə'brɔ:d]
ins Ausland abroad [ə'brɔ:d]
ausländisch alien ['eɪliən]; foreign ['fɒrɪn]
ausleihen to loan [ləʊn]
ausliefern to deliver [dɪ'lɪvə]
auslösen *(Alarm)* to set off [set‿'ɒf]
Auslöser button ['bʌtn]
ausmachen to matter ['mætə]; to put out [pʊt‿'aʊt]
ausrauben to rob [rɒb]
Ausreißer/Ausreißerin runaway ['rʌnəˌweɪ]
ausruhen to rest [rest]
sich ausruhen to rest [rest]
Ausrüstung equipment [ɪ'kwɪpmənt]
ausschalten to switch off [ˌswɪtʃ‿'ɒf]; to turn off [tɜ:n‿'ɒf]
ausscheren to swerve [swɜ:v]
ausschließen to ban [bæn]
Ausschreitung riot [raɪət]
aussehen to look [lʊk]
Aussehen look [lʊk]
außer beside [bɪ'saɪd]; but [bʌt]; except [ɪk'sept]
außerhalb outside [aʊt'saɪd]
Außerirdischer/Außerirdische alien ['eɪliən]
Aussicht view [vju:]
Ausstattung equipment [ɪ'kwɪpmənt]
aussteigen to get out [get‿'aʊt]
aussteigen aus to get off [get‿'ɒf]
Austausch exchange [ɪks'tʃeɪndʒ]
Australier Australian [ɒs'treɪliən]
australisch Australian [ɒs'treɪliən]
Auswahl choice [tʃɔɪs]
auswählen to choose [tʃu:z]
Auswahlmöglichkeit option ['ɒpʃn]
Auswahlverfahren tryout ['traɪaʊt]
auswandern to emigrate ['emɪgreɪt]
auswechseln to substitute ['sʌbstɪtju:t]
ausweichen to swerve [swɜ:v]
Auszeichnung award [ə'wɔ:d]
ausziehen to take off [ˌteɪk‿'ɒf]
Auszug bit [bɪt]
Auto car [kɑ:]
Autobahn Interstate *(AE)* [ˌɪntə'steɪt]
Autogramm autograph ['ɔ:təgrɑ:f]
Autopanne breakdown ['breɪkdaʊn]

B

Baby baby, babies *(pl)* ['beɪbi; 'beɪbiz]
Bach stream [stri:m]
Bäcker/Bäckerin baker ['beɪkə]
Backofen oven ['ʌvn]
Badeanzug swimsuit ['swɪmsu:t]
Badewanne bathtub ['bɑ:θtʌb]
Badezimmer bathroom ['bɑ:θrʊm]
Badminton badminton ['bædmɪntən]
Bagel bagel ['beɪgl]
Baguette baguette [bæg'et]
Bahnhof station ['steɪʃn]
Bahnsteig platform ['plætfɔ:m]
bald soon [su:n]
Ball ball [bɔ:l]
Ballkönigin homecoming queen [ˌhəʊmkʌmɪŋ 'kwi:n]
Ballsaal ballroom ['bɔ:lrʊm]
Banane banana [bə'nɑ:nə]
Band band [bænd]
Bande band [bænd]; gang [gæŋ]
Bank bank [bæŋk]
Bann ban [bæn]
bannen to ban [bæn]
Bar bar [bɑ:]
Bär/Bärin bear [beə]
Barkeeper barman, barmen *(pl)* ['bɑ:mən, 'bɑ:men]
Barmann barman, barmen *(pl)* ['bɑ:mən, 'bɑ:men]
Bart beard [bɪəd]
Base base [beɪs]
Baseball baseball ['beɪsbɔ:l]
Basis base [beɪs]
Basketball basketball ['bɑ:skɪtbɔ:l]
Bass bass [beɪs]
Batterie battery ['bætri]
Bauch stomach ['stʌmək]
bauen to build [bɪld]
Bauer/Bäuerin farmer ['fɑ:mə]
Bauernhaus farmhouse ['fɑ:mhaʊs]
Bauernhof farm [fɑ:m]
Baum tree [tri:]
Beamter/Beamtin officer ['ɒfɪsə]; official [ə'fɪʃl]
beanspruchen to claim [kleɪm]
Bedarf need [ni:d]
bedauerlich sad [sæd]
bedeuten to mean [mi:n]
Bedeutung sense [sens]
von Bedeutung sein to matter ['mætə]
bedienen to operate ['ɒpəreɪt]
Bedienung waiter ['weɪtə]
Bedingung condition [kən'dɪʃn]
bedrohen to threaten ['θretn]
Bedürfnis need [ni:d]
Beeil dich! Hurry up! [ˌhʌri‿'ʌp]
beenden to end [end]; to finish ['fɪnɪʃ]
beerdigen to bury ['beri]
Beerdigung funeral ['fju:nrəl]
Befähigung qualification [ˌkwɒlɪfɪ'keɪʃn]
Befehl order ['ɔ:də]
befestigen to fix [fɪks]
befolgen to follow ['fɒləʊ]
befördern to carry ['kæri]
Beförderung transport *(no pl.)* ['trænspɔ:t]
befristet temporary ['temprəri]
Beginn beginning [bɪ'gɪnɪŋ]; start [stɑ:t]
beginnen to begin [bɪ'gɪn]
Begleitperson chaperon ['ʃæprəʊn]
begraben to bury ['beri]
begreifen to get it ['get‿ɪt]
behalten to keep [ki:p]
Behandlung treatment ['tri:tmənt]
beherrschen to control [kən'trəʊl]
Behinderung disability [ˌdɪsə'bɪləti]
Behörde agency ['eɪdʒənsi]
bei at [æt; ət]; with [wɪð]
beide both [bəʊθ]
Beifahrer/Beifahrerin passenger ['pæsndʒə]
Bein leg [leg]
beinahe almost ['ɔ:lməʊst]
zum **Beispiel** for example [fər‿ɪg'zɑ:mpl]
beißen to bite [baɪt]; to sting [stɪŋ]
Beistand aid [eɪd]
beitreten to join [dʒɔɪn]
sich **beklagen** to moan [məʊn]
bekommen to get [get]

belästigen to disturb [dɪ'stɜ:b]
belebt busy ['bɪzi]
Beleg record ['rekɔ:d]; slip [slɪp]
beleidigen to diss *(slang)* [dɪs]
Belgier/Belgierin Belgian ['beldʒən]
belgisch Belgian ['beldʒən]
beliebt popular ['pɒpjələ]
bellen to bark [bɑ:k]
Bellen bark [bɑ:k]; barking ['bɑ:kɪŋ]
bemerken to notice ['nəʊtɪs]
benennen to label ['leɪbl]; to name [neɪm]
benötigen to need [ni:d]; to require [rɪ'kwaɪə]
benutzen to use [ju:z]
Benzin gas *(AE)* [gæs]
beobachten to watch [wɒtʃ]
bequem comfortable ['kʌmpftəbl]
bereit ready ['redi]
Berg hill [hɪl]; mountain ['maʊntɪn]
Bericht report [rɪ'pɔ:t]
Beruf career [kə'rɪə]
beruflich professional [prə'feʃnl]
Berufs- professional [prə'feʃnl]
Berufsberatung careers advice [kə'rɪəz əd,vaɪs]
berühmt famous ['feɪməs]
berühren to touch [tʌtʃ]
Besatzung crew [kru:]
beschädigen to damage ['dæmɪdʒ]
beschäftigt busy ['bɪzi]
Bescheinigung certificate [sə'tɪfɪkət]
Beschränkung limit ['lɪmɪt]
beschreiben to describe [dɪ'skraɪb]
beschriften to label ['leɪbl]
Beschriftung label ['leɪbl]
beschützen to protect [prə'tekt]
besichtigen to visit ['vɪzɪt]
besitzen to have got [hæv 'gɒt]; to own [əʊn]
Besitzer/Besitzerin owner ['əʊnə]
besonders special ['speʃl]; especially [ɪ'speʃli]
besorgen to get [get]
besorgt sein to be worried [bi: 'wʌrid]
Besprechung meeting ['mi:tɪŋ]
besprühen to spray [spreɪ]
besser better ['betə]
bestehen to pass [pɑ:s]; to survive [sə'vaɪv]
besteigen to climb ['klaɪm]
bestellen to order ['ɔ:də]
bester/beste/bestes best [best]
am **besten** best [best]
bestürzt sein to be upset [bi: ʌp'set]
Besuch visit ['vɪzɪt]
besuchen to see [si:]; to visit ['vɪzɪt]
Besucher/Besucherin visitor ['vɪzɪtə]
sich **beteiligen** to enter ['entə]
Betonung stress [stres]
betrachten to view [vju:]
betreten to enter ['entə]
Bett bed [bed]
beunruhigen to worry ['wʌri]
beunruhigt sein to be worried [bi: 'wʌrid]
Bevölkerung population [,pɒpjə'leɪʃn]
bevor before [bɪ'fɔ:]
bewachen to guard [gɑ:d]
bewegen to move [mu:v]
  sich bewegen to move [mu:v]
Bewegung motion ['məʊʃn]; move [mu:v]; movement ['mu:vmənt]
sich **bewerben (um)** to apply (for) [ə'plaɪ]
Bewerber/Bewerberin applicant ['æplɪkənt]
Bewerbung application [,æplɪ'keɪʃn]
bezahlen to pay (for) [peɪ]
Bezahlung pay [peɪ]
Bezeichnung title ['taɪtl]
Bezirk borough ['bʌrə]
Bezug reference ['refrns]
Bibliothek library ['laɪbri]
Bild picture ['pɪktʃə]
bilden to form [fɔ:m]
Bildschirm screen [skri:n]
Bildung education [edʒʊ'keɪʃn]
billig cheap [tʃi:p]
Bindeglied link [lɪŋk]
Bindfaden string [strɪŋ]
Birne pear [peə]
bis till [tɪl]; to [tʊ; tə]; until [ʌn'tɪl; n'tɪl]
  Bis .... See you around! [,si: jə ə'raʊnd]
  Bis dann! See you! ['si: jə]; See you around! [,si: jə ə'raʊnd]
  bis zu up to ['ʌp tə]
Biss bite [baɪt]
ein **bisschen** a bit [ə 'bɪt]
Bissen bite [baɪt]
Bistro bistro bar [,bi:strəʊ 'bɑ:]
bitte please [pli:z]
  Bitte schön! Here you are! ['hɪə ju:‿ɑ:]
  Bitte sehr! You're welcome. [jʊə 'welkəm]
bitten (um) to ask (for) ['ɑ:sk fə]
blasen to blow [bləʊ]
Blatt leaf, leaves *(pl)* [li:f; li:vz]
blau blue [blu:]
Blei lead [led]
bleiben to stay [steɪ]
Bleistift pencil ['pensl]
Blende shutter ['ʃʌtə]
Blick look [lʊk]
  einen vernichtenden Blick zuwerfen to give … a dirty look [,gɪv‿ə dɜ:ti 'lʊk]
blind blind [blaɪnd]
blinken to flash [flæʃ]
blitzen to flash [flæʃ]
Blitzen flash [flæʃ]
blöd stupid ['stju:pɪd]
blond blond [blɒnd]; blond(e)-haired ['blɒnd ,heəd]; fair [feə]
bloß only ['əʊnli]
Blume flower ['flaʊə]
Blut blood [blʌd]
blutig bloody ['blʌdi]
Boden ground [graʊnd]
Bohne bean [bi:n]
Bohrer drill [drɪl]
Bohrmaschine drill [drɪl]
Bombe bomb [bɒm]
Bonbon sweet [swi:t]
Boot boat [bəʊt]
borgen to borrow ['bɒrəʊ]
bösartig fierce [fɪəs]
böse angry ['æŋgri]
  böse sein auf to be angry with [bi: 'æŋgri wɪð]
Bosheit venom ['venəm]
Boss boss [bɒs]
Boulevard boulevard ['bu:ləvɑ:d]
Branche business ['bɪznɪs]
brand- brand [brænd]
Brand fire [faɪə]
brauchen to need [ni:d]; to require [rɪ'kwaɪə]; *(Zeit)* to take [teɪk]
braun brown [braʊn]
Breakdance tanzen to break-dance ['breɪkdɑ:nts]
brechen to break [breɪk]
brennen to burn [bɜ:n]; *(Licht)* to be on [bi:‿'ɒn]
Brennmaterial fuel ['fju:əl]
fossiler **Brennstoff** fossil fuel ['fɒsl ,fju:əl]
schwarzes **Brett** notice board ['nəʊtɪs bɔ:d]
Brief letter ['letə]

Briefmarke stamp [stæmp]
Brieftasche wallet ['wɒlɪt]
Briefumschlag envelope ['envələʊp]
Brille glasses *(pl)* ['glɑːsɪz]
bringen to bring [brɪŋ]; to take [teɪk]
es weit bringen to go far [gəʊ 'fɑː]
nach Hause bringen to take home [ˌteɪk 'həʊm]
britisch British ['brɪtɪʃ]
Brot bread [bred]
belegtes Brot sandwich ['sænwɪdʒ]
Brücke bridge [brɪdʒ]
Bruder brother ['brʌðə]
Buch book [bʊk]
buchen to book [bʊk]
Bücherei library ['laɪbri]
Büchse tin [tɪn]
Buchstabe letter ['letə]
buchstabieren to spell [spel]
Bude stall [stɔːl]
bügeln to iron [aɪən]
Bühne stage [steɪdʒ]
Bumm! Crash! [kræʃ]
Bundesstraße highway *(AE)* ['haɪweɪ]
bunt colored *(AE)* ['kʌləd]; colorful *(AE)* ['kʌləfl]
Burg castle ['kɑːsl]
bürgen to guarantee [ˌgærn'tiː]
Bürger/Bürgerin citizen ['sɪtɪzn]
Bürger- civil ['sɪvl]
bürgerlich civil ['sɪvl]
Bürgerrechte civil rights *(pl)* [ˌsɪvl 'raɪts]
Bürgerrechtsbewegung Civil Rights Movement (CRM) [ˌsɪvl 'raɪts ˌmuːvmənt]
Büro office ['ɒfɪs]
bürsten to brush [brʌʃ]
Bus bus, buses *(pl)* [bʌs; 'bʌsɪz]
im Bus on the bus [ˌɒn ðə 'bʌs]
Busch bush [bʊʃ]
eine **Busfahrt machen** to take a bus tour [ˌteɪk‿ə 'bʌs tʊə]
Bushaltestelle bus stop ['bʌs ˌstɒp]
Butter butter ['bʌtə]

C

Café café ['kæfeɪ]; snack bar ['snæk ˌbɑː]
Cafeteria cafeteria [ˌkæfə'tɪəriə]
Camp camp [kæmp]
Camping camping ['kæmpɪŋ]
Canyon canyon ['kænjən]
Cartoon cartoon [kɑː'tuːn]
Casino casino [kə'siːnəʊ]
Catering catering ['keɪtrɪŋ]
CD CD [ˌsiː'diː]
CD-Player CD player [ˌsiː'diː ˌpleɪə]
Celsius Celsius (C) ['selsiəs]
Cent *(Währung)* cent [sent]
Champagner champagne [ʃæm'peɪn]
Chaos chaos ['keɪɒs]
chaotisch messy ['mesi]
Charts charts *(pl)* [tʃɑːts]
Chatroom *(Internetforum, wo man sich online unterhalten kann)* chat room ['tʃæt rʊm]
Cheerleader *(Mädchen, das in einer Gruppe eine Sportmannschaft anfeuert)* cheerleader ['tʃɪəˌliːdə]
Chef/Chefin boss [bɒs]
Chemikalie chemical ['kemɪkl]
chemisch chemical ['kemɪkl]
chillen to chill out [tʃɪl‿'aʊt]
chinesisch Chinese [tʃaɪ'niːz]
circa about [ə'baʊt]
Coca coca ['kəʊkə]
Code code [kəʊd]
Cola coke [kəʊk]
College college ['kɒlɪdʒ]
Comic comic ['kɒmɪk]
Comicheft comic ['kɒmɪk]
Computer computer [ˌkəm'pjuːtə]
cool cool [kuːl]
Cornflakes cornflakes ['kɔːnfleɪks]
aus **Cornwall** Cornish ['kɔːnɪʃ]
Couch sofa ['səʊfə]
Couchpotato couch potato ['kaʊtʃ pəˌteɪtəʊ]
Countdown countdown ['kaʊntdaʊn]
Countrymusik country ['kʌntri]
Cousin/Cousine cousin ['kʌzn]
Cowboy cowboy ['kaʊbɔɪ]
Creme cream [kriːm]
Crew crew [kruː]
Curry *(Gewürz oder Gericht)* curry ['kʌri]

D

da there [ðeə]
da drüben over there [ˌəʊvə 'ðeə]
da ist there is [ðer‿'ɪz]
da sind there are [ðer‿'ɑː]
Dach roof [ruːf]
Dancehall *(Musikrichtung)* dancehall ['dɑːntshɔːl]
dänisch Danish ['deɪnɪʃ]
dank thanks to ['θæŋks tə]
danke thanks [θæŋks]; thank you ['θæŋk‿juː]
danken to thank [θæŋk]
dann then [ðen]
darauf zu towards [tə'wɔːdz]
Darlehen loan [ləʊn]
darstellen to pose [pəʊz]
sich darstellen to pose [pəʊz]
Darstellung demo ['deməʊ]
quer **darüber** across [ə'krɒs]
das the [ðə; ði]; that [ðæt]
Datum date [deɪt]
dauerhaft permanent ['pɜːmnənt]
dauern to last [lɑːst]; to take [teɪk]
Decke blanket ['blæŋkɪt]
dein/deine your [jɔː]
Dein … *(in Briefen)* Yours [jɔːz]
Deine … *(in Briefen)* Yours [jɔːz]
Dekompression decompression [ˌdiːkəm'preʃn]
Dekoration decoration [ˌdek'reɪʃn]
Deli deli *(AE)* ['deli]
dem whom [huːm]
Demo demo ['deməʊ]
Demonstrant/Demonstrantin protester [prə'testə]
Demonstration demo ['deməʊ]
denken to think [θɪŋk]
dennoch though [ðəʊ]; still [stɪl]
der the [ðə; ði]; whom [huːm]
der/dem/den/die *(Relativpronomen)* who [huː]
der/dem/den/die/das *(Relativpronomen)* which [wɪtʃ]
deren whose [huːz]
derselbe/dieselbe/dasselbe the same [seɪm]
Desaster disaster [dɪ'zɑːstə]
deshalb that's why ['ðæts ˌwaɪ]
Designer/Designerin designer [dɪ'zaɪnə]
dessen whose [huːz]
Dessert dessert [dɪ'zɜːt]
Detektiv/Detektivin detective [dɪ'tektɪv]
deuten (auf) to point (to) [pɔɪnt]
deutsch German ['dʒɜːmən]
Deutscher/Deutsche German ['dʒɜːmən]
Dezember December [dɪ'sembə]

Dialog dialogue ['daɪəlɒg]
Diamant diamond ['daɪəmənd]
Diät diet [daɪət]
eine Diät machen to go on a diet [ˌgəʊ‿ɒn ə 'daɪət]
dich you [ju:; jə]
Dichter/Dichterin poet ['pəʊɪt]
dick thick [θɪk]
die the [ðə; ði]
Diener/Dienerin servant ['sɜ:vnt]
Dienst service ['sɜ:vɪs]
Dienstag Tuesday ['tju:zdeɪ]
dies this [ðɪs]
dieser/diese/dieses this [ðɪs]
an diesem Abend that evening [ˌdæt‿'i:vnɪŋ]
diese these [ði:z]
diese dort those [ðəʊz]
diese hier these [ði:z]
digital digital ['dɪdʒɪtl]
Ding thing [θɪŋ]
dir you [ju:; jə]
direkt direct [dɪ'rekt]
Direktor/Direktorin director [dɪ'rektə]
Disko disco ['dɪskəʊ]
Diskriminierung discrimination [dɪˌskrɪmɪ'neɪʃn]
Distanz distance ['dɪstns]
DJ DJ [ˌdi:'dʒeɪ]
Dokument paper ['peɪpə]
Dokumentarfilm documentary [ˌdɒkjə'mentri]
dokumentiert on record [ɒn 'rekɔ:d]
Dokusoap docu soap ['dɒkju ˌsəʊp]
Dollar *(Währung)* dollar ['dɒlə]
Dom cathedral [kə'θi:drl]
Donnerstag Thursday ['θɜ:zdeɪ]
Doppelgänger double ['dʌbl]
das **Doppelte** double ['dʌbl]
Dorf village ['vɪlɪdʒ]
dort there [ðeə]
Dose tin [tɪn]
Down Under *(Spitzname für Australien)* Down Under [ˌdaʊn‿'ʌndə]
Drache dragon ['drægn]
Drama drama ['drɑ:mə]
dramatisch dramatic [drə'mætɪk]
draußen outside [aʊt'saɪd]
Dreck dirt [dɜ:t]
Drehbuch script [skrɪpt]
drehen to turn [tɜ:n]
drin inside [ɪn'saɪd]
dringend urgently ['ɜ:dʒntli]
dritter/dritte/drittes third [θɜ:d]
Drittel third [θɜ:d]
Droge drug [drʌg]
drohen to threaten ['θretn]
dröhnen to roar [rɔ:]
drücken to press [pres]; to push [pʊʃ]
drucken to print [prɪnt]
Druckverminderung decompression [ˌdi:kəm'preʃn]
du you [ju:; jə]
Du bist dran. It's your turn. [ɪts jɔ: 'tɜ:n]
Duft odour ['əʊdə]
dumm silly ['sɪli]; stupid ['stju:pɪd]; thick [θɪk]
Dummkopf idiot ['ɪdɪət]; silly ['sɪli]
dunkel dark [dɑ:k]
Dunkelheit dark ['dɑ:k]
durch through [θru:]
quer durch across [ə'krɒs]
durchdrehen to go bananas [ˌgəʊ bə'nɑ:nəz]
durcheinander messy ['mesi]
Durcheinander chaos ['keɪɒs]; mess [mes]
durchgehend non-stop [ˌnɒn'stɒp]
im **Durchmesser** across [ə'krɒs]
Durchsage announcement [ə'naʊntsmənt]
durchschnittlich average ['ævrɪdʒ]
durchstehen to survive [sə'vaɪv]
dürfen can [kæn]; may [meɪ]
nicht dürfen mustn't ['mʌsnt]
Dusche shower ['ʃaʊə]
DVD DVD [di:vi:'di:]
DVD-Player DVD player [ˌdi:vi:'di: ˌpleɪə]

E

Ebene level ['levl]
echt real [rɪəl]
Ecke corner ['kɔ:nə]
egal welche whatever [wɒt'evə]
Es ist mir egal. I don't care. [aɪ dəʊnt 'keə]
Ehefrau wife, wives *(pl)* [waɪf; waɪvz]
ehrenamtlich voluntary ['vɒləntri]
ehrlich honest ['ɒnɪst]
Ei egg [eg]
eifersüchtig (auf) jealous (of) ['dʒeləs]
eigener/eigene/eigenes own [əʊn]
es **eilig haben** to be in a hurry [bi:‿ɪn‿ə 'hʌri]
ein/eine a, an [ə; ən]
ein paar a few [ə 'fju:]
einander each other [ˌi:tʃ‿'ʌðə]
Einband cover ['kʌvə]
Einbrecher/Einbrecherin burglar ['bɜ:glə]
einfach easy ['i:zi]
Einfall idea [aɪ'dɪə]
Einfangen der Rinder mit dem Lasso roping ['rəʊpɪŋ]
einflussreich important [ɪm'pɔ:tnt]
einführen to launch [lɔ:nʃ]
Einführung launch [lɔ:nʃ]
eingeboren native ['neɪtɪv]
einheimisch local ['ləʊkl]; native ['neɪtɪv]
einige a few [ə 'fju:]; any ['eni]; some [sʌm]; a couple of [ə 'kʌpl‿əv]
Einkauf shopping ['ʃɒpɪŋ]
einkaufen to shop [ʃɒp]
Einkaufen shopping ['ʃɒpɪŋ]
Einkaufswagen trolley ['trɒli]
einladen to invite [ɪn'vaɪt]
Einladung invitation [ˌɪnvɪ'teɪʃn]
einmal once [wʌnts]
einrichten to set up [set‿'ʌp]
einsam lonely ['ləʊnli]
einschalten to switch on [swɪtʃ‿'ɒn]; to turn on [ˌtɜ:n‿'ɒn]
einschicken to send in [send‿'ɪn]
einschieben to put in [pʊt‿'ɪn]
einschließlich including [ɪn'klu:dɪŋ]
einsetzen to put in [pʊt‿'ɪn]
einst once [wʌnts]
einsteigen *(in Zug, Bus …)* to get on [get‿'ɒn]
einsteigen *(Bus)* to get onto [get‿'ɒntə]
einsteigen in *(Auto)* to get into [get‿'ɪntə]
einstellen to set [set]
Einstellung shot [ʃɒt]
Eintrag entry ['entri]
Eintragung entry ['entri]
eintreten to enter ['entə]
Eintritt verboten! Keep out! [ki:p‿'aʊt]
Eintrittskarte ticket ['tɪkɪt]
Einwanderer/Einwanderin immigrant ['ɪmɪgrənt]
einwandern to immigrate ['ɪmɪgreɪt]
Einwanderung immigration [ˌɪmɪ'greɪʃn]
Einzelkind only child ['əʊnli ˌtʃaɪld]
einziger/einzige/einziges only ['əʊnli]

Eis ice [aɪs]; ice-cream [aɪs 'kriːm]
Eisbahn ice rink ['aɪs rɪŋk]
Eiscreme ice-cream [aɪs 'kriːm]
Eishockey ice hockey ['aɪs ˌhɒki]
ekelhaft yukky ['jʌki]
Elefant elephant ['elɪfənt]
elektrisch electric [ɪ'lektrɪk]
Elektrizität electricity [ˌelɪk'trɪsəti]
Element panel ['pænl]
Ellbogen elbow ['elbəʊ]
Elle *(Längenmaß: 0,914 m)* yard [jɑːd]
Eltern parents *(pl)* ['peərənts]
E-Mail e-mail ['iːmeɪl]
  E-Mail schreiben to e-mail ['iːmeɪl]
  per E-Mail schicken to e-mail ['iːmeɪl]
emigrieren to emigrate ['emɪgreɪt]
Empfang reception [rɪ'sepʃn]
empörend outrageous [aʊt'reɪdʒəs]
Ende end [end]
enden to end [end]; to end up [ˌend‿'ʌp]
endlich at last [ət 'lɑːst]; finally ['faɪnli]
Energie energy ['enədʒi]
Engländer/Engländerinnen English ['ɪŋglɪʃ]
englisch English ['ɪŋglɪʃ]
entdecken to discover [dɪ'skʌvə]
Entfernung distance ['dɪstns]
entkommen to escape [ɪ'skeɪp]; to get out [get‿'aʊt]
entlang along [ə'lɒŋ]
entlanggehen to go down [gəʊ 'daʊn]
entschärfen to defuse [ˌdiː'fjuːz]
entscheiden to decide [dɪ'saɪd]
Entschuldigung! Excuse me! [ɪk'skjuːz mi]
sich **entspannen** to chill out [tʃɪl‿'aʊt]; to rest [rest]
jmdn. **enttäuschen** to let sb down [let 'daʊn]
enttäuscht disappointed [ˌdɪsə'pɔɪntɪd]
entwerfen to design [dɪ'zaɪn]
Entzücken glee [gliː]
er he [hiː]
Erbe/Erbin inheritor [ɪn'herɪtə]
Erbse pea [piː]
Erd- global ['gləʊbl]
Erdbeere strawberry ['strɔːbri]
Erde earth [ɜːθ]; world [wɜːld]
Erderwärmung global warming [ˌgləʊbl 'wɔːmɪŋ]
Erdkunde Geography [dʒi'ɒgrəfi]
Erdteil continent ['kɒntɪnənt]
Ereignis event [ɪ'vent]
erfahren to learn [lɜːn]
Erfahrung experience [ɪk'spɪəriənts]
Erfassung registration [ˌredʒɪ'streɪʃn]
erfinden to invent [ɪn'vent]; to make up [meɪk‿'ʌp]
Erfinder/Erfinderin inventor [ɪn'ventə]
Erfindung fiction ['fɪkʃn]; invention [ɪn'ventʃn]
Erfolg success [sək'ses]
erfolgreich successful [sək'sesfl]
Erfordernis need [niːd]
erforschen to explore [ɪk'splɔː]
sich **erfreuen** to enjoy [ɪn'dʒɔɪ]
erfüllen to fulfill *(AE)* [fʊl'fɪl]
Ergebnis result [rɪ'zʌlt]
sich **erinnern (an)** to remember [rɪ'membə]
in **Erinnerungen schwelgen** to reminisce [ˌremɪ'nɪs]
erkennen to realise ['rɪəlaɪz]
erklären to explain [ɪk'spleɪn]
erklingen to ring out [ˌrɪŋ‿'aʊt]
erkunden to explore [ɪk'splɔː]
Erlaubnis permission [pə'mɪʃn]
erläutern to explain [ɪk'spleɪn]
Erlebnis experience [ɪk'spɪəriənts]
erledigen to complete [kəm'pliːt]; to finish ['fɪnɪʃ]
erlöschen to go out [gəʊ‿'aʊt]
ermahnen to warn [wɔːn]
Ermordung murder ['mɜːdə]
Ernährung nutrition [njuː'trɪʃn]
Ernährungslehre nutrition [njuː'trɪʃn]
erreichen to catch [kætʃ]; to get to ['get tə]; to reach [riːtʃ]
erschießen to shoot [ʃuːt]
erschrecken to scare ['skeə]
ersetzen to substitute ['sʌbstɪtjuːt]
erst only ['əʊnli]
erstaunt surprised [sə'praɪzd]
erster/erste/erstes first [fɜːst]
ersticken to choke [tʃəʊk]
ertönen to ring out [ˌrɪŋ‿'aʊt]
Erwachsener/Erwachsene adult ['ædʌlt]
Erwärmung (global) warming [ˌgləʊbl 'wɔːmɪŋ]
erwarten to expect [ɪk'spekt]
erzählen to tell [tel]
  nochmals erzählen to retell [riː'tel]
Erzählung story ['stɔːri]
Erzeuger/Erzeugerin producer [prə'djuːsə]
Erziehung education [edʒʊ'keɪʃn]
es it [ɪt]
  es gibt there are [ðer‿'ɑː]; there is [ðer‿'ɪz]
  Es lautete .... It said .... [ɪt 'sed]
  es sei denn, (dass) ... unless [ən'les]
essen to eat [iːt]
Essen food [fuːd]
  Essen zum Mitnehmen takeaway ['teɪkəweɪ]
Essig vinegar ['vɪnɪgə]
Esszimmer dining room ['daɪnɪŋ rʊm]
et cetera etc. [ɪt'setrə]
Etikett label ['leɪbl]
etikettieren to label ['leɪbl]
etliche many ['meni]
etwa about [ə'baʊt]; around [ə'raʊnd]
etwas any ['eni]; anything ['eniθɪŋ]; some [sʌm]; something ['sʌmθɪŋ]
euch you [juː; jə]
euer/eure your [jɔː]
  Euer ... *(in Briefen)* Yours [jɔːz]
  Eure ... *(in Briefen)* Yours [jɔːz]
Eukalyptus eucalyptus [juːk'lɪptəs]
Euro *(Währung)* euro ['jʊərəʊ]
exakt exact [ɪg'zækt]
Examen exam [ɪg'zæm]
existieren to exist [ɪg'zɪst]
Experiment experiment [ɪk'sperɪmənt]
Export export ['ekspɔːt]
exportieren to export [ɪk'spɔːt]

F

fabelhaft fabulous ['fæbjələs]
Fabrik factory ['fæktri]
fachlich technical ['teknɪkl]
Fackel torch, torches *(pl)* [tɔːtʃ; 'tɔːtʃɪz]
Fahne flag [flæg]
Fähre ferry ['feri]
fahren to drive [draɪv]; to ride [raɪd]
  fahren *(Schiff)* to sail [seɪl]
Fahrenheit Fahrenheit (F) ['færnhaɪt]
Fahrer/Fahrerin driver ['draɪvə]
Fahrplan timetable ['taɪmteɪbl]
Fahrrad bike [baɪk]
  mit dem Fahrrad by bike [baɪ 'baɪk]
Fahrschein ticket ['tɪkɪt]
Fahrspur lane [leɪn]
Fahrt journey ['dʒɜːni]; ride [raɪd]; tour [tʊə]
fair fair [feə]
Fakt fact [fækt]

Fall fall [fɔ:l]
in der **Falle sitzen** to be trapped [bi: 'træpt]
fällen to cut down [kʌt 'daʊn]
fallen to fall [fɔ:l]; to drop [drɒp]
fallen lassen to drop [drɒp]
falls if [ɪf]
Fallschirmspringen parachuting ['pærəˌʃu:tɪŋ]
falsch wrong [rɒŋ]
falsch machen to get … wrong [get … 'rɒŋ]
Familie family ['fæmli]
Fan fan [fæn]
fangen to catch [kætʃ]
Fänger/Fängerin catcher ['kætʃə]
fantastisch fabulous ['fæbjələs]; fantastic [fæn'tæstɪk]
Farbe colour ['kʌlə]; paint [peɪnt]
färben to dye [daɪ]
farbig colored *(AE)* ['kʌləd]; colorful *(AE)* ['kʌləfl]
Farbiger/Farbige colored *(AE)* ['kʌləd]
Farm farm [fɑ:m]
fast almost ['ɔ:lməʊst]; nearly ['nɪəli]
Fastfood-Restaurant burger bar ['bɜ:gə ˌbɑ:]
Februar February ['februəri]
Federball badminton ['bædmɪntən]
Federmäppchen pencil case ['pensl ˌkeɪs]
fehlen to be missing [bi: 'mɪsɪŋ]; to miss [mɪs]
Fehler mistake [mɪ'steɪk]
Feier party ['pɑ:ti]
eine Party **feiern** to have a party [ˌhæv‿ə 'pɑ:ti]
Feiertag holiday ['hɒlədeɪ]
fein fine [faɪn]
Feind/Feindin enemy ['enəmi]
Feld field [fi:ld]
Felsen rock [rɒk]
Fenster window ['wɪndəʊ]
Ferien holiday(s) ['hɒlədeɪ(z)]; vacation *(AE)* [və'keɪʃn]
Ferienhaus cottage ['kɒtɪdʒ]
fern remote [rɪ'məʊt]
Fernbedienung remote control [rɪˌməʊt kən'trəʊl]
sich **fernhalten** to keep away [ki:p‿ə'weɪ]
Fernsehen TV [ˌti:'vi:]
Fernseher TV [ˌti:'vi:]
Fernsehglotzer/Fernsehglotzerin couch potato ['kaʊtʃ pəˌteɪtəʊ]
Fernsteuerung remote control [rɪˌməʊt kən'trəʊl]
fertig ready ['redi]
Fertigkeit skill [skɪl]
fertigstellen to complete [kəm'pli:t]
Fest festival ['festɪvl]
Festival festival ['festɪvl]
festnehmen to arrest [ə'rest]
Feuer fire [faɪə]
Feuerstelle fire [faɪə]
Feuerwehr fire brigade ['faɪə brɪˌgeɪd]
Feuerwerk firework ['faɪəwɜ:k]
Feuerwerkskörper firework ['faɪəwɜ:k]
Figur figure ['fɪgə]
Fiktion fiction ['fɪkʃn]
Film film [fɪlm]; movie *(AE)* ['mu:vi]; picture ['pɪktʃə]
filmen to film [fɪlm]
finden to find [faɪnd]
Finger finger ['fɪŋgə]
Finsternis dark ['dɑ:k]
Firma company ['kʌmpəni]; firm [fɜ:m]
Firmenzeichen logo ['ləʊgəʊ]
Fisch fish, fish *(pl)* [fɪʃ]
fischen to fish [fɪʃ]
Fischen fishing ['fɪʃɪŋ]
Fischer fisherman, fishermen *(pl)* ['fɪʃəmən; 'fɪʃəmen]
fit fit [fɪt]
flach flat [flæt]
Fläche area ['eəriə]
Flagge flag [flæg]
Flamme flame [fleɪm]
Flasche bottle ['bɒtl]
Fleck mark [mɑ:k]
Fleisch meat [mi:t]
fliegen to fly [flaɪ]
Flosse fin [fɪn]
flüchten to escape [ɪ'skeɪp]
Flug flight [flaɪt]
Flügel wing [wɪŋ]
Fluggesellschaft airline ['eəlaɪn]
Flughafen airport ['eəpɔ:t]
Fluglinie airline ['eəlaɪn]
Flugzeug plane [pleɪn]
Flur corridor ['kɒrɪdɔ:]; hall [hɔ:l]
Fluss river ['rɪvə]
flüstern to whisper ['wɪspə]
flutartige Überschwemmung flash flood ['flæʃ ˌflʌd]
folgen to follow ['fɒləʊ]
folgend/folgender/folgende/folgendes following ['fɒləʊɪŋ]
Fön hairdryer ['heəˌdraɪə]
Football American football [əˌmerɪkən 'fʊtbɔ:l]
Förderung aid [eɪd]
Form form [fɔ:m]; shape [ʃeɪp]
formal formal ['fɔ:ml]
formell formal ['fɔ:ml]
formen to form [fɔ:m]
förmlich formal ['fɔ:ml]
Formular form [fɔ:m]
Forschung research [rɪ'sɜ:tʃ]
fortfahren to continue [kən'tɪnju:]
fortgeschritten advanced [əd'vɑ:nst]
Forum forum ['fɔ:rəm]
fossil fossil ['fɒsl]
fossiler Brennstoff fossil fuel ['fɒsl ˌfju:əl]
Fossil fossil ['fɒsl]
Foto photo ['fəʊtəʊ]; shot [ʃɒt]
Fotos machen to take pictures [teɪk 'pɪktʃəz]
Fotoapparat camera ['kæmrə]
Fotograf/Fotografin photographer [fə'tɒgrəfə]
Fotografie photo ['fəʊtəʊ]; photography [fə'tɒgrəfi]
fotografieren to take pictures [teɪk 'pɪktʃəz]
Foul foul [faʊl]
Frage matter ['mætə]; question ['kwestʃn]
fragen to ask [ɑ:sk]
fragen nach to ask (for) ['ɑ:sk fə]
französisch French [frentʃ]
Frau woman, women *(pl)* ['wʊmən; 'wɪmɪn]; *(Anrede)* Miss [mɪs]; Mrs ['mɪsɪz]
frei free [fri:]
Freiheit freedom ['fri:dəm]
Freitag Friday [fraɪdeɪ]
freiwillig voluntary ['vɒləntri]; volunteer [ˌvɒlən'tɪə]
Freiwilliger/Freiwillige volunteer [ˌvɒlən'tɪə]
Freizeitpark theme park ['θi:m ˌpɑ:k]
fremd alien ['eɪliən]; foreign ['fɒrɪn]
Fremder/Fremde alien ['eɪliən]; stranger ['streɪndʒə]
fressen to eat [i:t]
Freund/Freundin friend [frend]
Freund *(in einer Paarbeziehung)* boyfriend ['bɔɪfrend]
Freundin *(in einer Paarbeziehung)* girlfriend ['gɜ:lfrend]
freundlich friendly ['frendli]

Freundschaft schließen (mit) to make friends (with) [ˌmeɪk 'frendz]
Friede peace [pi:s]
friedlich peaceful ['pi:sfl]
frieren to be cold [bi: 'kəʊld]
frisch fresh [freʃ]
Frischkäse cream cheese [ˌkri:m 'tʃi:z]
Friseur/Friseurin hairdresser ['heəˌdresə]
Frisur style [staɪl]
froh glad [glæd]; happy ['hæpi]
Frucht fruit [fru:t]
früh early ['ɜ:li]
Frühling spring [sprɪŋ]
Frühstück breakfast ['brekfəst]
frühstücken to have breakfast [hæv 'brekfəst]
frustriert frustrated [frʌs'treɪtɪd]
fühlen to feel [fi:l]
sich fühlen to feel [fi:l]
Führer/Führerin leader ['li:də]
Führerschein driver's license *(AE)* ['draɪvəz ˌlaɪsnts]; driving licence *(BE)* ['draɪvɪŋ ˌlaɪsnts]
füllen to fill [fɪl]
Füller pen [pen]
Fundbüro Lost and Found ['lɒst ˌənd 'faʊnd]
Funk *(Musikrichtung)* funk [fʌŋk]
funktionieren to work [wɜ:k]
für for [fɔ:; fə]
Für und Wider pros and cons [ˌprəʊz‿ənd 'kɒnz]
furchtbar awful ['ɔ:fl]; frightening ['fraɪtnɪŋ]; horrible ['hɒrəbl]; terrible ['terəbl]
sich **fürchten (vor)** to be afraid (of) [bi:‿ə'freɪd]
fürsorglich thoughtful ['θɔ:tfl]
Fuß foot, feet *(pl)* [fʊt; fi:t]
Fuß *(Längenmaß: 30,48 cm)* foot, feet *(pl)* [fʊt; fi:t]
zu Fuß on foot [ɒn 'fʊt]
Fußball football ['fʊtbɔ:l]; soccer *(AE)* ['sɒkə]
Fußboden floor [flɔ:]
füttern to feed [fi:d]

G

Gabel fork [fɔ:k]
Gang corridor ['kɒrɪdɔ:]
Gang *(Menü)* course [kɔ:s]
Gang gang [gæŋ]
im Gange sein to be on [bi:‿'ɒn]
Gangster/Gangsterin gangster ['gæŋkstə]
ganz all [ɔ:l]; full (of) [fʊl]; whole [həʊl]
ganz schön pretty ['prɪti]
im Ganzen in all [ɪn‿'ɔ:l]
garantieren to guarantee [ˌgærn'ti:]
Garderobe wardrobe ['wɔ:drəʊb]
Garten garden ['gɑ:dn]
Gas *(BE)* gas [gæs]
Gasse lane [leɪn]
Gast guest [gest]
Gastgeber host [həʊst]
Gastronomie catering ['keɪtrɪŋ]
Gate gate [geɪt]
Gebäude building ['bɪldɪŋ]
geben to give [gɪv]
Gebiet area ['eəriə]
gebrochen broken ['brəʊkn]
Geburt birth [bɜ:θ]
gebürtig native ['neɪtɪv]
Geburtstag birthday ['bɜ:θdeɪ]
Gedicht poem ['pəʊɪm]
geeignet suitable ['su:təbl]
Gefahr danger ['deɪndʒə]
gefährlich dangerous ['deɪndʒrəs]
Gefängnis jail [dʒeɪl]
Gefühl feeling ['fi:lɪŋ]
gegen- anti ['æntɪ]
gegen against [ə'genst]
sich **gegenseitig** each other [ˌi:tʃ‿'ʌðə]
Gehalt pay [peɪ]
geheim secret ['si:krət]
Geheimnis mystery ['mɪstəri]
gehen to go [gəʊ]; to leave [li:v]; to walk [wɔ:k]
Geh … entlang. Go down … . ['gəʊ daʊn]
gehören (zu) to belong (to) [bɪ'lɒŋ]
Geist ghost [gəʊst]; mind [maɪnd]; spirit ['spɪrɪt]
gelangweilt bored [bɔ:d]
gelb yellow ['jeləʊ]
Geld money ['mʌni]
Geldbeutel wallet ['wɒlɪt]
Geldbuße fine [faɪn]
Geldstrafe fine [faɪn]
Gelegenheit opportunity [ˌɒpə'tju:nəti]
geloben to pledge [pledʒ]
gemein mean [mi:n]
Gemeinde community [kə'mju:nəti]
Gemeinderat council ['kaʊnsl]
Gemeinschaft community [kə'mju:nəti]
Gemüse vegetable ['vedʒtəbl]
genannt werden to be called [bi: 'kɔ:ld]
genau exact [ɪg'zækt]
genau genommen in fact [ɪn 'fækt]
genießen to enjoy [ɪn'dʒɔɪ]
genug enough [ɪ'nʌf]
genügen to fulfill *(AE)* [fʊl'fɪl]
genügend enough [ɪ'nʌf]
geöffnet open ['əʊpn]
Geografie Geography [dʒi'ɒgrəfi]
Gepäck luggage ['lʌgɪdʒ]
Gepäckwagen trolley ['trɒli]
Geplauder chat [tʃæt]
Geräusch noise [nɔɪz]; sound [saʊnd]
gerecht fair [feə]
gern haben to like [laɪk]
gern mögen to love [lʌv]
Gern geschehen! You're welcome. [jʊə 'welkəm]
Geruch odour ['əʊdə]; smell [smel]
Gesamtschule comprehensive school [kɒmprɪ'hensɪv ˌsku:l]
Geschäft business ['bɪznɪs]; shop [ʃɒp]; store [stɔ:]
Geschäftsmann businessman ['bɪznɪsmən]
geschäftstüchtig enterprising ['entəpraɪzɪŋ]
geschehen to happen ['hæpn]
Geschenk present ['preznt]
Geschichte History ['hɪstəri]; story ['stɔ:ri]
geschichtlich historical [hɪ'stɒrɪkl]
Geschick skill [skɪl]
geschieden von divorced from [dɪ'vɔ:st frɒm]
geschmeidig smooth [smu:θ]
geschockt shocked [ʃɒkt]
Geschöpf creature ['kri:tʃə]
Gesellschaft company ['kʌmpəni]; firm [fɜ:m]; society [sə'saɪəti]
Gesellschaftstanz ballroom dancing [ˌbɔ:lrʊm 'dɑ:ntsɪŋ]
Gesetz law [lɔ:]
Gesetzgebung law [lɔ:]
Gesicht face [feɪs]
Gesichtspunkt aspect ['æspekt]
Gespenst ghost [gəʊst]
Gespräch dialogue ['daɪəlɒg]; talk [tɔ:k]
Gestalt figure ['fɪgə]
Gestank smell [smel]
gestern yesterday ['jestədeɪ]
gestern Abend last night [lɑ:st 'naɪt]
gestern Nacht last night [lɑ:st 'naɪt]

gestrandet stranded ['strændɪd]
gesund healthy ['helθi]
Gesundheit health [helθ]
Getränk drink [drɪŋk]
Gewächshaus greenhouse ['gri:nhaʊs]
gewagt outrageous [aʊt'reɪdʒəs]
Gewalt violence ['vaɪələnts]
gewaltfrei non-violent [ˌnɒn'vaɪələnt]
gewaltig huge [hju:dʒ]
Gewalttätigkeit violence ['vaɪələnts]
Gewicht weight [weɪt]
gewinnen to win [wɪn]
jmdn. dafür gewinnen, etw. zu tun to make sb do sth [meɪk]
Gewinner/Gewinnerin winner ['wɪnə]
gewiss certainly ['sɜ:tnli]
gewöhnlich usually ['ju:ʒli]
Gift *(z. B. von Schlangen und Insekten)* venom ['venəm]
Gitarre guitar [gɪ'tɑ:]
Gitter grid [grɪd]
glamourös glamorous ['glæmrəs]
Glas glass [glɑ:s]
glatt smooth [smu:θ]
glauben to believe [bɪ'li:v]; to think [θɪŋk]
gleich equal ['i:kwəl]; the same [seɪm]
gleich right away [raɪt‿ə'weɪ]
Gleich- equal ['i:kwəl]
Gleichaltriger/Gleichaltrige peer [pɪə]
gleichwertig equal ['i:kwəl]
Gleitschirmfliegen paragliding ['pærəˌglaɪdɪŋ]
global global ['gləʊbl]
Globalisierung globalisation [ˌgləʊblaɪ'zeɪʃn]
Glocke bell [bel]
Glück luck [lʌk]
du hast Glück you're lucky [ˌjʊə 'lʌki]
Viel Glück! Good luck! [ˌgʊd 'lʌk]
glücklich happy ['hæpi]; lucky ['lʌki]
glücklicherweise luckily ['lʌkɪli]
Glühbirne light bulb ['laɪt bʌlb]
Gold gold [gəʊld]
Mein **Gott!** My God! [maɪ 'gɒd]
göttlich divine [dɪ'vaɪn]
Grab grave [greɪv]
Grabstein gravestone ['greɪvstəʊn]
Grad degree (°) [dɪ'gri:]
Graffiti mural ['mjʊərl]
Gramm gramme (g) [græm]
Gras grass [grɑ:s]
grau grey [greɪ]
greifen to grab [græb]
Grenze border ['bɔ:də]; limit ['lɪmɪt]
Grieche/Griechin Greek [gri:k]
griechisch Greek [gri:k]
Grill barbecue ['bɑ:bɪkju:]
Grillparty barbecue ['bɑ:bɪkju:]
grob raw [rɔ:]
groß big [bɪg]; great [greɪt]; large [lɑ:dʒ]; tall [tɔ:l]
großartig fantastic [fæn'tæstɪk]; great [greɪt]; wicked ['wɪkɪd]
Größe height [haɪt]
Großstadt city ['sɪti]
grün green [gri:n]
Grund reason ['ri:zn]
gründen to found [faʊnd]; to set up [set‿'ʌp]
Grundlinie back line [ˌbæk 'laɪn]
Grundsatz policy ['pɒlɪsi]
Grundschule elementary school *(AE)* [elɪ'mentri ˌsku:l]; primary school ['praɪməri ˌsku:l]
Gruppe group [gru:p]
gruselig scary ['skeəri]
gültig valid ['vælɪd]
Gummi rubber ['rʌbə]
Gummistiefel rubber boots *(pl)* [ˌrʌbə 'bu:ts]
gut good [gʊd]; fine [faɪn]; all right [ɔ:l 'raɪt]
Es geht uns gut. We're OK. [ˌwɪər‿əʊ'keɪ]
Guten Morgen! Good morning! ['gʊd 'mɔ:nɪŋ]
gut mit … umgehen können to be good with … [bi: 'gʊd wɪð]
ich bin gut in … I'm good at … [aɪm 'gʊd‿ət]
Güter goods *(pl)* [gʊdz]
Gymnasium grammar school ['græmə ˌsku:l]

H

Ha! Ha! [hɑ:]
Haar, Haare hair [heə]
haben to have [hæv]; to have got [hæv 'gɒt]
keine Ahnung haben to have no clue [ˌhæv nəʊ 'klu:]
Hafen harbor *(AE)* ['hɑ:bə]; port [pɔ:t]
Hähnchen chicken ['tʃɪkɪn]
Hai shark [ʃɑ:k]
halb half [hɑ:f]
halb (drei) half past (two) ['hɑ:f pɑ:st]
eine halbe Stunde half an hour [ˌhɑ:f‿ən‿'aʊə]
zum halben Preis half-price [ˌhɑ:f'praɪs]
Halbschwester half-sister ['hɑ:fˌsɪstə]
Hälfte half [hɑ:f]
Halle hall [hɔ:l]
Hallo! Hello! [he'ləʊ]; Hi, there! ['haɪ ðeə]
halten to keep [ki:p]
Haltestelle stop [stɒp]
Hand hand [hænd]
Hände weg! Hands off! [hændz‿'ɒf]
Handel deal [di:l]; trade [treɪd]
handeln to act [ækt]
Handkarren trolley ['trɒli]
Handlung action ['ækʃn]
Handschuh glove [glʌv]
Handtasche handbag ['hænbæg]
Handwerker workman, workmen *(pl)* ['wɜ:kmən; 'wɜ:kmen]
handwerklich technical ['teknɪkl]
Handy cell phone *(AE)* ['sel ˌfəʊn]; mobile ['məʊbaɪl]
hart hard [hɑ:d]; tough [tʌf]
Hass hate [heɪt]
hassen to hate [heɪt]
hätte(n) gern would like [wʊd 'laɪk]
Haupt- main [meɪn]
Haus house [haʊs]
zu Hause at home [ət 'həʊm]
Hausaufgabe(n) homework ['həʊmwɜ:k]
Hausmeister/Hausmeisterin caretaker ['keəteɪkə]
Haustier pet [pet]
Heavy Metal heavy metal [ˌhevi 'metl]
Heft exercise book ['eksəsaɪz ˌbʊk]
heilig sacred ['seɪkrɪd]
Heim home [həʊm]
Heimat home [həʊm]
Heimat- home [həʊm]
heimlich secret ['si:krət]
Heimweh haben to feel homesick [ˌfi:l 'həʊmsɪk]
heiraten to marry ['mæri]
heiß hot [hɒt]
heißen to be called [bi: 'kɔ:ld]
Ich heiße … . My name is … . [maɪ 'neɪm‿ɪz]
Heißluftballon balloon [bə'lu:n]
Heizung heating ['hi:tɪŋ]

German – English

Held hero, heroes *(pl)* ['hɪərəʊ; 'hɪərəʊz]
Heldin heroine ['herəʊɪn]
helfen to help [help]
Helfer/Helferin helper ['helpə]
Helikopter helicopter ['helɪˌkɒptə]
hell fair [feə]; light [laɪt]
Helm helmet ['helmət]
Hemd shirt [ʃɜ:t]
heraus out [aʊt]
herausbringen to launch [lɔ:nʃ]
herausfinden to find out [faɪnd‿'aʊt]
herausnehmen to take out [teɪk‿'aʊt]
Herbst autumn ['ɔ:təm]
herein in [ɪn]
hereinkommen to come in [kʌm‿'ɪn]
Herr *(Anrede)* Mr ['mɪstə]
Herrscher/Herrscherin ruler ['ru:lə]
herstellen to produce [prə'dju:s]
Herstellung production [prə'dʌkʃn]
herüberkommen to come over [kʌm‿'əʊvə]
herüberreichen to pass [pɑ:s]
(um …) **herum** around [ə'raʊnd]; round [raʊnd]
herumalbern to mess around [ˌmes‿ə'raʊnd]
herumlungern to hang around [ˌhæŋ‿ə'raʊnd]
herumreisen to go places [ˌgəʊ 'pleɪsɪz]
herumspringen to jump about [ˌdʒʌmp‿ə'baʊt]
sich **herumtreiben** to hang out [hæŋ‿'aʊt]
herunter down [daʊn]; off [ɒf]
herunterfallen to fall off [fɔ:l‿'ɒf]; to fall [fɔ:l]
herunterkommen to come down [kʌm 'daʊn]
herunterladen to download [ˌdaʊn'ləʊd]
hervorrufen to cause [kɔ:z]
Herz heart [hɑ:t]
Herzliche Grüße love [lʌv]
Herzschrittmacher pacemaker ['peɪsˌmeɪkə]
heute today [tə'deɪ]
heute Abend tonight [tə'naɪt]
heute Nacht tonight [tə'naɪt]
Hi! Hi! [haɪ]
hier here [hɪə]
high-tech high-tech [ˌhaɪ'tek]
Highway highway *(AE)* ['haɪweɪ]
Hilfe aid [eɪd]; help [help]
hilflos helpless ['helpləs]
hilfreich helpful ['helpfəl]
Himmel sky [skaɪ]
hinauf up [ʌp]
(auf …) hinauf onto ['ɒntu:; 'ɒntə]
die Treppe **hinaufrennen** to run upstairs [ˌrʌn‿ʌp'steəz]
hinaufschauen to look up [lʊk‿'ʌp]
hinaus out [aʊt]
hinausgehen to go out [gəʊ‿'aʊt]
hinauslehnen to lean out [li:n‿'aʊt]
sich hinauslehnen to lean out [li:n‿'aʊt]
hinausstellen to put out [pʊt‿'aʊt]
hineingehen to go in [gəʊ‿'ɪn]
hinfallen to fall [fɔ:l]
hingehen to walk up to [wɔ:k‿'ʌp tə]
hinlegen to lie down [laɪ 'daʊn]
sich hinlegen to lie down [laɪ 'daʊn]
hinnehmen to accept [ək'sept]
sich **hinsetzen** to sit down [sɪt 'daʊn]
hinter behind [bɪ'haɪnd]
Hinter- back [bæk]
Hintergrund background ['bækgraʊnd]
hinterhergehen to follow ['fɒləʊ]
Hintern ass *(AE)* [æs]
hinüber across [ə'krɒs]
hinübergehen to go over [gəʊ‿'əʊvə]
hinüberrennen to run over [rʌn‿'əʊvə]
hin- und hergerissen torn [tɔ:n]
hinunter down [daʊn]
hinuntergehen to go down [gəʊ 'daʊn]
Hinweis clue [klu:]
hinzufügen to add [æd]; to put in [pʊt‿'ɪn]
Hip-Hop hip hop ['hɪp hɒp]
hispanisch Hispanic [hɪ'spænɪk]
historisch historical [hɪ'stɒrɪkl]
Hit hit [hɪt]
Hitparade charts *(pl)* [tʃɑ:ts]
Hitze heat [hi:t]
Hobby hobby, hobbies *(pl)* ['hɒbi; 'hɒbiz]
hoch high [haɪ]; tall [tɔ:l]
Hochmoor moor [mɔ:]
Hochmut pride [praɪd]
hochspringen to jump up [dʒʌmp‿'ʌp]
höchster/höchste/höchstes supreme [su:'pri:m]
Hochwasser flood [flʌd]
Hockey hockey ['hɒki]
hoffen to hope [həʊp]
höflich polite [pə'laɪt]
Höhe height [haɪt]
holen to get [get]
Hölle hell [hel]
Holz wood [wʊd]
Homecoming *(Schulfest an amerikanischen High Schools)* homecoming ['həʊmkʌmɪŋ]
hören to hear [hɪə]
Horoskop horoscope ['hɒrəskəʊp]
Hose trousers *(pl)* ['traʊzəz]
kurze Hose shorts *(pl)* [ʃɔ:ts]
Hosentasche pocket ['pɒkɪt]
Hotel hotel [həʊ'tel]
Hotelsuite hotel suite [həʊ'tel ˌswi:t]
Hotline hotline ['hɒtlaɪn]
Hubschrauber helicopter ['helɪˌkɒptə]
Hügel hill [hɪl]
Huhn chicken ['tʃɪkɪn]
Hund dog [dɒg]
mit dem Hund spazieren gehen to walk the dog [wɔ:k ðə 'dɒg]
hundemüde dog-tired [ˌdɒg 'taɪəd]
hundert hundred ['hʌndrəd]
Hunger bekommen to get hungry [get 'hʌŋgri]
Hungersnot famine ['fæmɪn]
hungrig hungry ['hʌŋgri]
Hut hat [hæt]

I

ich I [aɪ]
Ich heiße …. My name is …. [maɪ 'neɪm‿ɪz]
Ich nehme …. I'm having …. [aɪm 'hævɪŋ]
ich würde gern I'd like to [ˌaɪd 'laɪk tə]
ich würde lieber I'd rather [aɪd 'rɑ:ðə]
Idee idea [aɪ'dɪə]
Idiot idiot ['ɪdɪət]
ihm him [hɪm]
ihn him [hɪm]
ihnen them [ðem]
Ihnen you [ju:; jə]
ihr you [ju:; jə]
ihr/ihre her [hɜ:]; their [ðeə]; its [ɪts]
Ihr/Ihre your [jɔ:]
Ikone icon ['aɪkɒn]
illegal illegal [ɪ'li:gl]
im Gange sein to be on [bi:‿'ɒn]
im Ganzen in all [ɪn‿'ɔ:l]
im unteren Teil at the bottom [ət ðə 'bɒtəm]

im vorderen Teil at the front [ət ðə 'frʌnt]
Imbiss snack [snæk]
Imbissstube snack bar ['snæk ˌbɑː]; deli *(AE)* ['deli]; diner *(AE)* ['daɪnə]
immer always ['ɔːlweɪz]
immer noch still [stɪl]
Immigrant/Immigrantin immigrant ['ɪmɪgrənt]
Immigration immigration [ˌɪmɪ'greɪʃn]
immigrieren to immigrate ['ɪmɪgreɪt]
improvisieren to freestyle *(slang)* ['friːstaɪl]
in in [ɪn]; at [æt; ət]; into ['ɪntə]
in Australien Down Under [ˌdaʊn‿'ʌndə]
in … hinein into ['ɪntə]
Independent *(Musikrichtung)* independent [ˌɪndɪ'pendənt]
Indianer/Indianerin Native American [ˌneɪtɪv‿ə'merɪkən]
Indie *(Musikrichtung)* indie ['ɪndi]
indisch Indian ['ɪndiən]
Industrie industry ['ɪndəstri]
Infokasten fact box ['fækt bɒks]
Information/Informationen information [ˌɪnfə'meɪʃn]
Informationszentrum information centre [ɪnfə'meɪʃn ˌsentə]
Inhaber/Inhaberin keeper ['kiːpə]
Inhalt content ['kɒntent]
inklusive including [ɪn'kluːdɪŋ]
Inlineskates skates *(pl)* [skeɪts]
Inlineskates fahren to skate [skeɪt]
innen inside [ɪn'saɪd]
innerhalb within [wɪ'ðɪn]
Insel island ['aɪlənd]
Inselbewohner/Inselbewohnerin islander ['aɪləndə]
insgesamt in all [ɪn‿'ɔːl]
Institut college ['kɒlɪdʒ]
intelligent intelligent [ɪn'telɪdʒnt]
interessant interesting ['ɪntrəstɪŋ]
Interesse interest ['ɪntrəst]
sich **interessieren** to get interested [get 'ɪntrəstɪd]
interessiert interested ['ɪntrəstɪd]
interessiert sein an to be into [biː‿'ɪntə]
interkulturell inter-cultural [ˌɪntə'kʌltʃrl]
international international [ˌɪntə'næʃnl]
Internet Internet ['ɪntənet]
im Internet online [ˌɒn'laɪn]
im Internet surfen to surf the Internet [ˌsɜːf ði‿'ɪntənet]
Internetauftritt website ['websaɪt]
Interview interview ['ɪntəvjuː]
interviewen to interview ['ɪntəvjuː]
IQ *(Intelligenzquotient)* IQ [ˌaɪ'kjuː]
Iren/Irinnen Irish ['aɪrɪʃ]
irgendetwas anything ['eniθɪŋ]
irgendjemand anybody ['eniˌbɒdi]
irgendwie somehow ['sʌmhaʊ]
irgendwo anywhere ['eniweə]; somewhere ['sʌmweə]
irisch Irish ['aɪrɪʃ]
Italiener/Italienerin Italian [ɪ'tæliən]
italienisch Italian [ɪ'tæliən]

J

ja yes [jes]; yeah *(slang)* [jeə]
Jacke jacket ['dʒækɪt]
Jackentasche pocket ['pɒkɪt]
Jagdhund hound [haʊnd]
Jagen hunting ['hʌntɪŋ]
Jahr year [jɪə]
Jahrbuch yearbook ['jɪəbʊk]
Jahreszeit season ['siːzn]
Jahrgangsstufe year [jɪə]
Jahrhundert century ['sentʃri]
-jährig year-old [jɪər‿'əʊld]
-Jähriger/-Jährige year-old [jɪər‿'əʊld]
Jahrmarkt fair [feə]
Januar January ['dʒænjuəri]
Jazz jazz [dʒæz]
je each [iːtʃ]
Jeans jeans *(pl)* [dʒiːnz]
jeder everybody ['evribɒdi]
jeder (beliebige) anybody ['eniˌbɒdi]
jeder/jede/jedes every ['evri]; each [iːtʃ]
jederzeit at any time [æt‿eni 'taɪm]
jemals ever ['evə]
jemand somebody ['sʌmbədi]; someone ['sʌmwʌn]
jene those [ðəʊz]
jenes that [ðæt]
jetzt now [naʊ]
jetzt gleich right now [ˌraɪt 'naʊ]
jeweils each [iːtʃ]
Job job [dʒɒb]
joggen to jog [dʒɒg]
Jogger/Joggerin jogger [dʒɒgə]
jucken to itch [ɪtʃ]
Jugend youth [juːθ]
jugendlich teenage ['tiːneɪdʒ]
Jugendliche/Jugendlicher teenager ['tiːnˌeɪdʒə]; teen [tiːn]
Jugendtreffen rally ['ræli]
Juli July [dʒʊ'laɪ]
jung young [jʌŋ]
Junge boy [bɔɪ]; lad [læd]
Juni June [dʒuːn]
Juwel jewel ['dʒuːəl]

K

Kaffee coffee ['kɒfiː]
Käfig cage [keɪdʒ]
Kakao cocoa ['kəʊkəʊ]
Kalender calendar ['kæləndə]
kalt cold [kəʊld]
Kamera camera ['kæmrə]
Kamerad/Kameradin buddy *(infml)* ['bʌdi]; mate [meɪt]
Kameramann cameraman, cameramen *(pl)* ['kæmrəmæn; 'kæmrəmen]
Kaminfeuer fire [faɪə]
Kampf fight [faɪt]; fighting ['faɪtɪŋ]
Kampf- fighting ['faɪtɪŋ]
kämpfen to fight [faɪt]
Kampfrichter judge [dʒʌdʒ]
Kanal channel ['tʃænl]
Känguru kangaroo [ˌkæŋgr'uː]
Kante edge [edʒ]
Kanu fahren to canoe [kə'nuː]
Kapelle band [bænd]
Kapitän captain ['kæptɪn]
Kappe cap [kæp]
Kapsel capsule ['kæpsjuːl]
kaputt broken ['brəʊkn]
kaputtmachen to break [breɪk]
Karotte carrot ['kærət]
Karriere career [kə'rɪə]
Karte card [kɑːd]
Kartoffel potato, potatoes *(pl)* [pə'teɪtəʊ; pə'teɪtəʊz]
Kartoffelchip crisp [krɪsp]
Käse cheese [tʃiːz]
Kasten box, boxes *(pl)* [bɒks; 'bɒksɪz]
Katastrophe disaster [dɪ'zɑːstə]
Kathedrale cathedral [kə'θiːdrl]
Katze cat [kæt]
kaufen to buy [baɪ]
Kaufhaus department store [dɪ'pɑːtmənt stɔː]; store [stɔː]
Kaufhausdetektiv/Kaufhausdetektivin store detective ['stɔː dɪˌtektɪv]

Kautschuk rubber ['rʌbə]
Kaviar caviar ['kævia:]
kein/keine no [nəʊ]
keine Ahnung no idea [ˌnəʊ‿aɪ'dɪə]
überhaupt kein/keine no … at all [ˌnəʊ … ət‿'ɔ:l]
keiner/keine none [nʌn]
Keks biscuit ['bɪskɪt]
Kelch cup [kʌp]
Kellergeschoss basement ['beɪsmənt]
Kellner waiter ['weɪtə]
kennen to know [nəʊ]
kennzeichnend typical ['tɪpɪkl]
Kerl bloke [bləʊk]; guy [gaɪ]
Kette chain [tʃeɪn]
Kickboard kickboard ['kɪkbɔ:d]
kicken to kick [kɪk]
Kilo(gramm) kilo (kg) ['kɪləʊ]
Kilometer kilometre ['kɪləʊˌmi:tə; kɪ'lɒmɪtə]
Kind child, children *(pl)* [tʃaɪld; 'tʃɪldrɪn]; kid [kɪd]
Kino cinema ['sɪnəmə]; movies *(AE)* ['mu:viz]; theater *(AE)* ['θɪətə]
Kirche church [tʃɜ:tʃ]
Kirsche cherry ['tʃeri]
Kiste box, boxes *(pl)* [bɒks; 'bɒksɪz]
klagen to moan [məʊn]
Klang sound [saʊnd]
Klappe shutter ['ʃʌtə]
klar clear [klɪə]
sich klar werden to realise ['rɪəlaɪz]
klären *(ein Problem)* to sort out [sɔ:t‿'aʊt]
Klasse class [klɑ:s]; grade *(AE)* [greɪd]
Klassenarbeit test [test]
Klassenzimmer classroom ['klɑ:srʊm]
klassisch classic ['klæsɪk]
klatschen to clap [klæp]
Kleid dress [dres]
Kleider clothes *(pl)* [kləʊðz]
Kleiderschrank wardrobe ['wɔ:drəʊb]
Kleidung clothes *(pl)* [kləʊðz]; dress [dres]
klein little ['lɪtl]; small [smɔ:l]
klettern to climb ['klaɪm]
klicken to click [klɪk]
Klima climate ['klaɪmət]
Klingel bell [bel]
klingeln to ring [rɪŋ]
Es klingelt. The bell rings. [ðə 'bel rɪŋz]
klingen to sound [saʊnd]
Klippe cliff [klɪf]
klopfen to knock [nɒk]
fest klopfen to bang [bæŋ]
Klopfen knock [nɒk]
Klub club [klʌb]
klug intelligent [ɪn'telɪdʒnt]; smart [smɑ:t]
Klunker bling bling *(slang)* [ˌblɪŋ 'blɪŋ]
knallen to pop [pɒp]
knallen lassen to pop [pɒp]
knarren to creak [kri:k]
Kneipe bar [bɑ:]
Knie knee [ni:]
Knopf button ['bʌtn]
knusprig crunchy ['krʌntʃi]
Koala koala [kəʊ'ɑ:lə]
Kobold goblin ['gɒblɪn]
Koch/Köchin chef [ʃef]; cook [kʊk]
kochen to cook [kʊk]
Kochen cooking ['kʊkɪŋ]
Kollegium staff [stɑ:f]
Kolonie colony ['kɒləni]
komfortabel comfortable ['kʌmpftəbl]
komisch funny ['fʌni]
kommen to come [kʌm]; to get [get]
Komm./Kommt. Come on. [kʌm‿'ɒn]
kommen nach to get to ['get tə]
kommen zu to get to ['get tə]
Kommunikation communication [kəˌmju:nɪ'keɪʃn]
Komödie comedy ['kɒmədi]
Kompanie company ['kʌmpəni]
Komparativ comparative [kəm'pærətɪv]
Kondition condition [kən'dɪʃn]
König king [kɪŋ]
Königin queen [kwi:n]
königlich royal ['rɔɪəl]
Konkurrent/Konkurentin rival ['raɪvl]
können can [kæn]
konnte/konnten could [kʊd]
könnte/könnten could [kʊd]; might [maɪt]
kann/könnte(n) vielleicht may [meɪ]
kontaktfreudig outgoing ['aʊtgəʊɪŋ]
kontaktieren to contact ['kɒntækt]
Kontinent continent ['kɒntɪnənt]
Kontrolle check [tʃek]
kontrollieren to check [tʃek]; to control [kən'trəʊl]
Konzert concert ['kɒnsət]
Kooperative co-operative [kəʊ'ɒprətɪv]
Kopf head [hed]
Kopfhörer headphones *(pl)* ['hedfəʊnz]
Kopfsalat lettuce ['letɪs]
kopieren to copy ['kɒpi]
Koralle coral ['kɒrəl]
Korallen- coral ['kɒrəl]
Kordel string [strɪŋ]
kornisch Cornish ['kɔ:nɪʃ]
Körper body ['bɒdi]
körperlich physical ['fɪzɪkl]
korrekt correct [kə'rekt]; right [raɪt]
Korridor corridor ['kɒrɪdɔ:]
kosten to cost [kɒst]
kostenlos free [fri:]
krabbeln to crawl [krɔ:l]
Krach! Crash! [kræʃ]
Kraft energy ['enədʒi]; power ['paʊə]
Krake octopus ['ɒktəpəs]
krank ill [ɪl]; sick [sɪk]
Krankenhaus hospital ['hɒspɪtl]
Krankenpfleger nurse [nɜ:s]
Krankenschwester nurse [nɜ:s]
Krankenwagen ambulance ['æmbjələns]
Krankmeldung sick note ['sɪk ˌnəʊt]
Kreatur creature ['kri:tʃə]
Kredit loan [ləʊn]
Kreis circle ['sɜ:kl]
kreuzen to cross [krɒs]
Kreuzfahrt cruise [kru:z]
Kricket cricket ['krɪkɪt]
kriechen to crawl [krɔ:l]
Krieg war [wɔ:]
Krimi detective story [dɪ'tektɪv ˌstɔ:ri]
Kriminalität crime [kraɪm]
kriminell criminal ['krɪmɪnl]
Krimineller/Kriminelle criminal ['krɪmɪnl]
Kritik review [rɪ'vju:]
Krokodil crocodile ['krɒkədaɪl]
Krone crown [kraʊn]
Küche kitchen ['kɪtʃɪn]
Kuchen cake [keɪk]
Küchenchef/Küchenchefin chef [ʃef]
Küchenschrank cupboard ['kʌbəd]
Kuh cow [kaʊ]
kühl cool [ku:l]
Kühlschrank refrigerator [rɪ'frɪdʒreɪtə]
sich **kümmern** to care [keə]; to take care [teɪk 'keə]
sich kümmern um to look after [lʊk‿'ɑ:ftə]
Kumpel mate [meɪt]; buddy *(infml)* ['bʌdi]; homie *(slang)* ['həʊmi]
Kunde/Kundin customer ['kʌstəmə]
kündigen to quit [kwɪt]
Kunst Art [ɑ:t]
Künstler/Künstlerin artist ['ɑ:tɪst]

Kurier courier ['kʊriə]
Kurs class [klɑ:s]; course [kɔ:s]
Kurve curve [kɜ:v]
kurz short [ʃɔ:t]
Kuss kiss [kɪs]
küssen to kiss [kɪs]
Küste coast [kəʊst]; seaside ['si:saɪd]
Küstenlinie coastline ['kəʊst,laɪn]

L

Labor lab(oratory) [læb; lə'bɒrətri]
lächeln to smile [smaɪl]
lachen to laugh [lɑ:f]
lackieren to spray [spreɪ]
Laden shop [ʃɒp]; store [stɔ:]
Lager camp [kæmp]
Lagerfeuer campfire ['kæmpfaɪə]
Lamm lamb [læm]
Lammfleisch lamb [læm]
Lampe lamp [læmp]
Land country, countries *(pl)* ['kʌntri; 'kʌntriz]; land [lænd]; state [steɪt]
landen to land [lænd]; to end up [,end‿'ʌp]
landesweit national ['næʃnl]
Landkarte map [mæp]
Landschaft scenery ['si:nri]
Landstraße road [rəʊd]
Landungssteg pier [pɪə]
Landwirt/Landwirtin farmer ['fɑ:mə]
lang long [lɒŋ]
langsam slow [sləʊ]
langweilig boring ['bɔ:rɪŋ]
Laptop laptop ['læptɒp]
Lärm noise [nɔɪz]
lassen to let [let]; to leave [li:v]
jmdn. im Stich lassen to let sb down [let 'daʊn]
Lasst uns .... Let's .... [lets]
Lassi *(Jogurtgetränk)* lassi ['lasɪ]
Lastwagen truck *(AE)* [trʌk]
Lastwagenfahrer/Lastwagenfahrerin trucker *(AE)* ['trʌkə]
lateinamerikanisch Hispanic [hɪ'spænɪk]
Laterne lantern ['læntən]
Latino Latino [lə'ti:nəʊ]
Latinomusik Latino [lə'ti:nəʊ]
Lauf run [rʌn]
Laufbahn career [kə'rɪə]
laufen to walk [wɔ:k]; to run [rʌn]; to be on [bi:‿'ɒn]
laufen gegen to run into [rʌn‿'ɪntə]
laufen mit *(Auto)* to run on ['rʌn‿ɒn]
Läufer/Läuferin runner ['rʌnə]
Laune mood [mu:d]
laut loud [laʊd]
Es **lautete ....** It said .... [ɪt 'sed]
leben to live [lɪv]
Leben life, lives *(pl)* [laɪf; laɪvz]
am Leben alive [ə'laɪv]
lebendig alive [ə'laɪv]
Lebens- vital ['vaɪtl]
Lebensart lifestyle ['laɪfstaɪl]
Lebenslauf curriculum vitae (CV) [kə'rɪkjələm 'vi:taɪ]
Lebensmittel food [fu:d]
lebenswichtig vital ['vaɪtl]
Lebenszeichen vital signs *(pl)* [,vaɪtl 'saɪnz]
Lebewesen creature ['kri:tʃə]
lecker yummy ['jʌmi]
leer empty ['empti]; dead [ded]
legal legal ['li:gl]
legen to put [pʊt]
sich legen to come down [kʌm 'daʊn]
Lehre apprenticeship [ə'prentɪʃɪp]
lehren to teach [ti:tʃ]
Lehrer/Lehrerin teacher ['ti:tʃə]; instructor [ɪn'strʌktə]
Lehrplan curriculum [kə'rɪkjələm]
leicht easy ['i:zi]; light [laɪt]
Leid tun to be sorry [bi: 'sɒri]
Tut mir leid. Sorry. ['sɒri]
leihen to borrow ['bɒrəʊ]; to lend [lend]
Leinwand screen [skri:n]
leise quiet ['kwaɪət]; silent ['saɪlənt]; soft [sɒft]
leiten to direct [dɪ'rekt]
lernen to learn [lɜ:n]; to study ['stʌdi]; to train [treɪn]
Lernen studies *(pl)* ['stʌdiz]
Lesebuch reader ['ri:də]
lesen to read [ri:d]
Leser/Leserin reader ['ri:də]
letzter/letzte/letztes final ['faɪnl]; last [lɑ:st]
Leuchte lamp [læmp]
leuchten to glow [gləʊ]
leuchtend brilliant ['brɪljənt]
Leuchtfeuer flare [fleə]
Leute people ['pi:pl]; folks *(Anrede)* [fəʊks]
Licht light [laɪt]
Lichtschein flare [fleə]
lieb dear [dɪə]
Liebe love [lʌv]
Liebe ... *(Anrede in Briefen)* Dear ... [dɪə]
lieben to love [lʌv]
ich würde **lieber** I'd rather [aɪd 'rɑ:ðə]
Lieber ... *(Anrede in Briefen)* Dear ... [dɪə]
Liebling pet [pet]
Lieblings- favourite ['feɪvrɪt]
Lied song [sɒŋ]
Liedtext lyrics ['lɪrɪks]
Lieferant/Lieferantin provider [prə'vaɪdə]
liefern to deliver [dɪ'lɪvə]
Lieferwagen van [væn]
liegen to lie [laɪ]; to rest [rest]
Liga union ['ju:njən]
lila purple ['pɜ:pl]
Limit limit ['lɪmɪt]
Limonade lemonade [,lemə'neɪd]
Limousine limousine [,lɪmə'zi:n]
Lineal ruler ['ru:lə]
Linie line [laɪn]
Link link [lɪŋk]
linker/linke/linkes left [left]
links left [left]; on the left [ɒn ðə 'left]
links abbiegen to turn left [tɜ:n 'left]
Lippenpflegestift lip balm ['lɪp bɑ:m]
Liste list [lɪst]
live live [laɪv]
Loch dump [dʌmp]
Löffel spoon [spu:n]
Logbuch logbook ['lɒgbʊk]
Logo logo ['ləʊgəʊ]
Lohn pay [peɪ]
lokal local ['ləʊkl]
löschen *(Text)* to delete [dɪ'li:t]
löschen to put out [pʊt‿'aʊt]
lösen to solve [sɒlv]
losgehen *(Alarm)* to go off [gəʊ‿'ɒf]
Löwe lion ['laɪən]
Luft air [eə]
keine Luft bekommen to choke [tʃəʊk]
Luftballon balloon [bə'lu:n]
lügen to lie [laɪ]
lustig funny ['fʌni]
sich lustig machen über to laugh at ['lɑ:f‿ət]
Lyrik poetry ['pəʊətri]

M

machen to do [du:]; to make [meɪk]
eine Diät machen to go on a diet [ˌgəʊ‿ɒn ə 'daɪət]
sich lustig machen über to laugh at ['lɑ:f‿ət]
Spaß machen to be fun [bi: 'fʌn]
Macht power ['paʊə]
Mädchen girl [gɜ:l]
Magazin magazine [mægə'zi:n]
Magen stomach ['stʌmək]
Mahlzeit meal [mi:l]
Mai May [meɪ]
mailen to e-mail ['i:meɪl]
makellos pristine ['prɪsti:n]
Make-up make-up ['meɪkʌp]
Mal *(zeitlich)* time [taɪm]
malen to paint [peɪnt]
Mama mum [mʌm]
man you [ju:; jə]; they [ðeɪ]
Manager/Managerin manager ['mænɪdʒə]
manchmal sometimes ['sʌmtaɪmz]
manipulieren to fix [fɪks]
Mann man, men *(pl)* [mæn; men]
Mannschaft crew [kru:]; team [ti:m]
Mantarochen manta ray ['mænta ˌreɪ]
Mantel coat [kəʊt]
Mappe folder ['fəʊldə]
markieren to mark [mɑ:k]
Markt market ['mɑ:kɪt]
Marmelade jam [dʒæm]
Marsch march [mɑ:tʃ]
marschieren to march [mɑ:tʃ]
März March [mɑ:tʃ]
Maschine machine [mə'ʃi:n]
Mast post [pəʊst]
Material material [mə'tɪəriəl]
Mathematik Maths [mæθs]
Mauer wall [wɔ:l]
Maultier mule [mju:l]
Maus mouse [maʊs]
Mechaniker/Mechanikerin mechanic [mə'kænɪk]
Medien media *(pl)* ['mi:diə]
Medikament drug [drʌg]
Meer sea [si:]
Meeresküste seaside ['si:saɪd]
mehr more [mɔ:]
mehrere several ['sevrl]
Mehrzahl plural ['plʊərəl]
Meile *(brit. Längenmaß)* mile [maɪl]
Meilenstein milestone ['maɪlstəʊn]
meilenweit for miles [fə‿'maɪlz]
mein/meine my [maɪ]
Mein Gott! My God! [maɪ 'gɒd]
mein Herr *(Anrede)* sir [sɜ:]
Meinung opinion [ə'pɪnjən]
einer Meinung sein to agree [ə'gri:]
das **meiste** most [məʊst]
die meisten most [məʊst]
Meldung report [rɪ'pɔ:t]
eine **Menge** a lot of [ə 'lɒt‿əv]
Mensch human ['hju:mən]
Menschen people ['pi:pl]
Menschenmenge crowd [kraʊd]
menschlich human ['hju:mən]
Menü menu ['menju:]
sich **merken** to remember [rɪ'membə]
merkwürdig strange [streɪndʒ]
Messe fair [feə]
Messer knife, knives *(pl)* [naɪf; naɪvz]
Messestand stand [stænd]
Metal *(Musikrichtung)* metal ['metl]
Metall metal ['metl]
Meter metre ['mi:tə]
Mexikaner/Mexikanerin Mexican ['meksɪkən]
mexikanisch Mexican ['meksɪkən]
mich me [mi:]
mich (selbst) myself [maɪ'self]
Miesmacher/Miesmacherin wet blanket [wet 'blæŋkɪt]
Miete rent [rent]
mieten to rent [rent]
Mikrofon microphone ['maɪkrəfəʊn]
Mikrowelle microwave ['maɪkrəʊweɪv]
Milch milk [mɪlk]
milchig milky ['mɪlki]
Milchmann milkman, milkmen *(pl)* ['mɪlkmən; 'mɪlkmen]
Milchshake milkshake ['mɪlkʃeɪk]
Million million ['mɪlɪən]
mindestens at least [ət 'li:st]
Mineral- mineral ['mɪnərəl]
Minestrone minestrone [ˌmɪnɪ'strəʊni]
Minute minute ['mɪnɪt]
mir me [mi:]
mischen to mix [mɪks]
Mission mission ['mɪʃn]
mit with [wɪð]
Mitarbeiter/Mitarbeiterin employee [ɪm'plɔɪi:]
mitbringen to bring [brɪŋ]
miteinander together [tə'geðə]
Mitfahrgelegenheit ride [raɪd]
mitführen to carry along [ˌkæri‿ə'lɒŋ]
Mitglied member ['membə]
mitnehmen to take [teɪk]
zum **Mitnehmen** to go [tə‿'gəʊ]
mitreißen to carry along [ˌkæri‿ə'lɒŋ]
Mitspieler/Mitspielerin player ['pleɪə]
Mittagessen lunch [lʌntʃ]; dinner ['dɪnə]
Mittagszeit lunchtime ['lʌntʃtaɪm]
Mitte middle ['mɪdl]
mittel medium ['mi:diəm]
Mittel- middle ['mɪdl]
Mittelpunkt centre ['sentə]
Mittelschule *(weiterführende Schule in den USA, Mittelstufe)* middle school *(AE)* ['mɪdl ˌsku:l]
Mitternacht midnight ['mɪdnaɪt]
Mittwoch Wednesday ['wenzdeɪ]
mixen to mix [mɪks]
Möbel furniture ['fɜ:nɪtʃə]
Mobiltelefon mobile ['məʊbaɪl]; cell phone *(AE)* ['sel ˌfəʊn]
möchte(n) gern would like [wʊd 'laɪk]
Mode fashion ['fæʃn]
Model model ['mɒdl]
Modell model ['mɒdl]
modern modern ['mɒdn]
modisch trendy ['trendi]
mögen to like [laɪk]
gern mögen to love [lʌv]
möglich possible ['pɒsəbl]
Möglichkeit opportunity [ˌɒpə'tju:nəti]
Mohrrübe carrot ['kærət]
Molkerei dairy ['deəri]
Moment moment ['məʊmənt]
Moment mal! Hang on! ['hæŋ‿ɒn]
momentan at the moment [ət ðə 'məʊmənt]
Monat month [mʌnθ]
Mond moon [mu:n]
Monster monster ['mɒnstə]
Montag Monday ['mʌndeɪ]
montags on Mondays [ɒn 'mʌndeɪz]
Mord murder ['mɜ:də]
Mörder/Mörderin killer ['kɪlə]
morgen tomorrow [tə'mɒrəʊ]
Morgen morning ['mɔ:nɪŋ]; *(Flächenmaß: 40,47 Ar)* acre ['eɪkə]
am Morgen in the morning [ˌɪn ðə 'mɔ:nɪŋ]
am nächsten Morgen the next morning [ˌnekst 'mɔ:nɪŋ]
Guten Morgen! Good morning! ['gʊd 'mɔ:nɪŋ]
Morgenappell assembly [ə'sembli]

Morgendämmerung dawn [dɔːn]
morgens in the morning [ˌɪn ðə ˈmɔːnɪŋ]
Motel motel [məʊˈtel]
Motor motor [ˈməʊtə]; engine [ˈendʒɪn]
Motorrad motorbike [ˈməʊtəbaɪk]
MP3 MP3 [empiːˈθriː]
MP3-Player MP3 player [empiːˈθriː ˌpleɪə]
müde tired [ˈtaɪəd]
Müll rubbish [ˈrʌbɪʃ]
Mülleimer bin [bɪn]
Müllkippe dump [dʌmp]
Mülltonne bin [bɪn]
multinational multinational [ˌmʌltiˈnæʃnl]
Mund mouth [maʊθ]
Museum museum [mjuːˈziːəm]
Musical musical [ˈmjuːzɪkl]
Musik music [ˈmjuːzɪk]
Musiker/Musikerin musician [mjuːˈzɪʃn]
müssen must [mʌst]; to have to [ˈhæv tə]; to need [niːd]
mutig brave [breɪv]
Mutter mother [ˈmʌðə]
Mutti mum [mʌm]
Mütze cap [kæp]
Mythos myth [mɪθ]

N

nach *(zeitlich)* after [ˈɑːftə]
nach *(Uhrzeit)* past [pɑːst]
nach to [tʊ; tə]
nach draußen outside [aʊtˈsaɪd]
nach drinnen inside [ɪnˈsaɪd]
nach Hause home [həʊm]
nach Hause bringen to take home [ˌteɪk ˈhəʊm]
nach unten down [daʊn]
Nachbar/Nachbarin neighbour [ˈneɪbə]
Nachbarschaft neighborhood *(AE)* [ˈneɪbəhʊd]
nacherzählen to retell [riːˈtel]
Nachmittag afternoon [ˌɑːftəˈnuːn]
am Nachmittag in the afternoon [ˌɪn ði ˌɑːftəˈnuːn]
nachmittags in the afternoon [ˌɪn ði ˌɑːftəˈnuːn]
Nachmittagstee afternoon tea [ˌɑːftənuːn ˈtiː]
Nachricht message [ˈmesɪdʒ]
Nachricht(en) news *(sg.)* [njuːz]
neueste Nachrichten breaking news [ˌbreɪkɪŋ ˈnjuːz]
nachschauen to have a look [ˌhæv‿ə ˈlʊk]
nachschlagen to look up [lʊk‿ˈʌp]
nächster/nächste/nächstes next [nekst]
am nächsten Morgen the next morning [ˌnekst ˈmɔːnɪŋ]
Nacht night [naɪt]
heute Nacht tonight [təˈnaɪt]
nachts at night [ət ˈnaɪt]
Nachtisch dessert [dɪˈzɜːt]; pudding [ˈpʊdɪŋ]
Nachtschwester night nurse [ˈnaɪt nɜːs]
Nacktschnecke slug [slʌg]
nahe close [kləʊs]; near [nɪə]
in der **Nähe von** near [nɪə]
Nahrung food [fuːd]
Name name [neɪm]
Nase nose [nəʊz]
die Nase voll haben to be fed up [biː ˌfed‿ˈʌp]
nass wet [wet]
national national [ˈnæʃnl]
National- national [ˈnæʃnl]
Nationalpark national park [ˌnæʃnl ˈpɑːk]
natürlich of course [əv ˈkɔːs]
Naturwissenschaft Science [ˈsaɪəns]
Nebel fog [fɒg]
neben next to [ˈnekst tə]; beside [bɪˈsaɪd]
nebenan next door [ˌnekst ˈdɔː]
Nebenprodukt spin-off [ˈspɪn‿ɒf]
neblig foggy [ˈfɒgi]
Neffe nephew [ˈnefjuː]
nehmen to take [teɪk]
Ich nehme .... I'm having .... [aɪm ˈhævɪŋ]
neidisch (auf) jealous (of) [ˈdʒeləs]
nein no [nəʊ]
nennen to call [kɔːl]; to name [neɪm]
neonfarben neon [ˈniːɒn]
Neoprenanzug wetsuit [ˈwetsuːt]
nervös nervous [ˈnɜːvəs]
nett nice [naɪs]; friendly [ˈfrendli]
Netz net [net]
neu new [njuː]
Neuigkeit(en) news *(sg.)* [njuːz]
nicht no [nəʊ]; not [nɒt]
auch nicht not ... either [ˌnɒt ... ˈaɪðə]
nicht einmal not even [nɒt‿ˈiːvn]
noch nicht not ... yet [jet]
nichts nothing [ˈnʌθɪŋ]
Nickel *(Währung)* nickel [ˈnɪkl]
nie never [ˈnevə]
nieder down [daʊn]
Niederländer/Niederländerinnen Dutch [dʌtʃ]
niederländisch Dutch [dʌtʃ]
niederlegen to lie down [laɪ ˈdaʊn]
niedlich cute [kjuːt]
niedrig low [ləʊ]
niemals never [ˈnevə]
niemand nobody [ˈnəʊbədi]; no one [ˈnəʊwʌn]
nirgendwo(hin) nowhere [ˈnəʊweə]
Niveau level [ˈlevl]
noch else [els]; still [stɪl]
noch ein/noch eine another [əˈnʌðə]
noch nicht not ... yet [jet]
non-stop non-stop [ˌnɒnˈstɒp]
Norden north [nɔːθ]
normal normal [ˈnɔːml]
normalerweise usually [ˈjuːʒli]
Note mark [mɑːk]; grade *(AE)* [greɪd]
Notfall emergency [ɪˈmɜːdʒnsi]
Notiz note [nəʊt]; notice [ˈnəʊtɪs]
Notlage emergency [ɪˈmɜːdʒnsi]
November November [nəʊˈvembə]
Nummer number [ˈnʌmbə]
nun now [naʊ]
nur only [ˈəʊnli]
nussig nutty [ˈnʌti]
nützlich useful [ˈjuːsfl]
nutzlos useless [ˈjuːsləs]

O

ob if [ɪf]
oben above [əˈbʌv]; up [ʌp]; upstairs [ʌpˈsteəz]; at the top [ət ðə ˈtɒp]
oberer/obere/oberes upper [ˈʌpə]
oberer Teil top [tɒp]
oberhalb above [əˈbʌv]
oberster/oberste/oberstes supreme [suːˈpriːm]
obligatorisch compulsory [kəmˈpʌlsri]
Observatorium observatory [əbˈzɜːvətri]
Obst fruit [fruːt]
obwohl although [ɔːlˈðəʊ]

oder or [ɔ:]
offen open ['əʊpn]
öffentlich public ['pʌblɪk]
offiziell officially [ə'fɪʃli]
öffnen to open ['əʊpn]
sich öffnen to open ['əʊpn]
Öffnungszeiten hours ['aʊəz]
oft often ['ɒfn]
ohne without [wɪ'ðaʊt]
ohne … auskommen to go without [ˌgəʊ wɪ'ðaʊt]
ohnmächtig werden to faint [feɪnt]
Ohr ear [ɪə]
Oje! Oh dear! [əʊ 'dɪə]
o.k. OK [əʊ'keɪ]
Öko- eco [i:kəʊ]
Oktober October [ɒk'təʊbə]
Oktopus octopus ['ɒktəpəs]
Öl oil [ɔɪl]
Oma grandma ['grændmɑ:]
Onkel uncle ['ʌŋkl]
online online [ˌɒn'laɪn]
Opa grandad ['grændæd]
Oper opera ['ɒprə]
operieren to operate ['ɒpəreɪt]
Option option ['ɒpʃn]
Orange orange ['ɒrɪndʒ]
Ordner folder ['fəʊldə]
Ordner mit Informationen (über) fact file (on) ['fækt faɪl]
Ordnung order ['ɔ:də]
in Ordnung all right [ɔ:l 'raɪt]
Organisation organisation [ˌɔ:gnaɪ'zeɪʃn]
Organisator/Organisatorin organizer ['ɔ:gənaɪzə]
organisieren to organize ['ɔ:gənaɪz]
Ort place [pleɪs]
örtlich local ['ləʊkl]
ortsansässig local ['ləʊkl]
Osten east [i:st]
das **Outback** the Outback ['aʊtbæk]
Ozean ocean ['əʊʃn]
Ozeandampfer ocean liner ['əʊʃn ˌlaɪnə]

P

ein **paar** a few [ə 'fju:]; a couple of [ə 'kʌpl‿əv]
Paar couple ['kʌpl]
Pacht rent [rent]
pachten to rent [rent]
Päckchen packet ['pækɪt]
packen to pack [pæk]
Paket packet ['pækɪt]
Palast palace ['pælɪs]
in **Panik geraten** to panic ['pænɪk]
Panter panther ['pæntθə]
Papa dad [dæd]
Papier paper ['peɪpə]
Parade parade [pə'reɪd]
Paradies paradise ['pærəˌdaɪs]
Paragliding paragliding ['pærəˌglaɪdɪŋ]
Park park [pɑ:k]
Parkaufseher/Parkaufseherin (park) ranger [ˌpɑ:k 'reɪndʒə]
Partner/Partnerin partner ['pɑ:tnə]
Party party ['pɑ:ti]
eine Party feiern to have a party [ˌhæv‿ə 'pɑ:ti]
Pass passport ['pɑ:spɔ:t]
Passagier/Passagierin passenger ['pæsndʒə]
passen to fit [fɪt]
passen zu to go with ['gəʊ‿wɪð]; to match [mætʃ]
passend suitable ['su:təbl]
das nicht dazu passende odd one out [ɒd wʌn‿'aʊt]
Passkontrolle passports *(pl)* ['pɑ:spɔ:ts]
Pastrami pastrami [pəs'trɑ:mi]
Patient/Patientin patient ['peɪʃnt]
Pause break [breɪk]
PC PC [ˌpi:'si:]
Pech bad luck [ˌbæd 'lʌk]
peinlich embarrassing [ɪm'bærəsɪŋ]
Pence *(Währung)* pence *(pl)* [pents]
perfekt perfect ['pɜ:fɪkt]
Periode period ['pɪəriəd]
permanent permanent ['pɜ:mənənt]
Person person ['pɜ:sn]
Personal staff [stɑ:f]
Perücke wig [wɪg]
Pfad path [pɑ:θ]
Pfannkuchen pancake ['pænkeɪk]
Pfeife pipe [paɪp]
Pferd horse [hɔ:s]
Pflanze plant [plɑ:nt]
pflücken to pick [pɪk]
Pflücker/Pflückerin picker ['pɪkə]
pflügen to plough [plaʊ]
Pforte gate [geɪt]
Pfosten post [pəʊst]
Pfund *(Währung)* pound (£) [paʊnd]
Pfund *(Gewicht)* pound (lb) [paʊnd]
physisch physical ['fɪzɪkl]
Pier pier [pɪə]
pikant spicy ['spaɪsi]
Pilot/Pilotin pilot ['paɪlət]
pink pink [pɪŋk]
Pionier/Pionierin pioneer [ˌpaɪə'nɪə]
Pitcher/Pitcherin pitcher ['pɪtʃə]
Pizza pizza ['pi:tsə]
Plakat poster ['pəʊstə]
Plan plan [plæn]
planen to plan [plæn]
Planet planet ['plænɪt]
platt flat [flæt]
Platte record ['rekɔ:d]; panel ['pænl]
Plattform platform ['plætfɔ:m]
Platz place [pleɪs]; room [ru:m; rʊm]; space [speɪs]
pleite broke [brəʊk]
plötzlich suddenly ['sʌdnli]; at once [ət 'wʌnts]
Plundergebäck Danish ['deɪnɪʃ]
Plural plural ['plʊərəl]
plus plus [plʌs]
Poet/Poetin poet ['pəʊɪt]
Poetry Slam *(Gedichtwettbewerb)* poetry slam ['pəʊətri ˌslæm]
Pokal cup [kʌp]
Politik policy ['pɒlɪsi]
politisch political [pə'lɪtɪkl]
politische Linie policy ['pɒlɪsi]
Polizei police [pə'li:s]
Polizist policeman, policemen *(pl)* [pə'li:smən; pə'li:smen]
Polizist/Polizistin cop *(AE)* [kɒp]
polnisch Polish ['pəʊlɪʃ]
Pommes frites French fries *(AE)* ['frentʃ ˌfraɪz]; chips *(pl)* [tʃɪps]
Pompon pompom ['pɒmpɒm]
Pony pony ['pəʊni]
Popmusik pop [pɒp]
populär popular ['pɒpjələ]
Porträt profile ['prəʊfaɪl]
posieren to pose [pəʊz]
Position position [pə'zɪʃn]
Postamt post office ['pəʊst‿ɒfɪs]
posten *(im Internetforum)* to post [pəʊst]
Poster poster ['pəʊstə]
Postkarte postcard ['pəʊstkɑ:d]
Prachtstraße boulevard ['bu:ləvɑ:d]
praktizieren to practise ['præktɪs]
präsentieren to present [prɪ'zent]
Preis price [praɪs]; prize [praɪz]; award [ə'wɔ:d]
zum halben Preis half-price [ˌhɑ:f'praɪs]
pressen to press [pres]

prima brilliant ['brɪljənt]; cool [ku:l]
Prinz prince [prɪns]
privat private ['praɪvɪt]
Privatschule public school *(BE)* [ˌpʌblɪk 'sku:l]
pro per [pɜ:]
Pro und Kontra pros and cons [ˌprəʊz‿ənd 'kɒnz]
proben to practise ['præktɪs]
proben *(ein Theaterstück)* to rehearse [rɪ'hɜ:s]
probieren to try [traɪ]
Problem problem ['prɒbləm]
Produkt product ['prɒdʌkt]
Produktion production [prə'dʌkʃn]
Produzent/Produzentin producer [prə'dju:sə]
produzieren to produce [prə'dju:s]
professionell professional [prə'feʃnl]
Profil profile ['prəʊfaɪl]
Programm programme ['prəʊgræm]; channel ['tʃænl]
Projekt project ['prɒdʒekt]
Protest protest ['prəʊtest]
protestieren to protest [prəʊ'test]
Protestierender/Protestierende protester [prə'testə]
Provider provider [prə'vaɪdə]
Prozent per cent (%) [pə 'sent]
prüfen to test [test]
Prüfung exam [ɪg'zæm]; check [tʃek]
Publikum audience ['ɔ:diəns]
Pudding pudding ['pʊdɪŋ]
Puder powder ['paʊdə]
Pulver powder ['paʊdə]
Punk punk [pʌŋk]
Punkmusik punk [pʌŋk]
Punkt point [pɔɪnt]; dot [dɒt]
Pünktchen dot [dɒt]
punkten to score [skɔ:]
Punktestand score [skɔ:]
pünktlich on time [ɒn 'taɪm]
Pute turkey ['tɜ:ki]
putzen to brush [brʌʃ]
Putzerstation cleaning station ['kli:nɪŋ ˌsteɪʃn]
Putzkraft cleaner ['kli:nə]
Puzzle puzzle ['pʌzl]

Q

Qualifikation qualification [ˌkwɒlɪfɪ'keɪʃn]
Qualle jellyfish, jellyfish *(pl)* ['dʒelifɪʃ]
Quallen-Schutzanzug stinger suit [ˌstɪŋə 'su:t]
quer durch across [ə'krɒs]
quietschen to creak [kri:k]
Quote quota ['kwəʊtə]

R

Radiergummi rubber ['rʌbə]
Radio radio ['reɪdiəʊ]
Radiosendung radio show ['reɪdiəʊ ˌʃəʊ]
Rallye rally ['ræli]
Ranch ranch [ræntʃ]
Rand edge [edʒ]
Ranger (park) ranger [ˌpɑ:k 'reɪndʒə]
Rap rap [ræp]
rappen to rap [ræp]
Rapper/Rapperin rapper ['ræpə]
Rasen grass [grɑ:s]
Rasierwasser aftershave ['ɑ:ftəʃeɪv]
Rasse race [reɪs]
Rassen- racial ['reɪʃl]
Rassentrennung segregation *(no pl)* [ˌsegrɪ'geɪʃn]
Rast rest [rest]
rasten to rest [rest]
Rastplatz rest area ['rest ˌeəriə]
Rat advice [əd'vaɪs]
raten to advise [əd'vaɪz]; to guess [ges]
Ratschlag advice [əd'vaɪs]
Rätsel mystery ['mɪstəri]; puzzle ['pʌzl]
rau tough [tʌf]
rauben to rob [rɒb]
Räuber/Räuberin robber ['rɒbə]
Rauch smoke [sməʊk]
rauchen to smoke [sməʊk]
Raum room [ru:m; rʊm]; space [speɪs]
Raumfähre shuttle ['ʃʌtl]
Raumpfleger/Raumpflegerin cleaner ['kli:nə]
Raumschiff spaceship ['speɪsʃɪp]
Razzia raid [reɪd]
R&B R&B [ˌɑ:r‿n'bi:]
Reaktion reaction [ri'ækʃn]; response [rɪ'spɒns]
Realität reality [ri'æləti]
Realityshow reality show [ri'æləti ˌʃəʊ]
Recherche research [rɪ'sɜ:tʃ]
Rechnung bill [bɪl]
Recht right [raɪt]; law [lɔ:]
Recht haben to be right [bi: 'raɪt]
rechter/rechte/rechtes right [raɪt]
rechtlich legal ['li:gl]
rechts on the right [ɒn ðə 'raɪt]; right [raɪt]
rechts abbiegen to turn right [tɜ:n 'raɪt]
Rechts- legal ['li:gl]
rechtswidrig illegal [ɪ'li:gl]
Rede speech [spi:tʃ]; talk [tɔ:k]
reden to talk [tɔ:k]
reden mit to talk to ['tɔ:k tə]
Referenz reference ['refrns]; *(Person)* referee [ˌrefr'i:]
Refrain chorus ['kɔ:rəs]; refrain [rɪ'freɪn]
Regal shelf, shelves *(pl)* [ʃelf; ʃelvz]
Regalbrett shelf, shelves *(pl)* [ʃelf; ʃelvz]
Regel rule [ru:l]
regelmäßig regular ['regjələ]
regeln *(ein Problem)* to sort out [sɔ:t‿'aʊt]
Regen rain [reɪn]
Regenguss shower ['ʃaʊə]
Regenschirm umbrella [ʌm'brelə]
Reggae reggae ['regeɪ]
Regie führen to direct [dɪ'rekt]
Regierung government ['gʌvnmənt]
Regisseur/Regisseurin director [dɪ'rektə]
registrieren to register ['redʒɪstə]
sich registrieren to register ['redʒɪstə]
Registrierung registration [ˌredʒɪ'streɪʃn]
regnen to rain [reɪn]
regnerisch rainy ['reɪni]
regulär regular ['regjələ]
reich rich [rɪtʃ]
Reihe row [rəʊ]
Reihenfolge order ['ɔ:də]
rein pristine ['prɪsti:n]
reinigen to clean [kli:n]
Reis rice [raɪs]
Reise journey ['dʒɜ:ni]; tour [tʊə]; trip [trɪp]; travel ['trævl]
Reisebus coach [kəʊtʃ]
reisen to travel ['trævl]
Reisepass passport ['pɑ:spɔ:t]
reiten to ride [raɪd]
Reiten horseback riding ['hɔ:sbæk ˌraɪdɪŋ]; riding ['raɪdɪŋ]
Religion religion [rɪ'lɪdʒn]
Religionsunterricht Religious Education (RE) [rɪˌlɪdʒəs‿edʒʊ'keɪʃn]

religiös religious [rɪ'lɪdʒəs]
rennen to run [rʌn]
Rennen race [reɪs]
reparieren to repair [rɪ'peə]; to fix [fɪks]
Reporter/Reporterin reporter [rɪ'pɔ:tə]
Reservat reservation [ˌrezə'veɪʃn]
reservieren to book [bʊk]
Reservierung reservation [ˌrezə'veɪʃn]
Resonanz reaction [ri'ækʃn]
Respekt respect [rɪ'spekt]
Respektlosigkeit disrespect [ˌdɪsrɪ'spekt]
Rest rest [rest]
Restaurant restaurant ['restrɒnt]
Restaurant mit Straßenverkauf takeaway ['teɪkəweɪ]
Resultat result [rɪ'zʌlt]
retten to rescue ['reskju:]; to save [seɪv]
Rettung rescue ['reskju:]
Rettungsschwimmer/Rettungsschwimmerin lifeguard ['laɪfgɑ:d]
Rezept recipe ['resɪpi:]
Rezeption reception [rɪ'sepʃn]
Richter judge [dʒʌdʒ]
richtig correct [kə'rekt]; right [raɪt]
richtig machen to get ... right [get ... 'raɪt]
in **Richtung** towards [tə'wɔ:dz]
riechen to smell [smel]
Riegel bar [bɑ:]
riesig huge [hju:dʒ]; large [lɑ:dʒ]
Riff reef [ri:f]
Rinderhirte cowboy ['kaʊbɔɪ]
Rindvieh cattle *(pl. only)* ['kætl]
Ring ring [rɪŋ]
riskieren to dare [deə]
etw. riskieren to take your chance [ˌteɪk jɔ: 'tʃɑ:ns]
Ritt ride [raɪd]
Ritter knight [naɪt]
Rivale/Rivalin rival ['raɪvl]
Robbe seal [si:l]
Roboter robot ['rəʊbɒt]
Rock skirt [skɜ:t]
rocken to rock [rɒk]
Rockmusik rock [rɒk]
Rodeo rodeo [rəʊ'deɪəʊ; 'rəʊdiəʊ]
roh raw [rɔ:]
Rolle role [rəʊl]; part [pɑ:t]
Roller kickboard ['kɪkbɔ:d]
rosa pink [pɪŋk]
rot red [red]
rot werden to go red [gəʊ 'red]
Rücken back [bæk]
rückenfrei backless ['bækləs]
Rucksack rucksack ['rʌksæk]
rückwärtig back [bæk]
rufen to call [kɔ:l]; to cry [kraɪ]; to shout [ʃaʊt]
rufen *(Eule)* to hoot [hu:t]
rhythmisch rufen to chant [tʃɑ:nt]
Rugby rugby ['rʌgbi]
Rugbyschuh rugby boot ['rʌgbi bu:t]
Ruhe quiet ['kwaɪət]; rest [rest]
jmdn. in Ruhe lassen to leave sb alone [ˌli:v‿ə'ləʊn]
ruhig calm [kɑ:m]; quiet ['kwaɪət]
rumhängen to hang around [ˌhæŋ‿ə'raʊnd]
Runde round [raʊnd]; run [rʌn]
Russe/Russin Russian ['rʌʃn]
russisch Russian ['rʌʃn]

S

Saal hall [hɔ:l]
Sache thing [θɪŋ]
Saft juice [dʒu:s]
sagen to say [seɪ]; to tell [tel]
Sahne cream [kri:m]
Saison season ['si:zn]
Salat salad ['sæləd]
Salz salt [sɔ:lt]
Salzwasser saltwater ['sɔ:ltˌwɔ:tə]
sammeln to collect [kə'lekt]
Samstag Saturday ['sætədeɪ]
Sand sand [sænd]
sandig sandy ['sændi]
Sandwich sandwich ['sænwɪdʒ]
sanft soft [sɒft]
Sänger/Sängerin singer ['sɪŋə]
Satellit satellite ['sætlaɪt]
sauber clean [kli:n]
säubern to clean [kli:n]
sauer sour ['saʊə]
Säugling baby, babies *(pl)* ['beɪbi; 'beɪbiz]
Schachtel box, boxes *(pl)* [bɒks; 'bɒksɪz]
Schaden harm [hɑ:m]
Schaf sheep, sheep *(pl)* [ʃi:p]
es allein **schaffen** to go it alone [ˌgeʊ‿ɪt‿ə'leʊn]
es schaffen to make it ['meɪk‿ɪt]
Schallplatte record ['rekɔ:d]
Schalter desk [desk]; switch [swɪtʃ]
scharf hot [hɒt]
Schatten shadow ['ʃædəʊ]; shade [ʃeɪd]
Schattierung shade [ʃeɪd]
Schatz *(Anrede)* dear [dɪə]
Schau show [ʃəʊ]
schauen to look [lʊk]; to have a look [ˌhæv‿ə 'lʊk]
schaukeln to rock [rɒk]
Schauplatz scene [si:n]
Schauspieler actor ['æktə]
Schauspielerin actress ['æktrəs]
Scheibe slice [slaɪs]
Schein slip [slɪp]
schenken to give [gɪv]
scherzen to joke [dʒəʊk]
Scheune barn [bɑ:n]
schicken to send [send]
per E-Mail schicken to e-mail ['i:meɪl]
schieben to push [pʊʃ]
Schiedsrichter/Schiedsrichterin ref(eree) [ˌrefr'i:]
schief gehen to go wrong [gəʊ 'rɒŋ]
schießen to shoot [ʃu:t]
Schiff boat [bəʊt]
Schifffahrt shipping ['ʃɪpɪŋ]
Schild sign [saɪn]
Schinken ham [hæm]
Schinkenspeck bacon ['beɪkn]
Schlaf sleep [sli:p]
schlafen to sleep [sli:p]; to be asleep [ˌbi:‿ə'sli:p]
schläfrig sleepy ['sli:pi]
Schlafsack sleeping bag ['sli:pɪŋ ˌbæg]
Schlafzimmer bedroom ['bedrʊm]
Schlag knock [nɒk]; shot [ʃɒt]
schlagen to bang [bæŋ]; to bat [bæt]; to hit [hɪt]; to knock [nɒk]
k.o. schlagen to knock out [nɒk‿'aʊt]
Schläger bat [bæt]
Schlagmann/Schlagfrau batter ['bætə]
Schlagzeile headline ['hedlaɪn]
Schlagzeug drums *(pl)* [drʌmz]
Schlagzeuger/Schlagzeugerin drummer ['drʌmə]
Schlange queue [kju:]; snake [sneɪk]
schlau smart [smɑ:t]
schlecht bad [bæd]; ill [ɪl]
schlechter worse [wɜ:s]
schlechtester/schlechteste/schlechtestes worst [wɜ:st]
schleichen to crawl [krɔ:l]

Schleiereule barn owl ['bɑːn‿əʊl]
schließen to close [kləʊz]
Schließfach locker ['lɒkə]
schließlich at last [ət 'lɑːst]; in the end [ɪn ðiː‿'end]
Schließung closing ['kləʊzɪŋ]
schlimmer worse [wɜːs]
schlimmster/schlimmste/schlimmstes worst [wɜːst]
Schlittschuhbahn ice rink ['aɪs rɪŋk]
Schloss castle ['kɑːsl]
Schlucht canyon ['kænjən]
schlürfen to sip [sɪp]
Schluss end [end]
zum Schluss in the end [ɪn ðiː‿'end]
Schlüssel key [kiː]
schmackhaft tasty ['teɪsti]; nutty ['nʌti]
schmecken to taste [teɪst]
Pizza schmeckt besser. Pizza is tastier. ['piːtsə ɪz ˌteɪstɪə]
Schmerz pain [peɪn]
Schminke make-up ['meɪkʌp]
Schmuck jewellery ['dʒuːəlri]
Schmuggler/Schmugglerin smuggler ['smʌglə]
Schmutz dirt [dɜːt]
schmutzig dirty ['dɜːti]
schnappen to grab [græb]
Schnappschuss snapshot ['snæpʃɒt]
Schnee snow [snəʊ]
schneiden to cut [kʌt]
schneien to snow [snəʊ]
schnell fast [fɑːst]; quick [kwɪk]
schnüffeln to sniff [snɪf]
schnuppern to sniff [snɪf]
Schnur string [strɪŋ]
schockiert shocked [ʃɒkt]
Schokolade chocolate ['tʃɒklət]
schön beautiful ['bjuːtɪfl]; fine [faɪn]; nice [naɪs]
schon already [ɔːl'redi]
High **School** *(weiterführende Schule in den USA, Oberstufe)* high school ['haɪ ˌskuːl]
schottisch Scottish ['skɒtɪʃ]
Schrank cupboard ['kʌbəd]
einen **Schrecken einjagen** to scare ['skeə]
schrecklich awful ['ɔːfl]; frightening ['fraɪtnɪŋ]; horrible ['hɒrəbl]; terrible ['terəbl]
Schrei cry [kraɪ]
schreiben to write [raɪt]
E-Mail schreiben to e-mail ['iːmeɪl]
Schreibtisch desk [desk]
schreien to cry [kraɪ]; to shout [ʃaʊt]
schreien *(Eule)* to hoot [huːt]
Schritt step [step]; footstep ['fʊtstep]; move [muːv]
schüchtern shy [ʃaɪ]
Schuh shoe [ʃuː]
den **Schulabschluss machen** to graduate ['grædjueɪt]
schulden to owe [əʊ]
Schule school [skuːl]
Schüler/Schülerin pupil ['pjuːpl]; student ['stjuːdnt]
Schulfach subject ['sʌbdʒɪkt]
Schulhof playground ['pleɪgraʊnd]
Schulklasse class [klɑːs]
Schulranzen school bag ['skuːl bæg]
Schultasche school bag ['skuːl bæg]
Schulter shoulder ['ʃəʊldə]
Schuppen shed [ʃed]
Schuss gunshot ['gʌnʃɒt]; shot [ʃɒt]
Schüssel bowl [bəʊl]
Schusswaffe gun [gʌn]
schütteln to shake [ʃeɪk]
Quallen-**Schutzanzug** stinger suit [ˌstɪŋə 'suːt]
schützen to protect [prə'tekt]
schwach weak [wiːk]
schwach werden to go weak [gəʊ 'wiːk]
Schwamm sponge [spʌndʒ]
schwarz black [blæk]
Schwarzer/Schwarze Black [blæk]
Schwein pig [pɪg]
Schweinefleisch pork [pɔːk]
schwenken to wave [weɪv]
schwer heavy ['hevi]
Schwester sister ['sɪstə]
schwierig difficult ['dɪfɪklt]; hard [hɑːd]
Schwierigkeit problem ['prɒbləm]
Schwimmbad swimming pool ['swɪmɪŋ ˌpuːl]
Schwimmbecken swimming pool ['swɪmɪŋ ˌpuːl]
schwimmen to swim [swɪm]
Schwimmer/Schwimmerin swimmer ['swɪmə]
Schwimmflosse fin [fɪn]
Schwimmreifen rubber ring [ˌrʌbə 'rɪŋ]
schwindlig dizzy ['dɪzi]
Sciencefiction science fiction [ˌsaɪəns 'fɪkʃn]
Scone *(Gebäck)* scone [skɒn]
Screenshot screen shot ['skriːn ˌʃɒt]
See lake [leɪk]
Seehund seal [siːl]
seekrank seasick ['siːsɪk]
Seele soul [səʊl]
Seelöwe sea lion ['siː ˌlaɪən]
Seewespe sea wasp ['siː ˌwɒsp]
segeln to sail [seɪl]
sehen to see [siː]; to look [lʊk]
Sehenswürdigkeit sight [saɪt]
sehr very ['veri]
Seife soap [səʊp]
Seifenoper soap [səʊp]
sein to be [biː]
an der Reihe sein to be on [biː‿'ɒn]
an sein to be on [biː‿'ɒn]
sein his [hɪz]; its [ɪts]
seit for [fɔː]; since [sɪnts]
seitdem since [sɪnts]
Seite side [saɪd]; page [peɪdʒ]
Sekretär/Sekretärin secretary ['sekrətri]
Sekunde second ['seknd]
(ich) **selbst** myself [maɪ'self]
Selbstständigkeit self-employment [ˌselfɪm'plɔɪmənt]
selbstverständlich of course [əv 'kɔːs]
selten seldom ['seldəm]
seltsam strange [streɪndʒ]
Sendung programme ['prəʊgræm]; show [ʃəʊ]
auf Sendung on the air [ˌɒn ði‿'eə]
September September [sep'tembə]
Serie series, series *(pl)* ['sɪəriːz]
Service service ['sɜːvɪs]
sich **setzen** to sit down [sɪt 'daʊn]
sich setzen zu to sit with ['sɪt wɪθ]
Shorts shorts *(pl)* [ʃɔːts]
Show show [ʃəʊ]
sicher safe [seɪf]; sure [ʃʊə]; certainly ['sɜːtnli]
sichergehen to make sure [meɪk 'ʃʊə]
sicherstellen to assure [ə'ʃʊə]; to guarantee [ˌgærn'tiː]
Sicherungskasten fuse-box ['fjuːzbɒks]
Sicht sight [saɪt]; view [vjuː]
sie she [ʃiː]; her [hɜː]
sie *(Mehrzahl)* they [ðeɪ]; them [ðem]
Sie *(Anrede)* mister ['mɪstə]
Siegel label ['leɪbl]
siegen to win [wɪn]
Sieger/Siegerin winner ['wɪnə]
Siegtreffer winning goal ['wɪnɪŋ gəʊl]

German – English

Signal signal ['sɪgnl]
simsen to text [tekst]
singen to sing [sɪŋ]; to chant [tʃɑ:nt]
sinken *(beim Tauchen)* to drop [drɒp]
Sinn sense [sens]
Sinnbild symbol ['sɪmbl]
Sintflut flash flood ['flæʃ ˌflʌd]
Sirup syrup ['sɪrəp]
Situation situation [ˌsɪtju'eɪʃn]
Situationskomödie sitcom ['sɪtkɒm]
Sitz seat [si:t]
sitzen to sit [sɪt]
in der Falle sitzen to be trapped [bi: 'træpt]
Sitzplatz seat [si:t]
Skateboard skateboard ['skeɪtbɔ:d]
skaten to skate [skeɪt]
Skifahren skiing ['ski:ɪŋ]
Sklave/Sklavin slave [sleɪv]
Sklaverei slavery ['sleɪvri]
SMS text message ['tekst ˌmesɪdʒ]
Snack snack [snæk]
Snowboarden snowboarding ['snəʊbɔ:dɪŋ]
so so [səʊ]
so (schlimm) that (bad) ['ðæt bæd]
so … wie … as … as [æz … æz; əz … əz]
Sofa sofa ['səʊfə]
sofort at once [ət 'wʌnts]; right away [raɪt‿ə'weɪ]
sogar even ['i:vn]
Sohn son [sʌn]
solange wie as long as [əz 'lɒŋ‿əz]
solar solar ['səʊlə]
Solar- solar ['səʊlə]
solch such [sʌtʃ]
sollte/sollten should [ʃʊd]
solo solo ['səʊləʊ]
Solo- solo ['səʊləʊ]
Sommer summer ['sʌmə]
Sommerfest summer fair ['sʌmə ˌfeə]
Sonne sun [sʌn]
Sonnen- solar ['səʊlə]
Sonnenbräune suntan ['sʌntæn]
Sonnenkollektor solar panel [ˌsəʊlə 'pænl]
Sonnensystem solar system ['səʊlə ˌsɪstəm]
sonnig sunny ['sʌni]
Sonntag Sunday ['sʌndeɪ]
sonst else [els]
sich **Sorgen machen** to worry ['wʌri]
sorgfältig careful ['keəfl]

Sorte kind [kaɪnd]; type [taɪp]
Soulmusik soul [səʊl]
Souvenir souvenir [ˌsu:və'nɪə]
Spa spa [spɑ:]
Spaghetti spaghetti [spə'geti]
spanisch Spanish ['spænɪʃ]
Spanisch Spanish ['spænɪʃ]
spannend exciting [ɪk'saɪtɪŋ]
Spannung suspense [sə'spents]
sparen to save [seɪv]
Sparschwein piggy bank ['pɪgi bæŋk]
Spaß fun [fʌn]
Spaß haben to have fun [ˌhæv 'fʌn]
Spaß machen to be fun [bi: 'fʌn]
Viel Spaß! Have fun! [ˌhæv 'fʌn]
spät late [leɪt]
zu spät late [leɪt]
spazieren gehen to go for a walk [ˌgəʊ fər‿ə 'wɔ:k]
Spaziergang walk [wɔ:k]
Speisekarte menu ['menju:]
Speisesaal dining room ['daɪnɪŋ rʊm]
spektakulär spectacular [spek'tækjələ]
Sperre ban [bæn]
Spezialität special ['speʃl]
speziell special ['speʃl]
Spiegelei sunny side up [ˌsʌni saɪd‿'ʌp]
Spiel game [geɪm]; match [mætʃ]; play [pleɪ]
spielen to play [pleɪ]; *(Theater)* to act [ækt]
Spieler/Spielerin player ['pleɪə]
Spielfeld court [kɔ:t]; pitch [pɪtʃ]
Spielplatz playground ['pleɪgraʊnd]
Spielstand score [skɔ:]
Spielzeug toy [tɔɪ]
Spinne spider ['spaɪdə]
Spitze top [tɒp]
Spitzname nickname ['nɪkneɪm]
Sport sport [spɔ:t]
Sport *(Schulfach)* Physical Education (PE) [ˌfɪzɪkl‿edʒʊ'keɪʃn]
Sport treiben to do sports [du: 'spɔ:ts]; to exercise ['eksəsaɪz]
Sportfest sports day ['spɔ:ts deɪ]
Sportgeschäft sports shop ['spɔ:ts ʃɒp]
sportlich sporty ['spɔ:ti]
Sportplatz sports field ['spɔ:ts fi:ld]
Sportzeug PE kit [ˌpi:‿'i: kɪt]
Sprache language ['læŋgwɪdʒ]; speech [spi:tʃ]
sprechen to say [seɪ]; to speak [spi:k]; to talk [tɔ:k]
sprechen mit to talk to ['tɔ:k tə]

Sprechen speech [spi:tʃ]
Sprecher/Sprecherin speaker ['spi:kə]
springen to jump [dʒʌmp]
sprühen to spray [spreɪ]
Spülbecken sink [sɪŋk]
Square Dance square dance ['skweə ˌdɑ:nts]
Staat state [steɪt]
staatlich state [steɪt]
staatliche Schule (USA) public school [ˌpʌblɪk 'sku:l]
Staats- civil ['sɪvl]
Staatsbürger/Staatsbürgerin citizen ['sɪtɪzn]
Stadion stadium ['steɪdiəm]; arena [ə'ri:nə]
Stadt city ['sɪti]; town [taʊn]
Stadtplan map [mæp]
Stadtteil borough ['bʌrə]
Stamm tribe [traɪb]
Stammkunde/Stammkundin regular ['regjələ]
Stand stand [stænd]; stall [stɔ:l]
Standbesitzer/Standbesitzerin stall holder ['stɔ:l ˌhəʊldə]
Standbild statue ['stætʃu:]
Standfoto still (picture) ['stɪl ˌpɪktʃə]
ständig always ['ɔ:lweɪz]
Stange bar [bɑ:]
Star star [stɑ:]
stark strong [strɒŋ]; hard [hɑ:d]
Stärke power ['paʊə]
Start start [stɑ:t]; launch [lɔ:nʃ]
starten to start [stɑ:t]; to take off [ˌteɪk‿'ɒf]; to launch [lɔ:nʃ]
Station station ['steɪʃn]; base [beɪs]
stattfinden to take place [teɪk 'pleɪs]
Statue statue ['stætʃu:]
Stau traffic jam ['træfɪk ˌdʒæm]
staubig dusty ['dʌsti]
stechen to sting [stɪŋ]
Steckbrief profile ['prəʊfaɪl]
Steckdose socket ['sɒkɪt]
Stecker plug [plʌg]
Steelband *(Band, deren Instrumente aus leeren Ölfässern bestehen)* steel band [ˌsti:l 'bænd]
stehen to stand [stænd]
im Weg stehen to get in the way (of) [ˌget‿ɪn‿ðə‿'weɪ]
stehlen to steal [sti:l]
steigen to climb ['klaɪm]; to rise [raɪz]
Stein stone [stəʊn]; rock [rɒk]
Stelle place [pleɪs]

stellen *(Uhr)* to set [set]
Stellenangebot vacancy ['veɪknsi]
sterben to die [daɪ]
Stern star [stɑː]
Sternwarte observatory [əb'zɜːvətri]
Stich bite [baɪt]
Stiefel boot [buːt]
Stiefvater stepdad ['stepdæd]
Stil style [staɪl]
still quiet ['kwaɪət]; silent ['saɪlənt]
Stille quiet ['kwaɪət]
Stimme voice [vɔɪs]
Stimmung mood [muːd]; spirit ['spɪrɪt]
stinken to stink [stɪŋk]
Stock stick [stɪk]
im oberen **Stock** upstairs [ʌp'steəz]
im unteren Stock downstairs [daʊn'steəz]
Stoff material [mə'tɪəriəl]
stöhnen to moan [məʊn]
Stollenschuh rugby boot ['rʌgbi buːt]
stolz auf proud of ['praʊd‿əv]
Stolz pride [praɪd]
Stöpsel plug [plʌg]
stören to disturb [dɪ'stɜːb]
stoßen to push [pʊʃ]; to knock [nɒk]
stoßen gegen to run into [rʌn‿'ɪntə]
Strafe sentence ['sentənts]
Sträfling convict ['kɒnvɪkt]
Strand beach [biːtʃ]
Straße street [striːt]; road [rəʊd]
Strauch bush [bʊʃ]
Streich trick [trɪk]
streichen to paint [peɪnt]
streiten to argue ['ɑːgjuː]; to fight [faɪt]
sich streiten to have an argument [ˌhæv‿ən‿'ɑːgjəmənt]
streng strict [strɪkt]
Stress stress [stres]
strikt strict [strɪkt]
Strom current ['kʌrnt]; electricity [ˌelɪk'trɪsəti]
Stromausfall blackout *(AE)* ['blækaʊt]
Strömung current ['kʌrnt]
Strömung, die nach oben zieht up current ['ʌp ˌkʌrnt]
Strophe verse [vɜːs]
Strumpfhose tights *(pl)* [taɪts]
Stück piece [piːs]; bar [bɑː]
Stückchen bit [bɪt]
Student/Studentin student ['stjuːdnt]
studieren to study ['stʌdi]
Studio studio ['stjuːdiəʊ]
Studium studies *(pl)* ['stʌdiz]
Stufe step [step]
Stuhl chair [tʃeə]
Stummfilm silent movie [ˌsaɪlənt 'muːvi]
Stunde hour ['aʊə]
eine halbe Stunde half an hour [ˌhɑːf‿ən‿'aʊə]
stundenlang for hours [fər‿'aʊəz]
Stundenplan curriculum [kə'rɪkjələm]; timetable ['taɪmteɪbl]
Sturm storm [stɔːm]
stürmisch stormy ['stɔːmi]
Sturz fall [fɔːl]
suchen nach to look for ['lʊk fə]
Süden south [saʊθ]
Südwesten southwest [ˌsaʊθ'west]
Superlativ superlative [suː'pɜːlətɪv]
Supermarkt supermarket ['suːpəˌmɑːkɪt]
Suppe soup [suːp]
Surfbrett surfboard ['sɜːfbɔːd]
surfen to surf [sɜːf]
im Internet surfen to surf the Internet [ˌsɜːf ði‿'ɪntənet]
Surfen surfing ['sɜːfɪŋ]
Surfer/Surferin surfer ['sɜːfə]
süß sweet [swiːt]; cute [kjuːt]
Süßigkeit sweet [swiːt]
Sweatshirt sweatshirt ['swetʃɜːt]
Symbol symbol ['sɪmbl]
System system ['sɪstəm]
Szene scene [siːn]

T

Tabak tobacco [tə'bækəʊ]
Tabelle grid [grɪd]
Tafel bar [bɑː]; board [bɔːd]; panel ['pænl]
Tag day [deɪ]
Einen schönen Tag. Have a nice day. [ˌhæv‿ə naɪs 'deɪ]
Einen schönen Tag noch. Have a nice day. [ˌhæv‿ə naɪs 'deɪ]
eines Tages one day [wʌn 'deɪ]
Tagesanbruch dawn [dɔːn]
Tagesfahrkarte day travel card [ˌdeɪ 'trævl ˌkɑːd]
täglich daily ['deɪli]
Talent talent ['tælənt]
Talkmaster host [həʊst]
Talkshow talk show ['tɔːk ˌʃəʊ]
Tante aunt [ɑːnt]
Tanz dance [dɑːnts]
tanzen to dance [dɑːnts]
Breakdance tanzen to break-dance ['breɪkdɑːnts]
Tanzen dancing ['dɑːntsɪŋ]
Tanzfläche dance floor ['dɑːnts flɔː]
tapfer brave [breɪv]
Tasche bag [bæg]
Taschendieb/Taschendiebin pickpocket ['pɪkˌpɒkɪt]
Taschengeld pocket money ['pɒkɪt ˌmʌni]
Taschenlampe torch, torches *(pl)* [tɔːtʃ; 'tɔːtʃɪz]
Taschenmesser penknife, penknives *(pl)* ['pennaɪf; 'pennaɪvz]
Tasse cup [kʌp]
tasten nach to feel for ['fiːl fə]
in der **Tat** in fact [ɪn 'fækt]
Tätowierung tattoo [tæt'uː]
Tatsache fact [fækt]
Tauch- dive [daɪv]; diving ['daɪvɪŋ]
Tauchbegleiter/Tauchbegleiterin buddy *(infml)* ['bʌdi]
tauchen to dive [daɪv]
Tauchen diving ['daɪvɪŋ]; diving ['daɪvɪŋ]
Taucher/Taucherin diver ['daɪvə]
Taucheranzug wetsuit ['wetsuːt]
Tauchgang dive [daɪv]
Tauchzentrum dive centre ['daɪv ˌsentə]
Tausch exchange [ɪks'tʃeɪndʒ]; swap [swɒp]
tauschen to change [tʃeɪndʒ]; to swap [swɒp]
tausend thousand ['θaʊznd]
Taxi taxi ['tæksi]
Team team [tiːm]
Technik Technology [tek'nɒlədʒi]
technisch technical ['teknɪkl]
Tee tea [tiː]
Teenager teenager ['tiːnˌeɪdʒə]
Teil part [pɑːt]; bit [bɪt]
teilen to share [ʃeə]
teilnehmen an to take part in [teɪk 'pɑːt‿ɪn]
Teilzeit- part-time (P/T) [ˌpɑːt'taɪm]
Telefon phone [fəʊn]
telefonieren to phone [fəʊn]
Telefonnummer phone number ['fəʊn ˌnʌmbə]
Telefonzelle phone box ['fəʊn ˌbɒks]
Teller plate [pleɪt]
Temperatur temperature ['temprətʃə]

temporär temporary ['temprəri]
Tennis tennis ['tenɪs]
Teppichboden carpet ['kɑ:pɪt]
Test test [test]
testen to test [test]
teuer expensive [ɪk'spensɪv]
Textnachricht (SMS) schicken to text [tekst]
Theater theater *(AE)* ['θɪətə]
Theaterstück play [pleɪ]
Thema subject ['sʌbdʒɪkt]; topic ['tɒpɪk]
Thriller thriller ['θrɪlə]
Ticket ticket ['tɪkɪt]
tief deep [di:p]; low [ləʊ]
Tier animal ['ænɪml]
Tierpark zoo [zu:]
Tierpfleger/Tierpflegerin zookeeper ['zu:ki:pə]
Tiger tiger ['taɪgə]
Tipp tip [tɪp]
Tisch table ['teɪbl]
den Tisch decken to set the table [ˌset ðə 'teɪbl]
Tischtennis table-tennis ['teɪblˌtenɪs]
Titel title ['taɪtl]
Titelseite cover ['kʌvə]
Toast toast [təʊst]
Tochter daughter ['dɔ:tə]
Tod death [deθ]
Todesfall death [deθ]
tödlich deadly ['dedli]
Toilette toilet ['tɔɪlɪt]
toll awesome ['ɔ:səm]; brilliant ['brɪljənt]; great [greɪt]; hot [hɒt]
tollpatschig clumsy ['klʌmzi]
Tomate tomato, tomatoes *(pl)* [tə'mɑ:təʊ; tə'mɑ:təʊz]
Ton sound [saʊnd]
Tonfilm talkie ['tɔ:ki]
Topf pot [pɒt]
Tor gate [geɪt]; goal [gəʊl]
ein Tor schießen to score [skɔ:]
Torwart goalkeeper ['gəʊlˌki:pə]
tot dead [ded]
töten to kill [kɪl]
Tour tour [tʊə]
Tourist/Touristin tourist ['tʊərɪst]
Tradition tradition [trə'dɪʃn]
tragen to carry ['kæri]
trainieren to train [treɪn]
Training training ['treɪnɪŋ]; practice ['præktɪs]
Traktor tractor ['træktə]
Träne tear [tɪə]
Transport transport ['trænspɔ:t]
transportieren to transport [træn'spɔ:t]
Traum dream [dri:m]
träumen to dream [dri:m]
traurig sad [sæd]
treffen to hit [hɪt]; to meet [mi:t]
sich treffen to meet [mi:t]
Treffen meeting ['mi:tɪŋ]
Treibhausgas greenhouse gas [ˌgri:nhaʊs 'gæs]
Treibstoff fuel ['fju:əl]
Treppe stairs *(pl)* [steəz]
die Treppe hinaufrennen to run upstairs [ˌrʌn‿ʌp'steəz]
treten to kick [kɪk]
Treue allegiance [ə'li:dʒns]
Tribüne platform ['plætfɔ:m]; stand [stænd]
Trick trick [trɪk]
trinken to drink [drɪŋk]
schluckweise trinken to sip [sɪp]
Trinkgeld tip [tɪp]
trocknen to dry [draɪ]
Trödelstand white elephant stall [ˌwaɪt 'elɪfənt stɔ:l]
tröpfeln to drip [drɪp]
tropfen (lassen) to drip [drɪp]
Trottel jerk *(slang)* [dʒɜ:k]
trotzdem though [ðəʊ]
Truck truck *(AE)* [trʌk]
Trucker trucker *(AE)* ['trʌkə]
Truthahn turkey ['tɜ:ki]
tschüss bye [baɪ]
T-Shirt T-shirt ['ti:ʃɜ:t]
tun to do [du:]; to make [meɪk]
Tunnel tunnel ['tʌnl]
Tür door [dɔ:]
türkisch Turkish ['tɜ:kɪʃ]
Türklingel doorbell ['dɔ:bel]
Turm tower ['taʊə]
Turnhalle gym [dʒɪm]
Turnier competition [ˌkɒmpə'tɪʃn]
Turnschuhe trainers ['treɪnəz]
Türstufe doorstep ['dɔ:step]
Tüte bag [bæg]
Typ type [taɪp]; bloke [bləʊk]; guy [gaɪ]
typisch typical ['tɪpɪkl]

U

U-Bahn underground ['ʌndəgraʊnd]
Übelkeit verspüren to feel sick [fi:l 'sɪk]
üben to exercise ['eksəsaɪz]; to practise ['præktɪs]
über above [ə'bʌv]; across [ə'krɒs]; over ['əʊvə]; about [ə'baʊt]
überall all over [ˌɔ:l‿'əʊvə]; anywhere ['eniweə]; everywhere ['evriweə]
Übereinkunft deal [di:l]
überleben to survive [sə'vaɪv]
Überleben survival [sə'vaɪvl]
überprüfen to check [tʃek]
Überprüfung check [tʃek]
überqueren to cross [krɒs]
überraschend surprising [sə'praɪzɪŋ]
überrascht surprised [sə'praɪzd]
Überschrift title ['taɪtl]; headline ['hedlaɪn]
Überschwemmung flood [flʌd]
flutartige Überschwemmung flash flood ['flæʃ ˌflʌd]
übertreiben to overdo [ˌəʊvə'du:]
überwachen to monitor ['mɒnɪtə]
übrig left [left]
übrigens by the way [ˌbaɪ ðə 'weɪ]
Übung exercise ['eksəsaɪz]
Übungsheft exercise book ['eksəsaɪz ˌbʊk]
Uhr clock [klɒk]
Uhr *(Zeitangabe)* o'clock [ə'klɒk]
Um wie viel Uhr …? What time … ? [wɒt 'taɪm]
Wie viel Uhr ist es, bitte? What's the time, please? [ˌwɒts ðə 'taɪm ˌpli:z]
umdrehen to turn over [ˌtɜ:n‿'əʊvə]; to turn round [tɜ:n 'raʊnd]
sich umdrehen to turn [tɜ:n]; to turn over [ˌtɜ:n‿'əʊvə]; to turn round [tɜ:n 'raʊnd]
Umfrage survey ['sɜ:veɪ]
Umgebung environment [ɪn'vaɪərnmənt]
umhauen to knock out [nɒk‿'aʊt]
umher around [ə'raʊnd]
umkehren to turn back [tɜ:n 'bæk]
Umsatz turnover ['tɜ:nˌəʊvə]
Umschlag envelope ['envələʊp]
sich **umsehen** to look round [lʊk 'raʊnd]
umsonst free [fri:]
umsteigen to change [tʃeɪndʒ]
Umwelt environment [ɪn'vaɪərnmənt]
die Umwelt betreffend environmental [ɪnˌvaɪərn'mentl]
Umwelt- eco [i:kəʊ]; environmental [ɪnˌvaɪərn'mentl]

umweltbedingt environmental [ɪnˌvaɪərn'mentl]
Umweltverschmutzung pollution [pə'lu:ʃn]
umziehen to move [mu:v]
Umzug parade [pə'reɪd]
unabhängig independent [ˌɪndɪ'pendənt]
und and [ænd]
unerlässlich vital ['vaɪtl]
Unfähigkeit disability [ˌdɪsə'bɪləti]
Unfall accident ['æksɪdnt]; crash [kræʃ]
unfreundlich unfriendly [ʌn'frendli]
ungefähr about [ə'baʊt]; around [ə'raʊnd]
ungeschickt clumsy ['klʌmzi]
ungesund unhealthy [ʌn'helθi]
unglücklich unhappy [ʌn'hæpi]
unheimlich scary ['skeəri]; spooky ['spu:ki]
Uniform uniform ['ju:nɪfɔ:m]
Union union ['ju:njən]
Universität university [ˌju:nɪ'vɜ:səti]
Universum universe ['ju:nɪvɜ:s]
unordentlich messy ['mesi]
Unordnung mess [mes]
Unrecht haben to be wrong [bi: 'rɒŋ]
unrechtmäßig illegal [ɪ'li:gl]
Unruhe riot [raɪət]
uns us [ʌs]
unser/unsere our ['aʊə]
Unsinn rubbish ['rʌbɪʃ]
unten down [daʊn]; below [bɪ'ləʊ]; at the bottom [ət ðə 'bɒtəm]; downstairs [daʊn'steəz]
nach unten down [daʊn]
unter under ['ʌndə]
ohne **Unterbrechung** non-stop [ˌnɒn'stɒp]
Unterdrückung oppression [ə'preʃn]
Unterführung tunnel ['tʌnl]
Untergeschoss basement ['beɪsmənt]
unterhalb below [bɪ'ləʊ]
sich **unterhalten** to chat [tʃæt]
Unterhaltung chat [tʃæt]
Unternehmen firm [fɜ:m]; organisation [ˌɔ:gnaɪ'zeɪʃn]
unternehmungslustig enterprising ['entəpraɪzɪŋ]
Unterricht class [klɑ:s]
unterrichten to teach [ti:tʃ]
Unterrichtsstunde lesson ['lesn]; period *(AE)* ['pɪəriəd]
Unterschied difference ['dɪfrns]
unterschreiben to sign [saɪn]
unterstreichen to underline [ˌʌndə'laɪn]
unterstützen to support [sə'pɔ:t]
untersuchen to check [tʃek]
Untersuchung research [rɪ'sɜ:tʃ]
Unterwasser- underwater [ˌʌndə'wɔ:tə]
Ureinwohner/Ureinwohnerin Australiens Aborigine [ˌæbə'rɪdʒni]
Ureinwohner/Ureinwohnerin Amerikas Native American [ˌneɪtɪv‿ə'merɪkən]
Urkunde certificate [sə'tɪfɪkət]
Urlaub holiday(s) ['hɒlədeɪ(z)]; vacation *(AE)* [və'keɪʃn]
Urteil sentence ['sentənts]
usw. etc. [ɪt'setrə]

V

Vater father ['fɑ:ðə]
Vati dad [dæd]
sich **verabreden** to date [deɪt]
Verabredung date [deɪt]
Verachtung disrespect [ˌdɪsrɪ'spekt]
verändern to change [tʃeɪndʒ]
verängstigt scared [skeəd]
jmdn. **veranlassen, etw. zu tun** to make sb do sth [meɪk]
veranstalten to hold [həʊld]
Veranstalter/Veranstalterin organizer ['ɔ:gənaɪzə]
Veranstaltung event [ɪ'vent]; session ['seʃn]
verärgert angry ['æŋgri]
verbannen to ban [bæn]
verbieten to ban [bæn]
verbinden to join [dʒɔɪn]; to link [lɪŋk]
Verbindung link [lɪŋk]
sich in Verbindung setzen mit to contact ['kɒntækt]
Verbot ban [bæn]
Verbrechen crime [kraɪm]
Verbrecher/Verbrecherin criminal ['krɪmɪnl]; gangster ['gæŋkstə]
verbrennen to burn [bɜ:n]
verbringen to spend [spend]
verdammt bloody ['blʌdi]; damn [dæm]
verdanken to owe [əʊ]
verdienen to earn [ɜ:n]; to deserve [dɪ'zɜ:v]
Verein club [klʌb]; society [sə'saɪəti]
Vereinigung union ['ju:njən]
verfehlen to miss [mɪs]
Vergangenheit past [pɑ:st]
vergessen to forget [fə'get]
vergleichen to compare [kəm'peə]
verhaften to arrest [ə'rest]
sich **verhalten** to act [ækt]
verheiratet mit married to ['mærid tə]
etw. verhindern to get in the way (of) [ˌget‿ɪn‿ðə‿'weɪ]
sich verirren to get lost [get 'lɒst]
sich verirrt haben to be lost [bi: 'lɒst]
verkaufen to sell [sel]
Verkäufer/Verkäuferin shop assistant ['ʃɒp‿əˌsɪstnt]
Verkaufsgespräch sales talk ['seɪlz tɔ:k]
Verkehr traffic ['træfɪk]
Verkehrsmittel transport *(no pl.)* ['trænspɔ:t]
verklappen to dump sb [dʌmp]
verknüpfen to link [lɪŋk]
Verknüpfung link [lɪŋk]
verlassen to leave [li:v]
verleihen to loan [ləʊn]; to present [prɪ'zent]
verletzen to hurt [hɜ:t]
verletzt hurt [hɜ:t]
Verletzung harm [hɑ:m]
verlieren to lose [lu:z]
verloren gehen to get lost [get 'lɒst]
vermissen to miss [mɪs]
vermuten to guess [ges]
vernünftig intelligent [ɪn'telɪdʒnt]; sensible ['sensɪbl]
verpassen to miss [mɪs]
Verpflegung catering ['keɪtrɪŋ]
verregnet rainy ['reɪni]
verrückt crazy ['kreɪzi]; mad [mæd]
verrückt machen to drive crazy [draɪv 'kreɪzi]
verrückt nach … sein to be nuts about [bi: ˌnʌts‿ə'baʊt]
verrückt werden to go bananas [ˌgəʊ bə'nɑ:nəz]
Vers verse [vɜ:s]
Versammlung assembly [ə'sembli]; rally ['ræli]
verschieden different ['dɪfrnt]
verschiedene several ['sevrl]
Verschiffung shipping ['ʃɪpɪŋ]
verschlafen sleepy ['sli:pi]
Verschluss shutter ['ʃʌtə]
Verschlüsselung code [kəʊd]
Verschmutzung pollution [pə'lu:ʃn]
verschneit snowy ['snəʊi]

verschwenden to waste [weɪst]
Verschwendung waste [weɪst]
verschwinden to disappear [ˌdɪsəˈpɪə]
versichern to assure [əˈʃʊə]
Versicherung insurance [ɪnˈʃʊərns]
verspätet late [leɪt]; delayed [dɪˈleɪd]
versprechen to promise [ˈprɒmɪs]
Verstand mind [maɪnd]
Verständigung communication [kəˌmjuːnɪˈkeɪʃn]
verstecken to hide [haɪd]
  sich verstecken to hide [haɪd]
verstehen to understand [ˌʌndəˈstænd]
  etwas verstehen to get it [ˈget‿ɪt]
versteinert fossil [ˈfɒsl]
Versuch attempt [əˈtempt]; experiment [ɪkˈsperɪmənt]
versuchen to try [traɪ]
Vertrag contract [ˈkɒntrækt]
vertrauen to trust [trʌst]
Vertreter/Vertreterin agent [ˈeɪdʒnt]
verursachen to cause [kɔːz]
Verurteilung sentence [ˈsentənts]
vervollständigen to complete [kəmˈpliːt]
Verweis reference [ˈrefrns]
verwenden to use [juːz]
verzeichnet on record [ɒn ˈrekɔːd]
verzögert delayed [dɪˈleɪd]
Video video [ˈvɪdiəʊ]
Vieh cattle *(pl. only)* [ˈkætl]
Viehtrieb cattle drive [ˈkætl ˌdraɪv]
viel a lot [ə ˈlɒt]; much [mʌtʃ]
  viel/viele a lot of [ə ˈlɒt‿əv]; lots (of) [ˈlɒts‿əv]
  Viel Glück! Good luck! [ˌgʊd ˈlʌk]
viele many [ˈmeni]
vielleicht maybe [ˈmeɪbi]
Viertel neighborhood *(AE)* [ˈneɪbəhʊd]; quarter [ˈkwɔːtə]
  Viertel nach quarter past [ˈkwɔːtə pɑːst]
  Viertel vor quarter to [ˈkwɔːtə tə]
Vierteldollar *(Währung)* quarter [ˈkwɔːtə]
violett purple [ˈpɜːpl]
virtuell virtual [ˈvɜːtʃuəl]
Vogel bird [bɜːd]
Volksmusik folk [fəʊk]
Volksstamm tribe [traɪb]
voll (von) full (of) [fʊl]
Volleyball volleyball [ˈvɒlibɔːl]
vollkommen perfect [ˈpɜːfɪkt]
Vollzeit- full-time (F/T) [ˌfʊlˈtaɪm]

von from [frɒm]; of [ɒv; əv]; by [baɪ]; in [ɪn]
vor before [bɪˈfɔː]; in front of [ɪn ˈfrʌnt‿əv]
  vor *(zeitlich)* ago [əˈgəʊ]
vorbei over [ˈəʊvə]; past [pɑːst]
vorbereiten to prepare [prɪˈpeə]
  sich vorbereiten to get ready [get ˈredi]
Vordergrund foreground [ˈfɔːgraʊnd]
Vorderseite front [frʌnt]
Vorhang curtain [ˈkɜːtn]
Vorhersage *(Wetter)* forecast [ˈfɔːkɑːst]
vorhersagen *(Wetter)* to forecast [ˈfɔːkɑːst]
Vormittag morning [ˈmɔːnɪŋ]
vormittags in the morning [ˌɪn ðə ˈmɔːnɪŋ]
  vormittags *(Uhrzeit)* a.m. [ˌeɪˈem]
vorne at the front [ət ðə ˈfrʌnt]
Vorort suburb [ˈsʌbɜːb]
Vorschrift rule [ruːl]
Vorsicht caution *(no pl)* [ˈkɔːʃn]
vorsichtig careful [ˈkeəfl]
Vorsingen audition [ɔːˈdɪʃn]
Vorspeise starter [ˈstɑːtə]
Vorsprechen audition [ɔːˈdɪʃn]
sich (etwas) **vorstellen** to imagine [ɪˈmædʒɪn]
Vorstellung performance [pəˈfɔːməns]
Vortanzen audition [ɔːˈdɪʃn]
Vor- und Nachteile pros and cons [ˌprəʊz‿ənd ˈkɒnz]
Vortrag talk [tɔːk]
vorüber over [ˈəʊvə]; past [pɑːst]
vorübergehen to pass [pɑːs]
vorübergehend temporary [ˈtemprəri]

W

wachsen to rise [raɪz]; to grow [grəʊ]
  wachsen lassen to grow [grəʊ]
Waffe weapon [ˈwepən]
wagen to dare [deə]
  etw. wagen to take your chance [ˌteɪk jɔː ˈtʃɑːns]
Wahl choice [tʃɔɪs]
wählen to choose [tʃuːz]; to vote [vəʊt]
wahr true [truː]
während as [æz; əz]; while [waɪl]
  während *(+ Nomen)* during *(+ noun)* [ˈdjʊərɪŋ]
wahrscheinlich probably [ˈprɒbəbli]

Waliser/Waliserin Welsh [welʃ]
walisisch Welsh [welʃ]
Wand wall [wɔːl]
Wandmalerei mural [ˈmjʊərl]
Wandtafel board [bɔːd]
wann when [wen]
Ware product [ˈprɒdʌkt]
Waren goods *(pl)* [gʊdz]
warm warm [wɔːm]
Warn- warning [ˈwɔːnɪŋ]
warnen to warn [wɔːn]
Warnung warning [ˈwɔːnɪŋ]; caution *(no pl)* [ˈkɔːʃn]
warten to wait [weɪt]
  Warte mal! Hang on! [ˈhæŋ‿ɒn]
  warten auf to wait for [ˈweɪt fɔː]
Wärter/Wärterin keeper [ˈkiːpə]; zookeeper [ˈzuːkiːpə]
Warteschlange queue [kjuː]
warum why [waɪ]
was what [wɒt]
  was auch immer whatever [wɒtˈevə]
  Was ist los? What's up? [ˌwɒts‿ˈʌp]
  Was ist mit …? What about …? [wɒt‿əˈbaʊt]
Waschbecken *(im Amerikanischen)* sink [sɪŋk]
Waschbrettbauch six-pack [ˈsɪkspæk]
(sich) **waschen** to wash [wɒʃ]
Wasser water [ˈwɔːtə]
Wasserhahn faucet *(AE)* [ˈfɔːsɪt]
Website website [ˈwebsaɪt]
Wechselgeld change [tʃeɪndʒ]
wechseln to change [tʃeɪndʒ]
wecken to wake [weɪk]
Wecker alarm clock [əˈlɑːm ˌklɒk]
weg away [əˈweɪ]
Weg way [weɪ]; path [pɑːθ]
  Er ist auf dem Weg zu …. He is on his way to …. [ˌhiː‿ɪz‿ɒn hɪz ˈweɪ tə]
  sich auf den Weg machen to set off [set‿ˈɒf]
Wegbereiter/Wegbereiterin pioneer [ˌpaɪəˈnɪə]
wegbleiben to keep away [kiːp‿əˈweɪ]; to stay out [steɪ‿ˈaʊt]
weggehen to leave [liːv]
wegnehmen to take [teɪk]
wegrennen to run away [rʌn‿əˈweɪ]
weh tun to hurt [hɜːt]
wehen to fly [flaɪ]
weich soft [sɒft]; smooth [smuːθ]
weil because [bɪˈkɒz]
weinen to cry [kraɪ]

weit far [fɑː]
weiter further ['fɜːðə]
es weit bringen to go far [gəʊ 'fɑː]
weit kommen to go far [gəʊ 'fɑː]
weiter- to … on [ɒn]
weitergeben to pass [pɑːs]
weitergehen to continue [kən'tɪnjuː]
weitermachen to continue [kən'tɪnjuː]; to go on [gəʊ‿'ɒn]
Weitsprung long jump ['lɒŋ ˌdʒʌmp]
welcher/welche/welches what [wɒt]; which [wɪtʃ]
Welle wave [weɪv]
Wellenreiten surfing ['sɜːfɪŋ]
Wellness-Center spa [spɑː]
Welt world [wɜːld]
Weltall outer space [ˌaʊtə 'speɪs]
Weltraum space [speɪs]; outer space [ˌaʊtə 'speɪs]; universe ['juːnɪvɜːs]
Weltraumstation space station ['speɪs ˌsteɪʃn]
weltweit worldwide [ˌwɜːld'waɪd]
wem who [huː]
wen who [huː]
wenig little ['lɪtl]
weniger less [les]
am wenigsten least [liːst]
wenige few [fjuː]
wenigstens at least [ət 'liːst]
wenn if [ɪf]; when [wen]
wenn nicht unless [ən'les]
wer who [huː]
Werbespot ad [æd]; advert ['ædvɜːt]
werden to become [bɪ'kʌm]; to get [get]
werden, werden nicht *(futurisch)* will ('ll), won't [wɪl; wəʊnt]
werfen to throw [θrəʊ]
Werk factory ['fæktri]
Werkstatt workshop ['wɜːkʃɒp]
Werktag weekday ['wiːkdeɪ]
wertvoll valuable ['væljuəbl]
wessen whose [huːz]
Westen west [west]
Western western ['westən]
Western- western ['westən]
westlich western ['westən]
Wettbewerb competition [ˌkɒmpə'tɪʃn]
wetten to bet [bet]
Wetter weather ['weðə]
Wettkampf match [mætʃ]
Wettlauf race [reɪs]
einen Wettlauf machen to run a race [ˌrʌn‿ə 'reɪs]

wichtig important [ɪm'pɔːtnt]
widerhallen to echo ['ekəʊ]
wie as [æz; əz]; *(Vergleich)* like [laɪk]
wie how [haʊ]
Wie alt bist du? How old are you? [haʊ‿'əʊld‿ɑː juː]
Wie geht es dir/Ihnen/euch? How are you? [ˌhaʊ‿'ɑː juː]
Wie heißt du? What's your name? [ˌwɒts jə 'neɪm]
Wie spät ist es, bitte? What's the time, please? [ˌwɒts ðə 'taɪm ˌpliːz]
wie viele how many [haʊ 'meni]
Wie viel kosten … ? How much are … ? [ˌhaʊ 'mʌtʃ‿ɑː]
Wie viel kostet … ? How much is … ? [ˌhaʊ 'mʌtʃ‿ɪz]
Wie viel Uhr … ? What time … ? [wɒt 'taɪm]
Wie viel Uhr ist es, bitte? What's the time, please? [ˌwɒts ðə 'taɪm ˌpliːz]
Wie wäre es mit …? What about … ? [wɒt‿ə'baʊt]
wieder again [ə'gen]
auf **Wiedersehen** goodbye [gʊd'baɪ]
wild wild [waɪld]
Willkommen (in) … Welcome (to) … ['welkəm tə]
willkommen heißen to welcome ['welkəm]
Wind wind [wɪnd]
windig windy ['wɪndi]
Windkraftanlage windmill ['wɪnmɪl]
Windmühle windmill ['wɪnmɪl]
Windrad windmill ['wɪnmɪl]
windsurfen to surf [sɜːf]; to windsurf ['wɪnsɜːf]
winken to wave [weɪv]
Winter winter ['wɪntə]
winzig tiny ['taɪni]
wir we [wiː]
wirklich real [rɪəl]; really ['rɪəli]
Wirklichkeit reality [ri'æləti]
wissen to know [nəʊ]
Wissenschaft Science ['saɪəns]
Wissenschaftler/Wissenschaftlerin scientist ['saɪəntɪst]
Witz joke [dʒəʊk]
Witze machen to joke [dʒəʊk]
wo where [weə]
Woche week [wiːk]
in der Woche a week [ə 'wiːk]
pro Woche a week [ə 'wiːk]
Wochenende weekend [ˌwiːk'end]

Wochentag weekday ['wiːkdeɪ]
Woher kommst du? Where are you from? [ˌweər‿ə jə 'frɒm]
wohin where [weə]
Wohltätigkeit charity ['tʃærɪti]
Wohltätigkeitsverein charity ['tʃærɪti]
wohnen to live [lɪv]
wohnen bei to stay with ['steɪ wɪð]
Wohnung flat [flæt]; apartment *(AE)* [ə'pɑːtmənt]
Wohnzimmer living room ['lɪvɪŋ rʊm]
Wolf wolf, wolves *(pl)* [wʊlf; wʊlvz]
Wolke cloud [klaʊd]
Wolkenkratzer skyscraper ['skaɪˌskreɪpə]
wolkig cloudy ['klaʊdi]
Wolldecke blanket ['blæŋkɪt]
wollen to want (to) ['wɒnt tə]
Workshop workshop ['wɜːkʃɒp]
Wort word [wɜːd]
Wörterbuch dictionary ['dɪkʃnri]
wunderschön beautiful ['bjuːtɪfl]
Wunsch wish [wɪʃ]
wünschen to wish [wɪʃ]
würde/würden would [wʊd]
Wurst sausage ['sɒsɪdʒ]
Würstchen sausage ['sɒsɪdʒ]
würzig spicy ['spaɪsi]
wütend furious ['fjʊəriəs]; mad [mæd]

Z

zäh tough [tʌf]
Zahl number ['nʌmbə]
zahlen to pay (for) [peɪ]
Zahn tooth, teeth *(pl)* [tuːθ; tiːθ]
Zahnarzt/Zahnärztin dentist ['dentɪst]
Zahnschmerzen toothache ['tuːθeɪk]
Zauberer wizard ['wɪzəd]
Zaun fence [fens]
Zeh toe [təʊ]
Zehncentstück *(Währung)* dime [daɪm]
Zeichen sign [saɪn]; signal ['sɪgnl]; symbol ['sɪmbl]
Zeichentrickfilm cartoon [kɑː'tuːn]
zeichnen to draw [drɔː]; to design [dɪ'zaɪn]
zeigen to show [ʃəʊ]
zeigen (auf) to point (to) [pɔɪnt]
Zeile line [laɪn]
Zeit time [taɪm]
Du liebe Zeit! Good grief! [gʊd 'griːf]
Zeitabschnitt period ['pɪəriəd]

Zeitalter age [eɪdʒ]
Zeitschrift magazine [mægə'zi:n]
Zeitschriftenhändler/ Zeitschriftenhändlerin newsagent ['nju:sˌeɪdʒənt]
Zeitung newspaper ['nju:sˌpeɪpə]; paper ['peɪpə]
Zelt tent [tent]
Zelten camping ['kæmpɪŋ]
Zentimeter centimetre (cm) ['sentɪˌmi:tə]
Zentrum centre ['sentə]
zerbrechen to break [breɪk]
zerbrochen broken ['brəʊkn]
Zeremonie ceremony ['serɪməni]
zerrissen torn [tɔ:n]
zerstören to destroy [dɪ'strɔɪ]
Zertifikat certificate [sə'tɪfɪkət]
Zeug stuff [stʌf]
Zeugnis report [rɪ'pɔ:t]; certificate [sə'tɪfɪkət]
ziehen to pull [pʊl]
Ziehen tug [tʌg]
Ziel goal [gəʊl]
ziemlich pretty ['prɪti]
Zigarette cigarette [ˌsɪgr'et]
Zimmer room [ru:m; rʊm]
freies Zimmer vacancy ['veɪknsi]
zirka around [ə'raʊnd]
zittern to shake [ʃeɪk]
zivil civil ['sɪvl]
Zoll customs *(pl)* ['kʌstəmz]
Zoll *(Längenmaß: 2,54 cm)* inch [ɪnʃ]
Zoo zoo [zu:]
zu to [tʊ; tə]
zuallererst first of all [ˌfɜ:st‿ɒf‿'ɔ:l]
zubereiten to prepare [prɪ'peə]
zuerst first [fɜ:st]; at first [ət 'fɜ:st]; first of all [ˌfɜ:st‿ɒf‿'ɔ:l]
zuflüstern to whisper ['wɪspə]
zufrieden sein mit to be pleased with [bi: 'pli:zd wɪð]
Zug train [treɪn]
Zugang access ['ækses]
zugehen auf to walk up to [wɔ:k‿'ʌp tə]
Zuhause home [həʊm]
zuhören to listen ['lɪsn]
Zukunft future ['fju:tʃə]
zulässig valid ['vælɪd]
zumachen to close [kləʊz]
zunächst at first [ət 'fɜ:st]; first of all [ˌfɜ:st‿ɒf‿'ɔ:l]
zunehmen to grow [grəʊ]; to rise [raɪz]
zuordnen to match [mætʃ]
Zupfen tug [tʌg]
zurück back [bæk]
zurückdenken to reminisce [ˌremɪ'nɪs]
zurückgehen to turn back [tɜ:n 'bæk]
sich **zurücklehnen** to sit back [ˌsɪt 'bæk]
zusammen together [tə'geðə]
Zusammenbruch breakdown ['breɪkdaʊn]
zusammenfügen to match [mætʃ]
Zusatz extra ['ekstrə]
zusätzlich extra ['ekstrə]
Zuschauer/Zuschauerin viewer ['vju:ə]
etw. **zusichern** to assure [ə'ʃʊə]
zustimmen to agree [ə'gri:]
zuzüglich plus [plʌs]
zweimal twice [twaɪs]
zweitens secondly ['sekndli]
zwingend compulsory [kəm'pʌlsri]
zwischen between [bɪ'twi:n]

In the classroom

What you can say …

… if you want to be polite:

I'm sorry (to bother you), but could I please borrow your mobile/…?	Entschuldige, (dass ich dich störe,) aber kann ich bitte dein Handy/… ausleihen?
I'm sorry about my homework/… .	Es tut mir Leid wegen meiner Hausaufgaben/… .
I'm sorry (that) I'm late.	Entschuldigung, dass ich zu/so spät komme.
Oh, I'm sorry!	Oh, Entschuldigung/Verzeihung!
That's OK./ No problem.	Macht nichts./Nichts passiert./In Ordnung!
Wait, I'll help you.	Warte mal! Ich helfe dir.
Thanks./Thank you (very much).	Danke! Vielen Dank!

… if there is a problem:

How are you?	Wie geht es dir?
Are you feeling sick?	Ist dir schlecht?
I'm fine, thank you.	Gut, danke.
I'm not feeling well.	Ich fühle mich nicht gut.
Can I open the window, please?	Darf ich bitte das Fenster öffnen?
Can I go to the toilet, please?	Darf ich bitte auf die Toilette gehen?

… if you want to ask for help:

Can you help me, please?	Kannst du/Können Sie mir bitte helfen?
I don't understand this.	Ich verstehe das nicht.
What's that in English/German?	Was heißt das auf Englisch/Deutsch?
Can I say: …?/What does … mean?	Kann ich sagen: …?/Was bedeutet …?
How do you do this exercise?	Wie macht man diese Übung?
Is this right? I'm not sure.	Ist das richtig? Ich bin mir nicht sicher.
Sorry, I don't know.	Tut mir Leid, das weiß ich nicht.
Can you write it on the board, please?	Können Sie das bitte an die Tafel schreiben?
Can I ask a question, please?	Kann ich bitte eine Frage stellen?
Pardon? Can you repeat the question/sentence, please?	Wie bitte? Können Sie die Frage/den Satz bitte wiederholen?
Can you play the CD again, please?	Können Sie die CD bitte nochmal abspielen?
Can we do another example, please?	Können wir noch ein Beispiel machen?

… if you have a discussion:

What do you think?	Was meinst du?
In my opinion … .	Meiner Meinung nach … .
I think you are right/wrong.	Ich denke, du hast Recht/nicht Recht/Unrecht.
On the one hand … , on the other hand … .	Einerseits … , andererseits … .

… if you give a talk/presentation:

Today I'd like to talk about … .	Heute möchte ich über … reden.
Here you can see … .	Hier seht ihr … .
On the left/right … .	Auf der linken/rechten Seite … .
I hope you liked the talk.	Ich hoffe, euch hat mein Vortrag gefallen.
Are there any questions?	Gibt es/Habt ihr Fragen dazu?
I am going to give a (PowerPoint) presentation on … .	Ich möchte eine (PowerPoint-) Präsentation über … halten.
The title of the presentation is … .	Der Titel der Präsentation ist … .
It will last about … minutes.	Sie wird etwa … Minuten dauern.
It would be good if you kept any questions until the end.	Es wäre gut, wenn ihr eure Fragen erst am Schluss stellen könntet.
I shall be happy to answer them after the presentation.	Ich beantworte sie gerne nach der Präsentation.

... if you work together:

Can I work with ...?	Kann ich mit ... zusammenarbeiten?
Can I have your ...?	Kann ich mal dein/e/n ... haben?
Whose turn is it?	Wer ist dran?
What are we going to do first?	Was machen wir als Erstes?
Let's write ... on our poster.	Lasst uns ... auf unser Poster schreiben.
Let's put this picture here.	Lasst uns das Bild hier hinsetzen/-kleben.
You can be ... and I'll be	Du kannst ... spielen und ich werde ... spielen.
Let's act the story/play a game.	Lasst uns die Geschichte/ein Spiel spielen.
I don't understand what you mean.	Ich verstehe nicht, was du meinst.
Can you repeat that, please?	Könntest du das bitte wiederholen?
I think we should ... first.	Ich denke, wir sollten zuerst ... .
What did you find on the Internet?	Was hast du im Internet gefunden?
I really like your idea.	Mir gefällt deine Idee sehr gut.
What do you suggest?	Was schlägst du vor?
Where shall we start?	Wo sollen wir anfangen?
I think we need	Ich denke, wir brauchen ... .

... if you want to talk about stories/poems/songs:

I like/don't like this story/poem/song/game.	Diese Geschichte/Dieses Gedicht/Lied/Spiel gefällt mir/gefällt mir nicht.
I think it's good/interesting/brilliant/funny/really exciting.	Ich finde sie/es gut/interessant/toll/ witzig/wirklich spannend.
I think it's sad/boring/terrible.	Ich finde sie/es traurig/langweilig/schrecklich.
It was OK but I've read better ones.	Sie/Es ist ganz nett, aber ich habe schon bessere gelesen.
I (don't) think this is right/wrong.	Ich glaube (nicht), dass dies richtig/falsch ist.

What the teacher says to you ...

Questions

Excuse me. Could you ...?	Entschuldigung, könntest du ...?
Could you help me, please?	Könntest du mir bitte helfen?
What's the problem?	Was ist das Problem?/Was ist los?
What's happening in the picture?	Was passiert (gerade) im Bild?
What do you know about the CRM/...?	Was wisst ihr über die „CRM"/...?
What do you think of ...?	Was haltet ihr von ...?
Have you got any other ideas?	Habt ihr andere/sonstige Ideen?
Can you find the mistakes?	Könnt ihr die Fehler entdecken?
What does ... mean?	Was bedeutet ...?

Instructions

Be careful with the word order/... .	Achtet auf die Satzstellung/... .
Make a grid (like this).	Macht eine Tabelle (wie diese).
Match the questions/pictures with the answers/sentences.	Ordnet den Fragen/Bildern die Antworten/Sätze zu.
Read the definitions.	Lest die Definitionen.
Define these jobs/... .	Erklärt diese Berufe/... .
Discuss with a partner.	Diskutiert mit einem Partner/einer Partnerin.
Give three reasons.	Nenne drei Gründe.
Find the places on the map.	Findet die Orte auf der Karte.
Close your books, please.	Macht eure Bücher zu.
Don't forget to check your spelling.	Vergesst nicht, die Rechtschreibung zu überprüfen.
Give your talk to the class.	Halte dein Referat vor der Klasse.
Present your topic/poster/... to the class.	Präsentiere dein Topic/Poster/... vor der Klasse.

List of irregular verbs

to **be** [bi:]	**was/were** [wɒz/wɜ:]	**been** [bi:n]	sein
to **become** [bɪ'kʌm]	**became** [bɪ'keɪm]	**become** [bɪ'kʌm]	werden
to **begin** [bɪ'gɪn]	**began** [bɪ'gæn]	**begun** [bɪ'gʌn]	beginnen, anfangen
to **bet** [bet]	**bet** [bet]	**bet** [bet]	wetten
to **bite** [baɪt]	**bit** [bɪt]	**bitten** ['bɪtn]	beißen
to **build** [bɪld]	**built** [bɪlt]	**built** [bɪlt]	bauen
to **blow** [bləʊ]	**blew** [blu:]	**blown** [bləʊn]	blasen
to **break** [breɪk]	**broke** [brəʊk]	**broken** ['brəʊkn]	(zer)brechen; kaputtmachen
to **bring** [brɪŋ]	**brought** [brɔ:t]	**brought** [brɔ:t]	bringen, mitbringen
to **burn** [bɜ:n]	**burnt** [bɜ:nt]	**burnt** [bɜ:nt]	(ver)brennen
to **buy** [baɪ]	**bought** [bɔ:t]	**bought** [bɔ:t]	kaufen
to **catch** [kætʃ]	**caught** [kɔ:t]	**caught** [kɔ:t]	fangen
to **choose** [tʃu:z]	**chose** [tʃəʊz]	**chosen** ['tʃəʊzn]	wählen, auswählen
to **come** [kʌm]	**came** [keɪm]	**come** [kʌm]	kommen
to **cost** [kɒst]	**cost** [kɒst]	**cost** [kɒst]	kosten
to **cut** [kʌt]	**cut** [kʌt]	**cut** [kʌt]	schneiden
to **dig up** [dɪg‿'ʌp]	**dug up** [dʌg‿'ʌp]	**dug up** [dʌg‿'ʌp]	ausgraben
to **do** [du:]	**did** [dɪd]	**done** [dʌn]	machen, tun
to **draw** [drɔ:]	**drew** [dru:]	**drawn** [drɔ:n]	zeichnen
to **drink** [drɪŋk]	**drank** [dræŋk]	**drunk** [drʌŋk]	trinken
to **drive** [draɪv]	**drove** [drəʊv]	**driven** ['drɪvn]	fahren
to **eat** [i:t]	**ate** [et / eɪt]	**eaten** ['i:tn]	essen, fressen
to **fall** [fɔ:l]	**fell** [fel]	**fallen** ['fɔ:ln]	fallen, herunterfallen, hinfallen
to **feed** [fi:d]	**fed** [fed]	**fed** [fed]	füttern
to **feel** [fi:l]	**felt** [felt]	**felt** [felt]	fühlen, sich fühlen
to **fight** [faɪt]	**fought** [fɔ:t]	**fought** [fɔ:t]	kämpfen
to **find** [faɪnd]	**found** [faʊnd]	**found** [faʊnd]	finden
to **fly** [flaɪ]	**flew** [flu:]	**flown** [fləʊn]	fliegen
to **forecast** ['fɔ:kɑ:st]	**forecast** ['fɔ:kɑ:st]	**forecast** ['fɔ:kɑ:st]	vorhersagen *(Wetter)*
to **forget** [fə'get]	**forgot** [fə'gɒt]	**forgotten** [fə'gɒtn]	vergessen
to **get** [get]	**got** [gɒt]	**got** [gɒt]	kommen, bekommen; werden
to **give** [gɪv]	**gave** [geɪv]	**given** ['gɪvn]	geben, schenken
to **go** [gəʊ]	**went** [went]	**gone** [gɒn]	gehen
to **grow** [grəʊ]	**grew** [gru:]	**grown** [grəʊn]	anbauen; zunehmen
to **hang out** [hæŋ‿'aʊt]	**hung out** [hʌŋ‿'aʊt]	**hung out** [hʌŋ‿'aʊt]	sich herumtreiben
to **hear** [hɪə]	**heard** [hɜ:d]	**heard** [hɜ:d]	hören
to **hide** [haɪd]	**hid** [hɪd]	**hidden** ['hɪdn]	verstecken, sich verstecken
to **hit** [hɪt]	**hit** [hɪt]	**hit** [hɪt]	schlagen, treffen
to **hold** [həʊld]	**held** [held]	**held** [held]	halten
to **hurt** [hɜ:t]	**hurt** [hɜ:t]	**hurt** [hɜ:t]	verletzen, weh tun
to **keep** [ki:p]	**kept** [kept]	**kept** [kept]	(be)halten
to **know** [nəʊ]	**knew** [nju:]	**known** [nəʊn]	wissen, kennen
to **lay** [leɪ]	**laid** [leɪd]	**lain** [leɪn]	legen
to **learn** [lɜ:n]	**learnt** [lɜ:nt]	**learnt** [lɜ:nt]	lernen
to **leave** [li:v]	**left** [left]	**left** [left]	lassen, verlassen, abfahren
to **lend** [lend]	**lent** [lent]	**lent** [lent]	leihen

to **lose** [lu:z]	**lost** [lɒst]	**lost** [lɒst]	verlieren
to **make** [meɪk]	**made** [meɪd]	**made** [meɪd]	machen, tun
to **mean** [mi:n]	**meant** [ment]	**meant** [ment]	bedeuten, meinen
to **meet** [mi:t]	**met** [met]	**met** [met]	treffen, sich treffen
to **overdo** [ˌəʊvəˈdu:]	**overdid** [ˌəʊvəˈdɪd]	**overdone** [ˌəʊvəˈdʌn]	übertreiben
to **pay** [peɪ]	**paid** [peɪd]	**paid** [peɪd]	(be)zahlen
to **put** [pʊt]	**put** [pʊt]	**put** [pʊt]	setzen, stellen, legen
to **quit** [kwɪt]	**quit** [kwɪt]	**quit** [kwɪt]	aufhören; kündigen
to **read** [ri:d]	**read** [red]	**read** [red]	lesen
to **ride** [raɪd]	**rode** [rəʊd]	**ridden** [ˈrɪdn]	fahren, reiten
to **ring** [rɪŋ]	**rang** [ræŋ]	**rung** [rʌŋ]	klingeln; anrufen
to **rise** [raɪz]	**rose** [rəʊz]	**risen** [ˈrɪzn]	steigen, wachsen, zunehmen
to **run** [rʌn]	**ran** [ræn]	**run** [rʌn]	rennen, laufen
to **say** [seɪ]	**said** [sed]	**said** [sed]	sagen, sprechen
to **see** [si:]	**saw** [sɔ:]	**seen** [si:n]	sehen; besuchen
to **sell** [sel]	**sold** [səʊld]	**sold** [səʊld]	verkaufen
to **send** [send]	**sent** [sent]	**sent** [sent]	schicken
to **set** [set]	**set** [set]	**set** [set]	stellen, einstellen
to **shake** [ʃeɪk]	**shook** [ʃʊk]	**shaken** [ˈʃeɪkn]	schütteln, zittern
to **shoot** [ʃu:t]	**shot** [ʃɒt]	**shot** [ʃɒt]	(ab)schießen, erschießen
to **show** [ʃəʊ]	**showed** [ʃəʊd]	**shown** [ʃəʊn]	zeigen
to **sing** [sɪŋ]	**sang** [sæŋ]	**sung** [sʌŋ]	singen
to **sit** [sɪt]	**sat** [sæt]	**sat** [sæt]	sitzen
to **sleep** [sli:p]	**slept** [slept]	**slept** [slept]	schlafen
to **smell** [smel]	**smelt** [smelt]	**smelt** [smelt]	riechen
to **speak** [spi:k]	**spoke** [spəʊk]	**spoken** [ˈspəʊkn]	sprechen
to **spell** [spel]	**spelt** [spelt]	**spelt** [spelt]	buchstabieren
to **spend** [spend]	**spent** [spent]	**spent** [spent]	verbringen, ausgeben
to **stand** [stænd]	**stood** [stʊd]	**stood** [stʊd]	stehen
to **steal** [sti:l]	**stole** [stəʊl]	**stolen** [ˈstəʊln]	stehlen
to **sting** [stɪŋ]	**stung** [stʌŋ]	**stung** [stʌŋ]	stechen, beißen
to **stink** [stɪŋk]	**stank** [stæŋk]	**stunk** [stʌŋk]	stinken
to **swim** [swɪm]	**swam** [swæm]	**swum** [swʌm]	schwimmen
to **take** [teɪk]	**took** [tʊk]	**taken** [ˈteɪkn]	nehmen, mitnehmen, bringen
to **teach** [ti:tʃ]	**taught** [tɔ:t]	**taught** [tɔ:t]	lehren
to **tell** [tel]	**told** [təʊld]	**told** [təʊld]	erzählen, sagen
to **think** [θɪŋk]	**thought** [θɔ:t]	**thought** [θɔ:t]	denken, glauben
to **throw** [θrəʊ]	**threw** [θru:]	**thrown** [θrəʊn]	werfen
to **understand** [ˌʌndəˈstænd]	**understood** [ˌʌndəˈstʊd]	**understood** [ˌʌndəˈstʊd]	verstehen
to **wake** [weɪk]	**woke** [wəʊk]	**woken** [ˈwəʊkn]	(auf)wecken
to **wear** [weə]	**wore** [wɔ:]	**worn** [wɔ:n]	anhaben, tragen
to **win** [wɪn]	**won** [wɒn]	**won** [wɒn]	gewinnen, siegen
to **write** [raɪt]	**wrote** [rəʊt]	**written** [ˈrɪtn]	schreiben

Lösungen/Lösungsvorschläge Check-out

Topic 1, page 17

Option 1

1 Describe a picture.

It's a photo of people, maybe tourists. They're in the Australian Outback. They're walking.

2 Talk about the history of Australia.

1770/discover	In 1770: Australia is discovered./Captain James Cook discovered Australia in 1770.
1788/convicts	In 1788: The first convicts arived at Sydney Cove. /The First Fleet brought the first convicts to Sydney Cove in 1788.
1842/city	In 1842: The colony at Sydney Cove became the city of Sydney.
1951/school	In 1951: A school called School of the Air started for Outback kids (in 1951).
1975/reef	In 1975: The Great Barrier Reef Marine Park opened (in 1975).
2000/Olympics	In 2000: The Summer Olympics took place here (in 2000).

3 Talk about activities in Australia.

I'd like to go diving in Australia because I'd love to see the coral reef. I'd also like to see Uluru because it must be fantastic! I wouldn't like to get lost in the Outback – that could be very dangerous. I wouldn't like to swim where there are jellyfish because some of them are deadly!

4 Talk about creatures in Australia.

1. shark: They are found in warm waters and you shouldn't swim there. 2. (Sea Wasp) jelly fish: If you are stung, use vinegar. 3. koala bear: The koala bear is not really a bear. It eats the leaves of eucalyptus trees.

Option 2

1 Understand a job ad.

1. Mat wouldn't get it. He doesn't have a Life-Saving Certificate.
2. Sharon wouldn't get it. She is too young (only 15).
3. Cora would get it. She is over 16, is looking for a temporary job and has a Life-Saving Certificate.
4. Mark wouldn't get it. He is looking for a job between March and July.

2 Apply for a job.

I enjoy working with children and I love swimming! I've got a valid Life-Saving Certificate. I am a member of our local swimming club. I give swimming lessons to children (8-10) in our club and I help out on Saturday mornings in our water play group (for children under 4 years).
What time do the swimming classes start? Which days of the week would I work? Can I teach children, too? How big is a swimming group?

Topic 2, page 35

Option 1

1 Use a picture to interview someone.

I'm the person on the left/right/in the middle. I'm with my gang/friends/mates. We're outside the park. We have to wash off the paint because the officials are furious. We love painting but we also like going to discos/poetry raps.

2 Choose a good friend.

1. I would like to have her as a friend because she brings you flowers when you are ill.
2. I wouldn't like to have her as a friend, because she laughs about other people behind their backs. I don't think that's nice/fair.
3. I'd like to have him as a friend because he listens to people who are unhappy or who have problems.
4. I wouldn't like to have him as a friend because posing in front of girls isn't cool.

3 Tell a story in your own words.

1. Yesterday I fell over my bag. I was really fed up. Then my best friend came to my house and brought me some flowers.
2. We have a new teacher in our class who is very nice. She's a bit big and heavy. Some of the others in our class laughed at her behind her back. That wasn't very nice.
3. My little brother fell off his skateboard yesterday. He hurt his leg and cried a lot. I helped him to get up. And we went home.
4. I saw Paul in town on Saturday. He was waiting for a friend, I think. Suddenly a really attractive girl walked past him and he started posing. What an idiot!

Option 2

1 Talk about job qualifications.

a) A-levels are like our 'Abitur'. GCSEs are like our 'Mittlere Reife'. NVQs are like our 'Gesellenprüfung'.

b) With A-levels you can train to do most jobs or you can go to university. With GCSEs you can become a zookeeper. With NVQs you can become a chef.

2 Choose a job which you would be good at.

1. Nurse: I would be good at working as a nurse. I'm good at Biology and hospitals are very important. I like working in a team and to help ill people. I'm friendly and I like being with people.
2. DJ: I would be a good DJ. I love music and discos. I've done the job before and it was great! I don't need to do any exams for it, but I can watch other DJs and learn from them. I'm good at organizing. I'd like to work in a club in a big city.
3. Painter: I'd like to become a painter. My skills are communicating and organizing, but I also like working on my own. As a painter you have to talk to people, you sometimes work in a team and sometimes you work on your own. I'm really interested in colours and I would like to make people's homes nicer.
4. Cowboy: I would be a great cowboy. I think I'm good with animals and I like being outside. I'm good at riding and I love ranches.

Topic 3, page 49

Option 1

1 Write about important events in the American CRM.

1929: M. L. King was born.1954: Segregation in schools ended. 1955: The police arrested Rosa Parks. 1956: Segregation on buses ended. 1963: Martin Luther King gave a famous speech. 1964: King got the Nobel Peace Prize. 1968: Someone shot M. L. King dead.

2 Recognise important figures in the CRM.

a) The man is Martin Luther King. He is giving a speech/leading a protest.

b) Rosa Parks is another important person in the CRM. She helped to end segregation because she didn't give up her seat for a white person and the police arrested her. After that the black people decided that nobody should go by bus. One year later the bus service ended segregation on buses.

3 Write about civil rights and freedom.

In my country you can vote when you are 18. You mustn't show discrimination because of colour, age, religion etc. You may choose a job you like. You can marry who you want. You may leave school when you are 16. You should fight for everyone's freedom.

Option 2

1 Compare employers and employees.

a) An employer can organize and manage the business. He/She is his/her own boss. An employer can't take a vacation or have a day off when he/she feels sick.
b) An employee may take a vacation or have a day off when he/she feels sick. An employee shouldn't give orders.
c) The secretary must clean (her boss's) shoes, she must buy cigarettes for him, make muffins and cut his hair.
d) I'd like to be the secretary because she can help her boss. I'd like to be the boss because he/she needn't make cakes or clean his/her shoes.

2 Give advice on starting a business.

organized, trained, independent, smart, enterprising

Topic 4, page 69

Option 1

1 Understand some aspects of globalisation.

a)
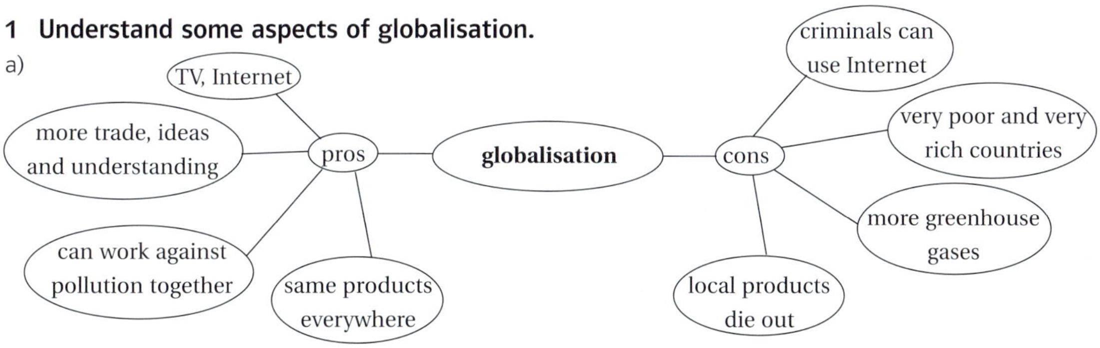

b) I think globalisation is good because we can meet people from lots of different cultures and we can buy lots of different things in our supermarkets: chocolate, pineapples, etc.
I think globalisation is bad because you can get ill in a foreign country, go back to your country and then people there can get ill, too. There is also a problem with some kinds of animals (birds, hens). They bring diseases which are dangerous to us. If we eat the meat, we can get ill, too.

2 Talk about the 'Fairtrade' label and chocolate.

a) Using labels first started in the late 1980s.
b) It helps farmers in Ghana. They work under good conditions and get a fair price for their work.
c) Musterlösung: My favourite chocolate is not so dark. It is sweet and has got lots of milk in it. It is soft inside. It is a long bar. It is quite expensive so I don't buy it very often.

3 Give a profile of a company.

a) Divine Chocolate Ltd. got its name on 1st January 2007. It's a company of the co-operative Kuapo Kokoo in Ghana and three British organizations who support projects in Africa. They produce good, fair trade chocolate and help the farmers in Ghana to get a guaranteed price for their cocoa beans. The company's turnover is more than 20 millon pounds

b) They give the cocoa farmers a guaranteed price for the beans. The farmers work under good working conditions.

4 Say what would happen if ...?

1. If they put farms together, they would make a co-operative.
2. If they grew cocoa beans, they would produce chocolate (bars).
3. If they changed their (company's) name, it would be 'Deli Chocolate Ltd.'.
4. If they opened a new office (company), it would be in Sydney.

Option 2

1 Describe an island in paradise and dangers to it.

a) I could see a blue sky, a fantastic beach with clean, white sand and the big, blue sea. Environmental problems could be: sea level rising (global warming), pollution (in the sea) or too much rubbish on the beaches

b) Yes, because I could swim in the sea, enjoy the sun and relax./No, because it would be a bit boring and I would want to see more of a country than just the beach and the sea.

2 Understand new words in a story.

Sea: manta ray, wetsuit, underwater shots, coral, current, fin, (diving group); **Hotel:** juice bar, spa, (manager); **People:** islanders, fisherman, diving group, tourists, manager, decompression

3 Talk about the characters in a story.

The islanders feel worried because large numbers of fish are dying. Zahra is unhappy because that could be bad for business. Amber feels excited because she sees a manta ray. Joel feels sick because maybe he needs decompression. Amber feels scared/unhappy because Joel is sick. And I think she also feels sad because her boyfriend has to go away.

4 Retell a story in your own words.

The story happened in London, in a café in summer. The main characters were a girl (Ann), a boy (Charles) and his friend (François) and a woman.

Charles was on holiday there. He went to a café with his friend François. They sat down at a table. There was a girl alone at a table near them. She had a book in her hand which looked very interesting. Her handbag was on the chair next to her. Suddenly a woman came closer to the girl and took her handbag. The two boys saw it and ran after the woman. They caught her and called the police. The girl was very happy and thanked the two boys.

I liked it because the boys had an exciting adventure when they ran after the woman through the streets. In the scene there were also lots of shots of famous places in London.

Lösungen/Lösungsvorschläge Test yourself!

Test yourself! 1, page 18–21

A Reading

1 a. 2; b. 3; c. 1; d. 3; e. 1; f. 3

2 a. Hervey Bay b. when he was five c. 16 finalists d. all seven states in Australia e. 21 years old f. the Outback g. to win the 'King of the Road' crown

B Language

1 a. truckies, b. pleased, c. points, d. difficult, e. scared, f. swap

2 a. a competition, b. a road train, c. states, d. test, e. expert, f. alone, g. the Outback, h. a crown

C Listening

1 a. wrong (She is a shop assistant.); b. right; c. wrong (She's 18.); d. right; e right; f. wrong (Her dream is to drive a road train.); g. wrong (Her brother and boyfriend are truckies); h. right

2 a. 2; b. 3; c. 1; d. 2

D Speaking

1 Describing

a. **Photo A:** department store, huge, lots of people, different things, no windows, noisy
Photo B: truck, alone, maybe a road train, no other vehicles in front or behind, green trees, red dust

b. I hate my job in the department store. It's huge and at the weekend there are always lots of people there. They sell so many different things but people always want something which we don't sell. There are no windows and it's often really noisy.
I love my job and I love my truck. It's great to be alone out in the Outback. Sometimes I see another truck or a road train. I like it best when there are no trucks in front of me or behind me. All I can see is green trees and the beautiful red dust of Australia.

2 Role Play

You: No. I know the roads because I often travel with my brother or my friend. They are both truckies.
You: That isn't a problem. I have already written to my boss.
You: I am planning to do it in a few years because the lessons are so expensive.
You: What towns will I visit? What will I transport? How much pay will I get?
How long are the working hours each day? Would I always drive the same truck?

E Mediation and communication

a. Man fährt links.
b. Nein. Das ist eine Spur auf einer mehrspurigen Straße.
c. Es heißt auf Deutsch „überholen".
d. Einen Riesenlaster zu überholen dauert lange.
e. Sie schalten manchmal ein Warschild ein, weil sie viel Platz brauchen, wenn sie links abbiegen.
f. Man darf auf keinen Fall überholen.
g. Wenn man hinter einem Riesenlaster fährt und es sehr viel Staub gibt.

F Writing

1 Skills

name	Ella Moore
age	18
address	16 Wongarooa Road, Sydney
normal trucker's licence	Yes: test passed on 23rd Sept
special trucker's licence	No (planned in 2–3 years)
truckie experience	Yes: three years

2 A job ad

18-year-old from Sydney is looking for a job as a truckie for normal trucks. Truckie's licence for one month. Three years experience of travelling with other truckies. Plans to do special licence in 2–3 years.

Test yourself! 2, page 36–39

A Reading

a. 2; b. 2; c. 1; d. 3; e. 1

B Language

1 a. the City Council b. the crew c. Riz Mirza and Greg Reidy d. GCSEs e. art folder f. finger paints/models 2

2 a. great b. different c. finished d. enemy e. hated f. bored g. part-time h. spend i. to forget j. difficult

C Listening

1 a. 3; b. 2; c. 4; d. 1

2 a. 2; b. 3

c. 1 wrong (She's one of the Art teachers at the college.); 2 right; 3 wrong (They're from a play group.); 4 right; 5 wrong (The shadows came from a lamp.); 6 wrong (She wanted to underline the shadows.); 7 wrong (They really enjoy singing.)

D Speaking

1 Describing

a. I'm with a mural group in town. I'm painting a wall. And it's quite funny. I think someone else is painting me at the same time! I can feel something on my legs and I'm laughing!

b. Look at that girl. She's painting the other girl's legs. It's really funny!
If you do that to my legs, I'll scream.

2 Role Play

You: Hey you two! Ruby, stop shouting please! What's happening?
You: Zara, please tell me what happend.
You: Well, Zara, I think you should explain where you were!
You: Ruby, I think you should say sorry.
You: I'm glad that we've sorted that out!

E Mediation and communication

a. Das ist Anthony Mackie.

b. Sie nehmen an einem *rap battle* teil.

c. Es ist der Name einer Straße in Detroit. Sie bezeichnet die Grenze zwischen Gebieten, wo Schwarze und Weiße wohnen.

d. Kim Basinger

e. Rabbit verlässt die Gang.
f. Er will zurück in die Fabrik und arbeiten.

F Writing

1 Skills

Individuelle Lösung

2 Your own profile

My name is … . I'm 15 years old. My hobbies are swimming and listening to hip hop. My favourite subject at school is Art. Painting murals would be an interesting job for me.

Test yourself! 3, page 50–53

A Reading

1 generation: Generation, mission: Mission, keyboard: Keyboard, lie: Lüge

2 a. the Coxes
b. Sydney and Adelaide
c. 'Took the Children Away'
d. near Berri, South Australia
e. the Altogethers
f. Time Magazine

3 a. 1; b. 3; c. 2; d. 1; e. 3

B Language

1 a. a mission house b. became famous around the world c. did an article about him
d. it moved many Australians e. offer them a break

2 a. foster parents; b. a difficult time; c. drinking a lot; d. the front cover

C Listening

a. Angie listened to Rudd's speech from outside the building where he spoke.
b. Rudd said he was sorry about the terrible life which the Stolen Generation had.
c. They took away Trevor's aunt when she was a baby and they changed her name.
d. Angie's grandad found his mother just before she died.

D Speaking

1 Fighting for your rights

a. In photo 1 there are a lot of young people on Broadway. Some of them are holding posters. They are fighting to save their dance center.
In photo 2 a teenager is holding a poster. It says that we should say 'no' to war.

b. I would choose the first photo. It would be more interesting for young people. You can see why the young people are protesting. There are a lot of them, so it must be important.
Or: I would choose the second photo. It makes you think because it isn't clear at first what the poster says. The flyer would be interesting to young people and to old people.

2 Role play

You: Hi, there. What is your protest about?
You: Es gibt einen tollen Platz hinter der Konzerthalle. Sie skaten dort immer. Jetzt will die Stadt es ihnen verbieten.
You: Oh, that's terrible. Why is the town against it?

You: Sie sind ziemlich laut – aber sie skaten nie, wenn es ein Konzert gibt. Er/Sie glaubt, dass manche Leute denken, dass sie gefährlich sind.

You: Why don't you write a letter to the newspaper – or tell a reporter about your problem?

You: Sie geben morgen Nachmittag um 17.15 ein Interview im Radio. Vielleicht kannst du es dir anhören.

You: Thank you. We'll listen to the interview.

E Mediation and communication

a. Junge Leute aus der Gegend haben diesen Flyer geschrieben.
b. Sie fordern, dass die Stadt ihre Disco nicht zumacht.
c. Sie planen eine 'Disco im Park'.
d. Sie werden mehrere Meilen in die nächste Disco fahren müssen. Sie befürchten auch, dass die Fälle von Trunkenheit am Steuer zunehmen werden.
e. Man kann das Problem in der Schule und zu Hause besprechen, an die Lokalzeitung schreiben, an der Parkdisco teilnehmen.

F Writing

If they close our youth club, then lots of young people won't have anything to do in town at the weekends. They will drive to the next town so that they can go to the youth club there. They will probably drink and then drive home. There will be a lot of accidents. How can you help us? Come to our street protest on Saturday and sign our supporters' list! Write to our local newspaper about the problem!

Test yourself! 4, page 70–73

A Reading

a. 2; b. 1; c. 3; d. 2

B Language

1 a. start; b. friends; c. talked; d. community; e. solar; f. humans

2 a. We talked about what the future would bring us.
b. It took a lot of time to decide how to organize our village.
c. Today, Greenford is 'our dream come true'.
d. Anyone who lives here must believe in our motto: 'Our Earth is Our Future'.
e. The Earth can go on without us but we can't live without it.

3 a. + d.

C Listening

Part I

1 a. 3; b. 2

2 a. The people are meeting to talk about the **fair** this year.
b. Karen and Mike are **new** in the village.
c. The best thing last year was the farmers' **market**.
d. In the three-legs football match two **people** play with three legs.
e. They had a disaster **after** the end of the match.
f. Suddenly two **pigs** destroyed the tea tent.

Part II

a. Mike, b. A couple, c. Karen, d. Angela, e. Mike, f. Angela

D Speaking

1 Describing

a. In the photo on the left I can see a woman. She is shopping in a supermarket. She is reading the information on a product because she wants to know how healthy the food is. In the other photo I can see four teenagers. They are shopping at a market. They are standing in front of a market stall. They are trying to decide what to buy because they are hungry.

b. **In the supermarket**: I don't know what to buy. There is so much choice. This looks good but it is very expensive.
At the market: I hope you'll decide soon because I'm hungry. Those apples look really good. Let's buy them or I'll buy one now.

place	pros	cons
A supermarket	big choice, cheaper than small shop	too many things, you buy things which you don't need
A market stall	the food is from local famers people are friendly	food is expensive you can't park near it

2 Role play

You: Yes, OK. But first I'd like to read what is in the pizzas.
You: Well, because there's often a lot of sugar and there are unhealthy things in pizzas.
You: Yes, but that could mean that maybe they have other things which aren't healthy.
You: Only buy organic food. So then you know that it's healthy.
You: Yes, I think what they write on the packet is true because there are strict rules for that.

E Mediation and communication

a. Nein, auf einer Insel in Neuseeland.
b. Der Strom kommt von Solarzellen und Windmühlen (nicht von Kraftwerken).
c. Es fällt genug Regen.
d. Ja klar!
e. Er hat gelernt, wie man Lehmziegel macht, wie Solarzellen Gebäude mit Strom versorgen und wie eine Windmühle eine Wasserpumpe antreibt.
f. Super war dass kein Verkehr war und dass man essen konnte, was man selber angebaut hatte. Die Ruhe auf der Insel tat so gut. Und es war eine schöne Atmosphäre dort, ein Gemeinschaftsgefühl.

F Writing

1 see how people live and survive in an eco-community, learn about eco-communities and how everything works there, have a different experience to city life, learn how alternative energy works, find out what I could do where I live to help the environment.

2 Dear Sir/Madam,
My name is Joshua Schneider and I have just finished school. I'm 18 and I live in Düsseldorf, a big city in Germany. I would like to do a project week at your eco-village as I'm very interested to see how people live in an eco-village. I would like to learn about how eco-villages work. I would also like to learn more about solar energy and about what I could do here in Germany to help the environment.
I would be very pleased if I could do a project week at your eco-community in August or September this year.
Yours faithfully,
…

Lösungen/Lösungsvorschläge Grammatik

Grammatikübungen (Grammar practice)

G 1 Vollverben und Hilfsverben

1 All on one trip!

a) lives, works, sends, flies, travel, work, find, love, save, ends, spend, feels, is

b) 2. No, Jeff doesn't live in Australia. His aunt lives there.
3. No, he doesn't visit his aunt in Perth. He visits her in Sydney.
4. No, he doesn't stay in the city for about a month. He stays there for about a week.
5. No, he doesn't go south with his cousin. He goes north (with him).
6. No, there they don't help on a cattle drive. They help on a cattle station.
7. No, they don't think the work is easy. They think it's hard.
8. No, they don't enjoy wide open doors. They enjoy wide open spaces.
9. No, they don't spend a week on a riding holiday. They spend a week on a diving holiday.
10. No, Jeff's trips to Australia don't make him very tired. They make him very happy.

c) 1. Do you want to fly to Australia again?
2. Does your cousin Lance go to school in Sydney?
3. Does Lance visit you in London sometimes?
4. Do you like life in the city or in the country better?
5. Does your holiday job on the station pay well?
6. Do you both go diving every year?
7. Do you plan to live in Australia one day?

d) 1. Yes, I really think that it's a great country!
2. No, he and a friend are on a dive instructor's course at the moment.
3. Yes, he usually comes over here in spring.
4. Well, I like both, in fact. But the ocean is the best of all!
5. Yes, it pays enough for us to have a great holiday after all that hard work!
6. No, not always. Sometimes we help on nature projects on the Great Barrier Reef.
7. Well, I think it's too early to make plans. But maybe when I finish school …

2 A report

Jeff's aunt sent him a ticket and he flew to Sydney. After about a week in the city he and his cousin Lance travelled to a cattle station in the north. They both worked there for about a month. They found farm life really hard but they loved the wide open spaces out there. Jeff and Lance saved all their money and when their job ended, they spent a week on a diving holiday together. Jeff felt very happy when he was in Australia!

G 2 Das Passiv im *simple present*

1 The American way

a) 1. is written, 2. isn't played, 3. is spoken, 4. is served, 5. is drawn, 6. isn't called

b) Mistakes are made. Presents are given. Questions are asked. Words are spoken. Songs are sung. Letters are written. Photos are taken. Autographs are signed. Prizes are won.

2 Out in nature

2. The forest isn't destroyed by music. It's destroyed by farmers (people).

3. Fish aren't caught in paper bags. They're caught in nets.
4. The reef isn't saved by tourists. It's saved by reef rangers.
5. Kangaroo meat isn't eaten by koala bears. It's eaten by people (in restaurants).
6. People aren't bitten by birds. They're bitten by spiders.

G 3 Modale Hilfsverben

1 Sayings

1. You can lead a horse to water but you can't make him drink. c. You can help a person to do something, but he/she must want to do it, too.
2. All good things must come to an end. d. Nothing lasts forever.
3. You should let sleeping dogs lie. b. Don't talk about a problem. Keep quiet about it.
4. People who live in glass houses shouldn't throw stones. e. Don't talk about other peoples' mistakes. Everyone makes mistakes!
5. A cat may look at a king. a. A poor person can do things that a rich person can do.

2 A big difference!

a) 1 C, 2 D, 3 A, 4 B

b) 1. So we needn't pack our anoraks. 2. You mustn't go into the water! 3. Thanks, but you needn't pick me up, Dad! 4. You really mustn't stay out in the sun so long.

3 A tourist brochure

1. You can't ride our cows but you may ride our horses if you want to.
2. Tourists shouldn't go walking without any water. They should always take some bottles with them.
3. You should wear a hat on the beach but you needn't wear a coat.
4. Visitors may take photos of the crocodiles but they mustn't get too close.
5. Parents must tell their kids not to play with snakes and they should know what to do in an emergency.
6. No one should swim where there are crocodiles. They can be dangerous.

G 4 Bedingungssätze (*if*-Sätze) Typ I

1 What if?

a) 2. d., 3. e., 4. a., 5. g., 6. b., 7. f.

b) 2. d. If we miss the last bus, I'll pay for a taxi. 3. e. If he's not at home, we'll go to the park.
4. a. If they're cold when we get home, I'll put them in our microwave. 5. g. If the shops are already closed, my brother will lend us his DVDs. 6. b. If they're too expensive, we'll buy a CD.
7. f. If they don't fit me, I'll ask for some larger ones.

G 5 Bedingungssätze (*if*-Sätze) Typ II

1 What would happen ...?

2. If Marley worked in a bank, she would (she'd) feel very bored.
3. If Ali and Shahid visited Australia, they wouldn't come back.
4. If Doug called 'TalkLine', he would (he'd) get some good advice.
5. If Jane tried a new sport, she would (she'd) enjoy it much more.
6. If Tom became a mechanic, he wouldn't need anyone to fix his car!

2 Winning the lottery

1. If I won the lottery, I would be rich. I wouldn't sit on the sofa. I'd travel round the world!
2. If I travelled round the world, I would take my girlfriend with me.
3. If I took my girlfriend …, we would (we'd) visit Las Vegas and we would (we'd) go to a casino.
4. If we went to the casino, I'd win lots of money.
5. Oh, I FORGOT!!! If I won the lottery, I wouldn't need to win money in a casino!

G 6 Gerundium

1 A dating profile

... I love watching films in the cinema, so it would be good if you loved that, too! Of course, dancing in clubs is also really cool and I'm crazy about hip-hop and rap music.
Playing football or doing most kinds of sports is not my thing, I'm afraid. I enjoy swimming but only in the sea and when it's warm. I really like listening to music. Girls who just can't stop talking about other nice guys are not for me! And if they only want to spend the weekend shopping in town then they needn't apply. ; -) So if you think we have similar interests and think that we would enjoy spending time together, just send me a message! I look forward to hearing from you! …

2 The driving test

You: … Now you can see why I'm looking forward to doing my driving test.
Dad: Oh, my God! Don't they know that sleeping on the streets is dangerous?
You: Oh, you're right! Lying on the streets is not a good idea! How can people be so stupid!
Dad: And giving alcohol to drivers is even worse!
You: … drinking and driving at the same time is really cool! I enjoy having a drink …
Dad: WHAT?? Oh no! I'll be frightened of going out on the streets when you get your license!
You: Dad, there is no sense in worrying! Stop being silly. … You know how I love making jokes. …
Dad: I just hope that you are as good at driving as you are at joking!

G 7 Indirekte Rede (sofort berichtet)

1 Things famous singers say …

3. Elton says that the great thing about rock 'n' roll is that almost anyone can become a star.
4. Natasha says (that it's a terrible article and) that they should call their newspaper The Daily Disaster!
5. Orville says that sometimes having more is really less …
6. Stevie says that his fans are important, but that he can't live his life for them.
7. Sean says that he would love to get an Oscar this time!

G 8 Indirekte Rede (später berichtet)

1 An interview

2. Then she wanted to know which school I went to.
3. After that she asked me if I did any sports.
4. Then she wanted to know why I wanted to work there.
5. Later she told me that they had 150 workers.
6. Then she added that the working hours were from 8 am to 4 pm.
7. After that she warned me that people didn't smoke in the building.
8. Last of all she advised me that I should wear a suit to work.

Textquellen:
S.22-25: "The Kiss" adapted from The Kiss by Rosie Rushton
Hörverstehenstext "Pride": Adam Clayton, Laurence Mullen, David Evans, Paul David Hewson © Universal Music Publ. G mbH, Berlin
Hörverstehenstext "Death of Luther King": Jack Dupree © Editions de Belmont SA, Montreux/Schweiz

Bildquellen:
Cover: Avenue Images GmbH (Photodisc), Hamburg; S.4: (1) shutterstock (RF/Kaspars Grinval), New York, NY; (2) Corbis (REUTERS/David Gray), Düsseldorf; (3) Wikimedia Foundation Inc. (PD), St. Petersburg FL; (4) Corbis (Atlantide Phototrave), Düsseldorf; (5) vario images, Bonn; (6) Joker (Karl-Heinz Hick), Bonn; (7) iStockphoto (Haider Yousuf), Calgary, Alberta; (8) Alamy Images RF (Matt Fagg), Abingdon, Oxon; S.5: (1) Corbis (Lehmann), Düsseldorf; (2) Corbis (Steve Schapiro), Düsseldorf; (3) iStockphoto (Quavondo Nguyen), Calgary, Alberta; (4) Avenue Images GmbH (BLEND IMAGES/Jupit), Hamburg; (5) laif (hemis), Köln; (6) Alamy Images RM (The Photolibrary Wal), Abingdon, Oxon; (7) Alamy Images RM (Visions of America,), Abingdon, Oxon; (8) Alamy Images RM (Greenshoots Communic), Abingdon, Oxon; S.8: Picture-Alliance (Jenny Evans), Frankfurt; S.9: (1) shutterstock (RF/Kaspars Grinval), New York, NY; (2) iStockphoto (RF/pamspix), Calgary, Alberta; (3) shutterstock (RF/Chee-Onn Leong), New York, NY; (4) Fotolia LLC (RF/Ian Scott), New York; S.10: (1) Fotolia LLC (RF/Dawn), New York; (2) iStockphoto (RF/Feng Yu), Calgary, Alberta; S.11: (1) JupiterImages (photos.com), Tucson, AZ; (2) JupiterImages (photos.com), Tucson, AZ; (3) iStockphoto (RainforestAustralia), Calgary, Alberta; (4) iStockphoto (vm), Calgary, Alberta; (5) Alamy Images RM (LOOK), Abingdon, Oxon; (6) Wikimedia Foundation Inc., St. Petersburg FL; S.12: (1) iStockphoto (RF/Michael Pettigr), Calgary, Alberta; (2) Fotofinder (Rodger Klein/WaterFr), Berlin; (3) Corbis (Joe McDonald), Düsseldorf; (4) Fotofinder (Bell/Wildlife), Berlin; (5) Wikimedia Foundation Inc. (PD), St. Petersburg FL; (6) Picture-Alliance (Horst Pfeiffer), Frankfurt; S.13: shutterstock (Ian Scott), New York, NY; S.14: (1) Alamy Images RF (RF), Abingdon, Oxon; (2) Getty Images (RR/Ralf Schultheis), München; S.17: (1) iStockphoto (François Marclay), Calgary, Alberta; (2) shutterstock (Ian Scott), New York, NY; (3) shutterstock (Nir Levy), New York, NY; (4) iStockphoto (Sawayasu Tsuji), Calgary, Alberta; S.18: (1) Getty Images (Martin Barraud), München; (2) Alamy Images RM (Karl Johaentges), Abingdon, Oxon; S.20: (1) shutterstock (Timur Kulgarin), New York, NY; (2) Alamy Images RM (Sindre Ellingsen), Abingdon, Oxon; S.26: (1) Alamy Images RM (Kuttig - People), Abingdon, Oxon; (2) vario images, Bonn; S.27: (1) Corbis (Mika/zefa), Düsseldorf; (2) Joker (Karl-Heinz Hick), Bonn; (3) mediacolor's P & F Müller (Dia), Zürich; S.28: Alamy Images RF (Matt Fagg), Abingdon, Oxon; S.29: (1) Dream Maker Software (RF), Colorado; (2) Dream Maker Software (RF), Colorado; (3) Alamy Images RF (Blend Images), Abingdon, Oxon; S.32: (1) Corbis (Reuters), Düsseldorf; (2) iStockphoto (Haider Yousuf), Calgary, Alberta; (3) Fotosearch RF (Corbis RF), Waukesha, WI; S.34: (1) Klett-Archiv, Stuttgart; (2) MEV, Augsburg; S.35: (1) iStockphoto (Rick Rhay), Calgary, Alberta; (2) iStockphoto (RichVintage), Calgary, Alberta; (3) iStockphoto (Lisa Kyle Young), Calgary, Alberta; (4) shutterstock (Lisa F. Young), New York, NY; (5) iStockphoto (Cynthia Baldauf), Calgary, Alberta; S.36: (1) iStockphoto (Dawna Stafford), Calgary, Alberta; (2) iStockphoto (Justin Horrocks), Calgary, Alberta; S.38: Alamy Images RM (Jim West), Abingdon, Oxon; S.39: Cinetext, Frankfurt; S.40: Alamy Images RM (StockShot/Tony Harri), Abingdon, Oxon; S.41: (1) Corbis (Arthur Siegel), Düsseldorf; (2) Avenue Images GmbH (BLEND IMAGES/Jupit), Hamburg; (3) Picture-Alliance (picture-alliance, Fr), Frankfurt; (4) Corbis (Lehmann), Düsseldorf; S.42: (1) Corbis (Flip Schulke), Düsseldorf; (2) Corbis (Brooks Kraft), Düsseldorf; S.43: Picture-Alliance (Larry W. Smith/epa), Frankfurt; S.44: (1) Corbis (Steve Schapiro), Düsseldorf; (2) Picture-Alliance (Jeff Kowalsky/epa), Frankfurt; (3) Interfoto, München; (4) Corbis (Bettmann), Düsseldorf; S.45: Avenue Images GmbH (Michael Siluk), Hamburg; S.46: (1) CartoonStock (Clive Goddard), Bath; (2) iStockphoto (Lise Gagne), Calgary, Alberta; (3) iStockphoto (Quavondo Nguyen), Calgary, Alberta; S.48: Picture-Alliance (PA), Frankfurt; S.49: (1) Picture-Alliance (ipol code), Frankfurt; (2) iStockphoto (andres balcazar), Calgary, Alberta; (3) Alamy Images RM (SIGRID DAUTH Stock P), Abingdon, Oxon; (4) Alamy Images RM (foodfolio), Abingdon, Oxon; (5) iStockphoto (Ilka-Erika Szasz-Fab), Calgary, Alberta; S.50: (1) Alamy Images RM (Jack Picone), Abingdon, Oxon; (2) Fotosearch RF (Maps Resources), Waukesha, WI; S.52: (1) Alamy Images RM (Richard Levine), Abingdon, Oxon; (2) Alamy Images RM (Rob Lacey/vividstock.net), Abingdon, Oxon; S.53: iStockphoto (Nicholas Monu), Calgary, Alberta; S.54: (1) JupiterImages (photos.com), Tucson, AZ; (2) JupiterImages (photos.com), Tucson, AZ; (3) Dinodia, Mumbai; (4) Picturefile (David Graham), London NW1 9UB; S.58: (1) Corbis (Barry Lewis), Düsseldorf; (2) Alamy Images RF (Brownstock Inc.), Abingdon, Oxon; S.59: (1) Corbis (Bettmann), Düsseldorf; (2) Alamy Images RM (The Photolibrary Wal), Abingdon, Oxon; (3) Corbis (Guenter Rossenbach), Düsseldorf; (4) Alamy Images RM (Olivier Asselin), Abingdon, Oxon; S.60: (1) iStockphoto (Deejpilot), Calgary, Alberta; (2) iStockphoto (SteveStone), Calgary, Alberta; (3) Fotofinder (EyeUbiquitous/Hutchison), Berlin; (4) Corbis (Alison Wright), Düsseldorf; S.61: (1) iStockphoto (Sonja Inselmann), Calgary, Alberta; (2) Alamy Images RM (Visions of America,), Abingdon, Oxon; S.62: (1) TransFair e.V., Köln; (2) Wikimedia Foundation Inc. (PD), St. Petersburg FL; (3) Alamy Images RM (Greenshoots Communic), Abingdon, Oxon; (4) Alamy Images RM (Greenshoots Communic), Abingdon, Oxon; (5) Alamy Images RM (Mark Boulton), Abingdon, Oxon; (6) Klett-Archiv (Hamida Aziz), Stuttgart; S.63: iStockphoto (Maceofoto), Calgary, Alberta; S.64: (1) laif (hemis), Köln; (2) shutterstock (Annetje), New York, NY; S.65: shutterstock (Annetje), New York, NY; S.66: shutterstock (Hiroyuki Saita), New York, NY; S.67: iStockphoto (Jason Stitt), Calgary, Alberta; S.68: (1) iStockphoto (Peeter Viisimaa), Calgary, Alberta; (2) iStockphoto (Peeter Viisimaa), Calgary, Alberta; S.69: (1) iStockphoto (giuseppe perrone), Calgary, Alberta; (2) iStockphoto (Vassili Koretski), Calgary, Alberta; S.70: (1) Alamy Images RM (Elizabeth Whiting &), Abingdon, Oxon; (2) shutterstock (PhotoSky 4t com), New York, NY; (3) iStockphoto (Liza McCorkle), Calgary, Alberta; (4) iStockphoto (Markus Guhl), Calgary, Alberta; S.72: (1) Alamy Images RM (David R. Frazier Pho), Abingdon, Oxon; (2) PhotoAlto (Patrick Sheandell O), Paris; S.73: iStockphoto (Rachel Dulson), Calgary, Alberta; S.79: CartoonStock (Mike Baldwin), Bath; S.80: Stockbyte, Tralee, County Kerry; S.91: (1) iStockphoto (Adam Dodd), Calgary, Alberta; (2) iStockphoto (gary milner), Calgary, Alberta; (3) iStockphoto (flavia bottazzini), Calgary, Alberta; (4) iStockphoto (Yuriy Soshnikov), Calgary, Alberta; S.92: (1) Fotolia LLC (RF/Dawn), New York; (2) iStockphoto (twobluedogs), Calgary, Alberta; (3) iStockphoto (Lee Daniels), Calgary, Alberta; (4) iStockphoto (Jan Rihak), Calgary, Alberta; (5) iStockphoto (Sandra Caldwell), Calgary, Alberta; (6) State Library of Tasmania (Allport Library an M), Hobart Tas Aust; (7) iStockphoto (Vik Thomas), Calgary, Alberta; (8) iStockphoto (KJA), Calgary, Alberta; (9) shutterstock (SexyGirls_Vehicles), New York, NY; (10) iStockphoto (Flavia Bottazzini), Calgary, Alberta; S.93: iStockphoto (Leon Bonaventura), Calgary, Alberta; S.94: (1) iStockphoto (Zoran Milic), Calgary, Alberta; (2) iStockphoto (bubaone), Calgary, Alberta; (3) iStockphoto (Miguel Angel Salinas Salinas), Calgary, Alberta; (4) iStockphoto (brett lamb), Calgary, Alberta; S.100: iStockphoto (RF/Clint Scholz), Calgary, Alberta; S.111: laif (Redux), Köln; S.113: (1) iStockphoto (IOANNIS DRIMILIS), Calgary, Alberta; (2) JupiterImages (photos.com), Tucson, AZ; (3) iStockphoto (Frances Twitty), Calgary, Alberta; (4) iStockphoto (Frances Twitty), Calgary, Alberta; S.114: shutterstock (Andrejs Pidjass), New York, NY; S.115: (1) shutterstock (Losevsky Pavel), New York, NY; (2) DNA Diligent Media Corporation Ltd. (Manjul), Mumbai; S.116: iStockphoto (James Pauls), Calgary, Alberta; S.119: (1) Comstock, Luxemburg; (2) iStockphoto (gary milner), Calgary, Alberta; S.124: Comstock, Luxemburg; S.128: (1) Comstock, Luxemburg; (2) Corbis, Düsseldorf; S.133: iStockphoto (Nicolas Loran), Calgary, Alberta

English-speaking countries

Countries in which English is the / an official language

NAME Independent Commonwealth sta

Name Dependent territories of Commonwealth states (in brackets) SCALE 1 : 88,000,000

Nutzer-Schlüssel
uHu7-Rw19-95Y8